POLICE IN SCHOOLS

This co-authored book critically reviews existing literature on school resource officer (SRO) programs and presents a thorough evaluation of an SRO program offered by Peel Regional Police in Ontario, Canada. The implementation of an SRO program is a controversial response to school violence and safety issues. While some call for an increased use of police in schools, others are pushing to remove police from schools, or at least to end their involvement in routine discipline. Though many SRO programs exist around the world, little systematic research has been conducted on the topic.

The study reported in this book represents the largest and most comprehensive assessment of such programs to date. The research by Duxbury and Bennell indicates that SRO programs can provide real value for students, school staff, policing organizations, and society, but benefits rely on having programs that are well-designed, that the right officers are selected for SRO roles, and that the initiative has support from major stakeholders. Given the current conversations regarding the costs and benefits of having police officers in schools, there is a clear need to determine the value that investment in these types of proactive policing programs creates.

The book provides researchers, SROs, police agencies, school boards, school administrators, teachers, parents, and students with information about: the activities that SROs are involved in, how SROs can collaborate with schools to create safe learning environments, and whether (and how) such programs benefit the police, schools, students, and society. Easy-to-digest charts facilitate understanding, and anonymized reflections from SROs, school staff, and students are presented throughout the book to provide context.

Linda Duxbury is Professor of Management and Strategy at Carleton University (Canada). She has published widely in both the academic and practitioner literatures in the areas of work–life balance, change management, supportive work environments, employee well-being, the use and impact of office technology, managing the new workforce and supportive management. Most of Linda's research focuses on using evidence to make the case for change (with respect to work–life, employee well-being, and recruitment/retention issues) in the public, private, and not-for-profit sectors.

Craig Bennell is a Professor of Psychology at Carleton University (Canada) where he teaches courses in forensic and police psychology. He also serves as Director of Carleton's Police Research Lab. Most of Craig's research examines evidence-based policing, with a particular focus on how research can be used to improve police investigations, police training, and police performance under pressure. This research is typically conducted in collaboration with police services.

POLICE IN SCHOOLS

An Evidence-based Look at the Use of School Resource Officers

Linda Duxbury and Craig Bennell

NEW YORK AND LONDON

First published 2020
by Routledge
52 Vanderbilt Avenue, New York, NY 10017

and by Routledge
2 Park Square, Milton Park, Abingdon, Oxon, OX14 4RN

Routledge is an imprint of the Taylor & Francis Group, an informa business

Library of Congress Cataloging-in-Publication Data
Names: Duxbury, Linda, 1962- author. | Bennell, Craig, author.
Title: Police in schools : an evidence-based look at the use of school resource officers / Linda Duxbury & Craig Bennell.
Description: Abingdon, Oxon ; New York, NY : Routledge, 2020. | Includes bibliographical references and index.
Identifiers: LCCN 2019013818 (print) | LCCN 2019980074 (ebook) | ISBN 9780367198855 (paperback) | ISBN 9780367198886 (hardback) | ISBN 9780429243905 (ebook)
Subjects: LCSH: School police—Ontario—Peel (Regional municipality)—Evaluation. | Schools—Ontario—Peel (Regional municipality)—Safety measures. | School violence—Ontario—Peel (Regional municipality)—Prevention. | Police-community relations—Ontario—Peel (Regional municipality) | Peel Regional Police.
Classification: LCC LB2866 .D88 2020 (print) | LCC LB2866 (ebook) | DDC 371.7/82—dc23
LC record available at https://lccn.loc.gov/2019013818
LC ebook record available at https://lccn.loc.gov/2019980074

ISBN: 978-0-367-19888-6 (hbk)
ISBN: 978-0-367-19885-5 (pbk)
ISBN: 978-0-429-24390-5 (ebk)

Typeset in Bembo
by Swales & Willis Ltd, Exeter, Devon, UK

CONTENTS

ACKNOWLEDGEMENTS

A research endeavor of this magnitude requires extraordinary levels of support from a number of people and institutions. Accordingly, the authors would like to acknowledge and thank Peel District School Board, Dufferin–Peel Catholic District School Board, Peel Regional Police, the school resource officers (SROs), and the administrators and students in the five high schools that participated in this research for the time and energy they devoted to this study. It would not have been possible to conduct this study without the high levels of cooperation and commitment from each of these groups. We would especially like to thank the individuals from these institutions that stepped up to take part in the Research Advisory Board and the Social Return on Investment (SROI) Steering Committee for the extra time that they gave to this project.

We would also like to specifically acknowledge the unwavering support of Jennifer Evans (Police Chief of Peel Regional Police at the time the study was being done) and Christopher McCord (Deputy Chief of Peel Regional Police at the time the study was being done). This study would not have been possible without their leadership.

We would also like to thank Oscar Castaneda, GIS Analyst, Intelligence Services, Peel Regional Police, who developed and tested the tool used by the SROs to collect the activity data reported in this book. The activity-tracking phase of the research would not have gone as smoothly as it did without his help.

Asking busy SROs to track all of their activities for almost half a year was no minor request. The research team was very lucky to have had complete cooperation from a group of dedicated Peel Regional police officers, all of whom diligently tracked their activities on a daily basis. We would like to thank them for their commitment to this project and for their contributions to its success. We would also like to thank them for the passion they bring to their job and the community they service.

Thanks are also owed to Brandy Doan, Manager, Research and Analytics, Evidence-Based Education Services Team, Hamilton-Wentworth District School Board, and Brittany Blaskovits, PhD student, Department of Psychology, Carleton University, for their help in analyzing the Time 1 and Time 2 student surveys. Thanks also go out to Gregory Dole, a PhD student in the Sprott School of Business at Carleton University. His ride-along experiences with the SROs provided the stories that form the backbone of Chapter 8 of this book. Greg also co-authored with Duxbury a report entitled *SROI Manual for Policing Services in Canada.* Material describing Peel Regional Police's SRO program (Chapter 1) and the SROI process (Chapter 3) was drawn from this report.

We would also like to thank the SiMPACT Strategy Group for the SROI analysis featured in Chapter 9. Their knowledge of SROI was invaluable to us during this step of our analysis.

Finally, both Linda and Craig would like to give special thanks to their families for their continuous love and support. Linda could not have done it without John Chinneck, Annie Chinneck, Cheryl Duxbury and Randy Moore. Craig would like to thank Cindy Bennell, Noah Bennell, and Elijah Bennell.

1

INTRODUCTION

In an era where the costs of policing are constantly under scrutiny from the governing municipalities, the time has come for policing organizations to re-evaluate the services they provide. To do this, these organizations need to answer questions relating to the value these services create in the communities they serve. In other words, they need to change the focus of the conversation from "what does this service cost" to "what value does this service provide."

This book summarizes key findings from a longitudinal (from 2014 to 2017) multi-method (quantitative, qualitative, and ethnographic data) case study undertaken to identify the value of school resource officers (SROs) that are employed by Peel Regional Police. Of particular note is the application of Social Return on Investment (SROI) techniques in this evaluation process. SROI, a methodology that emerged from the not-for-profit sector, helps researchers identify sources of value outside of those considered through traditional valuation techniques, such as cost–benefit analysis.

We began our study by undertaking a review of the existing academic literature in this area. This review showed that most research on SRO programs is limited to descriptions of SRO officers and the activities they perform (e.g., what they do on a daily basis, typical traits of SRO officers, perceptions of such programs). While we did identify a few evaluations of the effectiveness of SROs (see Chapter 2), none of these assessments looked at, or quantified, the value SROs provide to students and/or communities. Research on this topic in Canada was particularly difficult to locate.

The research team also discovered that, although SROI techniques have been widely used by organizations in the not-for-profit sector to quantify social value creation, there is no evidence of this technique being used by police services in Canada (or elsewhere) to assign value to any of the roles they play, including the assignment of police officers to schools. In other words, while the costs associated with SRO programs are high and very visible, the value of such programs has not been reasonably demonstrated. Given the current conversations regarding the costs of policing and whether or not there is merit in having police officers in schools, there is a clear need to demonstrate the value (if any) created by investment in these types of policing programs. Such was the goal of our program of research.

Research Objectives

There appears to be a real need for research examining the value offered by SRO programs. The communities that have "protected" the SRO role spend considerable resources on such services and need to know and be able to communicate to their key stakeholders: (1) whether these investments are meeting their stated goals, and (2) the value such programs create (if any) and for whom. The research program summarized in this book has, therefore, two main objectives.

First, the research seeks to provide answers to communities, politicians, and school boards who question the value of SRO programs. Second, the research adds to the existing body of work on the subject of public value measurement in general and SROI techniques in particular. This study fills a critical gap in our understanding of the SRO role and should assist other policing services who seek to demonstrate the value that such programs deliver to their governing bodies (e.g., municipalities and provincial or state-level governments). It also illustrates how SROI methodologies can be used to quantify the value of proactive community-based policing activities.

Background

In 2012, a team of researchers from Carleton University in Ottawa, Ontario, Canada received funding from the Social Sciences and Humanities Research Council (SSHRC) to conduct research focusing on the changes that were required to make public policing in Canada more sustainable. They were tasked with developing an action-oriented framework for managing change in this sector. The SSHRC initiative was guided by a research advisory board (RAB) that included individuals representing the Canadian Police Association, the Canadian Association of Chiefs of Police, the Canadian Association of Police Boards, the Federation of Canadian Municipalities, the Canadian Police College, and the Staff Relations Representative Program of the Royal Canadian Mounted Police (RCMP) and the Ontario Provincial Police (OPP). This advisory board assisted us by providing feedback on proposed initiatives and helping us analyze and interpret key findings.

Working with a group of stakeholders from six police services across Canada, as well as other members of the policing and community safety communities in Canada, the research group worked to determine: (1) common challenges facing policing services in Canada, and (2) the vision the various stakeholders have for making public police services more sustainable.

Several of the participating police services asked the research team to focus on identifying and specifying a methodology that their organizations could use to demonstrate to the community they serve, as well as those who fund police services in Canada, the potential "value" of selected roles that they perform in their capacity as police. More specifically, these police services were looking for a methodology that extended the focus of value beyond dollars; they wanted a methodology that captured a greater diversity of inputs than the currently employed methodologies of Return on Investment (ROI) and crime-based data analysis.

The research initiative described in this book was undertaken with Peel Regional Police (often referred to in this report as the "Peel Police"). Key to their participation was the formation of a research steering committee (RSC) specific to this service. The Peel RSC, which was charged with identifying how Peel Regional Police wished to move forward with respect to addressing issues associated with the sustainability of public policing in Canada, was made up of 17 individuals: 11 people who worked for Peel Regional Police (Deputy Chief, Staff Superintendent, Superintendent, Inspector, Detective, Staff Sergeant, three Sergeants/Acting Sergeants, and two Constables), and six civilians who represented the public sector and private sector. These 17 individuals each participated in an hour-long interview to help inform the research to be undertaken in their community.

All members of the Peel RSC agreed that any initiative undertaken within Peel Region should meet two criteria: (1) it should focus on the community as a whole and its relationship with the service, and (2) it should provide insights into how the police could better communicate what they did, as well as the value they provided, to the external community. The Peel RSC was then asked, given these priorities, where they would like the research team to focus their efforts.

After much discussion, the Peel RSC asked the research team to determine the "value" of their existing Neighborhood Police Unit (NPU). More specifically, they wanted the team to focus on the potential value provided by one specific facet of this program – the School Resource Officer or SRO.

Peel Regional Police's SRO Program

Peel Regional Police Service polices the Peel region of Ontario, Canada. It is the second largest police service in Ontario, following the Toronto Police Service. The police service employs over 2,000 uniformed police officers and almost 1,000 support staff. The area policed by Peel Regional Police contains approximately 1.5 million people, including people from many different cultures. The area includes Toronto's international airport.

Peel Regional Police assign a full-time police officer to all secondary schools operating in the area policed by their service. The officers who are assigned to area high schools are known as School Liaison Officers (SLOs), School Resource Officers (SROs), or Neighborhood Police Officers (NPOs). Throughout this book, we use the term NPU when talking about the unit to which the school officer is assigned, and SRO to talk about the officer working in this unit, as these are the terms currently in use by the Peel Police.

The SRO program was set up to ensure that all high school students within the Peel Region encounter a safe and positive school setting in which they can live, work, visit, and learn. On their website, Peel Regional Police describe the program as follows:

> The primary responsibility of the School Resource Officer (SRO) is to strive to create a safe learning environment at our Secondary Schools. This is achieved by forming positive partnerships with students and school administration. It is encouraged that officers use a proactive style of policing and interact with youth in a non-enforcement manner on a regular basis.

Evaluation of this program was motivated by two primary factors. First, the costs of this program are both easy to identify and significant. Second, it is very challenging to identify the value (if any) that this program provides to students and the community, and, hence, to justify the costs in a time where budgets are being scrutinized. The challenges of quantifying the value offered by assigning full-time SROs to Canadian high schools is evidenced by the fact that such programs are rare in Canada, as police services have responded to pressures to economize by removing officers from schools and eliminating the role of the SRO.

Description of the Program

The NPU was originally designed to focus on street crime enforcement. In 2003, following the implementation of the Street Crime Unit within the Peel Regional Police, the NPU was given a revised mandate to focus on creating a safe learning environment in the region's secondary schools. SROs assigned to this unit were tasked with dealing with issues in secondary schools as well as liaising between the Peel Regional Police and the region's secondary schools.

The 2003[1] mandate for the program stated that SROs were responsible for each of the following activities and programs within the secondary school to which they were assigned:

- the enforcement of Federal, Provincial, and Municipal statutes;
- investigations of all such incidents, along with appropriate follow-ups;
- the creation of projects targeting behaviour that interferes with a safe learning environment;

- the monitoring of youth gang activity;
- the delivery of lectures to student groups;
- liaising between school officials and Peel Regional Police; and
- liaising between school officials at assigned feeder schools (Grades 7 and 8 schools) and Peel Regional Police.

In 2011, the Peel Regional Police's SRO program was given a second revised mandate[2] that featured the following nine specific directives:

- enhance the safety and security of the community;
- reduce the amount of violent crimes in the schools;
- reduce the involvement of youths in property crimes;
- create safe school environments which promote respect, responsibility, and civility;
- reduce occurrences of drug abuse through education;
- reduce the incidents of lawless public behavior within the school population;
- provide proactive policing in parks, plazas, and other public places where youth are known to congregate;
- increase the involvement of youths in crime reduction strategies and in youth programs; and
- maintain a proactive approach towards suspected gang-related activities.

While the program has gone through a few iterations of its mandate over time, the core objectives are to assign sworn police officers to work in the region's high schools so as to develop a relationship with the youths living in the region and to enhance perceptions of safety and security in high schools and the community. In that capacity, the SROs work directly with teachers, parents, and the community to ensure that the youths are either on the right path to a positive future or that they can get back to the right path.

There are 60 SROs working in the schools and school catchment areas in Peel Region. These SROs are supervised by eight Sergeants and four Staff Sergeants. The Staff Sergeants have other NPU responsibilities along with the SRO program. The total cost of the program is $9,004,900[3] per year (excluding costs for uniforms, law enforcement supplies, etc.).

Using SROI Methodologies to Evaluate the Peel Regional Police's SROs

A number of facts support the need to use SROI methodologies to assign value to Peel Regional Police's SRO program. First, the research team found that Peel Regional Police's investment in the SRO program is among the highest in the country, as many services in Canada, in an attempt to save money, have either eliminated the program altogether or assigned responsibility for multiple schools to one officer. Discussions with a number of Canadian police services revealed that many services have cut these programs because of funding challenges and that many police services do, in fact, feel that these programs provide value. Furthermore, all services that we talked to expressed a strong desire to have access to the SROI analysis so that they could use it to support the reintroduction of such a program in their community if the data showed that it had value.

Second, as noted earlier, a review of the literature indicated that very few systematic evaluations of the effectiveness of SRO programs have been undertaken. Rather, most of the research in the area is descriptive and focuses on what SROs do on a daily basis, the typical traits of these officers, and the perceptions of the program as articulated by key stakeholders. Moreover, the research in this area that did look at the value such programs offered focused on the level to which school administrators and parents expressed satisfaction with the SRO rather than more quantitative measures of value.

Third, Peel Regional Police have never conducted this type of evaluation of their SRO program. Given that Peel Regional Police invests a substantial amount of resources to maintain a police presence in schools, an evaluation of this program using SROI techniques will help them determine the extent to which this program is successful in meeting its stated goals.

We were then faced with the following question: What is the best way to explore the value that is being produced by Peel Regional Police's investment in the SRO program? As a first step to answering this question, the research team interviewed a group of current SROs and the Staff Sergeants who supervised these officers (as well as those who had held this role in the past). The interview focused on the role of the SROs in their schools and the value that these officers perceived they were delivering to the stakeholders they were serving. From the responses provided by these officers and the Staff Sergeants, it was clear that they perceived value being produced. It was also clear that capturing this value would be challenging.

We felt that the logical place to start was with the goals of the program. If the program's goals matched the outcomes, then it could be said that the program was achieving, or had achieved, what it set out to do. A subsequent literature review, coupled with discussions with Peel RSC members and representatives from both the Peel Regional Police and the school boards operating in the region, indicated that school administrators sought several benefits from the introduction of the SROs into their schools. More specifically, school administrators wanted the SRO program to deliver:

- increased safety in and around the schools;
- increased perceptions of safety on the part of the students, teachers, and parents;
- improved response times from the police to calls for service from the schools;
- decreases in student truancy rates; and
- an overall reduction in the number of distractions facing students.

Given the lack of existing research data on SRO programs, it was very difficult to know the extent to which these desired benefits were being realized. That being said, the fact that all the school administrators we talked to were able to clearly articulate what they wanted from the program indicated the potential for value to be created (i.e., if the actions of the SROs were creating the school administrators' desired benefits, then there was a tangible connection between the officers' work and value being created). This preliminary work also reinforced our perception that:

- a better understanding of the value of the SRO program required a methodology that went beyond the common metrics of costs and crime statistics; and
- SROI methodologies could inform the discussion through the development of an outcome map, which would link the actions or activities of the SROs with the desired goals/outcomes that inspired the creation of the SRO program in the first instance.

Road Map to the Research and the Book

"SROI is a complex and revealing methodology which avoids the imprecision of qualitative and blandness of quantitative evaluation" (MBA Associates, 2015, p. 4). SROI analysis combines stories about the difference made by a particular program or service with monetary value so things can be compared. Measuring SROI can be very expensive and time consuming, particularly when outcome data to measure the program does not exist. The fact that it took over 2.5 years to complete this study attests to the challenges one is likely to face when using SROI to evaluate a program.

Value was determined in a number of ways in this study, using a variety of different sources of data. This approach was taken to increase our confidence in, and generalizability of, our findings. Data collected during the SRO evaluation process are listed in Table 1.1. This book comprises ten chapters (including this one), each using a different source of data to discuss and determine value. In the section below, we provide a short description of each of the chapters included in this book.

The book itself is very comprehensive, so to increase the readability we begin each chapter with a short summary of key findings that are relevant to the chapter topic. Starting with Chapter 3, we also provide a short summary at the end of each chapter that lists key findings with respect to the value of the SRO program identified in that specific section of the book. Finally, it should be emphasized that it is the stories provided by key stakeholders, such as school administrators, grade 9 students, the officers that manage the SROs, and the SROs themselves that vividly illustrate the value provided to the community, high school students, and Peel Regional Police by this program. As such, we include stories where appropriate throughout the book to illustrate instances of value creation.

The second chapter in this book, "The Value of SROs: The View from Inside the Ivory Tower", provides a very brief review of the academic literature examined in the course of our research. The chapter is divided into two main sections. The first part summarizes academic research evaluating SRO programs, while the second part looks at the relationship between students' perceptions of violence in schools, school safety, and academic achievement. This second body of literature is important, given the focus in this book on the value of students' perceptions of safety.

In the third chapter, "How Do SROs Spend Their Time?", we summarize our key findings with respect to the activities undertaken by the SROs during the course of a typical work week. These activities served as the inputs to the SROI analysis.

TABLE 1.1 Summary of data

	2014	*2015*	*2016*
Interviews (qualitative data)	10 SROs	5 SROs and 5 school administrators (August); 10 school administrators (December)	29 school administrators (January–March); 8 SROs (January–March); 11 Peel Police stakeholders (Sergeants and Staff Sergeants) (March–April); 8 student interviews (April)
SRO activity data		Daily records kept by SROs working in the 5 participating high schools (September–December)	Daily records kept by SROs working in the 5 participating high schools (January–February)
Student surveys (quantitative data)		Surveyed students in Grade 9 in the 5 participating high schools in September (beginning of term) ($n = 610$)	Surveyed students in Grade 9 in the 5 participating high schools in March (end of term) ($n = 655$)
Ride-alongs (ethnographic data)		5 of 10	5 of 10

SROI analysis requires the collection of a variety of indicators of value (i.e., desired outcomes of the SRO program). Indicator data were collected over several years, and in several formats, and required complete cooperation and commitment from the various stakeholders. It is a fact that this study could not have been done without this high level of co-operation from the two school boards in Peel, Peel Regional Police, the SROs, and the administrators in the five participating schools. Outcome data and stories collected from a variety of key SRO stakeholders are presented and discussed in Chapters 4 through 8.

The key outcome explored in this study (perceptions of a safe learning environment) requires that data be collected from students. For example, how can you use an indicator that asks whether exposure to an SRO has an impact on students' feelings towards the police, or perceptions of safety at school, without somehow soliciting that information from the students? Chapter 4, "The Value of SROs: Views from Within (High School Students)", presents and discusses qualitative and quantitative data collected from the Grade 9 students attending the five[4] Peel District high schools participating in this study.

The challenges we faced when designing our study were exacerbated by the fact that the SRO program in Peel Region has been in place for more than two decades. This made it impossible for us to calculate value using pre–post comparisons. The fact that Peel Police's SRO program does not, however, operate in middle or elementary schools within the region gave us another option, as it implies that students would not regularly interact with an SRO until they began Grade 9. Accordingly, in this study, we collected survey data that enabled us to compare relevant student attitudes and outcomes at two points in time: (1) when the student started in Grade 9 (i.e., September, 2015) and (2) at the end of the first semester of Grade 9 (i.e., March, 2016).

Collecting quantitative survey data from the students in the five participating high schools was fundamental to the success of this research initiative. The research team was, therefore, incredibly fortunate to get buy-in for this study from the administrators at the five schools participating in the study, as they needed to take time from their busy schedules at two different time periods to organize and administer the student surveys. While we would have liked to interview a number of high school students, this was very difficult given the many privacy and ethical hurdles we would have to navigate to get such participation. As it was, the research team was happy to have been able to interview eight student volunteers attending one of the five schools in our study. Their comments and stories helped us interpret the survey data.

The fifth chapter of the book, "The Value of SROs: Views from Within (School Administrators)", looks at the SRO program through the eyes of the 29 school administrators (five Principals, 13 Vice Principals, seven guidance counsellors, and four social workers/psychologists) working in the five high schools that participated in this study.

In Chapter 6, "The Value of SROs: Views from Within (School Resource Officers)", we present and discuss key findings gleaned from multiple interviews conducted with the SROs working in the five high schools that participated in our study.

The seventh chapter of the book, "The Value of SROs: Views from Above (Staff Sergeants)", summarizes the opinions of the 11 Peel Staff Sergeants who regularly interact with the SROs. Coordinating the interviews with these stakeholders was challenging because they often needed to set aside as much as an hour of their time during their workday to complete the interview. Inevitably, there were interview cancellations/postponements that could be linked to the fact that many of these stakeholders work in environments that require that they respond to crises (e.g., police investigations). Again, we appreciated the cooperation we received from Peel Police throughout the course of this study and attribute their willingness to make themselves available as another indicator of the value they place in this program.

Chapter 8, "The Value of SROs: Insider Views from Officer Ride-Alongs", focuses on ethnographic data that were collected by having one of the PhD students who was involved in this study (Greg Dole) spend nine entire days with the various SROs involved in this study. During the ride-alongs, the student took great care to observe the SROs' activities and interactions with students, school administrators, and the community. Ride-alongs were organized through the NPU Staff Sergeants.

Chapter 9, "The Value of SROs: Social Return on Investment (SROI)", uses the data presented in earlier chapters of the book (inputs, indicators, outcomes) to monetize the value of the SRO program. This chapter includes a brief description of the SROI methodology, followed by information on SROI stakeholders, inputs, indicators, and outcomes. Also included in this chapter is a discussion of the challenges faced by those who want to use this methodology to identify the value of a particular police program or activity, along with suggestions on how these can be addressed.

The final chapter in the book, "The Value of SROs: Summary of Key Findings and Conclusions", presents a summary of findings on the value of Peel Regional Police's SRO program.

Notes

1 Peel Regional Police. (2003, April). Peel Regional Police (PRP) Regional N.P.U. Mandate. Unpublished internal document.
2 Peel Regional Police. (2011, August). Peel Regional Police Directive Issue No. I-B-416 (F). Unpublished internal document.
3 Deputy C. McCord, 2017, Email.
4 The five Peel Region high schools that participated in this study were selected in such a manner to ensure that we had schools from both school boards operating in the region. The schools were located in a diversity of neighborhoods: two were designated "urban-grant" schools and were located in socio-economically challenged areas in Peel Region; two schools were situated in "middle class" communities; and one school was in an affluent community. Four of these five schools had student populations that were ethnically diverse.

2

THE VALUE OF SROS

The View from Inside the Ivory Tower

WordMap: 25 most common words in Chapter 2: "The Value of SROs: The View from Inside the Ivory Tower"

Key Learnings

Despite the fact that School Resource Officers (SROs) are now commonplace in many schools, especially in the United States (US), academic research that offers insights into the value provided by these officers lags behind the increasing popularity of these programs.

Research that does exist covers a range of topics, including (1) the impact of SRO programs, (2) the role of the SRO, (3) the relationship between SRO programs and the potential criminalization of students, and (4) the value being created by these programs. We can say the following things based on this research:

- Research examining the impact of SRO programs has focused on how SROs impact variables such as crime and violence, perceptions of safety, and police–student relations. Across each of these areas, available research is decidedly mixed. In other words, some research suggests that SRO programs can have a positive impact on crime/violence, perceptions of safety, and police–student relations, whereas other research suggest that such programs have no effect, or even a negative effect;
- In terms of the role that SROs play, there appears to be little agreement in the literature, including what tasks should be included in the role of the SRO;
- While claims are often made that SRO programs will criminalize students, thus contributing to the "school-to-prison pipeline," little research exists that can be used to clearly establish a causal link between the presence of SROs and increased processing through the criminal justice system. One of the main challenges in this area is conducting methodologically strong studies (e.g., including relevant comparison groups, controlling for variables that may influence criminalization), which can establish such a link;
- As far as we are aware, only one study has examined the value of SRO programs. While this study suggested that the program was cost-effective, more research on this topic is clearly needed.

A second body of related research examines the relationship between students' perceptions of violence in schools and school safety, and academic achievement. The following conclusions can be reached based on this research:

- In general, research appears to support a connection between exposure to violence and lower academic achievement, which suggests that if SRO programs can have a positive impact on the degree of violence encountered at school, academic achievement may be improved;
- Based on existing research, there appears to be a strong link between the perception of safety and academic success. Our review suggests that it is the *perception* of safety, rather than actual safety, that is key to our understanding of why exposure to violence can be so detrimental to academic achievement.

SROs (also known as School Liaison Officers [SLOs] or Neighborhood Policing Unit [NPU] Officers) are increasingly common in the hallways of schools around the English-speaking world (Theriot, 2009). It is difficult to pinpoint exactly when and where SRO programs originated (Brown, 2006). While some researchers identify the first SRO program in the US as being in Flint, Michigan during the 1950s (Theriot & Orme, 2016), others argue that school–police partnerships existed before that time (Brown, 2006). What seems to be beyond doubt, however, is the fact that the number of school–police partnerships has increased over time in the US.

The late 1990s were a seminal moment for SRO programs in the US because of the Columbine High School massacre. The response to the subsequent public outcry against school violence was the US Department of Justice's Community Oriented Policing Services (COPS) funding for SRO training (James et al., 2011). The number of SRO programs in the US has grown considerably since this time because of federal incentives (Theriot & Orme, 2016). The 2012 mass shootings at Sandy Hook Elementary School in the US spurred further investment in SRO programs, as these programs became a focus for former President Barack Obama (Theriot & Orme, 2016). Currently, in the US, both sides of the political ideological spectrum support increasing the number of SRO programs (Chrusciel et al., 2015; Wolf, 2014).

Less is known about the use of SROs in the other parts of the world, although SROs are clearly relied on in other countries, including Canada (e.g., Kaplan Research Associates, 2014).

Unfortunately, academic research that offers insights into the value provided by such officers lags behind the increasing popularity of these programs (Na & Gottfredson, 2013; Wolfe et al., 2015). While academic research is being conducted more widely in the US, academic research conducted in other countries, including Canada, is particularly difficult to find. Also rare are academic studies looking at the relationship between violence in schools (real and perceived) and academic achievement. Given the sizeable public investment in education, and the prioritization of school safety by school boards in the US, Canada, and other developed economies over the past several decades, the lack of academic inquiry into this subject is puzzling.

This chapter is divided into two parts. We begin in part one by providing the reader with a brief review of academic research relating to SRO programs. Included in this part of the chapter are sections summarizing studies that have evaluated the impact of SRO programs, investigations into the roles played by SROs, studies that have looked at the relationship between SRO programs and the potential criminalization of students, and research exploring value being created by these programs. The second part of this chapter focuses on what research tells us about the relationship between students' perceptions of violence in schools and school safety and academic achievement. Included in this part of the chapter are summaries of literature that discuss how exposure to violence in schools and perceptions of safety impact academic achievement. We end the chapter by summarizing key findings from existing literature on SRO programs, and the relationship between students' perceptions of violence in schools and school safety, and academic achievement

Academic Research on SRO Programs

To identify research on SRO programs of relevance to this chapter, a search was conducted using various databases. Keywords and terms such as "school resource officer," "school liaison officer," "neighborhood policing officer," "neighborhood policing unit," and "neighborhood policing program(me)" were used to gather scholarly articles that might be relevant. This collection was then pared down to a working list of 50 titles that specifically addressed the SRO program phenomenon. We could locate very little published research outside of the US that examined SROs or SRO programs (e.g., in Canada, we only found two studies and these examined cyber-bullying and the role that SROs play in dealing with this activity [Broll, 2016] and the perceptions that officers have towards cyber-bullying [Broll & Huey, 2015]).

The academic literature on SRO programs can be broken into several categories, three of which are summarized below: (1) evaluations and impact assessments of SRO programs, (2) investigations into the role of SROs, and (3) the potential criminalization of students by SRO programs. While other papers relating to the SRO phenomenon were identified, most were either literature reviews or reflections from the SROs themselves. We also note that many of the papers we reviewed noted the need for more research into many aspects of SRO programs, including evaluations of the effectiveness of SROs and the value these officers provide students and communities. In fact, James and McCallion (2013) concluded their congressional review of law enforcement officers in schools by noting that there are very few studies evaluating the effectiveness of such programs.

Evaluation and Impact Assessments of SRO Programs

Researchers evaluate SRO programs by conducting investigations into the impact of these programs and by examining whether or not the program has been effective in achieving goals, such as the reduction of crime. Some impact studies were more exploratory in nature, focusing on the more esoteric. By way of example, Theriot (2016) looked at how an SRO program engendered a feeling of school connectedness and Wolfe et al. (2015) sought to identify key factors that influenced stakeholders' opinions of SROs.

While most researchers used survey tools during the evaluation process, samples varied widely from study to study. Researchers such as Hopkins et al. (1992), Johnson (1999), Jackson (2002), Jennings et al. (2011), Chrusciel et al. (2015), Crawford and Burns (2016), Theriot (2016), Wright (2016), and Eklund et al. (2018) quantified the impact of the SRO by surveying stakeholders such as school administrators, students, and law enforcement officers. May et al. (2011) analyzed survey data obtained from the SROs themselves, while Na and Gottfredson (2013) used existing data from the US School Survey on Crime and Safety to assess the impact of SRO programs. Rogers (2004) employed existing data from several governmental agencies in Alabama for a similar impact assessment approach.

Our review of this literature identified three different types of SRO evaluation research: (1) impact of the SRO on the reduction of serious crime and violence, (2) impact of the SRO on perceptions of safety, and (3) impact of the SRO on police–student relations. Details from each of these literatures of relevance to this study are provided below.

Reduction of School Crime

The evidence on the relationship between the presence of SROs in schools and the reduction in crime and/or serious violence is conflicting (Wolfe et al., 2015). Johnson (1999) finds that the number of crimes declined in middle schools and high schools following the introduction of SROs. Support for this view comes from Jennings et al. (2011), who note that the presence of SROs in schools acts as a deterrent to serious crime.

Maskaly et al.'s (2011) review of research on the association between SROs and violent crime in schools, on the other hand, determined that the evidence that SROs are effective in reducing school crime is mixed. They suggested that school characteristics, such as school size, might be more important predictors of school crime. While Maskaly et al.'s (2011) study concluded that SROs may indeed reduce the amount of school-related gang activity, all of the findings related to the relationship between SRO programs and crime in schools were inconclusive.

Other studies concluded that SRO programs have little impact on school safety. Stevenson's (2011) doctoral thesis research, which explored whether or not school incidents of aggression decreased following the implementation of an SRO program, found that the SRO did not effect a decrease in the number of such incidents at school. Rogers' (2004) doctoral thesis explored whether or not the implementation of an SRO program in a school system had engendered overall positive changes in the schools, including an enhanced learning environment and a decline in negative student behaviors. Rogers reported no measurable overall positive quantitative change from the implementation and continued presence of the SRO program.

Finally, a number of researchers point out that the body of research in this area does not allow for any definitive conclusions to be reached regarding the relationship between having SROs in schools and school violence. Na and Gottfredson (2013), for example, state that SRO programs have not been subjected to the sort of rigorous evaluation that could allow for causal conclusions to be reached. They also note a lack of longitudinal research in the area, comparing the situation before the SRO program was implemented to conditions after the program was in place. After reviewing 11 SRO evaluations, Petrosino et al. (2012) concluded: "the evidence base in terms of evaluation studies is still premature to make definitive conclusions about whether policing schools has an impact on crime and disorder in the schools" (p. 92). Clearly, more studies are needed in this area.

Perceptions of Safety

Our review identified a subset of research on the impact of SRO programs that relates to the relationship between SROs and perceptions of safety among various stakeholders (e.g., students and their parents, school administrators, the nearby community). Again, the findings were mixed. Studies by Johnson (1999) and May et al. (2004), for example, found that there was a positive correlation between SROs and the perception of safety in schools. In their study into the relationship between availability of a SRO and school administrators' perceptions of school safety, May et al. (2004) found that the most important predictor of this outcome was the frequency with which administrators met with their SROs. They also found that the school administrators in their study linked SRO effectiveness to good communication between themselves and the SROs. In fact, the school administrators surveyed in this study felt that positive communication between themselves and the SRO was a more important determinant of SRO effectiveness than any particular form of SRO training (May et al., 2004).

Other studies find quite different and mixed results. Tillyer et al. (2011), for example, observed that student safety strategies, including police patrol presence in schools, did not significantly diminish the students' perception of risk, instead finding that fear of crime and perception of safety was more rooted in students' actual victimization experience(s). Bracy (2011) found that students believe security strategies, such as SROs, are unnecessary because they perceive their schools to be safe places. Bracy (2011) also found that students did not believe their school safety could be attributed to the presence of SROs. Brown (2006) found that the majority of students who participated in his study believed that SROs helped to keep the schools safe, but had little impact on drugs and weapons being present in their school buildings.

McDevitt and Panniello's (2005) research found that students' overall impression of SROs can affect their perceptions of safety. More to the point, their results showed that perceptions of safety among students is moderated by whether or not students have a positive opinion of the SROs, and that the more positive a student's opinion of SROs, the safer the student feels. While Theriot and Orme (2016) also found that students with positive opinions of their SRO reported increased perceptions of safety, they identified a number of other factors, such as neighborhood crime, past victimization, and gender that also affected perceptions of safety. They note, for example, that students who perceive that crime in their neighborhood is low feel safer at school, while students who have experienced victimization feel less safe than students who have not been victimized (see McDevitt & Panniello, 2005). Theriot and Orme (2016) also observed that the students' perception of safety was strongly affected by whether these students had experienced victimization and/or school violence.

Theriot and Orme (2016) found that interactions with SROs did not affect students' perceptions of safety. The authors felt that these findings could be due to the fact that only half of students in their sample reported interacting with SROs.

It would appear that further research in this area is needed before any conclusions can be drawn about the impact SROs have on perceptions of school safety. Support for this conclusion comes from several sources. First, James and McCallion (2013) noted in their paper that positive studies of SRO programs typically collected data related to participant perceptions of safety as opposed to any objective evidence. Similarly, Na and Gottfredson (2013) report a lack of research demonstrating that SRO programs are achieving a fundamental goal of increasing school safety. Finally, in a recent paper, Theriot and Orme (2016) call for continued research on SROs and their impact on students' "feelings of safety, perceptions of school, and experiences with school violence" (p. 143).

Police–Student Relations

It is intimated in many of the papers we reviewed that SROs might be a useful step in creating better relations between youth and police. James et al. (2011) make an unsubstantiated claim that SROs with proper training do improve the image of law enforcement in the eyes of youth. The research in this area to date, while not particularly extensive, tells a different story. In terms of SROs and liaison officers having a positive effect on police–student relations, Hopkins et al. (1992) found that SROs had a negligible positive effect on improving the image of police with youth. A decade later, Jackson (2002) echoed this claim, finding that interactions with SROs did not change students' perceptions of police and observed that, on occasion, SROs were viewed by students to be more threatening than even gang members or bullies. Bracy (2010) echoed these observations in her ethnographic study of two high schools, concluding that the presence of SROs might negatively influence school climate.

Investigations into the Role of SROs

Establishing a clear definition of the role of the SRO is difficult given the diffusion of responsibilities that arise when one is a law enforcement officer in an educational environment. Although researchers have explored the role of SROs, relatively recent work by Lambert and McGinty (2002), and Brown (2006), noted that there is a real lack of clarity in our understanding of what it is that the SRO is supposed to do.

Lambert and McGinty's (2002), and Brown's (2006), critiques prompted several studies designed to help key stakeholders better understand and calibrate the role of the SRO. This research has taken various forms. Coon and Travis (2012), for example, employed surveys; Cray and Weiler (2011) analyzed a random sample of 178 public school districts from the US National Center for Educational Statistics; Lynch et al. (2016) analyzed data from the 2006 US School Survey on Crime; Choi et al. (2016) used semi-structured interviews; and Gill et al. (2016) performed qualitative analysis on a variety of source materials. In stark contrast to these aforementioned studies, Daniels et al. (2011) focused on interviews with three different SROs who had dealt with captive-taking scenarios, while Rhodes (2015) focused directly on the officers themselves, conducting surveys of SROs as well as uniform patrol officers.

Reviewing this body of literature, one is left with the impression that there is little agreement on what should and should not be included in the role of the SRO. Lambert and McGinty's (2002) paper surveyed principals, law enforcement administrators, and SROs to determine what characteristics and skills were important for SROs, only to discover that the various stakeholders held differing views and the role was ambiguous. Some years later, Brown's (2006) literature review urged the relevant stakeholders (e.g., SROs, school officials, policy makers, etc.) to properly conceptualize the role of the SRO so as to provide SROs with a defined set of duties and goals to pursue and accomplish.

Further underscoring the issue of SRO role ambiguity, Cray and Weiler (Cray & Weiler, 2011; Weiler & Cray, 2011) set out to determine the extent to which the SRO role was defined and documented, only to find that approximately 40% of schools in the study sample did not have clear guidelines for the SROs. Interestingly, but not necessarily contrary to other studies on SROs' job role, Rhodes (2015) determined that SROs do not have as much role ambiguity and conflict as do their road patrol policing counterparts. The author suggests that perhaps this can be attributed to the well-defined nature of the school setting and the greater autonomy enjoyed by SROs, as opposed to their road patrol counterparts (Rhodes, 2015).

Lynch et al.'s (2016) study attempted to address the issue of SRO role ambiguity by looking at the influence of context on the expectations placed on the SRO. This study found evidence that schools with more social and educational disadvantages require more law enforcement work from their SROs. These findings might go some way towards explaining some of the leeway in policy guidelines on SRO roles.

The Potential Criminalization of Students by SRO Programs

Many papers have been written exploring the potential causal links between SRO programs and student criminalization – a path that has been given the moniker, "the school-to-prison pipeline." The general premise of this line of research is that having SROs in schools, and interacting frequently with students, might result in unintended negative consequences for the students.

Virtually all research in this area has been conducted in the US. The US bias is important because, as Merkwae (2015) notes, there are significant differences between the SRO programs in the UK and Canada as compared with the US. To wit, when Bough (1998) examines the SRO practice in schools, it is done from the perspective of the US constitution and the fourth amendment provisions regarding lawful/unlawful searches and seizures. A further example of the US bias is in Berger (2002), wherein the author presents a literature review of existing US judicial decisions that suggest the diminishing rights of students in schools with SROs.

Studies in this particular area of SRO research run the gamut when it comes to research methodology and samples. Theriot (2009) evaluated the impact of SROs by performing a statistical analysis of school-based arrest rates of a sample of schools (13 with SROs and 15 without). Bracy (2011) used an ethnographic and in-depth interview approach to determine the effect of SROs on students' rights. Robles-Piña and Denham (2012) used a mixed methods approach of open-ended interviews as well as survey instruments to evaluate the differences between SROs contracted by independent schools and SROs contracted from local law enforcement agencies. May et al.'s (2016) paper used an analysis of statistical data to examine how the so-called school-to-prison pipeline plays out in rural areas. Owens (2017) studied correlations between US government grants for SRO programs and the relevant crime stats.

So, what conclusions came out of these studies? After reviewing the above studies, we conclude that evidence supporting the idea that SROs will increase the criminalization of students is decidedly murky. It is challenging to determine what comes first: the student committing criminal acts or the presence of SROs. As Owens (2017) points out, there remains very little research on the causal effect of SROs in schools.

The most persuasive papers are those that are the most rhetorical in nature, such as Merkwae (2015), Bracy (2011), and Kupchik and Monahan (2006). They argue that SRO programs introduce and normalize students to the prison system and negatively impact youth of colour and youth with disabilities. The papers that rely on more objective findings, on the other hand, present more nuanced findings. Theriot's (2009) study, which we mentioned above, is a case in point. Applying regression models to data collected from 13 schools with SROs and 15 schools without, he found a mixed pattern of results: the presence of SROs was associated with a decrease in arrests for assault and weapons charges, but an increase in arrests for disorderly conduct. SROs did not predict higher total arrests of students in Theriot's study.

A significant challenge associated with research in this area is that many studies have methodological weaknesses. For example, numerous studies do not include adequate comparison groups (e.g., Johnson, 1999) and many studies are based on inadequate samples (e.g., just one school; Dohrn, 2001). Controlling for other factors that can influence the criminalization of students is another challenge (e.g., zero tolerance school policies, requirements for schools to report certain incidents to the police, limited constitutional protection of students in US schools). Without controlling for a range of variables, it isn't possible to isolate the effect that SROs have on the criminalization process. Nance (2016) recently carried out such a study, and found that the presence of police in schools increased the odds that school officials referred students to the police for a range of offence types. However, based on the data he had access to, Nance wasn't able to determine how often the students were actually arrested by the police.

Based on our assessment of the literature, we must conclude that while logically there may indeed be a causal link between SRO presence and student criminalization, sufficient research evidence to confirm or deny such a connection is not available at this time. Once more research becomes available, especially research that relies on the sort of sophisticated analysis used by Nance (2016), we may be able to understand the role that SROs play (or don't play) in the criminalization process.

What Do We Know About the Value of SRO Programs?

The literature on SROs rarely speaks to the value being created by these programs. Some papers, such as Jennings et al. (2011), skate around the topic: "The preponderance of evidence to date and including the current research suggest that there is an inherent value of SROs on school campuses" (p. 122). The question then becomes – what is this inherent value? The paper's authors do not explore the characteristics of this value that could logically be teased out and measured. By and large, the field of study related to SRO programs has not moved towards capturing and elucidating the value being created by the investment in such programs.

Perhaps the closest evaluation of the value of SROs was performed by Carroll et al. (2010), who assessed the efficiency of the program in the Broward (Florida) Sheriff's Office. From the perspective of efficiency, Carroll et al. (2010) analyzed the relationship between the program's outcome(s) and the program's budget, and concluded that the SRO program was efficient because, in ten of the 12 years they looked at, the cost of crime was a little higher than program costs.

While Carroll and colleagues' (2010) work provides some insights into the efficiency of investments in SRO programs by creating a ratio of the yearly cost of juvenile crime versus the yearly SRO program costs, the insights still do not generate a greater understanding of the value being created by the program, which is beyond the scope of Carroll et al.'s (2010) study. That being said, Carroll et al.'s (2010) study represents the only attempt we found in the academic literature to put real numbers on the return on the investment in SRO programs.

What can be concluded from this review, then, is that there is a need to better understand the value being created by SRO programs. As with all aspects of SRO programs, more research is needed. With respect to the value question, exploratory research is needed because there has not yet been a focus on value in the existing literature.

Critique: Academic Studies into SRO Programs

Given the significant public investment in SRO programs in the US, and the fact that the Obama administration gave priority to funding for these programs, it is curious that research into the effectiveness or value offered by such programs has not been particularly extensive. A literature review revealed approximately 50+ research papers on the topic, many of which were not actual studies of SRO programs, but, rather, literature reviews and *de facto* opinion pieces. The three main categories of research on SRO programs identified in our review (i.e., program evaluations, clarification of the SROs role, and the relationship between SRO programs and the criminalization of students) have produced mixed findings. Many researchers have called for more investigations in each of these areas to move the field forward. We also note that, at this point in time, there seems to be a fundamental lack of recognition within the research community that SROs are producing outcomes that can be captured and evaluated.

To date, very little has been done to determine the value of SROs, and, in most cases, the conversation has not moved beyond examining the perception of safety. Unfortunately, we could not find any research that attached any sort of value to this outcome (i.e., what is the value of feeling safe in schools?). The analysis done in this book fills this critical gap in our understanding. With respect to SRO programs and how they affect police–youth relations, this too could be assessed from the perspective of the value of positive police–youth relations – the caveat being that more research is needed to determine causal links between SRO programs and positive police–youth associations. Finally, in terms of how SRO programs potentially criminalize students, the phenomenon could be turned on its head to investigate if SRO programs divert students from criminality. In that scenario, the larger value question emerges of what is the value of diverting students (read young people) from criminalization.

The Relationship between School Violence and Academic Achievement

To identify research linking perceptions of school violence (and actual school violence) to academic achievement, we conducted another literature search using various databases. Given that this particular area of academic inquiry has not been explored in great detail, there is no specific term or terms that tie together the literature available. As such, several different search terms were employed in an attempt to locate all the relevant research papers and studies. Search terms included: "school violence," "school violence and academic success/achievement," "school safety," "perception of safety in schools," "perception of safety and academic achievement," "early childhood/childhood exposure to violence," "adolescent exposure to violence," "community exposure to violence and academic achievement," and "community exposure to violence and cognitive development."

This search determined that most research in this area has centered around the effect of violence on academic achievement. Most recently, Burdick-Will (2016) looked at the effect of neighborhood violence on standardized test scores; Graham et al. (2016) looked at the learning problems of refugee children; Ullah et al. (2016) studied the effects of US military drone strikes on students' academic performance; Hopson et al. (2014) explored how school climate affected student behavior and grades; Sharkey et al. (2012) examined whether the burden of violence in a community (operationalized as local homicide) had an effect on classroom learning; Ripski and Gregory (2009) looked at victimization as a predictor of high school achievement; Solberg et al. (2007) studied the influence of exposure to community violence on academic achievement; Ratner et al. (2006) examined how community violence affected cognitive outcomes; Flannery et al. (2004) evaluated students' exposure to school violence and academic attainment; Margolin and Gordis (2000) reviewed the extant literature to do with children's reactions to three types of violence; Gronna and Chin-Chance (1999) studied the effect of school safety on academic achievement in mathematics and reading (which is available through analysis of SAT scores); and Osofsky (1995) looked at how exposure to violence affected children.

Of relevance to this research is the fact that our extensive search of the academic literature in this area did not uncover any research that has looked at the value being created by the various investments in school safety using outcomes such as academic achievement. In other words, the question of what the value is of the investment in creating safe environments for students has not been posed by researchers.

Researchers have employed myriad research methodologies and used a variety of information sources when examining the relationship between school violence and perceptions of safety and academic achievement. Many researchers address these issues by analyzing data compiled in reports such as the US National Crime Victimization Survey. Still others mine data from the likes of SAT scores, the US National Study of Adolescent Health, the US School Success Profile, and the 1999 Metlife Survey. Other authors use more localized data, such as Burdick-Will's (2016) analysis of the data from the Chicago Police Department and Chicago Public Schools.

There were also a small number of studies that examined the relationship between exposure to violence and academic achievement. Ullah et al. (2016) analyzed data from 403 students chosen randomly from schools in Pakistan. Ratner et al. (2006) conducted a longitudinal study of 656 eligible children in the Detroit (MI) area. Solberg et al. (2007) surveyed 789 students in a large American Midwestern city. Flannery et al. (2004) conducted two studies, with a total sample of 5,969 students in Grades 9 through 12. Skiba et al. (2004) surveyed 2,465 students in two junior high/middle schools and three high schools in the American Midwestern states. Noaks and Noaks (2000) surveyed 29 boys and 32 girls in Year 9 at a school in Wales (UK). Gronna and Chin-Chance (1999) studied Grade 8 students in 46 of the 50 eligible schools in the state of Hawaii. Several of these studies were commissioned by US government organizations.

In the sections below, we review literature within the two main themes in this larger body of research: (1) the relationship between exposure to violence in school/the community and academic achievement, and (2) the relationship between perceptions of safety and academic achievement.

The Relationship between Exposure to Violence in School and Academic Achievement

Research examining the relationship between exposure to violence and cognitive abilities/academic achievement can be classified several different ways. First, a distinction can be made between studies drawing on samples of children versus samples of young adults (teenagers/high schoolers). Second, a distinction can be made between exposure to violence at school and exposure to violence in the local community surrounding the school.

In general, our review supports a connection between exposure to violence and lower academic achievement. Margolin and Gordis (2000) argue that, while exposure to violence is not a mediator variable for academic achievement/success, exposure to violence is not without its effects. Osofsky (1995) points out that the exposure of children to violence can vary from temporary upset to post traumatic stress disorder (PTSD).

Ratner et al. (2006) offer what might be the definitive work on the subject of early childhood exposure to violence and cognitive development. While not entirely related to the focus of our study, there are, nonetheless, insights from Ratner et al.'s research that may be tangentially applied to our study, which conceptualizes a safe learning environment as a key outcome of value. Ratner et al.'s (2006) study focused on six- and seven-year-olds in Detroit (MI) and showed that exposure to violence could potentially damage a "wide range of cognitive skills and abilities [in these children] and that these relations were still statistically significant even after the effects of many indices of poverty" (p. 278). Ratner et al. attribute this relationship between community violence exposure (CVE) and cognitive development to the "fight or flight" response, which they argue is triggered by CVE and inhibits typical cognitive processing. They base this argument on the idea that CVE activates a neurotransmitter response (noradrenaline) that, in turn, may inhibit a student's ability to focus, pay attention, and recall information (Ratner et al., 2006).

Walkley and Cox's (2013) review of the relevant literature on exposure to violence cites findings from Perry (2009), which is consistent with the above argument: "when a child is threatened, various neurophysiological and neuroendocrine responses are initiated. If they persist, there will be 'use-dependent' alterations in the key neural systems involved in stress response" (p. 1). Walkley and Cox (2013) then draw a connection between these physiological responses and the potential for impaired cognitive development. Perry's (2009) review of the existing literature on how trauma affects development also cites multiple ways in which trauma (in all its forms) may affect cognitive development from *in utero* through childhood. Much like Ratner et al. (2006), Perry (2009) cites the overstimulation of the "fight or flight" response as an impediment to cognitive development.

As mentioned, Ratner et al. (2006) found that community violence exposure has been linked to negative academic outcomes. This link is further supported by Sharkey (2010), who cites research finding that both direct and indirect exposure to violence can negatively affect cognitive performance. Sharkey also reports data supporting the idea that environmental stress affects cognitive performance, with specific reference to memory. Echoing those findings, Osofsky's (1995) literature review found that school-aged children exposed to violence could struggle with paying attention and concentrating.

Sharkey's (2010) research found, in a particular sample, that violence had a substantially negative affect on children's cognitive function. While Sharkey's findings were not found to be generalizable, they indicated that a strong negative relationship might exist between the after-effects of violence and cognitive function. Sharkey et al.'s (2012) subsequent study found that parental distress in reaction to localized violence was a pathway for such violence to affect a child's performance in cognitive assessment. Sharkey concluded that a parent's exposure to violence can negatively affect their child/children. This is notable because it indicates a more complex pathway for children's cognitive abilities to be affected by localized violence and, therefore, gives credence to the caution advised by Margolin and Gordis (2000) in terms of attributing causality.

Solberg et al.'s (2007) study of 789 high school youth found that there was indeed a relationship between violence and academic outcomes. Cluster analysis undertaken by these authors determined that higher exposure to violence did, in fact, translate into lower grades as well as lower retention in school. These authors also report that, in both resilient and not-at-risk groups of students, exposure to violence was a mediating variable between violence and grade scores.

Ullah et al.'s (2016) study of 403 students in Pakistan, while not related to violence in school but, rather, to US drone strikes in the Pakistani North Waziristan region, does conclude that exposure to violence negatively affects academic achievement. This being said, it is somewhat challenging to apply the learnings from this study on US military drone strikes in Pakistan to more common forms of school violence found in the Western world.

The literature includes a few studies that offer more definitive connections between exposure to violence in schools and diminished academic achievement. One of the earliest studies examining the relationship between school safety and academic achievement was Gronna and Chin-Chance's (1999) examination of a sample of middle schools in Hawaii. The researchers started with the research question: To what extent does the maintenance of a safe school influence individual student achievement? The authors report a statistically significant relationship between increased student learning and higher levels of perceived safety in schools. They concluded that students in schools deemed safer had higher levels of academic performance than students in schools deemed less safe. This study also found that maintaining school order and a quiet atmosphere had a consistent influence on students' performance in mathematics and reading. In particular, these researchers found that "every one standard deviation increase in school safety produced a .12 standard deviation change in mathematics achievement. Similarly, for every one standard deviation increase in school safety a .12 standard deviation change in reading achievement occurs" (Gronna & Chin-Chance, 1999, p. 13).

As Flannery et al. (2004) point out, there are very few studies focused on violence in schools and its effect on students. Interestingly, reported rates of exposure to violence in schools are higher than reported rates of direct victimization. In either case, a trauma occurs and is related to various emotional and behavioral problems (Flannery et al., 2004). The authors' 2004 study indicated strong correlations between school violence and student trauma. Furthermore, as the authors write, school violence has the capacity to affect the entire school:

> Where school violence is prevalent, students tend to be more cautious in order to avoid becoming the next victim. They can become hyper-vigilant and wary of people around them. The entire school suffers, not just perpetrators and victims. Where violence is prevalent, the climate of the entire school can be affected and can contribute to the continuation of the cycle of violence exposure, victimization, and perpetration of violence on school grounds.
>
> *(Flannery et al., 2004, p. 570)*

Flannery et al. (2004) also make the argument that victimization negatively impacts students' abilities to learn in school:

> It is hard to concentrate on academic subjects unrelated to daily life when students are constantly worrying about the next time they will be harassed, what they can do to get revenge on their tormentor, or if they will become the next victim. Students may become withdrawn, isolated, or inattentive in class. These effects will negatively impact their motivation and ability to learn, as well as their socialization with peers and the quality of their relationships with adults at their school.
>
> *(p. 570)*

In a review of the relevant literature, Cornell and Mayer (2010) find there is a relationship between delinquent student behavior and academic achievement. There is also a relationship between students' delinquent behavior and their victim's academic achievement. Student anxiety over fears for their own personal safety is also a concern. Finally, there is a relationship between the delinquent behavior of students and the engagement of their teachers. Both students and teachers are compromised by delinquent behavior in schools.

Bowen and Bowen (1999) review the relevant literature and make similar claims: that the delinquent behavior of students draws attention away from teachers and, thus, adversely interferes with their teaching objectives as well as the time that these teachers actually devote to teaching. Bowen and Bowen also cite research finding that one in four teens reported that the "threat of violence at their school interfered with teaching effectiveness" (Bowen & Bowen, 1999, p. 323).

Perception of Safety and Academic Achievement

While it may be challenging to conclude definitively that exposure to violence directly impacts academic achievement, a review of the literature indicates that there are very strong links between the perception of safety and academic success. In other words, it is the *perception* of safety, rather than actual safety, that is key to our understanding of why exposure to violence can be so detrimental to academic achievement. Ratner et al.'s (2006) study found a statistically strong relationship between a negative perception of safety and diminished academic achievement. More specifically, students who perceived their environment as being unsafe did not perform as well on cognitive and achievement outcome measures as did students who perceived their environment as being safe (Ratner et al., 2006). It is important to note that this study was limited to children in the age range of six to seven. As such, it is problematic to draw conclusions from this study that similar conditions would exist for high school students. Nevertheless, the study indicates that there is a relationship between perceptions of safety and cognitive outcomes, and that this relationship could very well hold true for students in older age groups.

Ratner et al. (2006) argue that the link between perceptions of safety and academic performance can be explained as follows: (1) students who feel safe experience less anxiety, (2) students with lower levels of anxiety are better able to direct more energy towards their schoolwork, and (3) students who spend more energy on their schoolwork experience better academic outcomes. In other words, they argue that it is this *feeling* of being safe that frees up time and focus that might otherwise not be dedicated towards learning tasks (Ratner et al., 2006).

Ratner et al. (2006) also report that "children who reported they felt safe, regardless of their actual exposure to community violence, performed better on most of the cognitive and achievement outcome measures" (p. 278). These authors provided an extensive background to speculate as to why their findings might be generalizable. Their reasoning included that feeling safe reduced feelings of anxiety/worry/stress that interfered with processing resources that could otherwise be focused on schoolwork. Following that line of logic, if a student is able to focus because they feel safe, they may have a greater likelihood of achieving better grades (Ratner et al., 2006).

Theriot and Orme (2016) find, in their review of the relevant literature, that students with higher grade point averages also report feeling safer in their schools. Their own research also showed that students' sense of safety is significantly affected by experiences with school violence. These findings support the idea that perception of safety affects students' learning experiences.

In their review of the literature, Perumean-Chaney and Sutton (2013) note that previous studies had found that, when students perceive their schools to be unsafe, they are more likely to skip school to avoid becoming a victim of violence. Perumean-Chaney and Sutton found other studies in which students who perceived their schools to be unsafe were then more likely to be focused on self-protection and, subsequently, more likely to give less attention to their studies, which then had detrimental effects on academic achievement.

Finally, by establishing the importance of school climate as a "determinant of behavior," Ripski and Gregory (2009) set a logical basis from which to explore the relationship between perception of victimization, as well as perception of hostility, and academic achievement. The study's limitations notwithstanding, the findings do indeed demonstrate that students who report their academic environments to be hostile, and report being victimized, have lower academic achievement (Ripski & Gregory, 2009).

Critique: Academic Studies on the Link Between School Safety and Academic Achievement

In conclusion, the above review of the literature provides strong support for the idea that exposure to violence at school (or in the community or home) has a negative impact on academic achievement. Margolin and Gordis (2000) point out, however, that causality remains an issue in many of these studies and that not all exposure to violence results in poorer academic achievement. What seems much clearer is that the perception of safety has been found to affect academic achievement, a finding that is relevant to our research on the value of the SRO. As is often the case, more research is needed. Given the seemingly clear relationship between feeling safe and academic achievement, there may be ample opportunity to make more definitive observations about how engendering positive perceptions of safety among students subsequently results in improved academic outcomes.

Summary and Conclusions

Despite the fact that SROs are now commonplace in many schools, especially in the US, academic research that offers insights into the value provided by these officers lags behind the increasing popularity of these programs. Research that does exist covers a range of topics, primarily focusing on: (1) the impact of SRO programs, (2) the role of the SRO, and (3) the relationship between SRO programs and the potential criminalization of students.

Research examining the impact of SRO programs has focused on how SROs impact variables such as crime and violence, perceptions of safety, and police–student relations. Across each of these areas, available research is decidedly mixed, with some research suggesting that SRO programs have a positive impact on these variables, some research suggesting that these programs have no effect, and still other research suggesting that these programs have a negative effect. In terms of the role that SROs play, there appears to be little agreement in the literature about what should (and shouldn't) be included in the SRO role.

Perhaps the issue that has received the most attention in the research literature is whether SRO programs criminalize students, thus contributing to the so-called "school-to-prison pipeline." Our review of existing literature suggests that few studies exist which can clearly establish a causal link between the presence of SROs and increased processing through the criminal justice system. One of the main challenges in this area is that most studies have important methodological weaknesses. For example, studies commonly lack relevant comparison groups, they often rely on small samples, and rarely do researchers control for variables that may influence criminalization in order to isolate the role that SRO programs might play in the criminalization process.

In contrast to this literature, more research, and higher quality research, exists on related topics, such as research focusing on the link between students' perceptions of violence in schools and school safety, and academic achievement. In general, this body of research appears to support a connection between exposure to violence and lower academic achievement, which suggests that if SRO programs can have a positive impact on the degree of violence encountered at school, academic achievement may be improved. Based on existing research, there also appears to be a strong link between the perception of safety and academic success. Our review suggests that it is the *perception* of safety, rather than actual safety, that is key to our understanding of why exposure to violence can be so detrimental to academic achievement.

3

HOW DO SROS SPEND THEIR TIME?

information
spent
officers Peel prevent
engage patrol
school required
report
community
hours
role
SROs activities Police
critical calls activity spend administrators
crime reactive
value
time
proactive

WordMap: 26 most common words in Chapter 3: "How Do SROs Spend Their Time?"

Key Learnings

The Social Return on Investment (SROI) methodology used in this project requires the researcher to identify key inputs to the system being evaluated. This means that anyone using this technique has first to identify the key inputs of interest (in this case, the various activities undertaken by the School Resource Officers [SROs] and then identify how best to quantify these inputs [in this case, the amount of time our SROs spent in each activity]). This chapter describes how we set about meeting these goals. It also provides data describing the various activities undertaken by SROs.

Our research supports the following conclusions:

- SROs spend almost a third of their time on information gathering activities to help prevent crime. These activities also serve to enhance relationships with key stakeholders;
- SROs spend almost a quarter of their time on administrative work;
- SROs spend approximately a quarter of their time using the knowledge they have gained to enforce the law and/or respond to a call for service;
- SROs spend approximately 10% of their work time engaged in each of the following four activities: (1) criminal calls for service at, or around, the school, (2) general patrol in the neighborhood around the school, (3) acting as a liaison between school administrators and Peel Regional Police, and (4) other patrol work.

Peel Police's Neighborhood Police Unit (NPU) was put in place to work with high school administration and staff to create a safe learning environment at secondary schools located within Peel Region. To this end, Peel Regional Police have placed an SRO in each of the high schools operating in Peel Region. Two SROs are assigned to each school and each SRO pair has responsibility for two different schools. SROs seek to create a safe learning environment by forming positive partnerships with students, school administrators, and staff, by working to prevent crime and victimization within the school and the school's catchment area, and by enforcing the law.

The SROI methodology used in this project requires the researcher to identify key inputs to the system being evaluated. This meant that before we could calculate the value of Peel Police's SRO program we had to:

- identify the various activities undertaken by the SROs (i.e., inputs to the SROI process);
- measure the amount of time each of the SROs operating in the five schools participating in our study spent on each of these activities; and
- link the various activities engaged in by the SROs to the likelihood of the SRO program achieving its goals (i.e., the creation of a safe learning environment).

To inform this process, we began by reviewing the academic and practitioner literatures in the area (see Chapter 2). Our review uncovered lists of the job duties SROs carry out when assigned to schools, lists of the different roles they are required to play, descriptions of the relationships they are expected to create and maintain, and a catalogue of key job functions that they are expected to deliver. We also scanned several job descriptions that police services across Canada and the US have used to recruit people to the SRO position and identified a diverse range of duties that were incorporated into the SRO role. We concluded from this review that the SRO is expected to be "everything to everyone," as most job descriptions are seeking someone who is familiar with the law, but can also function as a public safety specialist, liaise with the community, solve unique problems on the fly, educate students on the law, and act as a positive role model. Job descriptions also typically discussed the desired characteristics of an SRO (e.g., good public speaker, self-disciplined, self-motivated). We even found anecdotal evidence from the media on what it was that SROs are supposed to do, as illustrated by the following quote from CNN (Botelho & Ellis, 2015):

> School resource officers, or SROs, supervise lunchrooms, coach sports, promote drug and alcohol awareness, and become confidants to teens who might have never thought they'd befriend a police officer. SROs may build relationships at a key time in many young people's lives.

With a few exceptions (see, for example, May & Higgins, 2011) we were unable to unearth a comprehensive list of the specific day-to-day activities that SROs are expected to execute in order to meet the role responsibilities listed above. In other words, we could not identify what SROs actually *did* to "create a school setting that is safe and secure and promotes learning." This type of information is critical to our ability to evaluate the SRO program and quantify the value provided by having SROs in schools. As such, we devoted considerable time and effort to identifying the activities undertaken by these officers, classifying these activities into major groups, and measuring the frequency with which the officers engaged in each of these key activities.

This chapter presents the key findings with respect to the activities undertaken by SROs operating in Peel District high schools. It is divided into five subsections. In the first, we discuss how we identified the different activities undertaken by Peel Regional Police's SROs. The second section outlines a typology we developed to classify these different activities, while the third discusses how we went about measuring officer participation in each of the activities identified. Key findings with respect to the amount of time spent in the various SRO activities are presented in the fourth section. The chapter ends by summarizing key findings from this stage of our analysis.

Identification of Activities Undertaken by SROs

To identify the main activities performed by Peel Police SROs we consulted three stakeholder groups: school administrators, the SROs themselves, and the steering committee guiding this research. Six months before the evaluation was to begin, we interviewed a school administrator at each of the five schools participating in this study and asked them to identify all the activities they had either observed or of which they had second-hand knowledge (e.g., heard from a parent or a student) of their SROs performing. At the same time, we also interviewed each of the eight SROs working at the five schools that were participating in this study and asked them to list the activities they engaged in when enacting their role. We used findings from these two sets of interviews to compile a list of SRO activities. We then met with our research steering committee (see Chapter 1) and asked them to validate the activities that had been identified and add any to the list that had been missed. At the end of this process we were left with a list of the 19 main activities that all parties agreed that SROs working in the Peel District secondary schools executed at work. We also included a twentieth category labeled "other" to our list to account for the possibility that there were additional activities that the key stakeholders had not mentioned. The activities that were agreed upon are listed in Table 3.1.

TABLE 3.1 Activities undertaken by SROs

Activities (Inputs)
SROs walk around the school with school administrators
SROs walk around targeted areas where students congregate
SROs patrol (on foot or in cars) the neighborhood around the school
SROs engage in extracurricular activities with students (e.g., sports, charity events) either at the school and/or within the community
SROs monitor social media (e.g., searching/researching social media sites)
SROs participate in Problem Oriented Policing (POP) projects within their community
SROs assist other Peel Regional Police bureaus with NPU-related investigations
SROs pass on relevant information to other bureaus within Peel Regional Police
SROs respond to requests for service/information from other school community members
SROs serve an educational role within their school(s) (i.e., educating them about the law)
SROs serve as a liaison between school administrators and Peel Regional Police
SROs use information they have gathered to prevent criminal activity from occurring (in the school and in the school's catchment area)
SROs engage in emergency preparedness exercises within the school
SROs respond to criminal calls for service at the school and in the school's catchment area (e.g., drugs, pimping, assaults, robberies, thefts, mischief, threats, extortion, child porn, harassment, sexual assault, etc.)
SROs respond to non-criminal (but critical) calls for service at the school and in the school's catchment area (e.g., trespassing, domestic violence, liquor infractions, fighting, etc.)
SROs enforce federal/provincial/municipal laws in the school and in the school's catchment area
SROs spend time dealing with critical incidents at the school and in the school's catchment area (e.g., mental health related, behaviour issues, etc.)
SROs conduct patrol work not related to NPU
SROs attend court
Other (report writing, training, etc.)

Classification of Activities

Examination of the list of SRO activities shown in Table 3.1 determined that the SROs engaged in activities that were either reactive or proactive in nature. Proactive policing is the practice of deterring criminal activity by showing police presence and engaging the public to learn about their concerns. The focus of proactive policing is to prevent crime from occurring in the first place. In contrast, responding to a complaint after a crime has been committed and/or responding to a call for service is reactive policing.

Oxford Bibliographies[1] provides an excellent discussion of these two concepts. The following definition is taken from this website:

> Proactive policing [sometimes referred to as community policing, problem-oriented policing, or intelligence led policing] can take on a variety of meanings. In the most general sense, it is the polar opposite of reactive policing, which is characterized by randomized patrol, rapid response to calls for service, and retrospective investigations. Instead of waiting for a crime to transpire, proactive policing entails striving to prevent crime before it ever comes to fruition . . . On the whole, proactive policing is the antithesis of traditional policing methods. Rather than reacting to crime as it comes to their attention, the proactive movement calls for the police to do everything they can to try to prevent crime from occurring in the first place.

Our interviews with the school administrators and the SROs determined that these officers engaged in reactive activities as a response to something that had already happened at the school or in the school's catchment area that required a response from the officer. In all reactive situations, the SROs undertook a variety of actions to resolve the matter effectively and re-establish a safe learning environment. All the activities in the proactive grouping, on the other hand, were actions taken by the SROs either to prevent a crime, avert the victimization of other students, or forestall antisocial activity. All proactive actions were undertaken to prevent crime/non-social behavior, thereby fostering a safe learning environment.

Our review of the literature (see Chapter 2) indicated that SROs' activities may be positively correlated with a reduction in the amount of school violence and criminal behavior (Dogutas, 2008), but provided no insights into which activities were more impactful. Our study addressed this gap in our understanding by looking at the relative value of having SROs engage in proactive versus reactive policing activities (see Chapter 9). In fact, part of the reason we elected to use SROI methodology in this study was that it offers a method to put a value on proactive policing activities and calculate the value of something like victimization or fighting *not* happening.

Further analysis of the data showed that the SRO activities listed in Table 3.1 could also be classified along a second dimension, which represented how information was viewed/used by the SRO when undertaking each of these activities. In this case, we note that some of the activities engaged in by the SROs involved information gathering while other activities required that the SROs use information that they had acquired, either as part of their training or when on the job, to carry out their various functions. The interviews with school administrators and SROs determined that information gathering activities contributed to the development of positive relationships with key stakeholders, while the appropriate use of information, skills, and training enhanced the credibility of these officers with the various stakeholder groups. Applying these different criteria to the tasks listed in Table 3.1 allows us to create the typology shown in Figure 3.1 to categorize the various activities undertaken by the SROs as they seek to meet their goal of making the school a safe place to learn.

Measurement of Activities

Prior to the beginning of the school term, the research team worked with the Peel Regional Police's analytics team to develop a method of tracking the amount of time each of the SROs working in the five schools that had agreed to participate in the SROI initiative spent in each of the activities listed in Table 3.1/Figure 3.1. This tool was developed and tested prior to the beginning of the school semester.

Several approaches were considered for the collection of the activity data. The first idea was to 'program' a list of activity codes on the officers' Motorola radios so they could punch in the code for the activity and the time spent as the activity occurred "in real time." This idea turned out to be technically and operationally impractical, and was not implemented. The second option we considered was to have the officers enter their time spent in various activities in an Excel spreadsheet at the end of their workday. Peel Police analytics officers would then compile and merge the data from all officers and provide them to the researchers at the end of the data collection period. This idea was also discarded for a variety of reasons.

In the end, Peel Police created a web form on their intranet that was used for data collection. SROs are required to use notepads to keep track of what they do during the course of the day. The researchers asked them not only to write down what they did each day, but also to note when they began and ended each task. Then, when they had time available during the day/week, we asked them to the launch the web form and enter their data. The web form

	Gather Information → Relationship Building	**Use Information and Expertise → Credibility Building**
Proactive (prevention)	• SROs walk around the school with school administrators • SROs walk around other targeted areas where students congregate • Police monitor social media • SROs patrol the neighborhood around the school • SROs conduct patrol work not related to NPU • SROs engage in extra-curricular activities with students (e.g., sports, charity events) and in the community	• SROs respond to requests from members of the school's broader community • SROs play an educational role in their school • SROs act as a liaison between Peel Police and administrators in the school • SROs use information they have gathered to prevent criminal activity from occurring (in the school and in the school's catchment area) • SROs engage in emergency preparedness exercises within the school
Reactive (enforcement)	• SROs participate in (POP) projects within their community • SROs pass on relevant information to other members of Peel Police, as appropriate • SROs assist other bureaus with NPU-related investigations	• SROs respond to criminal (e.g., drugs, robberies) and non-criminal (e.g., trespassing, liquor, fighting, suicide attempts) calls for service at the school and in the school's catchment area; in other words, they use their training and information they have gathered to enforce the law • SROs deal with non-criminal critical incidents in the school (e.g., trespass, suicide attempts) • SROs spend time dealing with critical incidents at the school and in the school's catchment area (behavioural and mental health issues) • SROs enforce federal/provincial/municipal laws in the school and in the school's catchment area • SROs attend court • SROs write reports and complete administrative duties

FIGURE 3.1 Typology of the different activities undertaken by SROs

was connected to a SQL server database. After the officer entered the data, the information became available immediately for analysis. This solution proved to be easy to use, quick, and very inexpensive.

Peel Police followed a number of principles when designing and implementing the web-based application. First, they wanted a product that could be built and delivered reasonably quickly (a 'robust' web application could take several months to build). Second, they wanted any system that was developed to be extremely easy for the officers to use (i.e., the form had to be self-explanatory). This would minimize the amount of time spent on training and increase the probability that the officers would provide accurate data. Third, not only did the form have to be easy to use, it was important that it did not take much time to enter data on the form (i.e., fast to use). This was also critical, as we were asking the officers to contribute their time to this research initiative for the duration of the project (five+ months). Finally, it was important to provide the officers with a high amount of flexibility and freedom with respect to when they could use the application to enter the data (i.e., it had to be available for use when it was convenient for the officers, not driven by the needs of the researchers). We noted that while officers often used the information in their notebook to enter their activities at the end of each workday, on some occasions they entered their data every couple of days or at the end of the work week. It should also be noted that the form that was designed and used allowed the officers to enter their activities for the day in a matter of minutes.

Data Collection: The Application

The web-based application was simple to use. After logging in the officer was presented with the SROI application home screen as shown in Figure 3.2.

The officers were presented with two options: a data entry form and a report where they could see their data. The data entry form (see Figure 3.3) asked for a date and the name of

FIGURE 3.2 SROI activity data: home screen

11/16/2017

SROI PEEL

Social Return On Investment (SROI)

SEP 2015 CANADA SECONDARY SCHOOL

Badge	Officer	Day	Month	Year	Activity	Description	From	To	Total
123	Cst. Smith	08	SEP	2017	A1	FP with Admin	0946	1015	0.48
123	Cst. Smith	08	SEP	2017	A3	GP in neighbourhood	1315	1600	2.75
456	Cst. Jones	08	SEP	2017	A1	FP with Admin	0946	1015	0.48
456	Cst. Jones	08	SEP	2017	A3	GP in neighbourhood	1315	1600	2.75
123	Cst. Smith	09	SEP	2017	A3	GP in neighbourhood	0831	1116	2.75
123	Cst. Smith	09	SEP	2017	A3	GP in neighbourhood	1315	1600	2.75
456	Cst. Jones	09	SEP	2017	A3	GP in neighbourhood	0831	1116	2.75
456	Cst. Jones	09	SEP	2017	A3	GP in neighbourhood	1315	1600	2.75
123	Cst. Smith	10	SEP	2017	A1	FP with Admin	1012	1050	0.63
123	Cst. Smith	10	SEP	2017	A3	GP in neighbourhood	1352	1600	2.13
456	Cst. Jones	10	SEP	2017	A1	FP with Admin	1012	1050	0.63
456	Cst. Jones	10	SEP	2017	A3	GP in neighbourhood	1352	1600	2.13
123	Cst. Smith	11	SEP	2017	A3	GP in neighbourhood	0913	0940	0.45
123	Cst. Smith	11	SEP	2017	A14	Criminal call for service at or around school	1303	1600	2.95
456	Cst. Jones	11	SEP	2017	A3	GP in neighbourhood	0913	0940	0.45
456	Cst. Jones	11	SEP	2017	A14	Criminal call for service at or around school	1303	1600	2.95
123	Cst. Smith	14	SEP	2017	A3	GP in neighbourhood	1342	1426	0.73
456	Cst. Jones	14	SEP	2017	A3	GP in neighbourhood	1342	1426	0.73
123	Cst. Smith	15	SEP	2017	A11	Liaison between school and PRP	0834	1018	1.73
123	Cst. Smith	15	SEP	2017	A3	GP in neighbourhood	1332	1600	2.47
456	Cst. Jones	15	SEP	2017	A11	Liaison between school and PRP	0834	1018	1.73
456	Cst. Jones	15	SEP	2017	A3	GP in neighbourhood	1332	1600	2.47
123	Cst. Smith	16	SEP	2017	A3	GP in neighbourhood	1231	1251	0.33
123	Cst. Smith	16	SEP	2017	A11	Liaison between school and PRP	1252	1600	3.13
456	Cst. Jones	16	SEP	2017	A3	GP in neighbourhood	1231	1251	0.33
456	Cst. Jones	16	SEP	2017	A11	Liaison between school and PRP	1252	1600	3.13
123	Cst. Smith	17	SEP	2017	A3	GP in neighbourhood	0832	1018	1.77
123	Cst. Smith	17	SEP	2017	A14	Criminal call for service at or around school	1225	1600	3.58
456	Cst. Jones	17	SEP	2017	A3	GP in neighbourhood	0832	1018	1.77
456	Cst. Jones	17	SEP	2017	A14	Criminal call for service at or around school	1225	1600	3.58
123	Cst. Smith	18	SEP	2017	A11	Liaison between school and PRP	1154	1223	0.48
456	Cst. Jones	18	SEP	2017	A11	Liaison between school and PRP	1154	1223	0.48
123	Cst. Smith	21	SEP	2017	A3	GP in neighbourhood	1315	1530	2.25
456	Cst. Jones	21	SEP	2017	A3	GP in neighbourhood	1315	1530	2.25
123	Cst. Smith	22	SEP	2017	A11	Liaison between school and PRP	1001	1130	1.48

http://hqanalysis2/sroi/index.html ½

FIGURE 3.3 SROI data entry form

the officer (or *officers*, as Peel Police SROs typically work in pairs). Then, for those officers, it asked for the school in which they were working, the day, month, and year their entry referred to, the activity code (each activity was assigned a code), and the beginning and end time of their participation in the activity. Pull down lists, which included all 20 activity codes, were used during data entry to save time, reduce errors, and increase the likelihood that the officers would actually complete the form. The following decision rules were imposed on the use of the form:

- if the officer was working with a partner for the entire shift, one officer would complete one timesheet to record activity times for the two officers;
- if the officer was working solo for their whole shift, they would complete a timesheet for that shift;
- if the officer was working solo for part of their shift and with a partner for part of their shift, they would complete one timesheet for them and their partner, listing the activities the officers did together, and then complete a separate sheet for those times that they were solo, listing only the activities that they performed when they were on their own.

These rules prevented double counting of time spent on the various activities. The report option was made as a way to provide the officers with an auditing tool to see what they had entered and to determine if they had missed anything or double counted activities.

The web-based form captures the data and saves it on a SQL database. There is a program running behind the scenes that calculates the time spent on the different activities. For example, if an officer said that they worked on Activity 3 from 0834 to 1018, then the program returns 1.73 hours as the time spent on Activity 3 and saves that value on the officer's record for that entry. The program also takes timesheets that include information from two officers and splits the times into two separate records so each officer's time is independently accounted for.

The advantage of having the web-based form is that it is convenient; officers can go to the website whenever they have time and Peel Police analytics officers who are working behind the scenes can get immediate access to all records in the database and run analytics whenever they see the need.

During the Fall semester, the nine SROs working in the five schools participating in this research (one pair jointly covered two of the schools in our study) created a daily record of how they spent their time. This step allows for a more precise breakdown of the amount of time spent on an activity that could then be evaluated based on the existing budget expenses of the Peel Regional Police's SRO program.[2]

Key Findings: Activity Data

Activity data were analyzed by school, by week, by month, by semester, and by officer. A number of observations were made by scanning these data. First, we note that there was variation between schools in the activities performed by the officers, reflecting the fact that officers respond to the types of issues and concerns common in the school they patrolled and its catchment area. Second, we identified variation in the time spent on various activities by day of the week and month, which seemed to correspond to school holidays, school testing periods, proximity to the weekend, etc. Third, we note that most SROs spend just over 40 hours a week on SRO-related activities. Finally, our calculations showed that officers spent almost a quarter of their time at work on "other activities." We were somewhat surprised by this and turned to the officers for help in

TABLE 3.2 Percentage of time SROs spent on different activities: Sept. 2015–Feb. 2016

Activity	*% of time*
Other (administrative work/report writing)	23
Criminal call for service at or around school	14
General patrol in neighborhood around school	13
SROs act as a liaison between school administrators and Peel Regional Police	8
Other patrol work	8
Non-criminal call for service at or around school	6
Foot patrol with school administrators	6
Problem Oriented Policing (POP) project	4
SROs in court	3
Assist other bureaus with NPU related investigations	2
Extracurricular activities with students	2
Critical incidents at or around school (mental health)	2
Educational role within the school	2
Enforce federal/provincial/municipal laws in or around the school	1
SROs monitor social media	1
SROs engage in emergency preparedness activity at school	1
SROs use information they have gathered to prevent a crime in or around the school	1
SROs performs foot patrol in targeted areas	1
Pass on relevant information to other Peel Police bureaus	1
SROs respond to requests from community members	1

Note: Numbers have been rounded up, and include activity data from the two weeks in February the officers worked prior to the break for exams.

Key	
	Use Information/Expertise to Enforce the Law (i.e., Enforcement/Apply Knowledge)
	Gather Intelligence to Enforce the Law (i.e., Enforcement/Gather Information)
	Gather Intelligence to Prevent Crime (i.e., Prevention/Gather Information)
	Use Information/Expertise to Prevent Crime (i.e., Prevention/Apply Knowledge)

understanding these data. All officers had essentially the same view of what was included in the "other" category – report writing. One officer explained as follows:

> "If we go by the calculation that a simple report takes around one hour to complete, then we are spending about three hours minimum a week on simple reports – all of which can be considered reactive in nature as we are required to do them after we have

> handled an incident at the school. So then we are dedicating at least 12 hours a month to reactive report writing for simple issues . . . Then of course there are the more complex reports, which are typically triggered by a critical incident at the school [e.g., an arrest, a mental health call] . . . In these cases, the time dedicated to reports may take as much as four hours. So, you add that to the mix and we are now talking about most of our time in the 'other' category [90%] being spent writing reports. Meaning that if we deal with a critical incident approximately three times a week, that is 12 hours a week and 48 hours a month of report writing. So that is a big chunk of our month's 'other' category."

Another concurred and provided additional information as follows:

> "It's not only report writing, but everything that accompanies it. Filling out property tags, lodging property, informing supervisors of cases, writing notes, assisting other officers with their packages, court package preparation, disclosure requests from Crown/Defense, email correspondence with co-workers/Crowns/other police services, reading alerts that have been distributed, etc. You could summarize this as 'administration' or 'paper work'."

Officers estimated that approximately 90% of the time spent in other activities was spent on some type of administrative work/report writing. Other activities included in this category (i.e., activities that account for the rest of the time coded as "other") include calls to the elementary schools in the catchment area and training.

We also asked the officers to help us understand what was involved when they spent time on Problem Oriented Policing (POP) projects. Officers noted that, when the study was being conducted, SROs focused their attention on gang activity in some of the schools (i.e., trying to stop gangs from fighting) and drug trafficking, either on school property or near the schools.

How Do SROs Spend Their Time?

Which activities consume most of the SROs' time? Which activities are performed less frequently? These questions are answered in a number of different ways. First, we looked at activity time data by school semester (i.e., September 2015 to February 2016) and calculated the percentage of this time the officers spent on each of the 20 activities that we identified as part of the SRO role. These data are shown in Table 3.2. A number of important observations can be made from this first set of calculations. First, SROs spend almost a quarter of their time doing administrative work. Second, SROs spend approximately 10% of their time on four activities: criminal calls for service at or around the school, general patrol in the neighborhood around the school, acting as a liaison between school administrators and Peel Regional Police, and engaged in other patrol work. Third, approximately 5% of the SROs work time is spent on four other activities: non-criminal calls for service at or around the school, foot patrol with school administrators, POP projects, and appearing in court. The other activities that are part of the role appear to be performed on an "as needs" basis and consume relatively small amounts of the officer's time over the course of a semester.

Second, we calculated the relative amount of time the SROs spent during the semester (i.e., September 2015 to February 2016) on the four different types of activities included in our activity typology (Figure 3.1), as well as on administrative activities/report writing. Results from these calculations are shown in Figure 3.4. This analysis supports a number of important observations with respect to SRO time use over the course of one high school academic semester. First, SROs spend more of their time on activities associated with proactive policing and crime prevention (43.8% of their time) than they do on reactive activities involving enforcement of the law and/or calls

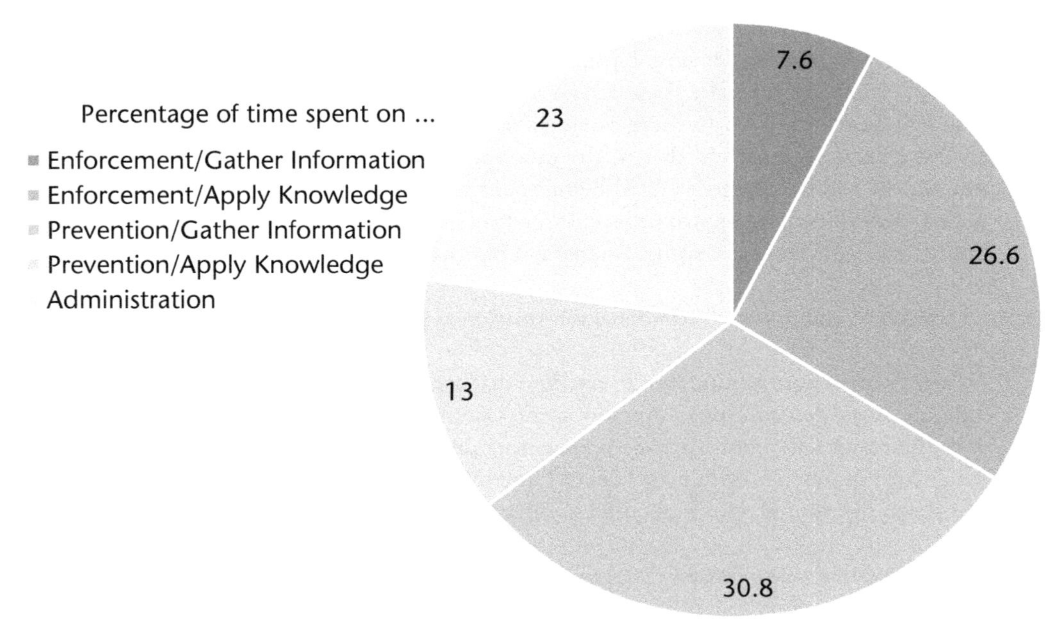

FIGURE 3.4 Percentage of time SROs spend on key activities: Sept. 2015–Feb. 2016 (%)

for service (34.2% of their time). Second, almost a third of the SROs' time is spent on information gathering activities to help prevent crime. These activities also serve to enhance relationships with key stakeholders. Third, officers also spend a substantial amount of their time either using the knowledge they have gained to enforce the law and/or respond to a call for service (26.6% of their time) or on follow-up administrative activities (23% of their time). Finally, we note that SROs spend relatively little time engaged in educational activities or emergency preparedness training (13% of their time is spent using their training and skills to engage in proactive policing) or on enforcement activities that involve knowledge gathering after the fact (7.6% of their time).

Third, our initial scan of the data showed us that the relative amount of time that the SROs spent on the four types of activities and report writing varied by month of the semester. To illustrate these differences, we show the percentage of the SROs' time per month spent per activity group numerically in Table 3.3 and in graphical form in Figure 3.5.

While the amount of time spent by the SROs on the different types of activities was relatively constant on a month-to-month basis throughout the term, there are a few variations that are important to note. First, the percentage of time spent on the various activities was observably different in

TABLE 3.3 Percentage of time SROs spend on key activities: by month

Activity	*Percentage of time on activity*					
	Sept.	*Oct.*	*Nov.*	*Dec.*	*Jan.*	*Total*
Use Information/Expertise to Enforce the Law	22.1	22.6	35.1	24.4	20.6	26.6
Gather Intelligence to Prevent Crime	32.8	34.4	27.5	30.6	31.9	30.8
Use Information/Expertise to Prevent Crime	15.6	12.8	12.9	11.8	13.5	13.0
Gather Intelligence to Enforce the Law	2.7	2.2	6.0	17.0	9.2	7.6
Other (report writing)	26.8	28.0	18.5	16.2	24.8	23.0

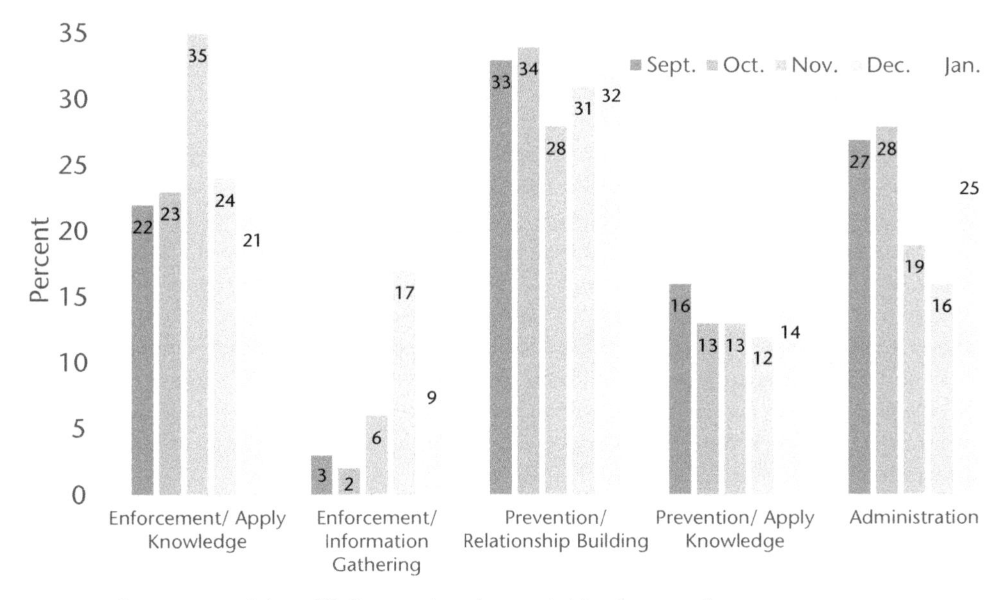

FIGURE 3.5 Percentage of time SROs spend on key activities: by month

November than in the other months of the term. In November, SROs spent substantially more of their time on activities where they were required to use their knowledge and expertise to enforce the law and less of their time on proactive information gathering activities and report writing. Second, we note that SROs spent considerably more of their time in December on reactive intelligence gathering activities (17% of their time). The amount of time spent in such activities in December is particularly remarkable when compared to the early months of the semester where officers spent relatively little time on enforcement activities that require the collection of information. The amount of time spent on administrative activities is also lower in December.

Summary and Conclusions

The role of the SRO involves participation in 20 different activities. These various activities can be classified in two different ways:

- the activities are either reactive and involve enforcement (n = 9) or proactive and relate to prevention (n = 11); and
- the activities require that information/intelligence either be gathered (n = 9) or used (n = 11).

Officers engage in reactive activities as a response to something that has already happened at the school or the school's catchment area. In all reactive situations, the SROs undertook a variety of actions to resolve the matter effectively and re-establish a safe school learning environment. All the activities in the proactive grouping are taken by the SROs either to prevent a crime, avert the victimization of other students, or forestall antisocial activity. Such activities can be considered to foster a safer learning environment. Information and intelligence gathering activities contribute to the development of positive relationships with key stakeholders while the activities that involve the use of information, skills, and training enhance the credibility of these officers within a variety of stakeholder groups.

Analysis of the activity data resulted in the following important observations and conclusions:

- SROs spend almost a quarter of their time on administrative work;
- SROs spend approximately 10% of their work time on each of the following four activities: criminal calls for service at or around the school, general patrol in the neighborhood around the school, acting as a liaison between school administrators and Peel Regional Police, and engaging in other patrol work;
- SROs spend approximately 5% of their time on each of the following four activities: non-criminal calls for service at or around the school, foot patrol with school administrators, Problem Oriented Policing projects, and appearing in court;
- the 11 other activities that are part of the SRO role appear to be performed on an "as needs" basis and consume relatively small amounts of the officer's time over the course of a semester;
- SROs spend more of their time on activities associated with proactive policing/crime prevention (44% of their time) than they do on reactive activities involving enforcement of the law and/or calls for service (34% of their time);
- a substantial amount of the SROs' time (30%) is spent on information gathering activities to help prevent crime. These activities also serve to enhance relationships with key stakeholders;
- officers spend a substantial amount of their time either using the knowledge they have gained to enforce the law and/or responding to a call for service (27% of their time), or in follow-up administrative activities (23% of their time);
- SROs spend less of their time applying their skills in a proactive way within the schools (i.e., 13% of their time is spent on educational activities or emergency preparedness training) or in enforcement activities that involve reactive knowledge gathering (8% of their time);
- while the amount of time spent by the SROs each month on the different types of activities is relatively constant over time, the activity pattern is somewhat different in November and December than the other months of the semester;
- SROs spent substantially more of their time in November on activities where they were required to use their knowledge and expertise to enforce the law. They spent less of their time involved in proactive information gathering activities and report writing;
- SROs spent considerably more of their time in December on reactive intelligence gathering policing activities (17% of their time). The amount of time spent on administrative activities was also lower in December.

Notes

1 www.oxfordbibliographies.com/view/document/obo-9780195396607/obo-978019539660 7-0183.xml

2 Asking busy SROs to track all of their activities for almost half a year was no minor request. The research team was very lucky to have had complete cooperation from a group of dedicated officers, all of whom diligently tracked their activities on a daily basis. We would like to thank them for their commitment to this project and for their contributions to its success.

4

THE VALUE OF SROS

Views from Within (High School Students)

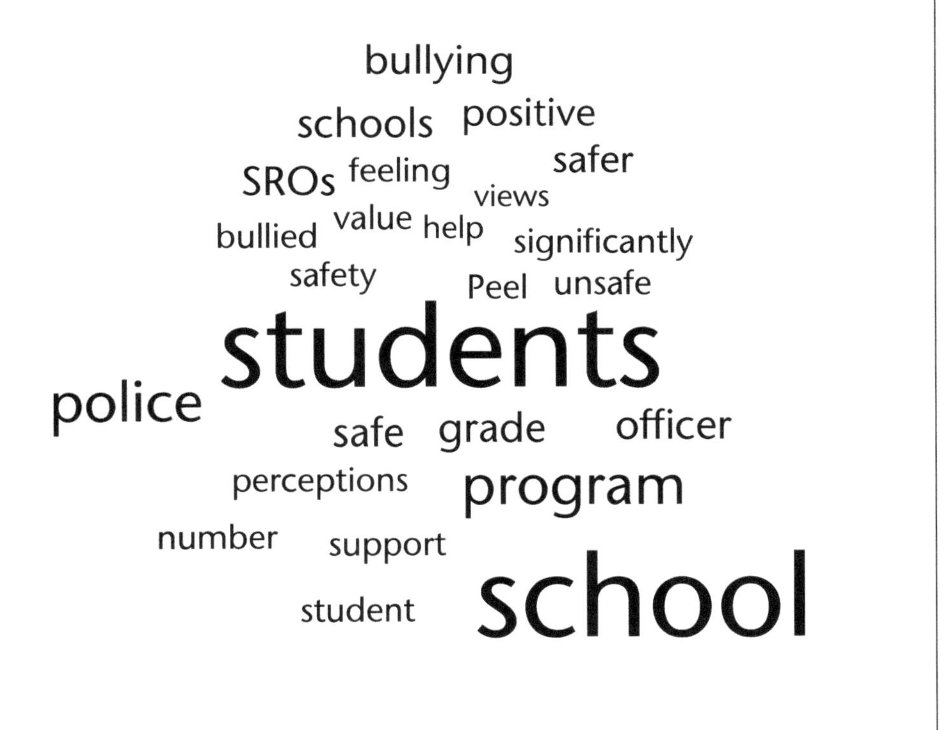

WordMap: 25 most common words in Chapter 4: "The Value of SROs: Views from Within (High School Students)"

Key Learnings

This chapter focuses on understanding a key stakeholder's perceptions of the value delivered by the School Resource Officer (SRO) program – that of the student. The data analyzed in this chapter comes from eight interviews undertaken with Grade 9 students attending one of the five schools participating in this study, and responses from 600 + Grade 9 students attending the five schools to surveys that were sent out the first week of the school semester (Time 1) and five months later at the end of the school semester (Time 2).

Does the presence of the SRO within the high school make students feel safer? Why does this matter (or does it)? What is more likely to occur when students feel safer? What is less likely to happen because students feel safer? Answers to these questions are provided in this chapter.

Interviews with Grade 9 Students Support the Following Observations and Conclusions

What do students perceive to be the most serious problem within their school at this time? The answer from this study is unequivocal: the threats they face from other students, such as thefts of electronics and phones, other students selling or taking drugs on school property, and verbal and physical bullying.

All of the students we talked to stated that they trusted the SRO at their school enough to talk to them if they knew about a crime that had occurred at their school.

All the students in our interview sample also agreed that having an SRO assigned to their school on a full-time basis made them feel safer, both at school and on their journey to and from school.

What value does the SRO program provide students? Interview responses indicate that:

- the SRO program stops students from making bad life choices (i.e., SROs act as deterrents);
- the SRO program creates (or enhances) a safe environment for learning and makes it easier for students to stay focused on their studies; and
- the SRO program gives the police a greater knowledge of the school and its students, which is invaluable in cases of emergencies.

Survey Data Collected from Grade 9 Students Support the Following Observations and Conclusions

The longitudinal survey data presented in this chapter provide strong support for the idea that the SRO program meets its goal of increasing students' perceptions of safety, both within the school and on the way to and from school, by reducing the amount of bullying taking place on school property and in the surrounding area.

Five months after becoming a student at a high school with a police officer on site, the Grade 9 students who responded to our survey:

- were more able to concentrate;
- were experiencing better mental health (i.e., reported less anxiety, stress, and depressed feelings);
- were less likely to report difficulties sleeping;
- were less likely to think about harming themselves or others; and
- were less likely to skip class, miss school, or think of dropping out.

Both school boards operating in Peel Region (Peel District School Board [PDSB] and Dufferin–Peel Catholic District School Board [DPCDSB]) emphasize the importance of student safety:

> The safety of our students and staff is at the core of everything we do. – PDSB
>
> The board strives to ensure that its schools and facilities are safe, caring, healthy and inclusive places in which to learn and to work. – DPCDSB

To help keep students safe, Peel Regional Police assign an officer working within their Neighbourhood Police Unit (NPU) to each high school in Brampton and Mississauga (Peel Regional Police's catchment area). These officers, which we refer to in this book as SROs, are given primary responsibility for the creation of a safe learning environment within the region's secondary schools. They do this by: (1) forming positive partnerships with students and high school administrators, (2) using a proactive style of policing whenever possible, and (3) interacting with youth in a non-enforcement manner on a regular basis.

This, however, poses the following questions: Does the presence of the SRO within the high school make students feel safer? Why does this matter (or does it)? What is more likely to occur when students feel safer? What is less likely to happen because students feel safer?

To answer these important questions, we consulted with the stakeholder at the heart of the SRO program – the student. Two very different types of data were collected from students attending the five Peel District high schools participating in this study: (1) qualitative interview data and (2) longitudinal, quantitative survey data. We focused our data collection efforts on Grade 9 students in particular, as these students had recently transitioned from feeder schools that were not part of the SRO program (i.e., there was no full-time SRO within these schools) to a high school with a full-time SRO. These students were, therefore, uniquely qualified to help us in our evaluation efforts.

This chapter is divided into three main sections. We begin by presenting and discussing findings from the interview phase of this research. We then present key findings from the two student surveys we completed during our evaluation of the SRO program. Finally, the chapter concludes with an overview of the value of the SRO program, as seen through the eyes of the students themselves.

The Student Interviews

In February 2016, we conducted interviews with eight high school students attending one of the two urban-grant schools[1] participating in this study. The interviews were done in person at the high school by a PhD student who worked as a researcher on this project. In all cases, parental consent was collected before the interviews were conducted. All students who engaged in this exercise volunteered to be interviewed. The interviews, which took approximately 30 minutes to complete, were recorded and transcribed. The same interview script was followed in all cases. Interviews were content coded using the methodology outlined in Cooper and Schindler (2006), and the responses were examined for commonalities of views and opinions. Many of the students provided multiple answers to a number of interview questions, which explains why response frequencies often exceed eight.

To help us interpret the data, we started the interview by asking the students some questions about themselves. Seven of the eight students were male. All students had started Grade 9 in September 2015. All students planned to go to university after they finished high school. Their career plans were diverse, ranging from computer engineering, film studies, science, accounting, social sciences, and air traffic control. None of the students we spoke to was Caucasian.

This section of the chapter is divided into five sections. We begin by examining questions that helped us understand how the students view the school that they attend. The next section focuses on the student's level of familiarity with the SRO program in their school. In the third section we focus on interactions between the SRO and the students in the school. This is followed, in the fourth section, with a discussion of data that speak to how the SRO program impacts perceptions of safety. The final section examines data that speak to the value attached by the students in our sample to having a police officer assigned to their school on a daily basis and whether they want the SRO program to continue at their school.

Students' Views of Their School

Responses to the following questions are presented in this section: (1) "If you were bragging about your school to a friend or colleague, what would you mention?"; (2) "What are the main challenges facing the students and staff at your school at this time?"; (3) "Which of these issues do you consider to be the most serious problem in your school at this time?"

If You Were Bragging About Your School to a Friend, What Would You Mention?

There was a high degree of consensus within the sample of Grade 9 students we interviewed with respect to what they felt made their school stand out in a positive way relative to other high schools. More than half of the students ($n = 5$) said they would brag about the quality of the sports program at their school ("we are known for our sports teams"). Half talked about the positive social atmosphere in their school:

> "A lot of people are friendly here and as a Grade 9 student I felt really welcome."

Perhaps most importantly, as pertains to this study, half talked about how their school felt like a safe place, especially when compared to the other schools they had attended:

> ". . . this school is a lot safer compared to the other school I was at."
>
> "I was bullied like throughout last year and that was a big issue for me. Like all of Grade 8 . . . this school is a lot safer compared to all the other schools . . . "

What Are the Main Challenges Facing the Students at Your School at This Time?

Students identified three types of challenges – social, academic, and those related to illegal activity – that occurred at their school.

Half the students said that they and their friends dealt with a number of social challenges. They found it hard to make friends and they felt pressured to make a good impression on other students and their teachers. Students who gave this response indicated that they felt more pressure to get to know new people than they did to do well at school.

Alternatively, half the students said that academic pressures they faced were the most challenging. They stated that they and their friends found getting used to the daily routine of high school stressful, noting that they felt pressure to complete school assignments and do well on tests. This group of students felt that they needed to focus on what is important, which in their case was doing well in school.

> "The main challenge is getting used to high school, like the way high school works."

Finally, three students responded to this question by talking about how their school had problems with drug use and stealing, particularly of electronics.

"Oh yes, I've been robbed here, of my ear buds. They were actually $100 . . . Yes, while I was in, during gym. So, we were playing, they were in my pocket, I don't know, came back, they weren't there, moved on."

What Is the Most Serious Problem in Your School at This Time?

While students identified the social and academic challenges that come with starting a new school as the main challenges facing students at their school, they gave a somewhat different answer when asked what they felt was the *most* serious problem within their school at this time. In this case, *all* the students we interviewed focused on the threats they faced from other students. The main threats they identified as serious included: (1) other students stealing things such as electronics and phones, (2) other students selling or taking drugs on school property, (3) verbal bullying ("the bullying just never goes away"), and (4) the sale of illegal goods on school property. Only one student talked about how difficult it was to stay focused on their school work and no one talked about the social challenges associated with being a high school student.

Students' Familiarity with the SRO Program

We then asked the students how familiar they were with the SRO program and, more specifically, what they thought that the SROs in their school actually did. Responses follow.

How Familiar Are You with the SRO Program within Your School?

Five of the eight students claimed that they were somewhat familiar with the SRO program in their school. The rest ($n = 3$) said that they were not that familiar (see Figure 4.1).

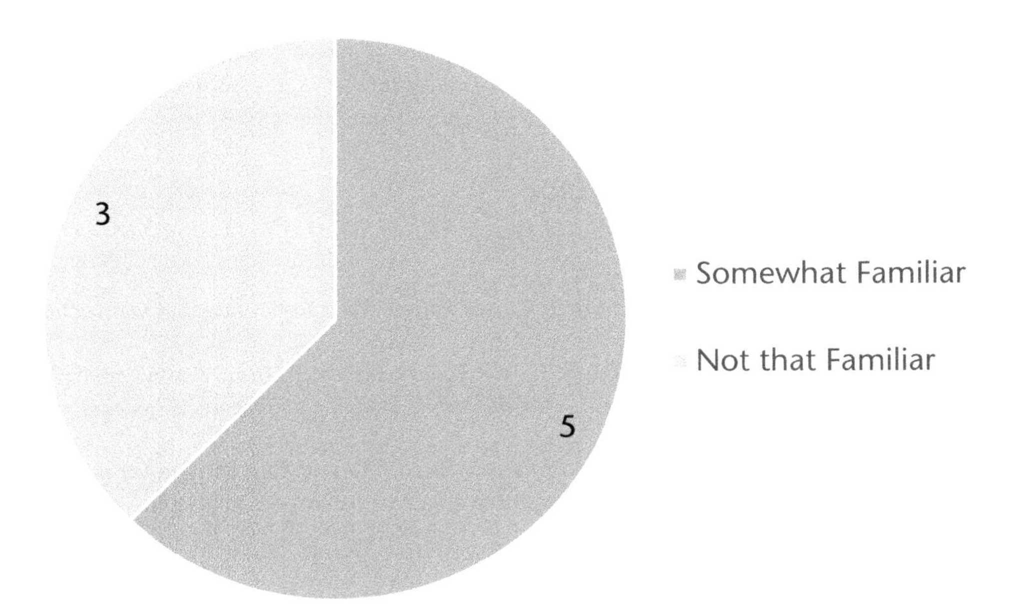

FIGURE 4.1 Familiarity with the SRO Program in your school ($n = 8$)

What Is the SRO Supposed To Do?

We then asked students to tell us what they thought the SROs in their school were there to do. Virtually all of the students we interviewed ($n = 6$) stated that SROs are supposed to keep the school and surrounding neighborhood safe by patrolling the area and keeping an eye out for problems and bad behavior. For example:

> "Well, I think they are trying to keep the school safe. If there is anything serious that goes down, like they are already here . . . They are here more for the safety of us, and it's not so much like how they would enforce things. It would just be more about safety in the school . . . Just in case, like a fight goes like haywire or something. They are there to control it but they are not here to specifically like search for something . . . They are just here just in case anything does go bad."

Three students also talked about how it is the SROs job to enforce the law in the school and the neighborhood:

> "They investigate when things like fights happen . . . They come to sort things out."

Three other students described the program as follows:

> "So basically, there are police officers that have been assigned to high schools and they are responsible to look after that high school and the students and the surrounding area. . .You can go to them if you have a problem."

Finally, one student said that they could not tell us what the SRO was supposed to do, claiming that they just did not know much about the program:

> "I'm not really sure what they do."

In sum, student responses to this question (e.g., keep the school safe, enforce the law, act as a resource to the students and the school) indicate that the sample of high school students we spoke with had a pretty good understanding of the SROs' role within their school.

Interactions between Students and SROs

We then asked our students the following questions:

- Have you ever had a talk with the SRO in your school about something that was bothering you or that you wanted advice on?
- Identify a time that you think the SRO assigned to your school really made a positive difference. Can you tell me about this occasion? What difference did it make that the SRO was around when this happened?
- Think about the SRO who is assigned to your school. Do you trust this person enough to go to him/her: about a problem that you know about at the school? A personal problem? A crime that you know has occurred?

Responses are provided below.

Talked to the SRO

None of the students we interviewed had ever spoken to the SRO at their school. When asked why this was the case, we received three responses. The most common response was that they had never had a reason to talk to the officers ("I just have never needed to . . . "). The six students who gave this response did, however, state that if they witnessed a crime or if one of their friends had a problem and needed help, then they would talk to the SRO. Two other responses were also noted. One student mentioned that they had never seen the SRO at their school. Another said that they avoided the SRO because they just did not want to get involved with other students' problems, preferring to talk to their parents instead (". . . if I do have a major problem I usually go to my parents first").

Situation where an SRO Made a Positive Difference

We then asked the students to identify and describe a time where they thought that the SRO assigned to their school had really made a positive difference. When asking this question, we emphasized that the occasion did not have to involve them directly, but had to be something that they personally knew about (i.e., they observed it happening, it impacted someone they knew). Only one student could not answer this question. This student said that while they saw their SRO walking through the school yard they were not sure what they were doing or with whom. Some of the students that did provide a response talked about situations where the SRO had intervened to break up a fight:

> ". . . when two girls were fighting . . . the police officer stopped them from trespassing and made sure nobody was hurt or doing anything wrong."
>
> "I have an older brother at this school too . . . An incident happened where it was kind of like an unprovoked assault against him. And it was just, like, completely out of nowhere. And so, then the police officer came and kind of like helped my brother and stuff, like, with the charges. And they dealt with the situation very well. They expelled the student . . . and he's been charged with assault."
>
> ". . . there was a fight that like happened last semester . . . they were here while that happened . . . They got that under control like as soon as that happened . . . I heard it on the announcement and all my friends were talking about it."

Two students talked about a session that they had attended where the SRO provided information about bullying and how to handle it to all new students at the school:

> "It is good that they talk to the Grade 9s about bullying and show that they care."
>
> "Like they want to show students that they can have fun and everything . . . but then they talk about bullying as well . . . They say you can make jokes but when someone is offended and they say stop you have to stop . . ."

The last student described a situation where the SRO investigated and resolved an issue involving a theft at the school:

> "My friend's phone was stolen. The police got the phone back and dealt with the guy who did it."

What Difference Did it Make that the SROs Were Around when this Happened?

Students identified three ways in which having a police officer at their school had a positive impact on the situation they described: (1) the officers were able to de-escalate the situation, (2) the officers helped students feel safer, and (3) the officers provided a visible reminder to others to respect boundaries. Details on each of these responses are provided below.

Just over half the students stated that the officer was able to stop the challenging condition before it escalated:

> "I don't want to fight, so I'm happy they are there to break it up."
>
> "It is really important that they help students who are being bullied."

Students who gave this response all valued the fact that the SRO was able to respond quickly to problematic situations and take control:

> "It was good because they listened and tried to do something about it right away. It didn't take very long to solve it . . . like within the week it happened."
>
> "The problem was solved much more quickly than it normally would have . . . It didn't go on for too long . . . Like they solved it immediately . . ."

Students also talked about how the officer's behavior in the situation they described increased their faith and trust of the police:

> ". . . it showed me that they actually, like, they'll come when they are needed . . . "

A majority of the students also talked about how they felt safer because the SRO was in the school. The link between feeling safe and enhanced learning was also mentioned by this group of students who linked feeling safe to an increased ability to concentrate on their studies:

> "Well it's a place of learning, you should always be feeling like welcomed there, you should be feeling like you're wanted there. You should be happy there . . . it is just like having your parents at the school . . . because you know if anything bad is going down or anything, or you need to talk to someone they're always there . . . "
>
> "They were looking out for everyone. Making sure nobody is hurt, keeping us safe . . . that everyone gets home safely . . . and this means we can focus on the important things."

Finally, two students said that the SRO makes a difference by just being there – by being visible. The students who gave this answer felt that the SROs provide a visible reminder to students in their school to respect the boundaries of good behavior when they are at school:

> ". . . it shows the kids that they can have fun without bullying and that they need to know when to stop."

Trust in SROs

We also asked the students in our sample if they trust the SRO who is assigned to their school enough to go to him/her about: (1) a problem at the school; (2) a personal problem; (3) a crime that they knew had occurred? Responses to these three questions are shown in Figure 4.2 and discussed below.

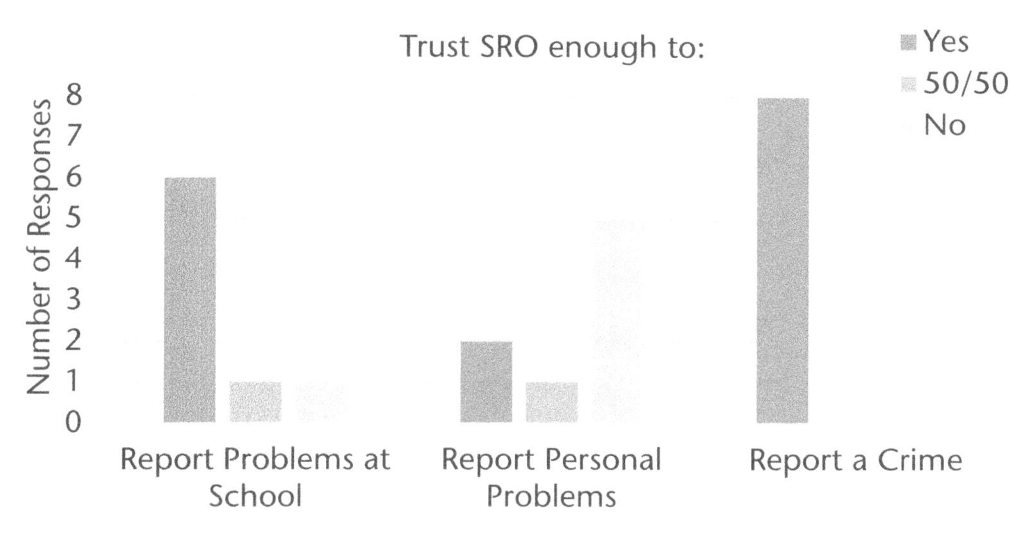

FIGURE 4.2 Interactions with SRO: trust

All of the students we talked to stated that they trusted the SRO at their school enough to talk to them if they knew about a crime that had occurred at the school. All but two would talk to the SRO about problems that were occurring at their school:

> "For sure. They are there to protect us so we shouldn't be afraid of them . . ."
>
> "For sure. Right away because they need to help as soon as possible. Especially if I knew someone who had been affected by a crime . . ."

In contrast, only two students said they would approach the SRO to talk about a personal problem with another student, indicating that they might have such a conversation if the situation was really problematic:

> ". . . 50/50 because they are still a stranger, not a friend."

Finally, the majority of students stated that they would not talk about personal problems with the SRO, preferring to deal with it by themselves or talk to their family about such issues:

> "I would stick to my family. Then, if it was really bad, then yes."

Impact of the SRO on Students' Perceptions of Safety

The goal of the SRO program is to increase student's perceptions of safety when they are at school and on their journey to and from school each day. We asked students a number of questions to help us quantify the extent to which the program achieves these goals. More specifically, we asked them:

- How safe do you feel your school is during school hours? Why do you feel this way?
- How do you get to and from school each day? How safe do you feel during your trip to and from school? Does the presence of an SRO in the neighborhood, around your school, in the after-school hours, affect you in any way?

- Does having an SRO assigned to your school on a full-time basis impact how safe you feel at school?
- What do you think would happen if the police officers were not in the school on a daily basis?

Responses to each of these questions are discussed below. Relevant data are also shown in Figure 4.3.

Perceptions of Safety while at School

We began by asking the students: "How safe do you feel your school is during school hours?" All eight students stated that they felt very safe or mostly safe at school. They attributed their feelings of safety to the visible presence of the SROs in their school. They noted that they could see the SROs patrolling the school for illegal or suspicious activity and found this reassuring:

> "I can see the police patrolling the area and I know they will spot any suspicious person before they can enter the school."

Students also attributed their perceptions of safety to the fact that there are enough teachers, supervisors, and principals present to monitor the school and take action if anything unsafe happens in the school:

> ". . . teachers, supervisors, SROs, and principals are present, making sure everything is going well . . . if there were a fight, it would be broken up quickly."

While all eight students described their school as very safe/mostly safe, five of them then went on to qualify their answer by talking about situations when they did not feel entirely safe in the school. These students gave two reasons for this reaction. First, they felt that there is always a risk that a stranger will enter their school and attack the students:

> ". . . the doors to the school aren't locked and people can just walk in."

Second, they noted that although they feel "mostly safe" when they were at school, they still felt unsafe when they were between classes. They said that between classes the hallways are crowded with students and there is little to no supervision. They described feeling uneasy going from class to class and talked about how it would be easy for something "bad" to happen without anyone seeing it:

> "So, it's not really safe during school hours because you could get into a fight right in the hall just by walking into them. It's not really a safe environment . . . I wouldn't pick the fight but some people do. Just coming at you for no reason."

Perceptions of Safety on way to and from School

We began this part of the interview by asking students how they got to and from school each day. Half the students said they walked to and from school each day, two mentioned that their parents drove them to school (dropping them off and picking them up at the entrance to the school), one student took a school bus, and one used public transport.

We then asked them how safe they felt during their trip to and from school. The two students whose parents drove them to and from school felt very safe, the students who walked and took the bus, on the other hand, either felt mostly safe or unsafe.

In school during school hours?

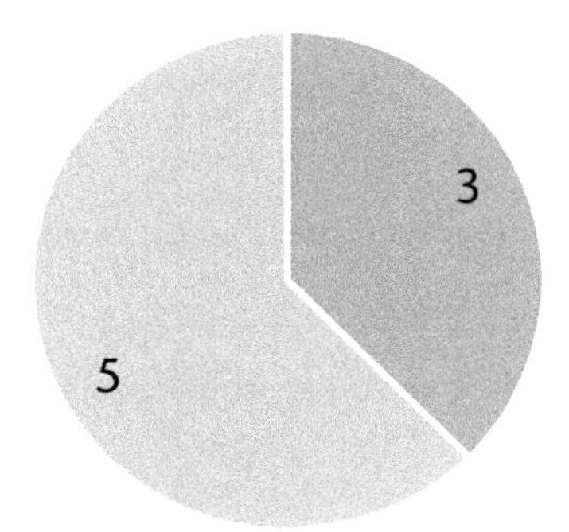

- Very safe
- Mostly feel safe
- Don't always feel safe

During your trip to/from school?

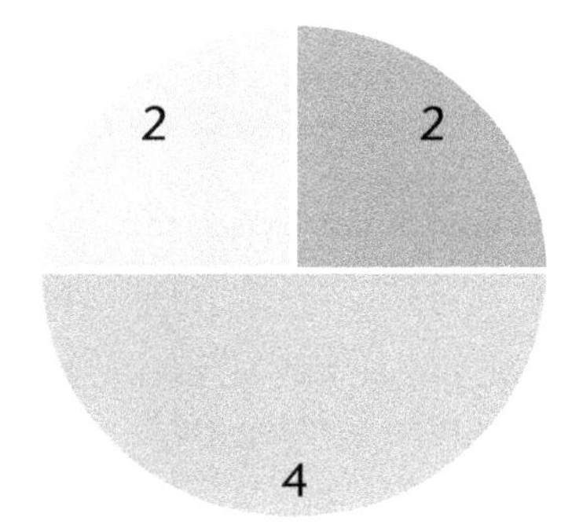

- Very safe
- Mostly feel safe
- Don't always feel safe

FIGURE 4.3 How Safe Do You Feel? (n = 8)

Surprisingly, when asked to explain why they gave the answer they did, the students who felt mostly safe gave similar reasons to the students who felt unsafe on their way to and from school. More specifically, both groups of students talked about how they felt nervous when they encountered groups of students engaged in suspicious activities (most mentioned dealing drugs) on the way to and from school:

> "Most of the time I'm very wary when I'm walking because the route I take, it's very short but it's kind of like through, like, a catwalk and it's on the side of the main street. And, on the main street, I mean . . . Well, first, on the catwalk, every so often I see drug dealers, like, and I have to, like, walk around them. It's a bit of a hassle. I don't want to see them and it scares me a bit."

Without being prompted these students went on to tell us what they did to reduce the risks they observed on their way to and from school. Key strategies included going home immediately when school ended, avoiding anyone they did not know (and often times avoiding some people that they did know), and, when possible, making the trip to and from school in the company of friends:

> "I leave at the bell and walk home as fast as possible."
>
> "I walk with friends and we don't talk to anyone else."
>
> "I sit with my friends on the school bus and don't talk to strangers."

To conclude this section of the interview, we asked students if the presence of an SRO in the neighborhood after school had ended for the day affected them in any way. Responses were mixed with half of the students saying that yes, having SROs patrol their community after school hours enhanced their feelings of safety; the other half of students reported no impact.

How does having SROs in the community after school hours enhance perceptions of safety? Analysis of the data shows that the mechanisms by which this occurs are similar to what we have heard with regard to perceptions of safety within the school. Students felt that the officers could respond quickly to unsafe situations (bullying, fighting) and criminal activity (dealing drugs, thefts):

> ". . . when school's out usually me and my friends are hanging out. We usually, like see, like, a police officer and then, like, later on that day we see someone bad. Like, my friends, they recently got their bikes stolen but the police officer drove right by before it happened . . . and they caught the guy and my friend got his bike back . . . So I feel like a bit more safe knowing the police officer in the neighborhood so that, like, as soon as something bad, like, happened to me I would just go tell them right away."

Students also felt that having an SRO in the community after school hours reduced the likelihood that others would engage in bullying or threatening behavior:

> "They make me feel safer walking home . . . because the kids see them around and it stops them from bullying me."

The students who denied any impact of the SROs presence in the community after school hours gave three different responses explaining why. The most common answer was given by the two students whose parents drove them into school and picked them up at the end of the day ("not an issue for me"). Their response is completely understandable given their circumstances. One student said that they did not see the officers enough to feel safe, and one student said he saw the officers, but he still felt nervous.

Impact of the SRO on Perceptions of Safety

We asked the eight students in our sample: "Does having an SRO assigned to your school on a full-time basis impact how safe you feel at school?" All the students affirmed that having an SRO assigned to their school on a full-time basis increased their feelings of safety at school:

> ". . . an SRO is like the feeling at the back of your mind that's like, if anything does go bad they are here. You always feel secure."

Why do students feel safer because of the SRO? Common reasons provided by these students included their perception that the SRO acts as a visible deterrent to students and others who might do harm, faster response times, and they are a resource the students can go to if they need advice or help. Details on each of responses are provided below.

SROs as a visible deterrent: Five of the eight students we interviewed linked two ideas – visibility and deterrence – when discussing why having an SRO increases their feelings of safety at school. These students stated that the presence of the SRO does more to enhance their feelings of safety than the presence of other members of the school staff because:

> "Teachers, admin, and students make me feel safe, but the police add an extra measure of safety because like I feel like they can enforce the rules . . . Teachers can't do what they [the police] can."
>
> "The teacher went out to go pick up something from the Science room . . . and as soon as she left these two guys started fighting . . . and then when the teacher came back she was really mad . . . and like they didn't respect the teacher . . . but the police can enforce the rules. . ."

The fact that half the students we talked to said that they feel nervous when the officers are not visibly present within their school underscores the strong association between the visible presence of an SRO within the school and students' perceptions of safety:

> "... when I don't see them, I don't feel safe ..."
>
> "... students take the rules more seriously because the police can enforce them ... it really does give a feeling of safety when I can see them ... and nervous when I can't."

SROs can respond quickly when needed: Three students indicated that the fact that the SRO was present in the school and could immediately take action to enforce the rules and the law if anything unsafe happened, increased their perceptions of safety at the school:

> "Because ... let's just say someone tries to break and enter into the school ... there would be an officer there and they could stop the person instead of going into lock-down position ... if we called 911 it would take the police like ten times longer to respond ... if there wasn't a police officer here anyone could break into the school or hurt someone and it would take the police officers a while to get from their station to the school."

SROs are a resource students can go to if they need help: Three students talked about how they saw the SROs as a resource that students can go to for help if they need it:

> "... because if there is a problem, I know there is someone there to talk to ..."

What if the SRO Was not in the School on a Daily Basis?

What would change if the SROs were not in the school on a daily basis? Two students said that they did not think much would change, but then qualified their answer as follows:

> "I don't think there would be a dramatic change ... but in another school, there might be more bullying and bad things."

The rest of the students stated unequivocally that if the officers were not in the school on a daily basis there would be more illegal activity and more school rules being broken. They also felt that there would be more fights, thefts, and drugs in the school:

> "I think there would be more fights, arguments, more like drugs and stuff ... and just, like, a lot of violence and mischief going around ... because, like, when people walk around the hallways and they see a police officer ... they know to be on the top of their game because if they do something wrong it's not like it's a principal who has caf [cafeteria] duty – you're just in trouble."
>
> "It's like having your parents at the school all the time. When you're around your parents you act one way but when you're around your friends you act another way. So, if you're around your parents you'd be like polite, do what they need you to do, you wouldn't like ... start swearing or fighting or anything, but if you're around your friends you're just a little looser and you just ... you know ..."

Student's Evaluation of the SRO Program

Five questions were included at the end of the interview to help us better understand how students viewed the SRO program and the value they attached to their SRO:

- What do you like most about having an SRO working in your school?
- What do you like least about having an SRO working in the school?
- Would you prefer to attend a school that has an SRO at the school full-time or a school that does not have an SRO in the school? Why do you say this?
- Do you think the SRO program should be continued or not? Why do you say this?
- In your opinion, what is the value of having the SRO program in your school?

Responses to each of these questions are provided and discussed in the sections below.

What Students Like about the SRO Program

What do the students like about the SRO program? Half liked that they felt safer at school because the SRO is there:

> "I feel secure knowing they are there . . . I feel protected at all times."
>
> "I like it . . . it lowers the amount of crimes and things happening in the school."

Half liked the fact that having the SRO at the school stopped students (including themselves) from making bad choices and doing stupid things and getting in trouble:

> "I like how like their presence affects other students and how students think twice because students are like . . . Oh if I do this then this will happen, and then it makes them realize that whatever they're about to do is a negative decision and they do the right decision instead of the wrong."
>
> "I feel like they enforce the rules and like people realize how serious they are . . . I feel like . . . their presence like affects other students' choices . . . They think twice about trying to sell some marijuana or steal so and so's cell phone."
>
> "My friends and I, like we always like think about what will happen when the police are around . . . and then we always end up doing the right decision. . .Like to be honest, like sometimes we like think about doing something we know is wrong . . . but then we go, oh no we can't do this, like we'll get caught and whatever it will be bad so we just end up not doing it . . . but then the fact that a police officer is . . . present . . . yes we think twice."

Three liked the fact that the SROs were able to take action immediately if anything unsafe happened in the school:

> "I like knowing that if there is a problem it can be dealt with quickly."

Finally, three students felt reassured that SROs were patrolling and monitoring the school at all times:

> "I like that the police are always watching . . ."

What Students Do not Like about the SRO Program

Six out of the eight students could not think of anything they did not like about having an SRO working in their school:

> "It's just a lot of pros, not really much cons."

One student felt that the SRO could be more visible and did not like it when the officer was not around:

> ". . . That I don't see them often enough . . . Want to see more of them."

The final student gave two responses to this question. This student felt that the presence of the SRO stopped students from acting freely because they felt they were being watched by the officers ("it restricts some activities"). The student also worried about possible overreaction by the officer to small things. When prompted though, this student admitted that he never observed any over-reactions by the SRO at his school, but stated that he was worried about this happening nonetheless.

Preference: School with SROs or School without SROs

All of the students reported that they would prefer to go to a high school that had a full-time SRO, rather than one without them. They justified their responses by listing four advantages of being in a school with an officer, and one disadvantage of being in a school without an officer.

The most commonly mentioned advantage of being in a school with an SRO (mentioned by six out of eight students) related to perceptions of safety. All of these students talked about how they felt safer at school because the SRO was there. In fact, three of them said that their parents also felt that they were safer because the officer was there:

> "When the police officer is there, you can do your work without having to worry about being safe."
>
> "My parents don't worry as much [be]cause the police are in the school."

The second most commonly mentioned advantage (given by half the students) was the perception that SROs stop illegal and unsafe activities from occurring in schools to which they are assigned:

> "Bad people are aware that the police are in our school all the time . . . So they just don't come here."
>
> "The police have more authority than VPs [vice principals] . . . Kids aren't afraid of being suspended but they are afraid of being arrested. So, they are more careful when the police are in the school."

The other two advantages were each given by only a couple of students. Two students felt that going to a school with an SRO really benefited the more vulnerable students since it reduced the amount of bullying that went on:

> ". . . having the police at the school helps all of us, but especially victims of bullying . . . it means you don't have to be a victim . . ."

Two other students mentioned that having an SRO in the school helped them focus on their school work by minimizing distractions and worry:

> "I can focus on my studying and long-term goals without worrying . . . [be]cause I know they are here."

Two students answered this question by talking about what they saw as the disadvantages of going to school without a full-time police officer. They felt that schools without an SRO are less safe than their school and that more illegal activity happens in such schools. It is interesting to note that these two students were the only ones who did not cite enhanced safety as an advantage of having an SRO present, preferring instead to talk about how students who went to a school without an officer felt unsafe. These two students had friends in schools in Toronto and based their answer on what they had heard about the situation there as compared to in Peel:

> "They don't have them in Toronto, and I hear from my friends that there are more problems there . . . and more crime too."

Should the SRO Program Be Continued?

All of the students we interviewed felt that the SRO program should be continued in its current format. They justified this response by repeating many of the answers they had given to earlier questions in the interview.

The most frequently given reason for wanting the program to continue related to the idea that the SRO program improves student well-being by enhancing students' feelings of safety in the school and "giving them the peace of mind to focus on their education." The five students who gave this response also talked about how having the SRO in the school had reduced how stressed they felt at school.

Half the students said that, in their opinion, the SRO program reduces the number of unsafe and illegal activities in their school ("they keep us from making stupid choices") and they want it to continue.

Finally, two students felt that the SRO program offered the students a place to go if they needed help or information:

> ". . . because they come to assemblies and provide information and you know they are there to help."

> ". . . they come in, like, I don't know, maybe . . . every few months. And they would just come and talk about, like, issues, like, bullying, cyberbullying and stuff. And I found that beneficial . . ."

What Is the Value of Having the SRO Program in Your School?

We concluded the interview by asking students: "All things considered, what value does having an SRO in the school deliver to you?" The students gave three responses to this question, many of which are similar to their responses to earlier questions.

Value – The SRO program stops students from making bad choices: A majority of the students we talked to felt that when the students saw the SRO in the school, they were motivated to make good choices. These students also noted that, in their opinion, the SRO really wanted to keep them out of trouble and out of jail:

> "I know some bad people and they can get in the way of someone learning things. Like, they can like, you know, get them addicted to drugs or create other problems. But with the police here, like they'll think twice about like messing with anyone or doing anything wrong."

Value – The SRO program creates/enhances a safer environment for learning: In a related response, five students mentioned that they felt safer because the SRO was in their school, and noted that when they felt safe, they were more able to stay focused on their studies:

> "They're just like our second parents, away from home. So, they're here to care for us, make sure we're safe, we're getting a good education, and no one's up to no good and everyone's, like, safe and sound."

Value – The SRO is familiar with the school and the students: One student felt the program was valuable because it gave the police greater knowledge of the school and its students. They felt that this familiarity would be very useful in case of emergencies:

> "I think having police in the school is better just because they're kind of familiar with the students in the school and like the location and what things happen in the school."

The Student Survey

Researchers conduct surveys to collect data to help them answer specific, important questions. Surveys are useful in that they:

- allow researchers to uncover answers in a non-intimidating, non-confrontational survey environment where anonymity is ensured;
- facilitate the collection of unbiased survey data, which allows decision makers to take action based on objective results;
- provide a snapshot of the attitudes and behaviors held by a target population at a particular point in time; and
- allow researchers to compare changes in key attitudes or outcomes over time.

This section of the chapter focuses on surveys that were administered to a randomly selected group of Grade 9 students who attended one of the five Peel District high schools participating in the study. The survey was designed to evaluate the extent to which the SRO program delivers on its goal of working with the schools to create a "safe learning environment" for students in Peel Region.

This section of the book is divided into five main sections. We begin by providing the reader with key information on the survey methodology, including the questions asked, how the survey was administered, and how the data were analyzed. The second section provides the reader with a description of who responded to the survey and the third examines data that speak to how the Grade 9 students who were surveyed feel about the police, stereotype the police, and evaluate the seriousness of a number of criminal offenses. The fourth section presents and discusses data relating to students' contact with, and their perceptions of, the SRO(s) assigned to their school and the SRO program in general. The fifth section presents and evaluates data relating to how safe students feel at school and makes the link between feeling safe at school and key outcomes such as learning, student well-being, etc. The final section explores how gender and past victimization impact the survey findings.

Methodology

The survey used in this study is based on one that was developed and tested in the UK by Dr. Nick Hopkins and his colleagues at the University of Dundee. Hopkins et al. (1992) undertook a study which sought to evaluate the impact of School Liaison Officers (SLOs) on young people's views and attitudes about the police and offending. Dr. Hopkins administered the survey to 1,245 secondary school students and compared students' views of police in schools with and without a full-time SLO. The following measures from that survey were used in our study:

- attitudes toward the police;
- perceptions of the seriousness of crime;
- perceptions of the likelihood of identification associated with crime;
- stereotypes of the police in general;
- stereotypes of the SRO; and
- degree of contact with the police inside and outside the school.

The questions in our survey on perceptions of safety, student quality of life (i.e., bullying), school attendance, and student well-being were either taken directly from, or were modified versions of, measures reported by Finn et al. (2004) in their important report that summarized key findings from case studies of 19 American SRO programs.

We employed a study design that was very similar to that of Hopkins et al. (1992). A randomly selected group of Grade 9 pupils were asked to complete a questionnaire at two points in time. The questionnaire was carried out by the administrators in each of the five schools participating in our study during a one-week period in September 2015 and March 2016. Standardized instructions and procedures were used in all five schools. Pupils were assured that their replies would be strictly confidential to encourage honest responding. Ethics clearance was obtained from Carleton University as well as the two Peel District school boards. A note was sent home to all parents telling them about the study and offering them the opportunity to withhold consent if they did not want their child to participate. Only three sets of parents withheld consent. Anonymity was ensured as we did not ask the students' names.

In total, 610 Grade 9 students (approximately 35% of the Grade 9 students attending one of the five high schools participating in the study) completed the survey in September 2015 (i.e., Time 1). These students had little to no exposure to the SRO program or SROs, as they had come from feeder schools where this program did not operate.

The Time 2 survey was administered in March of 2016. The 655 students who completed the survey in March 2016 were slightly older and had been exposed to the SRO program for just over half a year. Unfortunately, confidentiality requirements meant that we could not use a repeated measures design (i.e., the exact same students responding to the survey at both Time 1 and Time 2). That being said, we expect that many of the students who responded to the Time 1 survey also filled out the Time 2 survey.

Finally, unless otherwise stated, it should be assumed that all of the measures identified above were included in both the Time 1 and Time 2 surveys.

With respect to data analysis, Cronbach's alpha was used to assess the validity of all scales used in our analysis. This testing procedure determined that, with two exceptions (the two and three item scales measuring student reactions to the SRO in their school), all measures used in this study had Cronbach's alphas between 0.80 and 0.97 and can be considered valid.

Factor analysis was conducted on all scales to ensure that their structure was the same as reported by Hopkins et al. (1992). Factor analysis[2] is a statistical technique that can be used to reduce a lot of data to a smaller data set that is more manageable and more understandable. In this chapter, whenever possible, we report respondents' total scale scores, which are calculated as the summed averages of all the factors together. These total scale scores provide an excellent summary of what the data are telling us.

As noted above, the goal of the SRO program is for "Peel police to work with the school to create a safe learning environment." If the program is meeting this goal, we would expect that students who responded to the survey at Time 2 would report feeling safer at school (and, by extrapolation, be less likely to experience the negative consequences of feeling unsafe) than students who responded at Time 1. Since the SRO program also aims to develop more positive perceptions of the police and more responsible orientations towards offending, we would also expect to see a more positive pattern of attitudinal changes in both of these areas over time.

Comparisons of the Time 1 and Time 2 data were undertaken using either chi-square tests (for frequency data) or *t*-tests (for continuous data).

Finally, while the analyses reported in this chapter of the book provide us with some degree of understanding about the extent to which the SRO program changes attitudes and perceptions over time, it is important to remember that other factors, such as peer pressure, the experience of starting a new school, parental involvement, etc., might also impact the attitudes and beliefs of these students.

Demographics

We collected a range of demographic data to help us interpret the responses to the survey. More specifically, we asked the students:

- what grade they were in;
- their gender (male, female, prefer not to say);
- their family situation (e.g., I live with my mother and my father, I live with my mother most or all of the time, I live with my father most or all of the time, I live with a family member other than my mother or my father, other);
- whether or not they have a part-time job (yes or no);
- whether or not they engage in any kind of volunteer work (yes or no);
- whether or not they are a member of any kind of club or sports team (yes or no); and
- whether or not they considered themselves to be a member of a minority group (yes or no).

In order to better contextualize the findings, we also asked respondents the following three questions:

- Have you ever been arrested or stopped by the police?
- Has anyone in your family ever been arrested or stopped by the police?
- Have any of your close friends ever been arrested or stopped by the police?

Demographic data for the Time 1 and Time 2 samples are shown in Table 4.1. It should be noted that, while these questions were placed at the end of the survey, they are reported first to help the reader situate the rest of the discussion.

Examination of the sample for the two different time periods shows that there were no statistically significant demographic differences between the Time 1 and Time 2 samples. More specifically, we note that in both samples:

- male and female students were equally likely to fill out the survey;
- approximately one out of every twenty students elected not to provide their gender;
- the vast majority of the students lived with their mother and father, although approximately one in ten students lived with only their mother;
- one in ten of the students had a part-time job;
- just over half the students engaged in volunteer work;
- just over half the students belonged to a club or were members of a sports team;
- approximately one in four students self-identified as a visible minority;[3] and
- approximately one in ten of students had been arrested/stopped by the police[4] approximately 40% of the students indicated that a family member has been arrested/stopped by the police; and approximately one in three of the students had a close friend or friends who had been arrested/stopped by the police.

TABLE 4.1 Demographics of the sample

	Time 1 *n = 610*	*Time 2* *n = 655*
Gender		
Male	47%	49%
Female	47%	47%
Prefer not to say	6%	5%
Family Situation		
Live with mother and father	75%	79%
Live with mother most of time	13%	10%
Live with father most of time	1%	1%
Live with family member other than parents	1%	2%
Other	9%	8%
Yes: Have a part time job	9%	10%
Yes: Engage in volunteer work	51%	56%
Yes: Member of club or sports team	52%	56%
Yes: Consider themselves a minority group	26%	27%
Yes: The student has been arrested/stopped by police	9%	9%
Yes: A family member has been arrested/stopped by police	40%	42%
Yes: Close friend(s) have been arrested/stopped by police	29%	30%

The fact that there are no demographic differences between the two samples implies that differences in attitudes and outcomes examined in this study across the two time periods may be heavily influenced by the students' exposure to the SRO program.

Attitudes Toward the Police

The first section of the survey includes a number of questions to help us understand how the students feel about the police. In the section below, we present an explanation of how each of these ideas was assessed, along with key findings with respect to each of these measures.

Feelings about the Police

Student's feelings about the police were quantified in this study using an eight-item scale taken from Hopkins et al. (1992). Four of the items were positive in tone: (1) police help protect people like me, (2) I feel I can rely on the police if I am in trouble, (3) the police make society a better place for everyone to live, and (4) all things considered, I like the fact that the police are around in my school. Four of the items were negative in tone: (1) the police pick on young people too much, (2) police often use unnecessary physical force, (3) the police often pick on people like me, and (4) the police tend to pick on visible minorities too much. Students were asked to use a seven-point Likert scale (1 = disagree strongly; 4 = neutral; 7 = agree strongly) to indicate the extent to which they agreed or disagreed with each of these eight statements.

Factor analysis of these eight items identified two strong factors that we labeled "Police A Positive Force in Society" (this factor included all of the positively worded items) and "Police Pick on Young People/Visible Minorities" (all of the negatively worded items grouped together on this factor). Figure 4.4 summarizes key findings relating to students' views on whether or not the police are a positive force in society and whether or not they pick on young people/visible minorities.

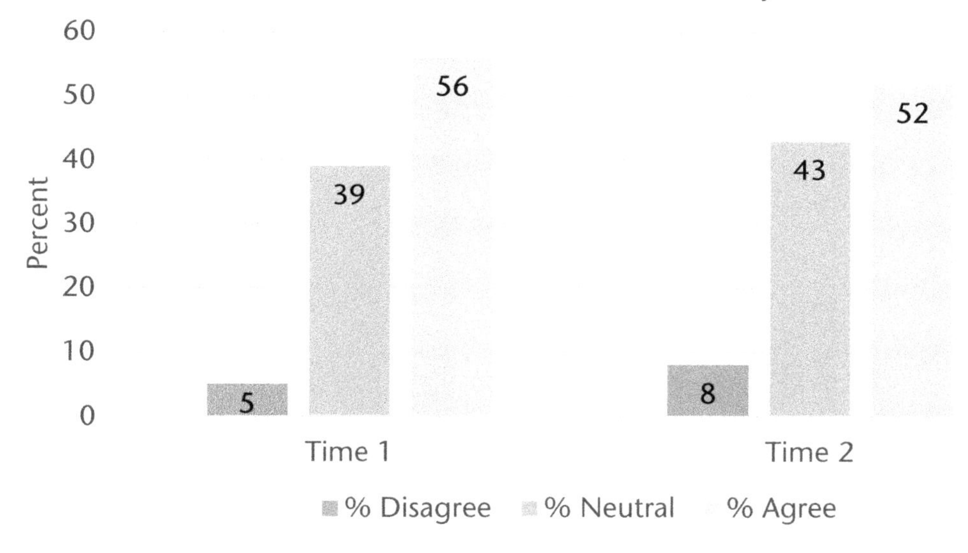

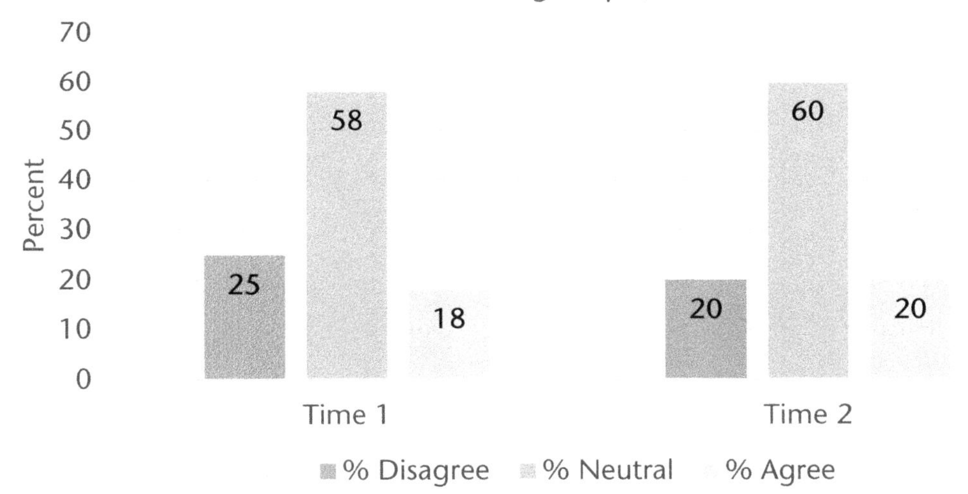

FIGURE 4.4 Feelings about the police

View of the Police in General

This measure was taken from Hopkins et al. (1992). It began with the following preamble: Different people have different views and images (i.e., stereotypes) of police officers. Please tell us how you view the police in general. The students were then presented with a list of eleven adjectives. Five of these adjectives were positive: (1) helpful, (2) trustworthy, (3) friendly, (4) fair, (5) approachable. Six of the adjectives were negative: (1) aggressive, (2) racist, (3) rude, (4) stupid, (5) useless, (6) strict. The students were given a seven point Likert scale (1 = no, not at all; 4 = half the time; 7 = all the time) to use in recording their responses. Factor analysis of the data identified two strong factors[5] as shown in Figure 4.5.

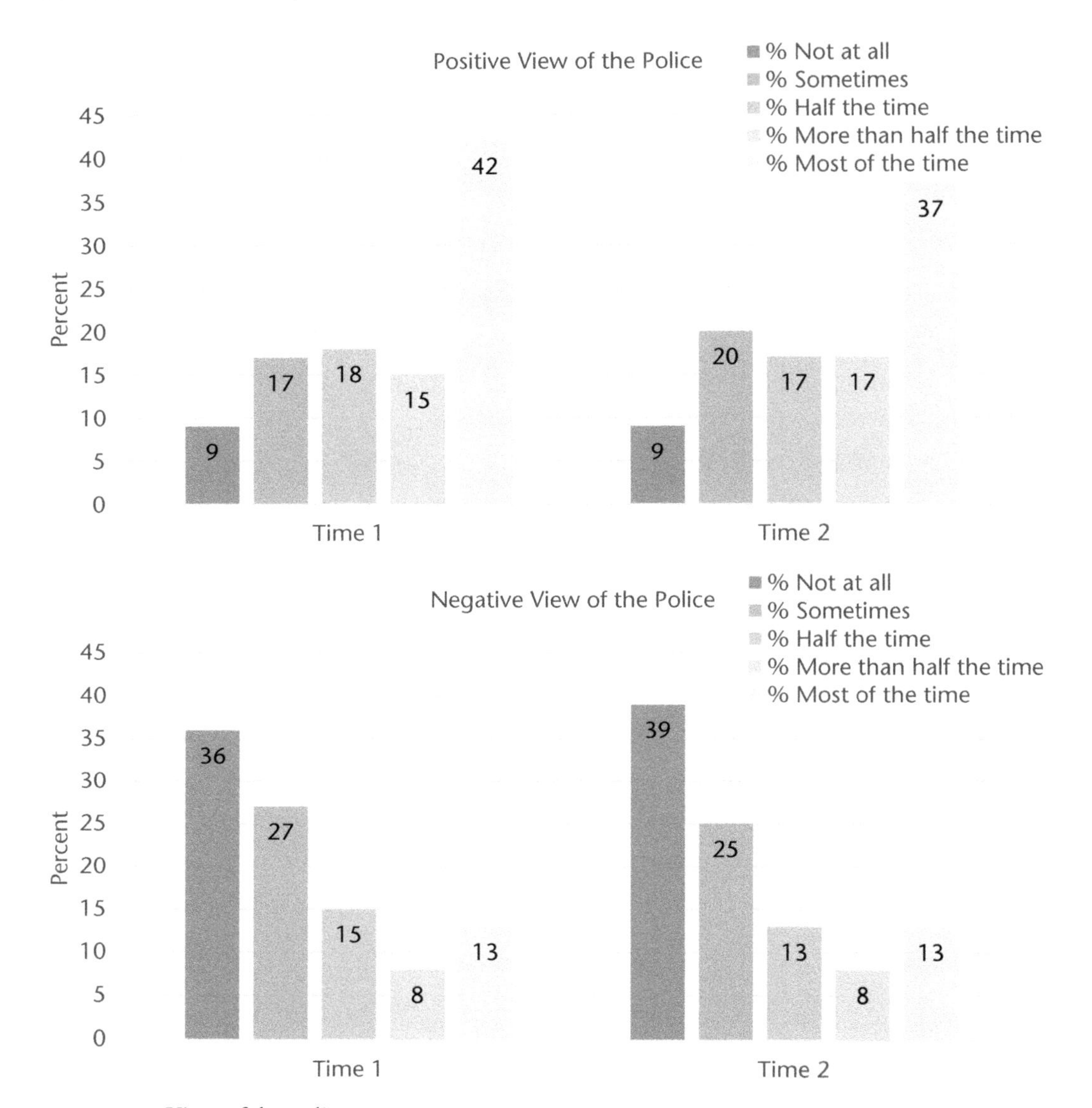

FIGURE 4.5 View of the police

The first factor, which we labelled "Positive View of the Police," included all the positive attributes included in the measure, along with the adjective "strict" (which we had initially viewed as a negative characteristic). It is interesting to note that "strict" negatively loaded on the "Negative View of the Police Factor." This loading pattern indicates that the more a student agrees that the police are aggressive, racist, rude, and stupid, the less likely they are to agree that the police officer is also strict. Instead, the data indicates that students who view the police as strict also see them as helpful, approachable, trustworthy, fair, and friendly. This finding suggests that the students appreciate the fact that the police are strict and demand that rules relating to behavior are observed and obeyed. This is consistent with the interview data. The following four negative adjectives – aggressive, racist, rude, and stupid – all loaded on the second factor, which we refer to as "Negative View of the Police."

The following observations can be made from the data in Figure 4.5. First, more students feel positively towards the police than do not. This conclusion is supported by the data showing that more than half the students (57% of respondents at Time 1 and 54% of respondents at Time 2) viewed the police positively more than half the time/all the time; double the number of students (26% of respondents at Time 1 and 29% of respondents at Time 2) who stated that they did not feel positively towards the police (i.e., gave a response of "sometimes" or "never"). Second, the majority of the students in our sample did not see the police as aggressive, racist, rude, and stupid (two-thirds of the students at both Time 1 and Time 2 rarely felt negatively about the police). Third, students' views of the police in general (both positive and negative) appear to be fairly stable over time. Finally, we note that 13% of the students at both Time 1 and Time 2 view the police negatively most of the time. Taken together, these findings suggest that the presence of an SRO in the school does not immediately lead to changes in how students view the police.

Contact with the Police at Your School

The second section of the survey included a set of questions that asked students about the amount of contact they had with the SRO(s) assigned to their school, as well as their perception of the SRO(s) and the SRO program in general. Details on how we measured each of these ideas, as well as key findings with respect to each of these topics, are summarized below.

Student Contact with the SRO in Their School

We began section two of the survey by asking students if they were aware that Peel Regional Police had assigned an officer to their school. Just over three quarters of the Time 2 survey respondents (78.1%) answered in the affirmative. Just over two-thirds of the students (68.5%) indicated that they knew the name of the SRO(s) working in their school, even though many had never talked to these officers.

We then asked the students who knew there was an SRO in their school: How much contact have you personally had with the police officers assigned to your school: (1) in the classroom, (2) when participating in school sports, (3) via a personal conversation at school, (4) via a personal conversation outside of school (e.g., plaza, community center), and (5) at a school assembly. In each case, we asked the students to use a seven-point Likert scale (1 = none at all; 4 = once a week; 7 = all the time) to record their responses. Analysis of the data showed that three-quarters of the respondents indicated that they had never had contact with their SRO in the classroom or at a sports event. A similar number said that they had never had a personal conversation with their SRO either at school or outside of school.

Where do almost all of the students in our sample make contact with the SRO at their school? School assemblies – a finding that is very consistent with what we heard in the interviews. While many students had little to no contact with their SRO, approximately 5% of students had personal conversations with their SRO weekly or daily at school, outside of school, or at school sports events.

We also asked students three single-item (yes/no) questions:

- Has your school police officer ever helped you out when you have had some sort of problem?
- Have you ever been questioned by your school police officer because he or she thought you did something wrong?
- Have you ever been questioned by your school police officer because you witnessed someone else doing something wrong?

Responses to these questions are summarized in Figure 4.6.

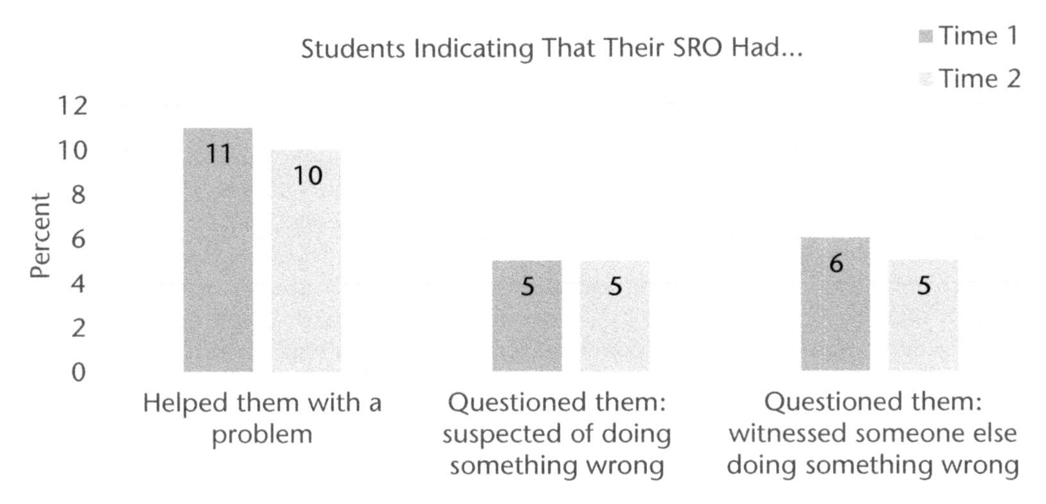

FIGURE 4.6 Contact with SRO

It is interesting to note that approximately one in ten students in both the Time 1 and Time 2 samples indicated that they had turned to their SRO for help when they had a problem – twice the number who had been questioned by their SRO because they were either personally suspected of doing something wrong or had witnessed someone else doing something wrong.

View of the SRO

To supplement the data looking at how Grade 9 students in Peel high schools view the police in general, we also asked them how they viewed the SRO within their school. This question began with the following preamble:

> The next couple of questions ask about how you view the police officers that work at your school (the SRO). Different people will have different views and images of these police officers. We are interested in how you personally view the police officers that work at your school. Please consider the officer that you deal with the most often when answering the questions below.

We then gave the students the same list of positive (helpful, trustworthy, friendly, fair, smart, approachable) and negative (aggressive, racist, rude, stupid, useless, and strict) adjectives that we had used to assess their views of police in general. Students were again asked to use a seven point Likert scale (1 = no, not at all; 4 = half the time, and 7 = all the time) to provide their responses.

These eleven adjectives loaded on two very different factors:

- positive view of the SRO: helpful, trustworthy, friendly, fair, smart, approachable, and strict; and
- negative view of the SRO: aggressive, racist, stupid, and rude.

As was the case when we asked about police in general, we note that "useless" did not load on either factor and that "strict", rather than clustering with the other negative adjectives, grouped with the positive SRO attributes. This reinforces the idea put forward earlier that many students do not view the SRO being strict as an undesirable characteristic, but instead appreciate the fact that their SRO demands that rules concerning behavior are observed and obeyed on school property.

This interpretation of the data is consistent with what we heard during the interviews. Responses showing how the students in our sample view their SRO can be seen in Figure 4.7.

The following observations can be made from the data in Figure 4.7. First, students were more than twice as likely to take the middle position (in both a positive and negative sense) when asked about the SRO in their school than when they were asked about police in general. Second, and perhaps most importantly, virtually none (5%) of the students indicated that they commonly (i.e., more than half the time) held negative views of their SRO. In comparison, 21% of the students commonly held negative views of the police in general. Finally, 80% of the Grade 9 students in our sample viewed their SRO positively at least half the time. These findings are consistent with the literature, which suggests that contact with the police in a non-confrontational environment may help break down the negative stereotypes youth hold about the police.

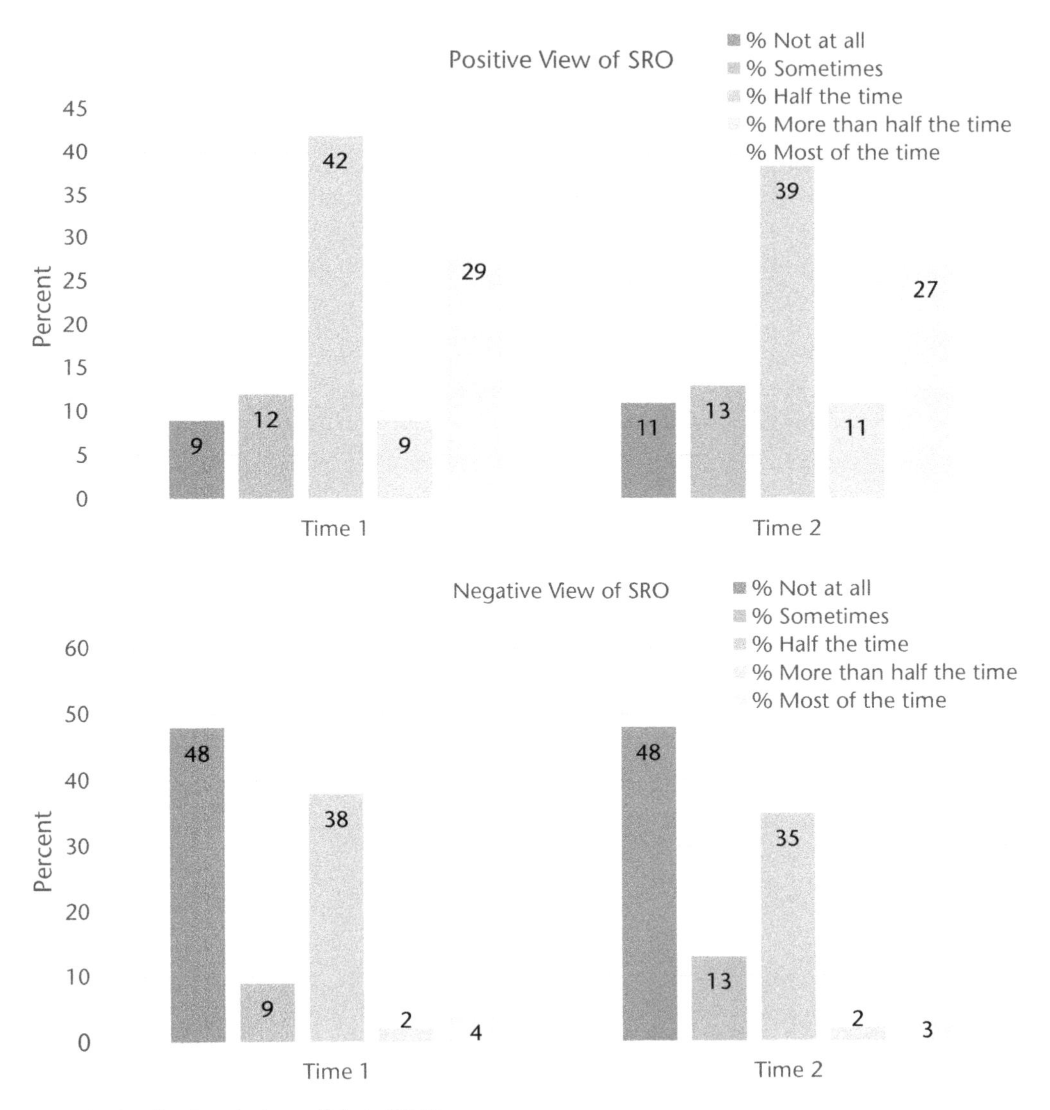

FIGURE 4.7 Students' view of their SRO

Reaction to SROs

We used items from Hopkins et al.'s (1992) surveys to measure students' reactions to the SRO in their school. This portion of the survey was phrased as follows: The next couple of questions ask about your relationship with the police officers that work at your school (the SROs), and how you react when you see them. We then asked them to use the following seven-point Likert scale (1 = never; 4 = half the time; 7 = all the time) to indicate how often, when they saw the SROs assigned to their school, they would: (1) say hi, (2) stop and chat, (3) feel anxious and stressed, (4) think twice about what they are about to do, and (5) feel safer. Students' responses to these five questions, taken from the Time 1 and Time 2 surveys, are shown in Figure 4.8. This analysis showed that the vast majority of the students in both the Time 1 and Time 2 samples feel safer when they see their school's SRO. That being said, the fact that one in three feel anxious when they see the SRO while half respond to the presence of the SRO by thinking before they act reinforces the idea (identified in the interviews) that the presence of the SROs in the school acts as a deterrent to inappropriate student behavior.

Attitude Toward SRO Program

We used items from Finn et al. (2004) to determine how students feel about the fact that there is a police officer assigned to work in their school. More specifically, we asked them to use a seven-point Likert scale (1 = strongly disagree; 4 = undecided; 7 = strongly agree) to indicate how much they agreed or disagreed with each of the following statements about the SRO program and their SRO:

- I think it is a good idea for the Peel Regional Police to assign officers to work in high schools;
- I feel safer because there is a police officer assigned to my school;
- I feel less stressed and anxious because there is a police officer assigned to my school;

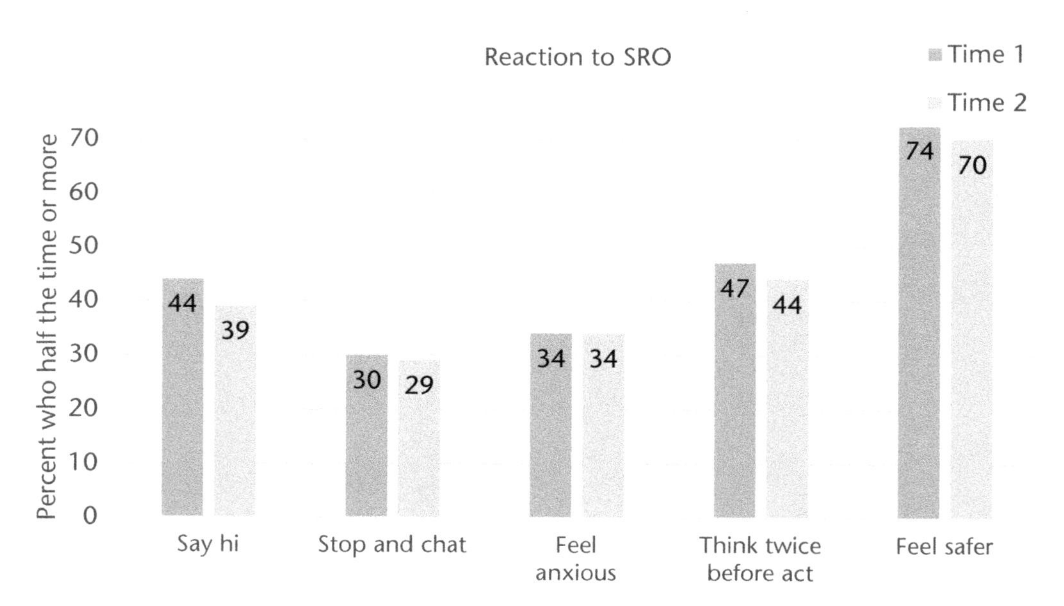

FIGURE 4.8 Reaction to school's SRO

- I would be comfortable approaching the police officer who works at my school to report a problem another student is having;
- I would be comfortable approaching the police officer who works at my school to report a crime; and
- I would be comfortable approaching the police officer who works at my school if I was being bullied or harassed.

Factor analysis determined that these questions loaded on two factors, one relating to attitudes towards the SRO program, the other speaking to the students' level of comfort with the SRO at their school. We labeled the one factor "Positive Attitudes Toward SRO Program" as it included items such as "It's a good idea to assign officers to work in high schools," "I feel safer because there is a police officer assigned to my school," and "I feel less stressed because a police officer is assigned to my school." We labeled the second factor "Level of Comfort with SRO" because it included items such as "I feel comfortable approaching the SRO at our school to report a problem another student is having," "I feel comfortable approaching the SRO at our school to report a crime," and "I would feel comfortable approaching the SRO at my school if I was being bullied or harassed." Results from this stage of the analysis are shown in Figures 4.9 and 4.10.

A number of key observations can be made from the data in Figures 4.9 and 4.10. First, the vast majority of students in both the Time 1 and Time 2 samples agree that the SRO program is a good idea, with half agreeing that they feel safer and one in three agreeing that they feel less stressed because the officer is around. These are very positive findings. Second, approximately one in three students agree that they would talk to their SRO about a problem another student was having, report a crime, and report if they were being bullied – more than double the number that disagree that they would take such actions. Third, while the number of students disagreeing that they would report a crime, report being bullied, and report a problem that another student was having remains unchanged over time, we note that five months after starting high school (i.e., at Time 2) students are less likely to agree that they would report such issues to their SRO. It is hard to say if these declines are because of something that the SRO has done, because of other issues such as peer pressure from other students, or because the student has matured and

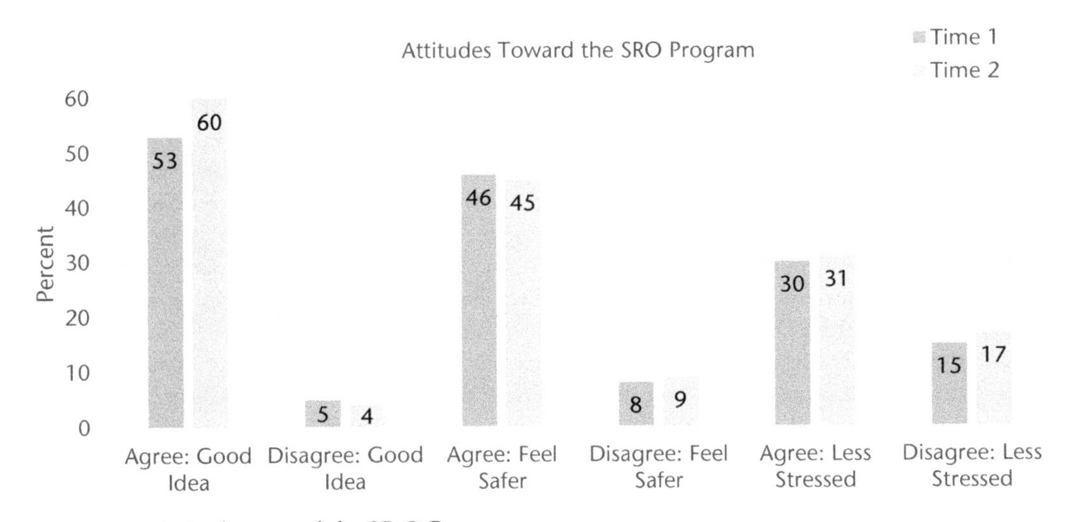

FIGURE 4.9 Attitudes toward the SRO Program

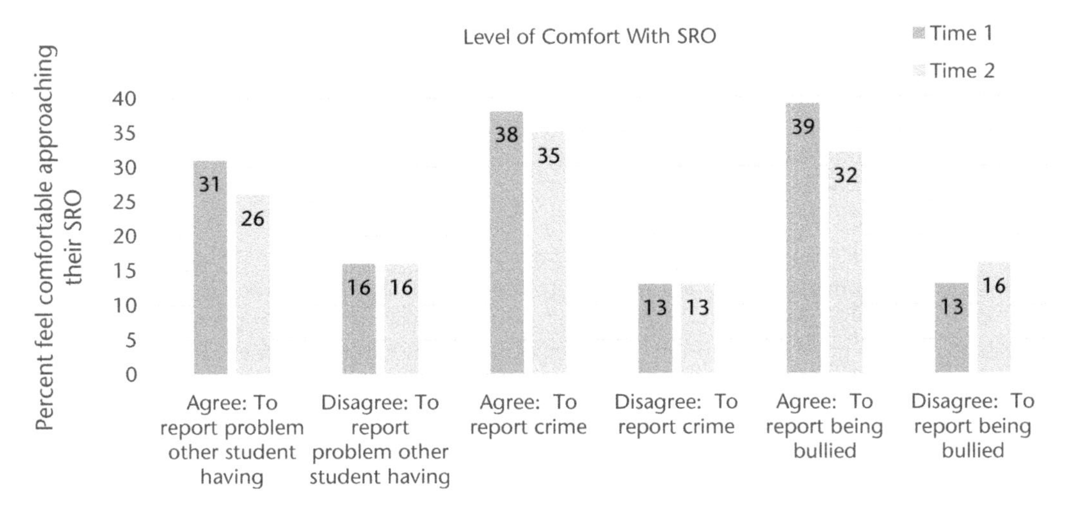

FIGURE 4.10 Level of comfort with SRO

prefers to use their own judgement with respect to these matters (i.e., the number of students who are undecided as to how they would handle each of these situations has increased over time).

How You Feel at School

The third and final section of the survey asked a number of questions designed to gauge students' perceptions of school safety, and make the link between feeling safe at school and key outcomes such as learning, student well-being, etc. Four sets of questions were included in this section to explore: feelings of safety at school, fear and anxiety at school, missing school, and consequences of feeling unsafe at school. All of the measures used in this section were based on work done by Finn et al. (2004) and all are important to our SROI calculations (see Chapter 9). Information about how each of these concepts were measured, along with key findings on each of these outcomes, is provided in the sections below.

Feelings of Safety at School

The first question in this section was included to help us understand how safe the students in our sample felt at school (in general) and in various locations around the school. More specifically, we asked students to use a seven-point Likert scale (1 = very safe; 4 = can't say; 7 = very unsafe) to indicate how safe they felt at school when they were in each of the following places: (1) the washrooms, (2) the locker room, (3) the gym, (4) the parking lot, (5) walking to and from school, (6) on the bus to and from school, (7) at school social events (e.g. dances), (8) in the cafeteria, and (9) stairs and hallways. We also asked them the following: All things considered, when I am at school I feel . . ."

The data show that, regardless of the time period when they were asked, students felt safest in the gym (66% responded safe) and the cafeteria (66% responded safe). Approximately half of the students indicated that they felt safe in the stairs and hallways of the schools, as well as in the locker room, at school social events, and in the school washrooms. Approximately 40% of the students agreed that they felt safe either walking or taking the bus to and from school. Where are Grade 9 students least likely to feel safe? The school parking lot (37% felt safe).

Finally, it should be noted that two-thirds of the students responded to the final question in this scale – "All things considered, when I am at school I feel . . ." by answering "safe" – regardless of the time period being considered.

All of these items loaded onto one factor so we created one summary score that we labeled "Feelings of Safety at School." Analysis of these data suggested that, in both September and March, 55% of students indicated that they felt safe at school, 40% felt safe sometimes, but not safe other times, and 5% felt unsafe.

Fear and Anxiety at School

Bullying and harassment are known to be an issue in many Canadian high schools. To get an indication of the extent to which a fear of bullying and being physically assaulted causes high school students stress and anxiety we asked them how anxious or afraid they were of being:

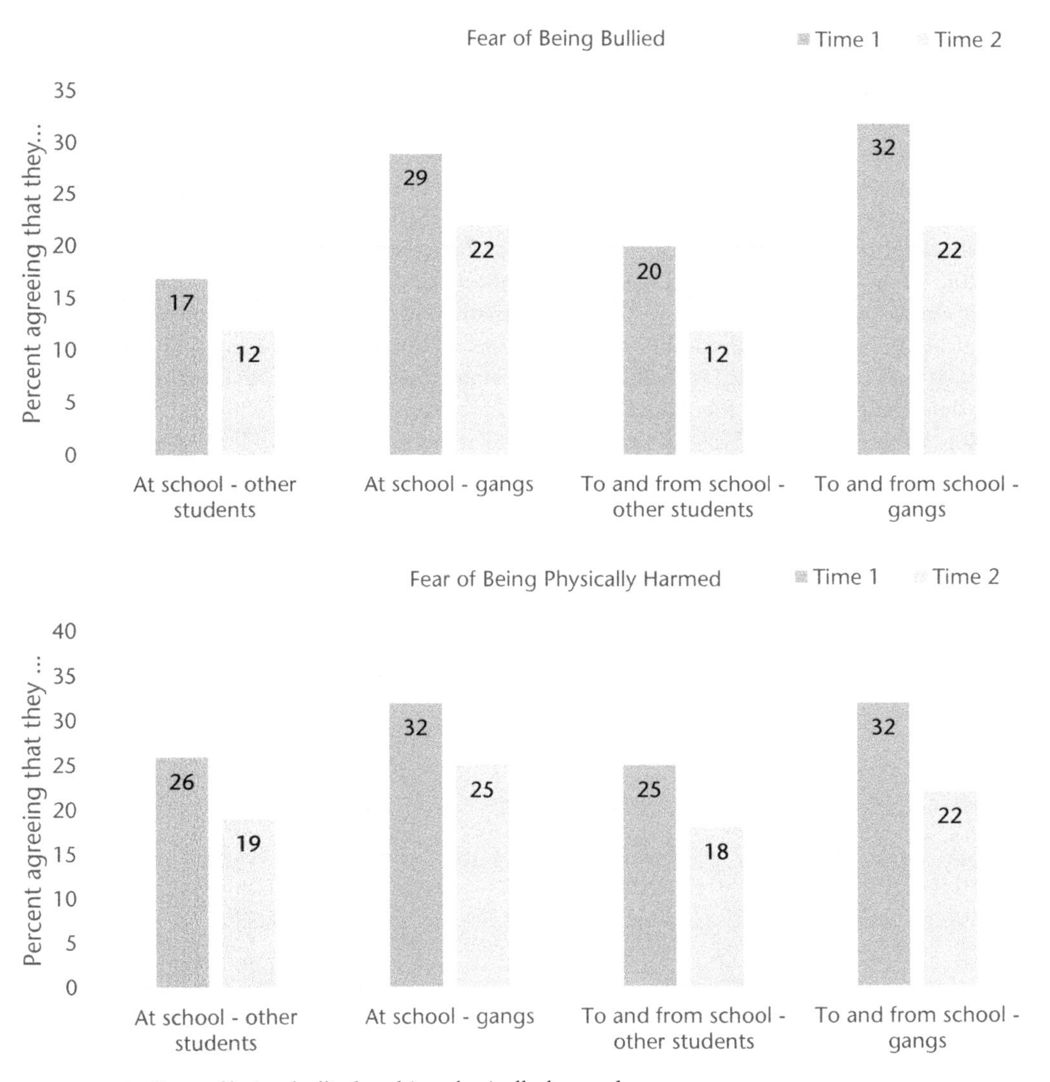

FIGURE 4.11 Fear of being bullied and/or physically harmed

- bullied or harassed by other students when they are at school;
- bullied by gang members when they are at school;
- bullied by other students when they are on the way to and from school;
- bullied by gang members when they are on the way to and from school;
- physically harmed by other students when they are at school;
- physically harmed by gang members when they are at school;
- physically harmed by other students when they are on the way to and from school; and
- physically harmed by gang members when they are on the way to and from school.

In all cases, students were asked to use a five-point Likert scale for their response where 1 = not at all afraid, 3 = somewhat afraid, and 5 = very afraid. Responses to each of these questions are shown in Figure 4.11. These data show that the Grade 9 students in our sample were significantly more likely to be afraid of being bullied or physically harmed by other students and gang members just after starting high school than they were five months later. These results provide support for the idea that the SRO program is increasing student's perceptions of safety both within the school and on the way to and from school.

During the interviews (with administrators, students, and SROs) we heard about how the SRO program reduced the amount of bullying and gang activities occurring at the high schools. These perceptions are supported by the quantitative survey data in Figure 4.11. Our findings from the survey with regard to bullying are also consistent with student reports admitting that because the SRO is around in the schools, they think twice before they act and are less likely to get into fights with others.

Finally, the data in Figure 4.11 supports the idea that gangs are an issue in Peel Region and contribute to problems in the schools and in neighborhoods around the school. Again, this was pointed out as an issue of concern in the administrators' interviews. Students seem to be more afraid of being bullied and physically harmed by gangs than they are of being bullied by other students. It is also noted that these fears decline over time, supporting the idea that the SROs may, in fact, deter gang activity in the school and its catchment area.

Factor analysis determined that the eight "fear and anxiety" questions all loaded on one factor, which we labeled "Stress and Anxiety at School." Figure 4.12 shows the percentage of students at Time 1 and Time 2 who are afraid/very afraid, sometimes afraid, and rarely/never afraid. We again

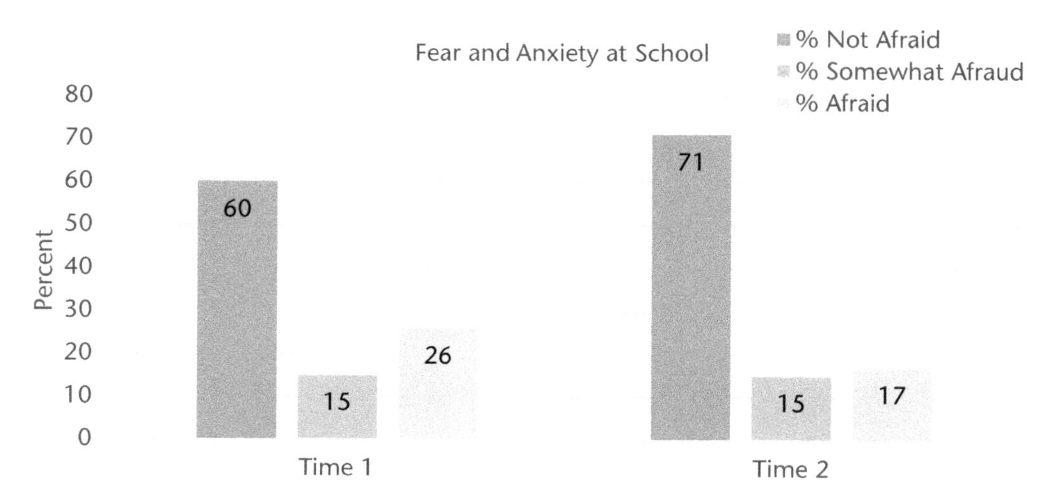

FIGURE 4.12 Fear and anxiety at school – total scale score

note that the percentage reporting that they are afraid at school declines significantly over time with a concomitant increase in the percentage reporting that they are rarely if ever afraid of being bullied or physically harmed. This again provides support for the idea that the SRO program is meeting a key program objective: making students feel safer at school and in the school's catchment area.

Missing School

Research has shown that students who are afraid of being bullied or harassed either at school or on their way to and from school are more likely to miss school. It can be expected, therefore, that any increase in student safety that comes about because of the SRO program will result in a visible decrease in the number of students who miss school or skip classes. This assumption was quantified in this study using a scale taken from Finn et al. (2004) to measure student absenteeism. In the Time 1 survey, we asked: How many times this semester do you think you will avoid going to school or skipping classes because:

- you are afraid of being bullied;
- you are afraid of being physically harmed;
- you have been bullied; and
- you have been physically harmed.

The wording was modified slightly in the Time 2 survey where we asked students to: Please think back to the last semester (the one that just ended). How often did you avoid going to school or skipping classes because:

- you were afraid of being bullied;
- you were afraid of being physically harmed;
- you were bullied; and
- you were physically harmed.

It should be noted that, when the students answered the Time 1 survey, they made their estimates based on their experiences in the previous year when they were at a school that did not have an SRO. When responding to the Time 2 survey, on the other hand, they were asked to think about their actual experiences when attending a school with a full time SRO. In both cases, responses were collected using the following scale: 1 = never; 2 = once; 3 = 2–3 times; 4 = 4–5 times, and 5 = 6 or more times.

As all four missing school items loaded on one factor, we elected to focus our discussion on the total "Missing School" score, which was calculated as the summed average of the four items in the scale. The data on missing school are shown in Figure 4.13. The trends observed with respect to missing school are very consistent with those noted from the data on fear of bullying and physical harm reported above and reinforce the idea that the reduction in fear and anxiety associated with being bullied and physically harmed can potentially be linked to the SRO program. These data also support the idea that the SRO program contributes to a decline in student absenteeism and, one can hope, increased learning.

Consequences of Feeling Unsafe at School

Finally, the survey included a scale to help us understand how feeling unsafe at school negatively impacted the students. The question was asked slightly differently in the Time 1 and Time 2 surveys.

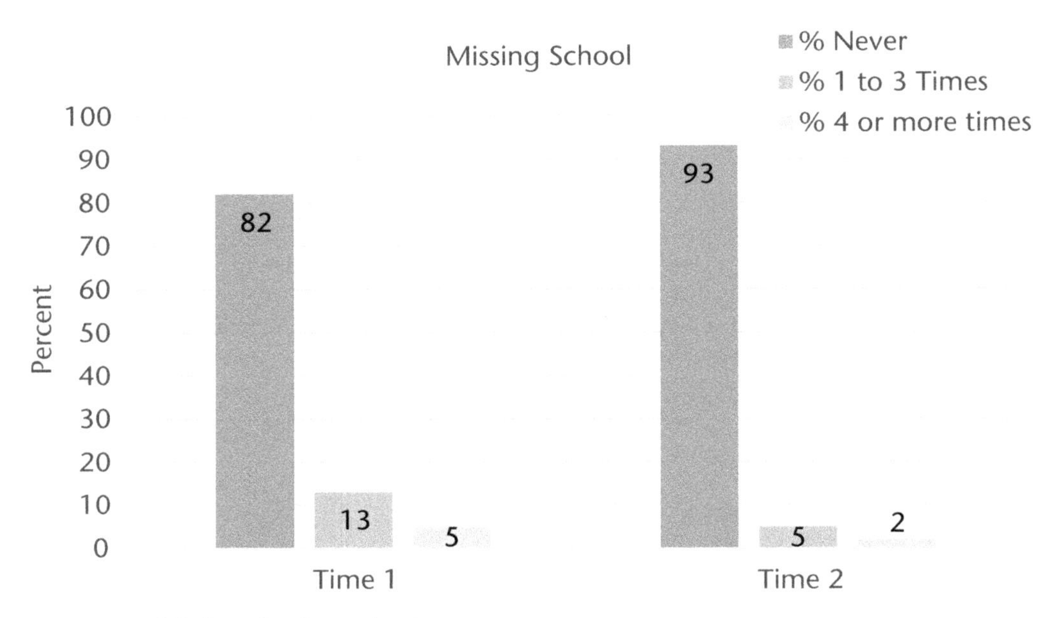

FIGURE 4.13 Missing school – total scale score

At Time 1, we asked the following: Please think about the second school semester last year (i.e., February to June, 2015). How often, during this semester, when you felt unsafe at school did it:

- make it difficult for you to concentrate on your schoolwork during class;
- make you feel anxious and stressed;
- make it difficult for you to sleep at night;
- make you think about harming yourself;
- make you think about harming someone else;
- make you feel depressed; and
- make you feel like dropping out of school.

In the Time 2 survey, we asked students the same questions but changed the question lead-in as follows: Please think back to the last semester (i.e., September 2015 to January 2016). How often during that semester did feeling unsafe at school . . ., followed by the same set of consequences listed above. In both cases, students were asked to record their answer using a seven-point Likert scale where 1 = never, 4 = once a week, and 7 = all the time.

When interpreting the answers, it should be noted that, when the students answered the Time I survey they were asked to think back to when they attended a school that did not have an SRO. In the Time 2 survey, on the other hand, they were asked to think about their time in their current high school where an SRO was present.

Responses to this set of questions probably provide the most compelling case in support of the SRO program as they reinforce the idea that SROs do, in fact, increase student perceptions of safety at school and decrease a number of the negative consequences associated with feeling unsafe. This conclusion is supported by the data in Figure 4.14 (individual items). Five months after becoming a student at a high school with a police officer on site, students reported that they were were significantly more able to concentrate, were experiencing better mental health (i.e., reported less anxiety, stress, and feeling depressed), were less likely to

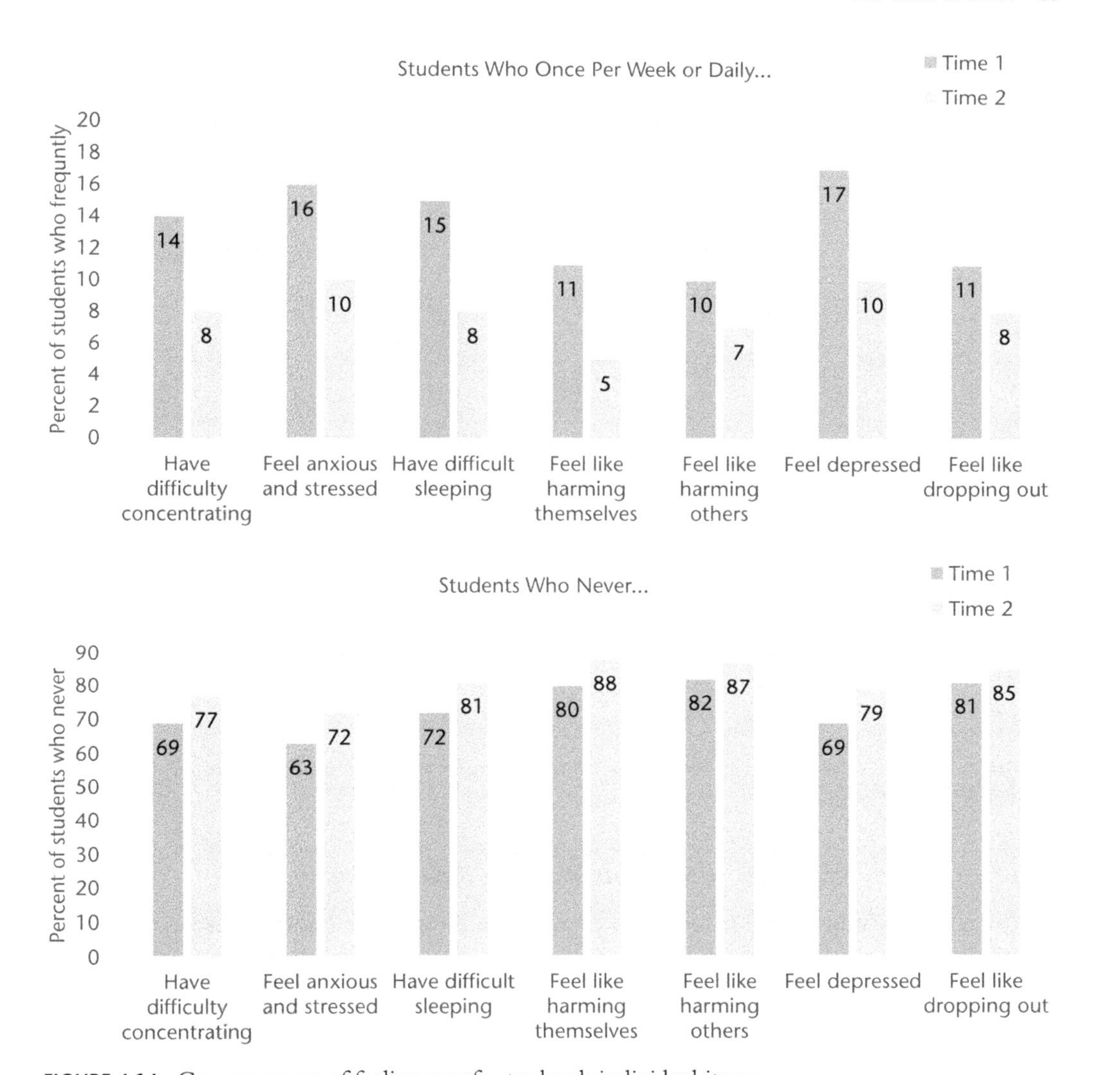

FIGURE 4.14 Consequences of feeling unsafe at school: individual items

report difficulties sleeping, and were less likely to think about harming themselves or others. They were also less likely to be thinking of dropping out of school, although this difference was not statistically significant.

These data provide support for the SRO program, as they link the presence of an SRO within the school to the students feeling safer which is, in turn, associated with a number of key student outcomes (improved mental health) and, we hope, better learning outcomes. These data are key to the value calculations presented in the SROI of the SRO program (see Chapter 9).

All seven items included in this scale loaded strongly on one factor, which we used to create a total scale score that quantifies the "Consequences of Feeling Unsafe at School." Not surprisingly, student scores on this scale (see Figure 4.15) provide further support for the idea that, when students feel safer at school, they are less likely to experience the myriad negative consequences that arise when they feel unsafe (and they are correspondingly more able to concentrate and learn at school). Of particular note are the data showing that the percentage of students

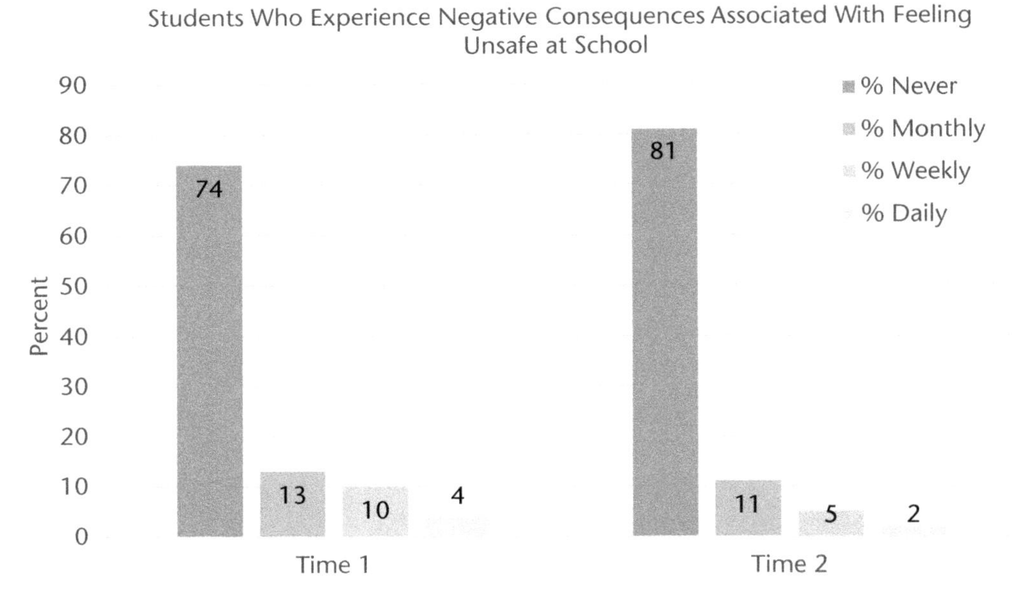

FIGURE 4.15 Consequences of feeling unsafe at school

reporting negative consequences weekly or more dropped from 14% of the Time 1 sample to 7% of the Time 2 sample.

Factors that May Impact how Students View the SRO Program

The student population in the schools we worked with differed on a number of factors, which may influence their perceptions of the SRO program or the impact this program had on them. Accordingly, in this section we provide data illustrating how each of the following factors impact the findings presented above: (1) contact with the SRO, (2) gender, (3) having been arrested/stopped by police, and (4) having been victimized.

Contact with the SRO

What is the association between contact with the SRO and the findings from this study? To answer this question, a summary measure was created that included student reports of any or all of the following forms of contact with their school SRO(s): (1) in the classroom, (2) while participating in school sports, (3) during school assemblies, and/or (4) personal conversations inside and/or outside the school. The measure was re-coded so that students who indicated that they had contact with their SRO(s) in any of these capacities "once in a while," "once a month," "once a week," "several times a week," "once a day," or "all the time" were considered to have "engaged with an SRO." Students who reported that they had "no [contact] at all" with their SRO in any of these situations were considered to have "no SRO engagement." Independent samples *t*-tests were then conducted to determine if there were significant differences between students who had some sort of personal contact with the SRO(s) assigned to their school and those who had no contact with the SRO(s), on the measure described above. The results of these analyses are available from the authors upon request. Statistically significant findings are shown in Figure 4.16 and summarized below.

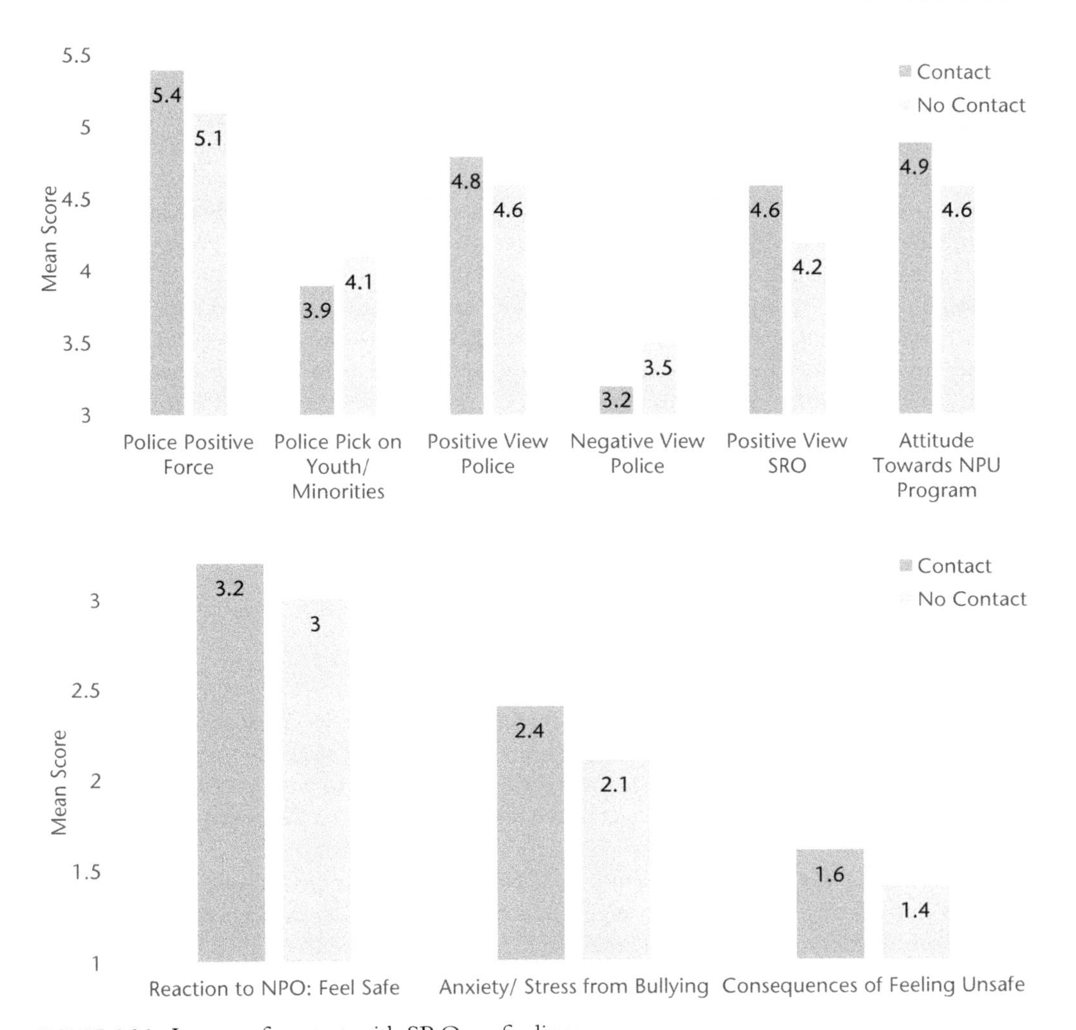

FIGURE 4.16 Impact of contact with SRO on findings

Compared to those who have never had contact with the SRO at their school, those who had contact are:

- significantly more likely to agree that the police are a positive force in our society;
- significantly more likely to have a positive view of the police in general;
- significantly more likely to have a positive view of the SRO in their school;
- significantly more likely to agree that they feel safer because the SRO is around; and
- significantly more likely to be favorably predisposed to the SRO program.

These findings support the idea that students who have more exposure to the police in a non-confrontational environment are more likely to develop positive views of the police and of their SRO(s) and/or that students with more positive views of the police are more likely to make contact with the SRO.

Our analysis also shows that those who have had contact with the SRO at their school are significantly more likely than those with no contact to report fear and anxiety due to bullying, to report that they have experienced negative consequences from feeling unsafe at school, and (as noted above) feel safer because the SRO is around. These findings imply that those who have had contact with an SRO may have been the victim of bullying and harassment, either in public school or in their current environment. They also provide support for the idea that the SRO program benefits the more vulnerable students attending Peel District high schools.

Unfortunately, we cannot determine from our results if positive views of the police lead the student to make contact with the SRO or if contact with the SRO results in positive views of the police (i.e., what is known as the direction of causality of a relationship). We face a similar issue when it comes to interpreting the findings showing that the students who have never had any contact with the SRO at their school are more likely than those who have had contact to have a negative view of the police (i.e., think they are aggressive and racist), as well as agree that police pick on youth/minorities. Do negative attitudes towards the police lead students to avoid the SRO within their school (i.e., have no contact) or does the lack of contact with the SRO result in the negative views towards the police (e.g., because the students have not formed a positive relationship with their SRO)? The findings from the interviews can be used to help us determine the direction of causality. Nonetheless, these data support the idea that contact with the school's SRO is associated with more positive views of the police and enhanced feelings of safety.

Gender

What is the association between gender and the findings from this study? To answer this question, tests were conducted to determine if there were significant differences between males, females, and students who did not wish to disclose their gender ("prefer not to say") on the various scales used in this study. Key findings with respect to the impact of gender on the findings are shown in Figure 4.17 and summarized below.

Before beginning our discussion of gender differences on the various attitudes and outcomes explored in this study, it is necessary to highlight a number of gender differences in the demographics of the samples that are worth pointing out. Males were more likely than females to have a part-time job, to live in an "atypical" family situation (i.e., not with their mother and/or their father), to have been arrested or stopped by the police prior to starting Grade 9, and to have a close

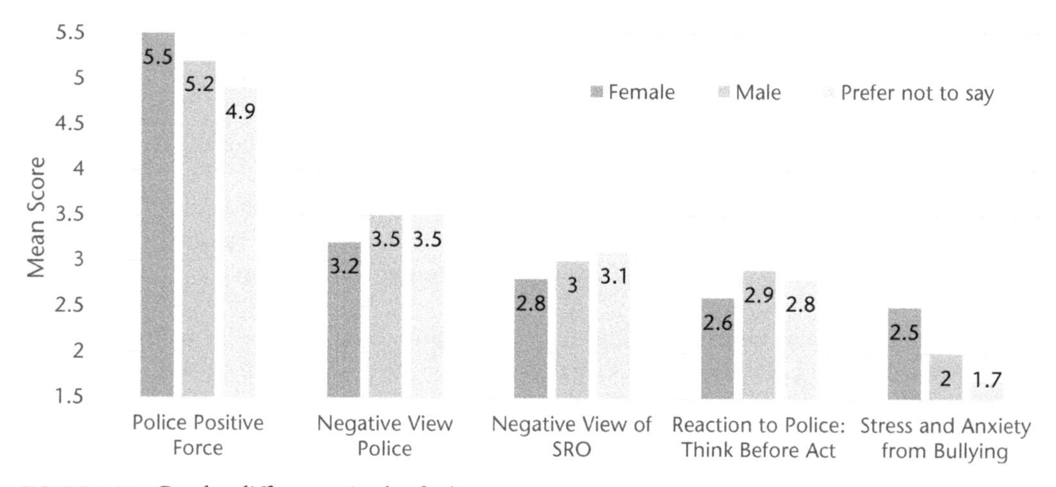

FIGURE 4.17 Gender differences in the findings

friend (or friends) who had been arrested or stopped by the police. Females were more likely than males to do volunteer work.

There were surprisingly few significant gender differences on the attitudes and outcomes of the study. Females held the most positive views of the police and their SRO (i.e., females were most likely to agree that police are a positive force in society and were less likely to hold a negative view of the police or their SRO). Males and those who preferred not to give their gender held the most negative views. The females in the sample were significantly more likely to report stress and anxiety due to bullying and harassment, whereas the males were more likely to indicate that they reacted to the police's presence in the school by thinking before they acted.

We used a two-way analysis of variance (ANOVA) to explore the extent to which these gender differences in the data were stable over time. This analysis helped us determine the extent to which males, females, and/or those who preferred not to disclose their gender changed their perceptions of the police, perceptions of their SRO, and/or their feelings of safety once they were exposed to the SRO program (i.e., between Time 1 and Time 2). For simplicity's sake, our discussion is limited to differences associated with either gender or time.[6]

A number of gender differences were stable over time. Regardless of when we asked them:

- females were more likely than males and those who did not disclose their gender to agree that the police were a positive force in society;
- males harboured significantly more negative views of the police, compared to females;
- males were significantly more likely than females to react to their SROs by thinking before acting; and
- females reported significantly higher feelings of anxiety and/or stress at school than the males.

Similarly, the following differences between responses provided at Time 1 as compared to Time 2 were stable, regardless of the gender of the respondent:

- all students, regardless of their gender, reported significantly higher feelings of anxiety and/or stress at Time 1 (i.e., before being exposed to the SRO program) compared to Time 2; and
- all students, regardless of gender, reported significantly higher negative consequences of feeling unsafe at school at Time 1 compared to Time 2.

Having Been Arrested/Stopped by the Police

What is the association between having been arrested/stopped by the police prior to starting high school and the findings from this study? To answer this question, independent samples *t*-tests were conducted to determine if there were significant differences on the various scales included in this study between students who attested to having been arrested or stopped by the police prior to starting high school and those who had never been arrested or stopped by the police. Key findings from this analysis are shown in Figure 4.18 and summarized below.

Examination of the data show that the students who have been arrested or stopped by the police prior to starting Grade 9 (9% of the sample) have very different attitudes towards the police and the SRO program than their peers who have not been arrested/stopped. They also report very different outcomes. Compared to those who have never been arrested or stopped by the police, those who have been arrested are significantly more likely to agree that police pick on young people/minorities and view the police and the SRO at their school negatively. Alternatively, those who have never been stopped by the police/arrested are significantly more likely than those who

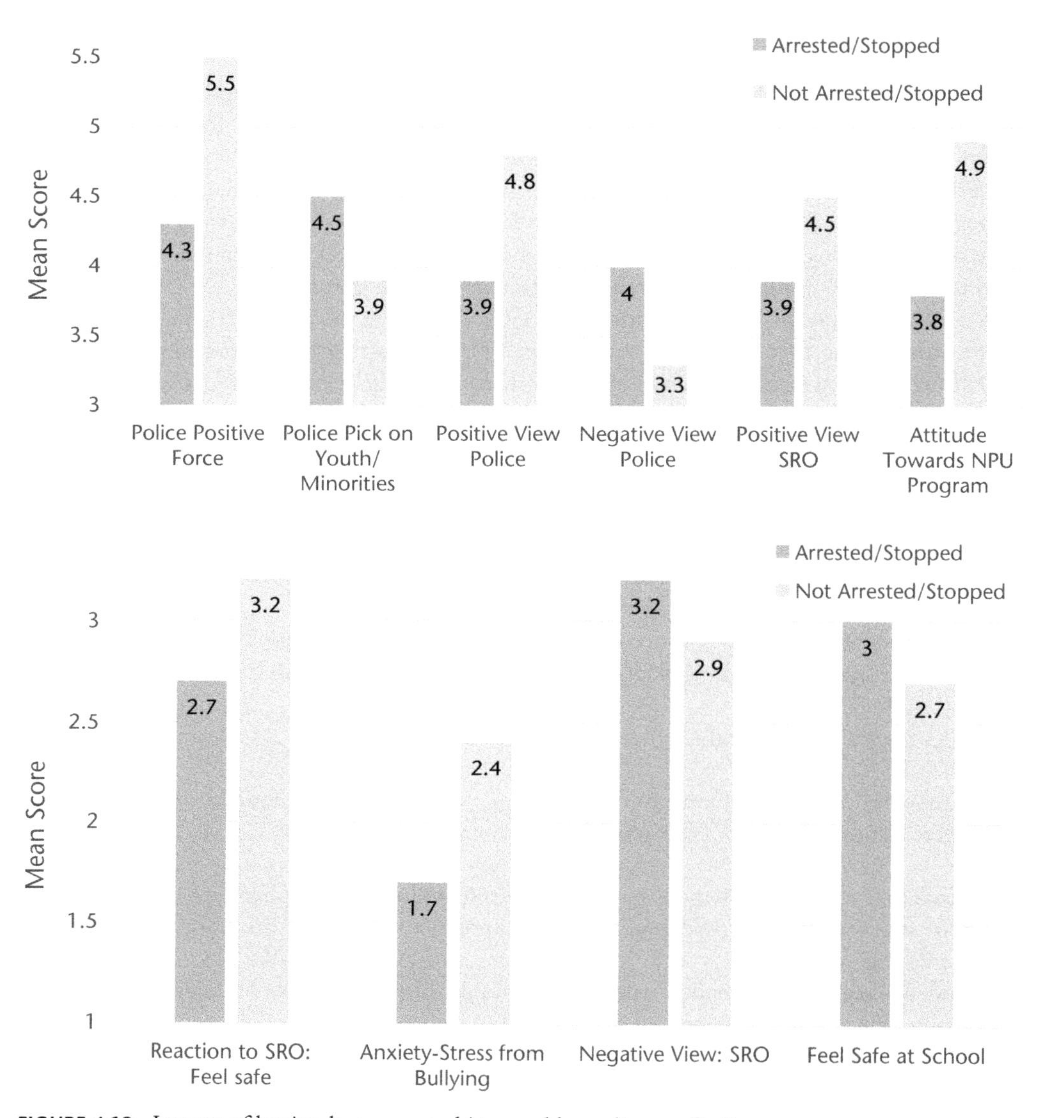

FIGURE 4.18 Impact of having been arrested/stopped by police on findings

have to agree that the police are a positive force in society, have a positive view of the police and their SRO, and agree that the SRO program is a good thing.

How these two groups of students react to the presence of the SRO in the school is also different, as those who have never been arrested/stopped by the police are significantly more likely to say that they feel safer because the SRO is around. Finally, those who have been arrested/stopped by the police are significantly more likely than those who have not to report that they feel safe at school and less likely to experience stress and anxiety at school because they are fearful of being bullied or harassed.

Again, there are multiple ways that these findings can be interpreted. Let us put forward two plausible scenarios:

Scenario one: The students in the arrested/stopped group committed a criminal offense before they started high school. They were stopped by the police, which has negatively colored their views of the police as well as their views of the SRO program. Rather than examine their own actions, they prefer to blame the police for their problems (i.e., police pick on young people and minorities). They feel safe at school and do not fear bullying because they are members of a gang that victimizes other students. Other students see that the presence of the SRO within the school deters students in this group from bullying others.

Scenario two: The students in the arrested/stopped group were unjustly stopped by the police before they started high school. As a result of this earlier experience with the police they view the police and their SRO quite negatively. They have unfavorable views of the SRO program. This interpretation of the data does not, however, explain why these students feel safer at a school with an SRO and are less likely to fear being bullied or physically harassed.

To determine if students with and without a history of being arrested and/or being stopped by the police change their perceptions of the police, their SRO, and/or their feelings of safety over time (i.e., post exposure to the SRO program), two-way ANOVAs were conducted to examine the effect of arrest and time on each of the scales included in this study.

All the differences between those who had been arrested/stopped by the police and those who had not been were stable over time. More specifically, across both time periods, students who had not been arrested/stopped by the police were significantly more likely than those who had been arrested/stopped to agree that the police are a positive force in society, to hold a positive view of the police, to report that they reacted to their school SRO(s) by feeling safer, by harbouring more favorable attitudes towards the SRO program, and by having higher feelings of anxiety and/or stress at school. Students who had been arrested/stopped by the police, on the other hand, were significantly more likely than those who had not to believe that the police pick on young people and/or minorities, to hold a negative view of the police, to hold a negative view of their SRO(s), and to report significantly higher feelings of safety at school.

Finally, and perhaps most importantly, our analysis of the data showed that all students in the sample, regardless of whether they had been arrested/stopped by the police or not, indicated that they felt safer at school at Time 2 (5+ months after exposure to the SRO program) compared to Time 1 (no exposure to the SRO program). The fact that this finding was statistically significant supports the idea that the SRO program benefits all students.

Previous Victimization

We also thought it important to examine the data to determine the extent to which being a victim of bullying and physical assault impacted the attitudes and outcomes included in the survey. To identify who had been victimized, we looked at those items in the survey that captured historical instances of: (1) actual bullying and (2) physical harm. Combining these factors produced a valid indicator of who had been bullied/victimized and who had not (Cronbach's alpha was satisfactory at 0.83). The new variable was then dichotomized so that anyone who indicated that they had been bullied or experienced physical harm (regardless of whether it was "once," "2–3 times," "4–5 times," or "6 or more times") was considered a "victim." Those who reported that they had never been bullied or physically harmed were designated "non-victims." Approximately 84% of the sample identified as non-victims while the remaining 16% had experienced either bullying and/or physical harm. Independent samples *t*-tests were then conducted to determine if there were significant differences with respect to any of the attitudes or outcomes included in this study between students who had not been victimized compared to those who had been victimized, on the various scales included in this study. The results of this analysis are shown in Figure 4.19 and summarized below.

Some of the biggest between-group differences were uncovered when we did this comparison. Compared to those who have not been victimized (i.e., bullied and/or physically harmed) those

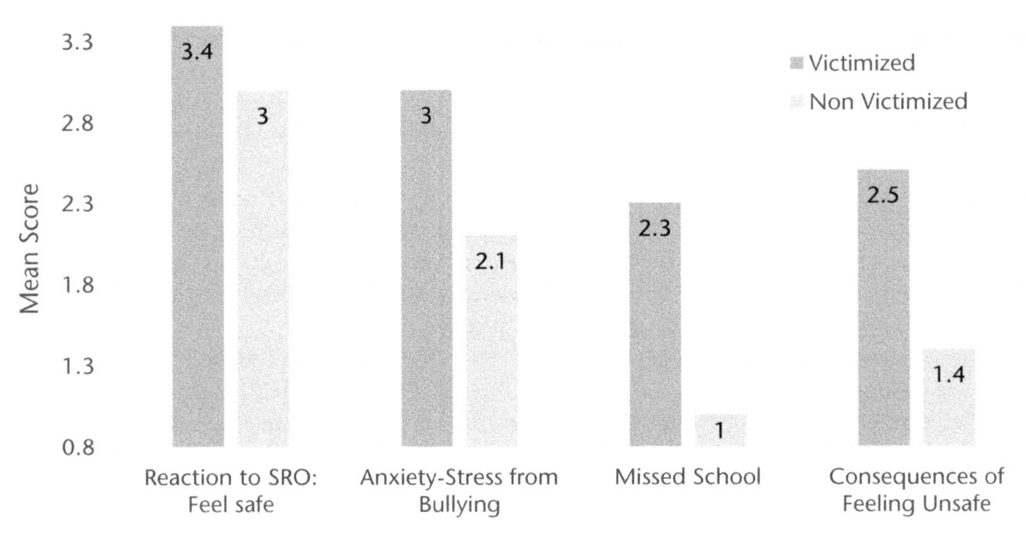

FIGURE 4.19 Impact of previous victimization on the findings

who had been victimized were significantly more likely to feel safe when they saw an SRO. This is important, as this group is significantly more likely, compared to those who have not been victimized, to report anxiety and stress due to a fear of bullying, to have missed school because they are afraid of being bullied, and to experience a number of negative mental health consequences that can be attributed to feeling unsafe. These data support the following conclusion: those who have been bullied (physically or mentally) can expect to gain the most from the presence of police in their high school.

To determine if students who had, or had not, been victimized changed their perceptions of the police, their SRO, and/or their feelings of safety once they were exposed to the SRO program, two-way ANOVAs were conducted.

There were a number of important between-group differences that were observed in the data across both time periods.[7] When compared to their peers who had not been victimized (i.e., bullied and/or physically harmed), students who had been victimized reacted to their SRO by indicating that they felt safer knowing the police were around and by saying that the police presence in their school contributed to a reduction in anxiety and/or stress at school. They were also significantly more likely to miss school than those who had not been victimized, regardless of the time period being considered.

There were also two important differences that were associated with the passage of time. More specifically, all students, regardless of whether or not they had been previously victimized, reported greater feelings of safety at school and lower feelings of anxiety and/or stress when responding to the Time 2 survey (5+ months after exposure to the SRO program) than at Time 1 (no exposure to SRO program). This reinforces the idea that all students realize measureable benefits from the presence of the SRO in their school.

Summary and Conclusions

In this chapter, we supply qualitative and quantitative data that provide support for the idea that SROs offer value to the students in the schools they service. The fact that the results from two very different studies were remarkably similar increase our confidence in the findings.

Key Findings from the Interview Data

The interview data indicate that having police officers in schools provide value to students in a number of important ways:

- they can respond more quickly when issues arise (i.e., faster response time);
- they are there when the students need them (i.e., students do not need to seek them out);
- the SROs' behavior increases students' faith in, and trust of, the police;
- they can stop problematic situations before they escalate;
- having an SRO assigned to their school makes students feel safer when they are at school and on their way to and from school;
- they reduce the likelihood that other students will behave inappropriately on school property; and
- they reduce the likelihood that students will be bullied or engage in fighting.

Why do students feel safer because of SROs in their school? The interview data identified three key reasons why this is the case:

- the presence of the SROs acts as a visible deterrent to students and others who might do harm (SROs can enforce the law, while teachers, vice principals, and the principal can only enforce school rules);
- they are at the school and can respond immediately if there is a problem; and
- they are a resource the students can go to if they need advice or help.

Students stated that they liked the following things about the SRO program:

- the SROs enhance feelings of safety in the school just by being there;
- the SROs stop students (including themselves) from making bad choices, doing stupid things, and getting into trouble;
- the SROs are able to take action immediately if anything unsafe happens in the school; and
- the SROs patrol and monitor the school at all times and act as a deterrent to students who bully or physically harm other students.

Students stated unequivocally that if the officers were not in the school on a daily basis there would be more illegal activity and more school rules broken. They also felt that there would be more fights, thefts, and drugs in the school.

All of the students we interviewed reported that they would prefer to go to a high school that had a full-time SRO. They justified their responses by listing the following four advantages of being in a school with an SRO:

- increased perceptions of safety for both the students and their parents;
- a reduction in the number of illegal and unsafe activities occurring within the schools to which the officers are assigned;
- a reduction in the amount of bullying occurring at the school and within the surrounding community; and
- an increased ability to focus on schoolwork without distraction from feelings of insecurity.

All of the students we interviewed indicated that the SRO program should be continued in its current format because:

- it improves student well-being by enhancing students' feelings of safety in the school, giving them the peace of mind to focus on their education and reducing how stressed they felt at school;
- it reduces the number of unsafe and illegal activities occurring in high schools; and
- it offers students a place to go if they need help or information.

Finally, the following quote from one of the students we talked to testifies to the value of the SRO program:

> "Would you talk to the police? Absolutely. My friends who go to schools where there are no police have a pretty different view though . . . like the police are bad and they don't want to have any communication with them . . . here it's more like, they are like your friends, you speak to them if you have any problems . . ."

Key Findings from the Survey Data

The quantitative data identified a number of ways in which the SRO program offers value to students.

First, a substantive number of students (one in ten of the Grade 9 students in both our Time 1 and Time 2 survey samples) stated that they have turned to their SRO for help when they have a problem.

Second, the data support the idea that the students in our sample relate to the SRO at their school in a different (and more positive) fashion than they do to the police in general.

Third, the vast majority of students in our sample seem to agree that the SRO program is a good idea, with a plurality either linking the presence of a police officer in their school to feeling safer or less stressed/anxious, or saying that the police officer has no impact on them at all.

Fourth, the data support the idea that the SRO program is effective at reducing the amount of bullying taking place on school property and in the surrounding area. The number of students who claimed to be afraid of being bullied or physically harmed by other students or by gang members either at school or during the commute to and from school decreased significantly over time. There was a concomitant increase in the percentage of students reporting that they are rarely, if ever, afraid of being bullied or physically harmed, and a significant decline in the number of students who avoided going to school or skipping classes because they either had been bullied or feared being bullied. These findings provide support for the idea that the SRO program meets its goal of increasing students' perceptions of safety, both within the school and on the way to and from school.

Fifth, the vast majority of the Grade 9 students we surveyed (approximately 75%) felt safer because there was a police officer assigned to their school. This poses the question: What value does the fact that students feel safer in a high school with a police officer offer the students (and, by extrapolation, the community and Canadian society)? The data from this study are fairly clear with respect to this issue. Five months after becoming a student at a high school with a police officer on site, the students who responded to our survey were significantly more able to concentrate, were in better mental health (i.e., reported less anxiety, stress, and feeling depressed), were less likely to report difficulties sleeping, and were less likely to think about harming themselves or others. Given the data showing that the students who feel safer are also less likely to skip class, miss school, and think about dropping out, we also expect that students who feel safer are also more able to take advantage of the learning opportunities at school.

Finally, while follow-up analysis determined that some groups realize more value from the SRO program compared to others, it is important to note our comparison of the Time 1 and Time 2 data determined that *all* students, regardless of their gender, their contact with an SRO, their arrest history, and/or their experience of victimization, indicated that they felt significantly safer at school and less stressed and anxious 5+ months after exposure to the SRO program than at the beginning of the semester (i.e., when they had no exposure to the SRO program). These findings support the following conclusion: all students realize measureable benefits from the presence of SROs in their school. That being said, the data also suggests that students who have been victimized (i.e., bullied and/or physically harmed) can expect to gain the most from the presence of police in high schools.

Methodological Issues to Consider

While our results support the conclusion that high school students realize measurable benefits from having SROs in their schools, several methodological issues should be considered by readers when reflecting on the findings reported in this chapter. First, the sample size for our interviews was small (n = 8) and, of course, it is possible that other students attending high schools in the Peel Region could have different views about the SROs in their school, or about the SRO program more generally. Second, because the exact same group of students may not have provided survey responses at Time 1 and Time 2 it is difficult to say precisely how attitudes changed over time within students who were exposed to the SRO program in Grade 9. Third, despite attempts to do so, it ended up being difficult to collect data from comparable "control" schools (i.e., schools that did not have an SRO, but were similar in other respects to the participating high schools). Such schools don't exist in the Peel Region and securing data from very similar schools in other jurisdictions proved too difficult. This would have allowed us to isolate the effects of SRO exposure to a greater degree and rule out other potential explanations for the differences we observed between Time 1 and Time 2 (e.g., students acclimatizing to high school in a more generalized way). The data presented in forthcoming chapters alleviates many of our concerns with these methodological issues. Collectively, these chapters examine how other stakeholders view the SRO program. As you will soon see, the views expressed by school administrators, SROs, staff sergeants who interact with the SROs, and a researcher who witnessed the SRO job first-hand are consistent with the conclusion reached in this chapter – that SROs have a significant positive impact on students attending high school in Peel Region.

Notes

1 The Province of Ontario has identified a set of 37 high schools that are located in urban centres across Ontario that face a number of challenges such as poverty, criminal and gang activity, and a lack of community resources, such as recreation centers or libraries. The government provides extra funding to these 37 schools as well as specific programming. Two of the five schools in our study have this designation. Interested readers can find out more information on these schools at: www.edu.gov.on.ca/eng/safeschools/urbanPriority.html
2 More information on factor analysis can be found at www.statisticshowto.com/factor-analysis/. Detailed information on the factor scores and factor loadings for all the scales used in this study are available from the researchers upon request.
3 Note that the number of visible minority students in several of the schools who participated in our study was significantly greater than 25%.
4 The students who gave this response in the Time 1 survey had been arrested/stopped by the police before they started high school.
5 The adjective "useless" did not load on either factor.
6 Note that although we identified two significant interactions between gender and time in the data, the findings added little to this discussion. These analyses are available from the authors on request.
7 We note four significant interactions in the data between victimization and time that are difficult to explain without doing follow-up interviews or study. Results from this analysis are again available from the authors upon request.

5

THE VALUE OF SROS

Views from Within (School Administrators)

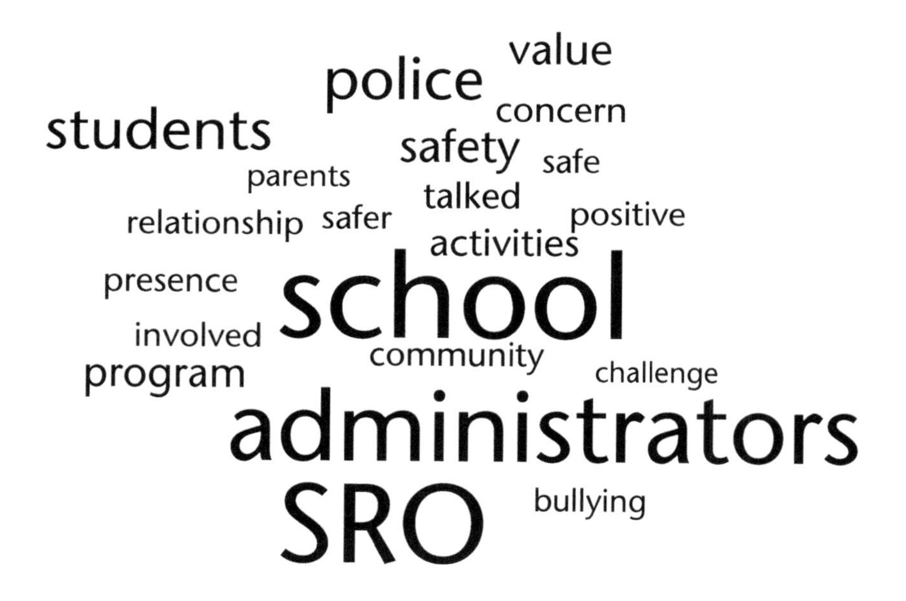

WordMap: 25 most common words in Chapter 5: "The Value of SROs: Views from Within (School Administrators)"

Key Learnings

This chapter focuses on understanding a second key stakeholder's perceptions of the value delivered by the School Resource Officer (SRO) program – the school administrators. The data analyzed in this chapter comes from interviews undertaken with 29 key administrators at the five schools participating in this study.

The Most Important Activities Executed by the SRO: The Administrators' Perspective

The majority of the administrators we spoke to felt that eight of the activities undertaken by the SRO were critical to ensuring a safe learning environment with the school:

- support the administration in their duties;
- be visible in the school because such visibility discourages students from committing crimes during school hours which, in turn, increases the sense of safety of students and staff;
- interact with students in a constructive manner (i.e., getting involved in student activities, counseling students individually or in groups, running workshops, and having pleasant conversations with the students) as such activities help the police build a positive relationship with the students;
- enforce the law, including charging and arresting students who commit crimes such as drug dealing;
- educate students and families on the role of police in Canadian society;
- act as a bridge between the school and the community;
- run wellness checks on students that are missing classes; and
- divert students from the justice system when appropriate.

Value Delivered by the SRO Program: The Administrators' Perspective

The results reviewed in this chapter make it clear that the administrators we talked to have a very positive view of the SRO program and felt that the program delivered real value to school administrators, students, and the community in which the school is located. According to these administrators, the value of the SRO program is multi-faceted and varied, and includes some combination of any or all of the following:

SROs can enforce the law: Students are not deterred by threat of school suspensions, but think twice when involved in a discussion with the police; parents are more likely to appreciate the severity of an issue if the police are involved. Both of these factors contribute to school safety.

Information sharing: Police have information or have access to information that the school administrators might not (e.g., assaults that occur off-campus, graffiti and gang-tagging that occurs on and off school grounds). The SRO ensures that such information is shared with the school.

SROs bring a different perspective to problem solving activities: Police bring a different perspective to the issues going on at the school than do the school administrators, who are often too close to the situation. The SROs' input improves the decision-making process and enhances school safety.

SROs reduce the amount of crime occurring on school property or within the school's catchment area: The presence of the police in the schools acts as a deterrent to those students who are thinking of behaving inappropriately.

(continued)

(continued)

The presence of the SROs results in enhanced perceptions of safety: The quick/easy access to the police ensured by the presence of the SROs makes students/parents/school personnel feel safer.

Familiarity with students and community increases police effectiveness: Any investigation is more effective when the SROs (rather than uniform patrol) are involved, as parents and students and administrators are more likely to communicate with the SROs than an officer that they do not know. The SROs are also aware of the student's circumstances and have a better appreciation of how to talk to teens.

Administrators agreed that if the SRO was not around, the volume of 911 calls and calls to the Peel Police would increase dramatically. They also envisioned myriad other negative consequences (the absence of which all contribute to the value of this program), including: the victims of a crime/bullying might not come forward and report the issue, it would be harder to coordinate any response to challenging incidents at the school between the police and the school, students would not be diverted and would end up dealing with the criminal justice system, school administration might never be able to identify the perpetrator of a crime that was impacting the school, and perpetrators of crimes might never be charged.

Sound program evaluation requires the evaluator to "reach out" to all key program stakeholders in order to get a clear and consensual understanding of the program's activities and outcomes. Stakeholders are defined as people or organizations invested in the program, interested in the results of the evaluation, and/or with a stake in what will be done with the results of the evaluation. Representing their needs and interests throughout the process is fundamental to good program evaluation.[1] In the introduction we described the various stakeholders we engaged with for our evaluation of the SRO program and the SROI process. This chapter provides the results from our consultations with school administrators during the SRO evaluation process.

In January of 2016, we conducted 29 interviews with key administrators at the five schools participating in this study. We also interviewed personnel at these five schools who had high familiarity with the Neighborhood Police Unit (NPU) program and the officers who worked within the program (SROs). More specifically, we interviewed the five Principals at the schools that were participating in the study, 13 Vice Principals, seven guidance counselors, and four social workers. In this chapter, we use the term "Administrator" to refer to this sample of principals, vice principals, guidance counselors, and social workers to minimize the likelihood that the people we talked to could be identified.

The 30–60-minute interviews were conducted in person at the school, recorded and transcribed. The same interview script was followed in all cases. Interviews were content coded using the methodology outlined in Cooper and Schindler (2006), and the responses examined for commonalities of views and opinions. Many of the administrators provided multiple answers to a number of interview questions, which explains why response frequencies often exceed 29.

As shown in Figure 5.1, the administrators we interviewed had worked at one of the five secondary schools participating in this study for between one and 18 years.

This chapter is divided into seven sections. The chapter begins with a short description of how the administrators in our sample perceive their job, the job of the SRO, and the school they work in. The second section examines data that speak to safety concerns that are common in these high schools and, we expect, other Canadian high schools. In the third section we analyze and report on data that speak to how the administrators in our sample interact and collaborate with the SROs assigned to their school. The fourth section continues this line of questioning and discusses what the administrators in our sample perceive to be the three most important activities undertaken by

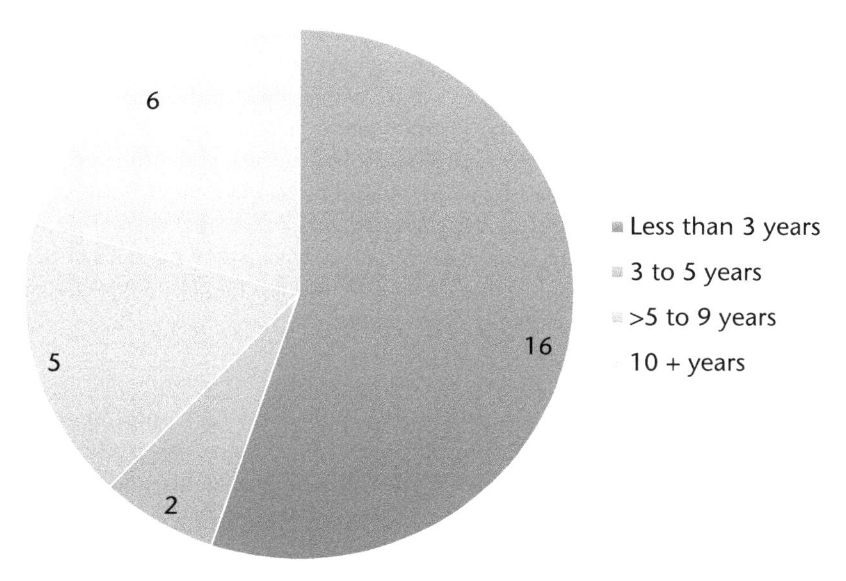

FIGURE 5.1 Years working at their current school (n = 29)

the SRO in their school. In the fifth section we examine administrators' perceptions of how having an SRO in their school has impacted their ability to do their job. The penultimate section summarizes our findings with respect to what the administrators feel about the SRO program overall and whether or not they feel it should be continued. The chapter ends by summarizing key findings with respect to the value offered by the SRO program as articulated by school administrators.

Administrators' Views of Their Schools

Responses to the following questions are presented in this section of the chapter:

- What do you do in a typical day?
- What are the key responsibilities of the SROs working in your school?
- If you were bragging about your school to a friend of colleague, what would you mention?
- What are the main challenges facing the students and staff at your school at this time?
- What makes your school "unique"?

The Job of a High School Administrator

The school administrators we spoke to perform a wide range of activities during a typical school day, as illustrated by the response given by one administrator when asked this question:

> "Well, how long is this interview supposed to take? I don't think we will have the time to discuss everything! Typically, I am dealing with crises. I am working with social workers and outside agencies. I am working with parents. I am working with the school board. I am working with interpreting board policies."

The breadth of activities undertaken by the administrators we talked to can be appreciated by noting that, during a typical day, virtually all of the administrators indicated that they spent time interacting with students, staff, teachers, and parents. Half of the administrators also spent time engaged in planning activities (e.g., curriculum) scheduling activities (e.g., school teams, school groups, guest speakers), program development (e.g., mental health initiatives, alternative education programs, student success programs), and interacting with the community.

Interactions with students were of two types: positive and negative. Three-quarters of the administrators talked about spending time in positive interactions with students (e.g., offering support to students, student course changes, academic and career planning, classroom visits, monitoring attendance, etc.). Sixty percent of the administrators mentioned spending time in more inauspicious interactions with students (e.g., disciplining students, enforcing the Safe Schools Act).

Finally, one administrator pointed out that there really was nothing like a typical day for someone in their job, a reflection that is certainly supported by the vast variety of activities mentioned by this group of administrators:

> "What I like to refer to as crisis management, depending on what's happening in our school. So it's kind of a combination of reacting to whatever's going on in the school on a day-to-day basis, along with the ongoing responsibilities that are part of my portfolio."

The Job of the SRO: As Perceived by School Administrators

What do the administrators working in the five schools in our study think are the key responsibilities and duties of the SROs working in high schools in Peel Region? Virtually all of the administrators we talked to agreed that the role of the SRO was to:

- create a positive relationship between the police, the students, the school, and the community (i.e., relationship building);
- act as the main point of contact between the school administrators and the Peel Regional Police (e.g., investigate incidents that occurred within the school or in the school's catchment area); and
- act as a resource to administrators, teachers, and students on anything involving the criminal justice system (i.e., education).

Additionally, half the administrators felt that the SRO should attend/participate in school activities (e.g., football games, prom, spirit runs, classroom presentations, etc.).

In other words, administrators want the SROs to focus their attention on activities that would create positive relationships between students and police, act as liaison between Peel Police and the school administration whenever a serious incident occurred at the school, and act as a resource (i.e., assist in solving and dealing with problems, educating students, etc.) to the school community writ large – administration, teachers, students, and parents. The following quote captures these ideas:

> "The program is designed to give the police a way to get to know the youth in our community. So many of our students are from other countries where they learn from a young age to be fearful of police, where their families for generations have distrusted the police. So the SRO is a way of educating students, especially those from immigrant families that have negative views of police based on their experiences in their own cultures, that the police can be a positive presence in their lives."

Strengths of Peel Regional High Schools

We began our interview by asking our school administrators the following question: "If you were bragging about your school to a friend or colleague, what would you mention?" Administrators gave three responses to this question. All but one of the administrators in our sample boasted about how their school provides a safe and caring community for students and staff (e.g., our school is respectful, inclusive, positive, and vibrant; there are strong relationships between staff, students, and administration within our school; our school provides excellent support services for students). One in three administrators either bragged about the extracurricular activities that were available at their school (e.g., sports teams, clubs, a very active student life, etc.) and/or boasted about the variety of programming offered at their school (e.g., we have a developmental disabilities program, we offer great vocational programs, etc.).

The following quote typifies what we heard from the administrators:

> "I would mention the strong relationship between staff and the admin, and staff and students, and the admin and students. Sort of this triangle of relationships that exists between those parties. And it is the single most positive example I've seen in any of the schools that I've worked at. The working relationship and the openness of communication, and sort of the level of trust between the groups has been quite remarkable."

What Makes Your School Unique?

Administrators responded with three different answers when asked "What makes your school unique?"

Programming: Sixty percent of administrators felt that the wide variety of programs for students offered at their school made them unique. Programs that were identified as unique included athletic programs, arts programs, extracurricular programs, credit recovery program for kids with mental health issues, and ESL programs.

Caring community: Forty percent of administrators felt that one of their school's unique strengths related to the fact that it provided students with a caring community. These administrators spoke with passion about how their school has a great culture and an atmosphere where students are put first, that the staff at the school are dynamic and caring, that the school is really the key focal point in the community, and that the school offers a sense of stability to students living in families from across the region. As noted by one administrator:

> "Because it's so busy, it's actually a hub, I find, in the community. So a lot of our students want to be here, like, they feel safe here, they're happy here, and they want to be here, they want to be committed to clubs and teams, they just want to hang here. Like, we have to go out every day at 2:30 and basically get them moving along, because they could be here till seven o'clock if we didn't do that, so it's just a safe hub for them."

High academic standards: Finally, one in four administrators spoke with pride about the high academic standards set by their school (e.g., challenging academics, Advanced Placement Program), which they felt set them apart.

The diversity of high schools within our sample reassures us that findings from this study can be widely generalized.

Challenges Facing Students and Staff in Peel Region High Schools

We asked the administrators in our sample: "What do you perceive to be the main challenges facing the students at your school at this time?" Approximately equal numbers of administrators identified three different challenges that they felt were facing students within their school.

Mental health issues: Almost half of the administrators identified mental health concerns as the major challenge within their school (e.g., students are overwhelmed, there is too much stress in their lives, there is too much pressure on them to achieve academically, social and emotional needs are contributing to mental health challenges).

Socio-economic challenges in the school's catchment area: One in three of the administrators talked about how socio-economic adversity was negatively affecting both their students and their student's families (e.g., families living on limited resources, many families are part of marginalized groups, parents working multiple jobs and do not have time for their children).

The following quote speaks to this issue:

> "We have a lot of poverty in this area. Most of our students are from immigrant families that are first generation. They do not have the financial supports at home. Our students are often caught between the culture of their parents and the culture they are growing up in, in Canada. There are mental health challenges as well. Most of our students are impacted by poverty as well and so they require a lot of additional support. It is definitely harder for our students to function because of all the day-to-day issues in their lives. I mean, how can I expect a student to function – to concentrate – when they show up at school hungry?"

Inconsistent engagement of students with the school: One in three of the administrators felt that the inconsistent engagement of the students in their school was very challenging. They attributed this lack of engagement to a diversity of factors, including outside distractions, the fact that many of their students had part-time jobs, and student drug use during and/or after school.

Safety Concerns

Peel Police's SRO program seeks to create safe school environments, which promote respect, responsibility, and learning. Analysis of data speaking to school administrators' perception of issues surrounding safety in their high schools at this time are summarized below.

Issues of Concern to the Schools

We asked the school administrators to tell us the extent to which they perceived the seven issues shown in Table 5.1 to be a cause for concern within their high school at the time the study was being conducted. Responses were coded using the following scale: not really a problem (=1), somewhat of a concern (=2), and poses a significant challenge within the school at this time (=3). Responses are summarized (in descending order from most challenging to least challenging) in Table 5.1 and Figure 5.2. Examination of these data support the following conclusions:

- the vast majority of school administrators agree that bullying, cyberbullying, drugs, and theft is either a significant challenge or somewhat of a concern within their school at this time;
- gangs are a source of concern in some schools (half the administrators are either somewhat concerned or very concerned about gangs operating within and near their school), but not others (half the administrators felt that gangs were not an issue in their school);
- while half the administrators felt that trespassing was not an issue within their school, the other half felt it was either a significant source of concern (10%) or somewhat of an issue (38%);

TABLE 5.1 Assessment of safety challenges in five Peel Region High Schools

Specific issue	*Not an issue*	*Somewhat of a concern*	*Significant challenge*
Bullying/Cyberbullying	0%	48%	52%
Drugs	3%	52%	45%
Theft	10%	59%	31%
Gangs	48%	42%	10%
Trespassing	52%	38%	10%
Assaults	38%	55%	7%
Racial/Ethnic conflict	31%	62%	7%
Religious conflict	93%	7%	0%

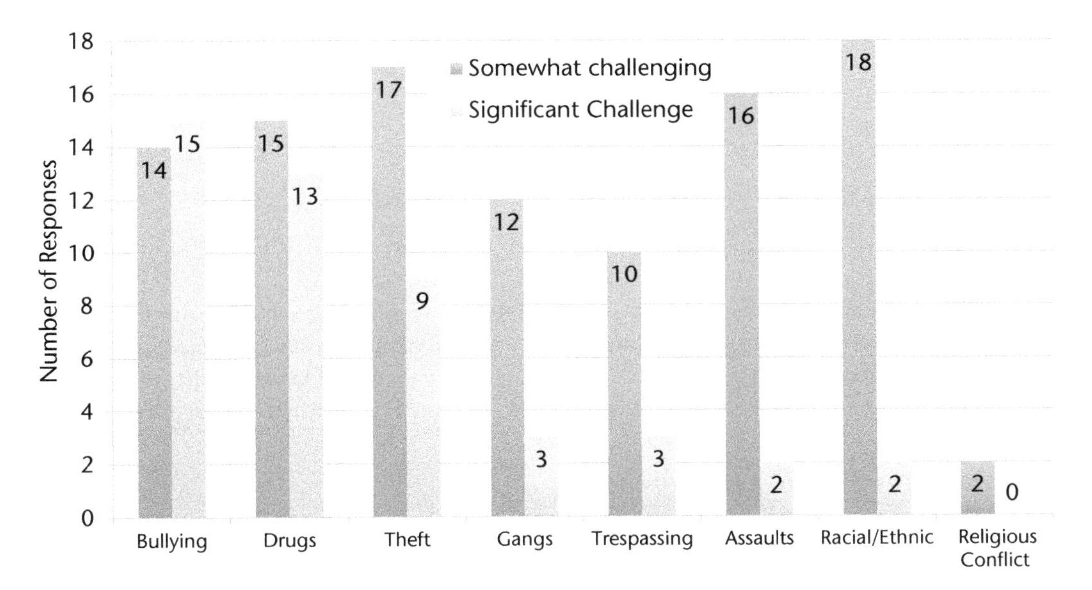

FIGURE 5.2 Challenges facing five Peel Region High Schools at this time

- while one in three administrators felt that neither assaults or racial/ethnic conflict were issues within their school, the rest were not as sanguine, with two-thirds of the administrators saying that this was either somewhat of a concern (62%) or presented a significant challenge (7%) within their school;
- there was a high degree of agreement within our sample of administrators (93%) that religious conflict was a not an issue within their school at this time.

Most Serious Challenges Within Their School at this Time

We then asked administrators to tell us which of these issues they felt was the *most* serious challenge facing their school at this time. Their responses to this question are summarized in Figure 5.3 and discussed below.

Almost half of the administrators identified the selling and using of drugs within their school as the issue that concerned them the most. Another one in three identified bullying and cyberbullying as the issue that they felt was the most significant problem in their school at this time. One in

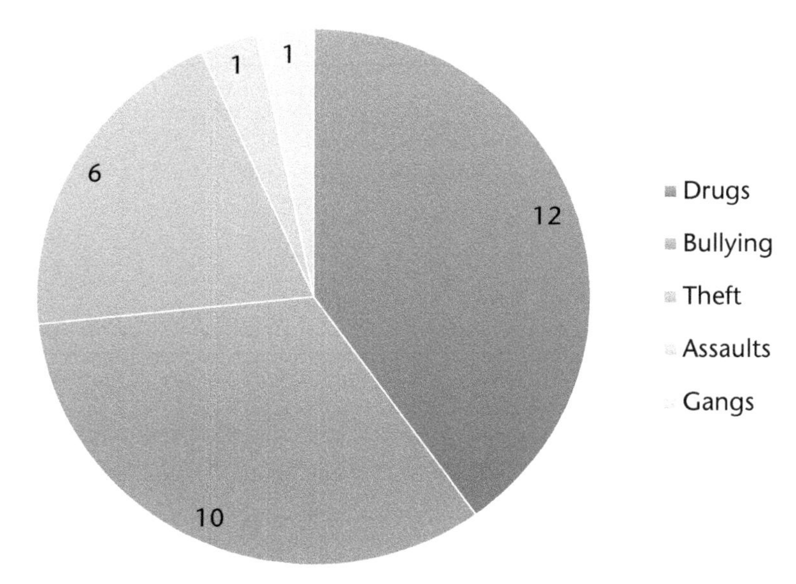

FIGURE 5.3 What is the most serious problem facing your school at this time? (*n = 29*)*

* There were multiple responses from one participant.

five administrators felt that theft was the most serious issue within their school at this time. One administrator stated that the biggest problem at their school was gangs while another administrator identified assaults as being the most problematic. No one identified racial, ethnic, or religious conflict, or trespassing, as the issue that they felt was the biggest concern at their schools.

Response of the SROs to Key Challenges

We then asked our school administrators to tell us "What are the SROs doing about this problem?" Responses to this question are presented below.

Four of the individuals in the administrator sample (those working as social workers and counsellors) indicated that they really did not know what the police were doing to address the issues of concern to the school. The rest of the administrators we talked to identified six different actions that the SROs were taking to address the issues of concern in the schools they were working in.

Sharing information: Two-thirds of the respondents stated that the SROs assisted the school administrators in dealing with the main issues of concern by sharing information with them, following up on leads generated at the school, running locker searches, etc. The administrators also noted that in their school the SROs acted as an "information" conduit between the community and the school. As police officers, SROs have access to a range of information about what is going on in the community at large. They also knew which of the school's students were involved in inappropriate or criminal activities outside of school hours. The administrators appreciated the fact that the SROs shared such information with them, as it allowed the school to take appropriate action.

Connecting the school to the community: Thirty percent of respondents talked about how the SRO attempted to make connections between what is happening in the school environment and the community at large. They felt that the SROs had greater access to needed information than those working within the school and observed that their SRO often acted as a "go-between" – sharing information about illegal activities carried out by students in the community at large and making school administrators aware of student activity off-campus.

Enforcing the law after the offense had occurred: One in three administrators spoke about how the officer dealt with the issue after the offense had occurred and the culprits were identified. They noted that in these cases the SRO either charged/disciplined the student(s) or gave a caution to the offending student(s). Two individuals also talked about how the SRO in their school made parents aware that their son/daughter was involved with drugs/bullying other students. In these conversations, the SRO gave the parents a warning about the consequences of their child continuing to display the behavior that was the source of concern (e.g., that cyberbullying could become a criminal charge).

Educating students on issues of concern: Four administrators talked about how the SRO had spent time educating the students via classroom presentations and/or school assemblies on how to prevent being bullied and how to avoid problems on social media.

Running investigations/apprehending suspects: Four other administrators talked about how the SROs ran investigations/surveillance/stakeouts on issues of concern to the school. They noted that these SRO-initiated investigations often resulted in the student or students who were causing the issue being apprehended. These administrators also talked about how the SROs monitored social media to reduce the amount of cyberbullying in the school.

Acting as a deterrent: Finally, three administrators stated that the SRO established a regular presence in school to act as a deterrent to students committing a crime.

To summarize, the actions taken by the SRO to deal with the issues of concern in the school they were working in depended very much on the problem being addressed. They consulted with the school administrator and took concrete actions when necessary. They engaged in information-sharing activities with the school, followed-up on leads generated at the schools, and took concrete steps, such as running locker searches. The following quote speaks to many of the above comments:

> "Oh my goodness, they've done a huge amount . . . in terms of the (drug) problem. They continue to do it. So, they're doing stakeouts. They're monitoring social media in order to figure out how they are dealing, where it's coming from, like where the drugs are being sold from. They're doing education with the kids. They're doing tons of other good things."

Perceptions of Safety

Finally, to appreciate the environment in which the SRO works, we asked our administrators a number of questions relating to whether or not they felt that their high school provided a safe learning environment for students.

We began by asking: "How serious do you consider your school's safety problems to be?" Responses to this question were coded using the following scale: 1= serious, 3 = moderately serious, 5 = not really any safety problems. The results are shown in Figure 5.4. We then asked our administrators why they gave the response that they did.

Three administrators stated that safety was a serious source of concern within their school at this time. These respondents stated that, "things at the school can get serious very quickly – they can turn from okay to dangerous in an instant." They attributed the safety issues in their school to the fact it was located in a socio-demographically challenged area of Peel. These administrators felt that "Without the SRO, we would be calling 911 all the time."

Just over half of the administrators we interviewed felt that safety was a moderately serious issue in their school at this time. These individuals clarified their answer by talking about how problems "can happen and have happened" that have resulted in major safety concerns (e.g., "so we have had a few instances this year – stabbings, drugs, gangs"). These individuals felt that the underlying issues that contributed to these safety issues ("socio-economically challenged community with large student body"; "students lack discipline in general"; "the parents are very critical of any attempt on the part of the school to discipline their children"; "mental health issues within the student body") had not been addressed by either the school board or the community. The vast majority of the administrators who awarded their school this rating noted that the presence of the SROs in the school diminishes the severity of the safety issue within their school significantly. In fact, almost all of the administrators said that the only reason they rated the safety issue as moderately serious as opposed to very serious was because they had the SROs to count on to help them address safety concerns.

Finally, one in three administrators felt that their school was safe and that any issues that did exist were manageable. Several of the administrators within this group did, however, note that the problems that "exist are more of students doing self-harm, drug overdoses, than harming others." These administrators worked in the one school in the sample that was located in a more socio-economically advantaged area.

The following quote illustrates what administrators told us with respect to safety concerns in their school:

> "I would say moderate, given that there are things that happen in the community that we don't even know about that involve kids that come to this school. We only know about these issues because the officers have to come in and question them. So, if you were to take all of what's happening in the community and bring it into the school and say okay, even though it's not maybe specifically happening in the school, it's still impacting us and the learning environment."

We also asked a number of follow-up questions during the interview to help us better understand issues around school safety (i.e., Are any areas less safe than others? Have you missed work because you were concerned about your safety? How often have concerns about your safety and security at work left you feeling stressed or anxious?). None of the administrators felt that their schools had any places that were less safe than others. None of the administrators stated that they had missed work out of fear for their safety. Administrators were, however, split down the middle with respect to whether or not they personally felt stressed or anxious at work because they

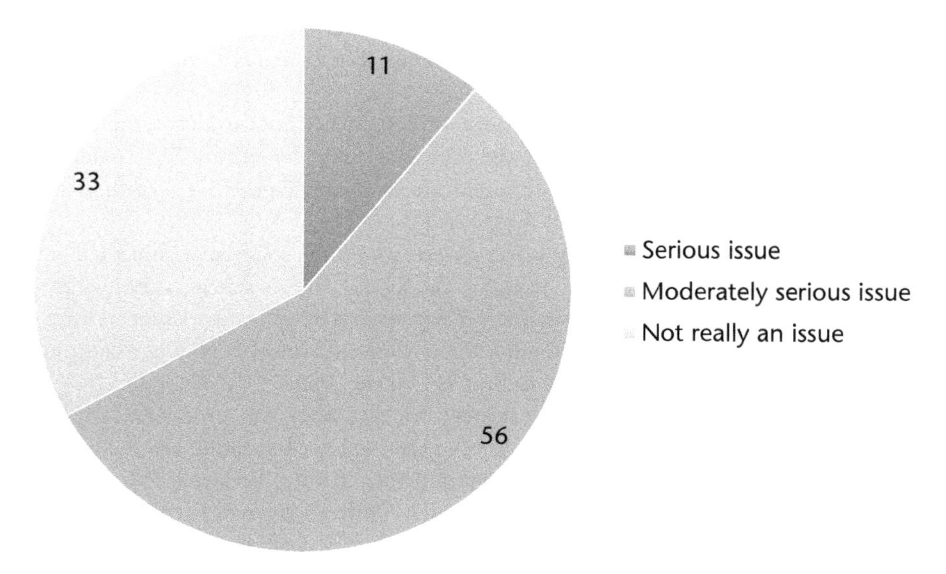

FIGURE 5.4 How serious do you consider your school's safety problems to be? (%)

felt their safety or security was compromised, with 15 administrators responding "never" and 14 saying "sometimes." The following quotes illustrate these responses:

> "Safety concerns cause me to feel anxious. I mean, absolutely. I've not had them in the last four years at this school, [school with an SRO] but I had them at my previous school that did not have an SRO assigned to it. At this school we had multiple stabbings, we had bank robbers. You know, there was a murder. I've been at schools where there's been two murders. So, in those schools there's a heightened sense of awareness, but it dissipates. It comes and goes, it's not a constant state of emergency."

> "Occasionally. If we've had an incident. Sometimes you know, there's some people lurking around. There's a bridge that goes over the river and sometimes people hang around there. And you know, there is a concern . . . but I walk out there and they see me looking at them and they'll take off usually. But sometimes when we've had a big fight I think okay, what's behind this? Is there some big picture that we're not getting? And it makes me feel anxious. But usually not."

Again, we note that the presence of the SRO in the school seems to alleviate the stress for many of the administrators we talked to.

Finally, we asked if concerns about their safety and security at work made it difficult for them to get a good night's sleep. For the most part the administrators we interviewed said they never felt as though concerns about their own safety made it difficult to get a good night's sleep. That being said, six of the administrators did agree that "sometimes their sleep was compromised by concerns about safety and security at the school as well as the safety and security of their students." For example:

> "I stay awake . . . the individual kid who's got some mental health issues . . . the kid who I can see is going down a pathway of criminal behavior . . . that keeps me awake thinking, okay, have we done everything for this kid? What else? Or if something happens to a kid, you know, what could we have done? Is there something we could have done to prevent that?"

Interactions between School Administrators and SROs

We began this section of the interview by asking our school administrators how often they collaborated with the SROs assigned to their school. Five respondents (social workers, counselors) rarely if ever dealt with the SROs directly and another four respondents had relatively infrequent interactions. In all of these cases the respondents noted that, at their school, the SROs collaborated with the main office and that any concerns they had would first be directed to either the vice principals or principals, and then brought to the SROs by the vice principals or principals as necessary. The rest ($n = 20$) interacted frequently (often daily) with the SROs, as shown in Figure 5.5.

Nature of the Collaboration

We then asked the administrators to describe the nature of their collaboration. The following seven responses were mentioned by least 10% of the administrators in the sample:

Touching base: Just under half of the administrators said that they regularly "touched base" with the SROs in their school. Touching base involved information-sharing on student issues, coordinating times to meet at school, getting updates on ongoing investigations, engaging in a personal conversation with the officers, and making sure that the officers knew about school social events.

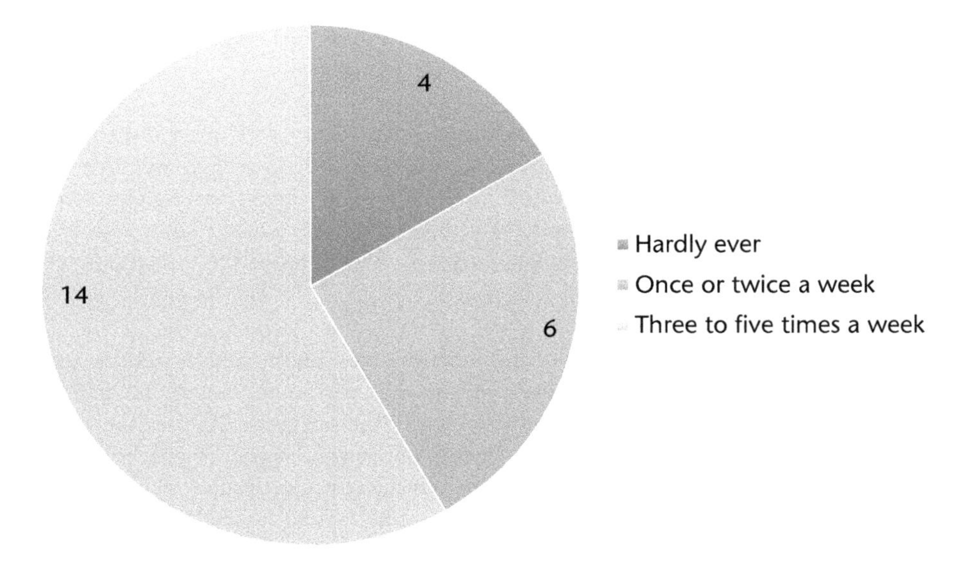

FIGURE 5.5 How often do you interact with the SROs in your school? (n = 24)

Collaborations that involved the sharing of information relating to student(s): Administrators also collaborated with their SROs in a variety of information sharing activities. One in three of the administrators identified each of the following ways in which they and their SRO engaged in this type of collaboration:

- SRO and the administrator engaged in information sharing involving students who were involved in an incident such as a theft or bullying;
- SRO and the administrator collaborated during investigations involving students; and
- SRO and the administrator shared information about students at the school who were involved in criminal incident(s) on and/or off school property where the student had been suspended, charged with a crime, arrested, or had conditions placed on them.

The following quote illustrates the varied nature of these collaborations:

> "Once a week – every time I contact them I am collaborating. The nature of the collaboration is about sharing information. So, for example, when [a mentally ill individual] came and wandered the halls of my school, this is something that I would collaborate with the police on. It turns out [this individual] had been in the community center across the road so the SROs had already heard about this as well and were able to deal with it quickly."

Higher level collaborations that involve the school, the students, and their families: One in five of the administrators talked about higher level collaborations that involved the SRO, the administrator, the student, and their parents/families. Such interactions typically involved the sharing of legal advice, career advice, or specific information on the criminal justice system.

Collaboration on issues that occurred within the community: Half the administrators gave examples of collaborations involving issues that had occurred off the school campus. These could involve investigations into social media, assaults, child abuse in a student's home, graffiti being painted in the community by students, or even monitoring students with challenging home lives. The following examples, taken from the interviews, illustrate the diversity of occasions in which SROs and school administrators cooperate to make the school a safer place for students and staff by dealing with issues that occurred not at school, but, rather, within the school's catchment area:

- *Example One*: A social media twitter feed that was publishing hate speech. The administrator suspected that it was from one of their students, but they had no way of finding out who was publishing the hate speech. An ongoing collaboration over many months involving both the administration and the SRO resulted in the identification of the student.
- *Example Two*: A fight/assault that happened off school property. It was a coordinated approach because arrests needed to be made and students needed to be expelled.
- *Example Three*: School administration collaborated with the SRO to investigate child abuse in the student's home. The school administrator notified the SRO of child abuse going on in a home where cultural sensitivity was an issue and uniform patrol was unable to get statements from the victim. The student's comfort level with the SRO allowed for dialogue to take place and the issue to be addressed.
- *Example Four*: School administrators collaborated with the SRO to investigate a case of illicit photo-sharing and bullying through Instagram.
- *Example Five*: School administrators collaborated with the SRO to stop a graffiti issue that had been happening in the community around the school.
- *Example Six*: School administrators and the SROs collaborated to monitor a vulnerable student in their school who was living on his own and sleeping in dumpsters. They were able to get the student help.
- *Example Seven*: The SRO alerted the school administration to an incident in the community that had the potential to affect many students (e.g., a suicide).

Collaboration relating to a safety issue at the school: One in four of the school administrators discussed how they and the SRO at their school collaborated to deliver a program or take actions with respect to a safety issue that they were aware of at the school. Examples included having the SRO run a safety audit, practice a school lockdown, deal with intimidating students and bullies, and investigate undocumented cars in the school parking lot.

Collaboration that related to a criminal code infraction that occurred on school grounds: One in five administrators spoke about how they and the SRO at their school collaborated on an incident that had taken place on the school campus that had criminal code implications. Examples given included: organizing an in-school arrest of a student, searching a drug dealer, laying a charge for sex assault, dealing with violent incidents that had occurred on school property (the case discussed involved a stabbing), and dealing with a bullying incident that was more layered than originally thought (i.e., involved a fight between a student and a youth that did not attend the school).

Collaboration that involved a diversion:[2] Four school administrators talked about how they and the SRO worked together on youth diversion programs. These administrators all talked about how the SROs were willing to help a student who had committed a criminal offense (as opposed to just charging them) because they had interacted with the student at the school and felt that the student was "essentially a good kid who had made a poor choice." The collaboration involved educating the students on making better choices.

Working Collaboratively: Details

To increase our understanding of the SROs'–school administrators' collaboration process, we then asked our respondents the following set of questions: "Please think back to a time that you worked collaboratively with the SRO assigned to your school that you remember clearly. Can you please describe this situation to us? What was the value to you of having the officer work with you on this issue?" The information we got using this approach was very detailed and rich, as illustrated by the quote below:

> "I'll just go back to last week with our semi-formal. You know, he was on paid duty, but . . . it's great when one of our SROs does the paid duty because they know our kids . . . anyway, this young lady, who was drunk and on something . . . the thing would have been handled, I think, very differently if he hadn't been there . . . and we worked together to, sort of, decide what was the best course of action.
>
> You know, unfortunately she was handcuffed and taken to the station, but . . . next morning our officer did let us know what had happened at the station . . . Was there more that we wanted him to do? And here's what the police decided to do, and how could we work together to, sort of, try to help this young lady? And I think that's, sort of, where their biggest strength is in their skills, when they know kids in your community and they're working to try to help kids versus just charge them and move on."

Analysis of the responses to these questions helped us identify the following six ways in which the SRO was perceived by the school administrators to provide value.

They can enforce the law: One in four administrators mentioned that the SRO has more authority than school administrators and can take investigations further and arrest perpetrators. These administrators all felt that their ability to access this authority as needed was very valuable within their school. They noted that, in collaborations that they could recall, the SRO reinforced the actions of the school administrators, which led to positive results for the school. They also described situations where the students at their school were not discouraged by threat of school suspensions, but thought twice about their actions when involved in a discussion with the police. Additionally, administrators felt that parents often did not understand the severity of an issue unless consequences were discussed by a police officer, who is perceived to be more of an authority figure than are school administrators.

Having a good relationship in place between police and school results in better outcomes for the student: One in five administrators talked about the value provided by having a good relationship in place between school administration and SROs when incidents occur requiring an investigation. These administrators felt that having an SRO lead such an investigation was more effective than involving uniform patrol, as the SRO was better able to get beyond superficial facts to what had happened. They gave a number of examples illustrating this source of value, including an incident at their school requiring lockdown and the case of one of their students who was living on the streets.

Information sharing: Four administrators felt that the main value of the SRO program was having access to SROs who had information and/or access to information that the school administrators might not (e.g., assaults that occur off-campus, graffiti and gang-tagging that occurs on-campus and off-campus).

Bring a different perspective: Four administrators stated that the fact that the SRO within their school brought a different perspective to the issues going on at the school helped them solve challenges they were facing in their school. They noted that the SRO's ability to step back from the issue provided value in those situations where the administrator was too close to the situation.

Deter crime and enhance perceptions of safety: Four administrators valued the fact that the presence of the SRO in the schools served as a deterrent to those students who were thinking of behaving inappropriately. By doing so, they made the school a safer place. One example given to make this case involved an online bullying incident where the officers were able to come in and address all of the students immediately and educate them about bullying and how it could hurt anyone in the school. After the lecture, there was less cyberbullying observed at the school.

Familiarity with students and community increases police effectiveness: Finally, four administrators emphasized the value of having a police officer in the school that understands the students and their lives (e.g., of having a police officer in the school who can put things in context, can understand better the lives of the students from a different cultural background, is familiar with how to deal with teenagers).

Finally, our analysis of the data showed that the value of having an officer working full time in the schools with administrators is multi-faceted and varied as illustrated by the following quote:

> "Yes, the value is they know the kids, they understand community needs, and they really work hard to work for the kids and not against the kids . . . About three weeks ago we had four or five kids jump a kid and rob him. Sometimes it's automatic: kids get charged and conditions not to return to the school imposed, but often the SRO gets involved and they'll have that conversation with us, and, you know what? Yes, it is important that these three boys or these three girls have conditions not to return because they're wreaking havoc in the whole school, and when these three kids can now be split up and each one going to a different school, it's helping those kids because they're getting away from that bad influence peer group. But it's also helping the school, sort of, return to a state of normal, where these kids aren't just, you know, creating drama and chaos, so they're really good about collaborating and having a conversation with us about best scenarios for kids."

What Would Happen if the Officer Was not Around?

We then asked our administrators: "What do you think would have happened in this situation if the officer was not around?" While six different responses were coded from the data, only four were given by four or more respondents, a finding which has more to do with the variety of collaborations described than anything else.

More calls to 911 and Peel Police: In a plurality of cases, the ramifications of not having an SRO were quite clear: the school would just call 911 or the Peel Regional Police switchboard. The administrators were not enamoured by this idea as they felt that they would not get the same level of support they currently enjoy (i.e., the call would be answered by police officers who were not familiar with the school and the community, or not as practiced in dealing with teenagers). Administrators expressed concern that uniform patrol officers who responded to the 911 call would probably not understand the context and culture of the school setting or know the details of a student, such as their cultural tendencies. Not only that, but they were worried that this option would increase the demands on the Peel Police and likely slow down response time. This shows that the SRO program offers value to both the school as well as the Peel Police.

Lose the value that the SRO brings to the school: Six administrators felt that, if the SRO had not been around, the school administrators would lose the capabilities that the SRO brings to any given situation at the school. More specifically, administrators talked about missing out on the following benefits they currently enjoy because they collaborate with the SROs in their school: the SROs reinforcement of the school administration's work would be lost, the SRO perspective would be missing, the ability to search a student for drugs in a timely manner would be jeopardized, the background knowledge of the school and students developed by the SROs would be missing, and the comfort level students might have with SROs, as opposed to uniform patrol, would be absent.

Myriad other negative consequences: What else would happen if the SRO was not available? Administrators identified numerous other negative impacts. First, they felt that victims might not come forward to confront the perpetrator (or even to report problematic incidents) without the support of the familiar SRO. Second, the administrators felt that, in the absence of an SRO, there would be no one to coordinate a response between the police and the school when things went wrong. In their minds, this would increase the likelihood that the situation would not be handled correctly, and that a small problem could escalate into a more significant issue. Third, they felt that the number of students who were diverted would decrease and more students would end up dealing with the criminal justice system. Fourth, the school administrators might not be able to find out the perpetrator of a particular crime (e.g., sex assault, publishing hate speech), which means that they could not take action to address the issue. Finally, the opportunity for a positive relationship to develop between student and the police would cease to exist.

No positive outcomes envisioned if the SRO program was to be terminated: It is interesting to note that none of the administrators envisioned a positive outcome occurring if the SRO was removed from the school. This reinforces the notion that the SRO program brings value to the schools within Peel Region and underscores the importance of the SRO program in the eyes of school administrators. The following quote reinforces this idea:

> "I've had situations where it could have gone sideways. We had a young lady who actually kicked him where it counted and . . . you know, somebody else who didn't maybe know her history and understand the challenges might have just said, that's it, honey, like, you're being charged with assault of a police officer and I'm done with you, you know? But that didn't happen in this case . . . You know, my last school I was at where my kids were cognitively challenged and when an officer would pick one up and bring them in and not understand the background of the kids, it was a very different conversation than I enjoy now when it is one of our SRO officers who deals with the kid."

Quality of the Collaboration: School and SROs

We then asked the 29 administrators in our sample: "How would you rate the quality of the collaboration between your school and the police officers with whom you work? Why do you say this?"

Nineteen administrators (66% of the sample) stated that the quality of the collaborations between themselves and their SRO was "excellent." The following quote typifies the sentiments expressed by this group of administrators:

> "We have a super positive working relationship with our SRO officer and their partner."

Administrators who felt that their collaboration with their SRO was "excellent" gave the following reasons for their response:

- we have constant communication/daily contact with our SRO;
- SROs are compassionate and understand how to deal with teenagers – they "understand that teenagers do stupid things";
- our SROs act as advocates for the school when communicating with Peel Police;
- we are all working for the same thing – school safety; and
- our SROs are really trying to help the students.

Another nine individuals (31% of the sample) rated the quality of their collaborations as "good." Those that gave this response gave a very different set of reasons from those who assess the relationship as excellent:

- "My department doesn't deal with the SROs as much as the main office . . . but overall any interaction I have had is pretty good."
- "It is good, but difficult in this current climate because in some cases the kids don't trust the police. They are constantly hearing in the media, in the community, and/or at home that they shouldn't – and that makes it hard for the SRO."
- "They are great and we have a good relationship in the school, but we still have problems in the school that need to be dealt with by the broader community" (e.g., drugs, bullying); and
- "Good, but sometimes we [school administrators] rely on them too much."

Finally, there was one administrator that said the relationship "needed improvement." Interestingly, they justified their response by stating that they wanted to see the SRO more frequently commenting: "The SRO is rarely in the building."

To end this section on a positive note, the following quote is typical of what we heard regarding the relationship between the SRO and school administrators:

> "Quality of collaboration is excellent . . . The SRO understands the culture of my building and can advocate to their hierarchy for help. Also, the kids understand who they are and respect them so it makes it more collaborative. Because the students understand who the SROs are and often have a better relationship with the SRO than they would with the general police that would come in if we called 911."

Quality of the Collaboration: School and Peel Police

We ended this section of the interview by asking the 29 administrators in our sample: "How would you rate the quality of the collaboration between your school and the Peel Police? Why do you say this?"

One in five of the school administrators indicated that they never had to contact Peel Police as their SRO was able to handle all of their policing needs. The rest of the school administrators (80%) stated that it was very easy to contact the Peel Regional Police when there was a matter that needed to be attended to. The interviews also revealed that the vice principals are the only administrators who would typically contact the police. Other members of the administration, such as the guidance department employees, would go through the vice principals if and when there was a concern. Almost all the administrators felt that the presence of the SRO in the school increased their access to Peel Police if such access was required:

> "To be honest, I go through my SRO and within seconds I'll get a response."
>
> "We never deal with uniform patrol. Like I never call them for assistance. Never."

Most Important Activities Undertaken by SRO: Administrators' Perspectives

Our work with the SROs revealed that the officers perform a wide variety of different activities (see Chapter 3). We asked a number of questions in the interview to help us determine which of the myriad activities performed by the school SRO are perceived by the school administrators to be the most useful.

Responses to the following three questions are addressed in this section of the chapter: "What do you feel are the three most important activities performed by the SRO assigned to your school? Why are each of these activities important? How satisfied are you with how your SRO performs each of these activities?" Responses to these questions are summarized in Table 5.2.

TABLE 5.2 Summary: administrators' view of three most important activities of SROs

Activity	*% identifying*	*Why important*
Support school administrators in their duties	66%	• Increases administrator's sense of safety • Officer helps administrator do job more effectively
Act as a deterrent to crime within the school	60%	• Reduces the amount of theft, assault, gang activity, and drug dealing/use at the school • Helps create the sense that school is a safe place
Build a positive relationship with the students by interacting with them in a constructive manner	52%	• Important that police are humanized • Reduces the sense of us versus them
Enforce the law	40%	• There are times when law enforcement is necessary and having police resources within the school who are familiar with school/teens speeds up resolution of the problem
Educating students/families on role of police in society	24%	• Teach students about the law and criminal justice system • Act as resource to parents about the law
Visit the school each day	15%	• This is a challenging community and the daily visit sets the tone (i.e., deterrent and relationship)
Act as bridge between school and community	15%	• Keep school administrators informed as to what is going on in the community • Parents/families might fear talking to police, but not the SRO
Run wellness checks on students that are missing classes	15%	• Increases awareness within the school of who is having mental health crisis/other health issues
Divert students when appropriate	15%	• Important to give students/children a second chance and not tarnish them for life

Key to Shading
Reactive Activity
Proactive Activity
Proactive and Reactive Activities

While nine different activities appeared in the "top three most important" list, four stand out as critically important as they were cited by more than half of the administrators: (1) support the administration in their duties, (2) act as a deterrent to the occurrence of crime within the school, (3) engage in behaviors that help build positive relationships with the students, and (4) enforce the law. Details on each are provided below.

Support administrators in their duties: Two-thirds of the school administrators we interviewed spoke about the importance of the support they received from their SRO to their ability to do their own job. This support was loosely defined to include both proactive and reactive activities and elements such as providing legal support and advice, providing insight on how to deal with a variety of challenges, cooperating with the administrator to address different issues and concerns as they occurred, being a resource and liaison for the school's administration, taking mentally ill students to hospital, and assisting the administrators in their efforts to deal with bullying within the school. This form of support also included being available by cell phone.

Administrators gave two reasons as to why they identified support from their SRO as very important. First, the knowledge that the SRO was just a phone call away increased their sense of safety, security, and wellbeing:

> "I appreciate the sense of familiarity;" ". . . the sense of consistency;" "it is great to know that they are there when we need them."

Second, they felt that the support from the SRO helped them do their own job better:

> ". . . when things are serious, they are here for us."
>
> "SRO support is important because they help us appreciate the severity of an issue – helps us put the issue into perspective."

Presence acts as a deterrent to crime in the schools: Most administrators we interviewed also mentioned how the SROs' presence and visibility in the schools discouraged students from committing crimes during school hours. Administrators who gave this response noted that the presence of police in their school had the important effect of limiting the amount of theft, gang activity, and drug dealing/use that occurred within their school. This resulted in an increased sense of safety for those at the school.

Build a positive relationship with the students by interacting with them in a constructive manner: According to half of the administrators in our sample, developing positive relationships with the students in the school was one of the most important things SROs did. Administrators noted that activities such as getting involved in student activities, counseling the students individually or in groups, running workshops, and having pleasant conversations with the students helped create a general atmosphere of support for the students within the school.

The administrators who identified such activities as important justified their response by noting that this form of relationship building "humanized police in the hearts and minds of the students" by "breaking down the 'us vs. them' sentiment."

Enforce the law: Just under half of the administrators in our sample identified the need for the SROs in the schools to arrest and charge students who were committing crimes, such as drug dealing. The administrators who gave this response felt that there were times when law enforcement was necessary (e.g., drug dealing) and felt that having an officer on the premises who is familiar with the school and teenagers helped resolve the problem quickly, efficiently, and often sensitively. These administrators felt that students who commit serious offences need to learn the consequences of their actions and that the victims of crime need to feel that they will be protected as well (e.g., assaults/bullying can create long-term problems).

Educating students and families on role of police in society: One in four administrators appreciated the fact that their SRO engaged in activities such as teaching civics classes and law classes, and giving presentations on police programs. They also had observed their SRO working with students and families to help them better understand the role of police in Canadian society. In a diverse region such as Peel with residents that come from cultures around the world, there is a real need to find a way to help residents to learn more about how Canada's legal system functions. Those administrators who said that such educational activities were important talked about how the SROs in their school had proven to be a great resource to students and families who wanted to understand how the law works and the role of the police in Canada.

Make daily visits to the school: The administrators who identified the importance of daily visits to the school (15% of the sample) noted that their schools were located in "challenging" communities and felt that the daily visit helped set the tone for life in the school. They felt that this visit had a dual value: it both deterred crime and facilitated positive interactions between the police and the students.

Act as a bridge between the school and the community: The administrators who identified the importance of being a bridge between school and community (15% of the sample) felt that it was important that students and their families were aware that the administrators knew about what was going on in the community. They also noted that the SRO program offered a way to make students and families in the area more comfortable talking to the police.

Run wellness checks on students who are missing classes: Administrators who mentioned this activity (15% of the sample) felt it was vital that school administrators were aware of mental health crises within their student populations and were available to help. Having checks done by the SROs on students who were missing class was felt to increase this awareness.

Diverting students from the justice system when appropriate: The 15% of administrators in the sample who identified the importance of diverting students who commit a crime away from the justice system (i.e., not charge them, but get them support) felt that that it was important to give students – who are "after all often just children" – a second chance.

Responses to the final question in this set indicates that, with one exception (run wellness checks), the administrators we talked to stated they were "very satisfied" with their SROs performance of the activities they felt were important. Administrators were "satisfied" with the officer's running of wellness checks.

Impact of SRO on Key Administrator Outcomes

We asked administrators to tell us how having an SRO in the school on a full-time basis impacted their workloads, their job satisfaction, and their ability to do their jobs effectively. Responses were collected using a 1 to 5 scale where 1 = Decreases it significantly, 3 = No impact, and 5 = Increases it significantly. We then followed up by asking the administrators to explain their answers. These data are summarized in Figure 5.6 and discussed in more detail below.

Workload: While the vast majority of the administrators we talked to felt that the SRO had little to no impact on their workloads, one in four administrators (mostly principals and vice principals) stated that having the SRO in their school had decreased their workload. They identified a number of reasons why this was the case. More specifically, they reported that: (1) the presence of the SRO within the school reduced the number of discipline issues they had to deal with, (2) the SRO performed a number of critical duties (e.g., conducting wellness checks, researching 'Do Not Attends,' and providing security within the school) that would need to be done by the administrators if the SRO was not there, and (3) their SROs made a real effort to address serious problems within the school and enhance school safety, which reduced workloads in the long run.

Finally, one in ten administrators (mainly school counsellors and social workers) felt that SROs increased their workload by bringing to the school's attention issues that they subsequently had to deal with (i.e., follow police protocol, contact other agencies, such as CAS).

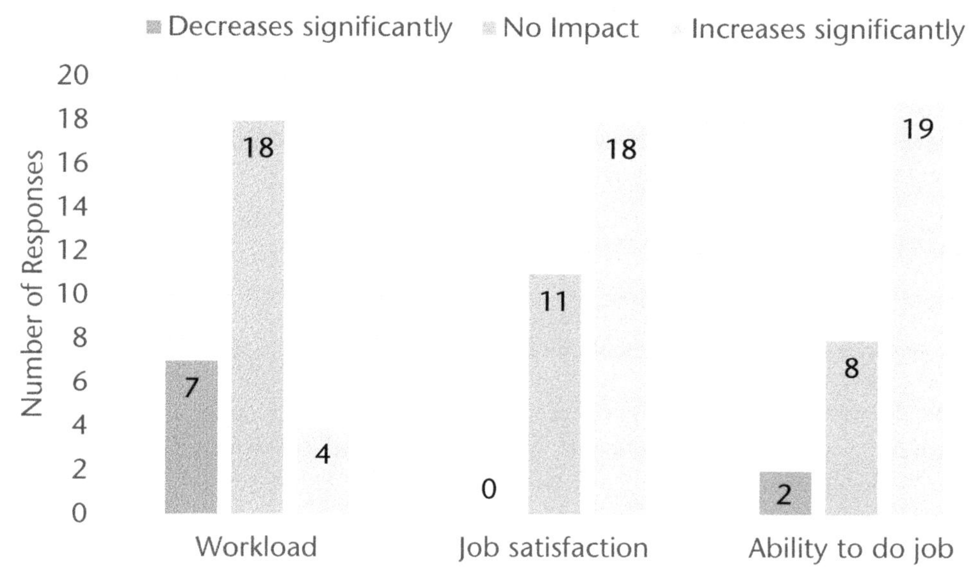

FIGURE 5.6 Impact of SRO on administrators' workload, job satisfaction, and ability to do job

Job satisfaction: None of the school administrators we talked to claimed that having an SRO at their school negatively impacted their job satisfaction. In fact, the majority stated that their job satisfaction was higher because they worked in a school with an SRO than it would be if the SRO were not there.

Those that said having an SRO in their schools had increased their job satisfaction gave a variety of reasons for their response, the most common of which are listed below:

- SROs are another resource in the school that can greatly help the school administrators resolve issues successfully (problem solving, someone else to consult, bring insight into a situation);
- SROs help administration provide a more enhanced learning environment and a better sense of community;
- SROs provide the school with information about what students are up to in the community, both good and bad;
- SROs make it easier for school administrators to deal with parents of children who have committed an offense (e.g., a parent is more likely to believe that their child/student is a drug dealer if an SRO tells them this as opposed to the school administrator); and
- SROs are very accessible and that personal connection is much better than dealing with 911 or Peel Police switchboard.

The rest of the administrators indicated that the SRO had no real impact on their job satisfaction.

Ability to do job effectively: A clear majority of the administrators (66%) in our sample felt that the SRO had positively impacted their ability to do their job. They provided a number of reasons for their response. Echoing what had been said before, many again talked about how the SRO made the administration's job easier by helping them maintain a safe and caring learning environment and by enhancing their ability to respond appropriately to situations as they arose. The following quotes typify the sentiments of the majority of the administrators we talked to:

> "Because it's a partnership: we deal with the educational aspect, they deal with the legal aspect, and a lot of the time an incident crosses both areas."

> "You know, some days there's no real impact on my job, but when there is a situation it certainly helps me. It doesn't hinder me. I don't feel like, oh God, they're here again. To me, I view them as a positive as they help me do my job . . ."

> "The SRO brings the force of the law to a given situation. . .they can advise both offenders and victims of their rights."

One in four felt that the SRO had no real impact on their ability to do their job, stating that their job would be the same with or without the SRO (e.g., "they are a resource, but it doesn't affect my work").

Finally, the two administrators who reported that the SRO decreased significantly their ability to do their job seemed to be suggesting that there was not enough collaboration between SROs and the school. This view was at odds with everyone else who we interviewed.

Perceptions of Safety

As shown in Figure 5.7, most administrators said that the presence of the SRO in the school made them feel either "much safer" (31%) or "somewhat safer" (34%). The rest (34%) stated that having an SRO in the school made no difference to their feelings of safety.

Those who responded that they felt a lot safer during work hours because of the SROs gave one of three reasons for this perception:

- they felt they could count on these officers to be available if they needed them ("they are always a phone call/text away");
- the SROs who worked in the school understood the school and the "troubled" students and were able to defuse problematic situations; and/or

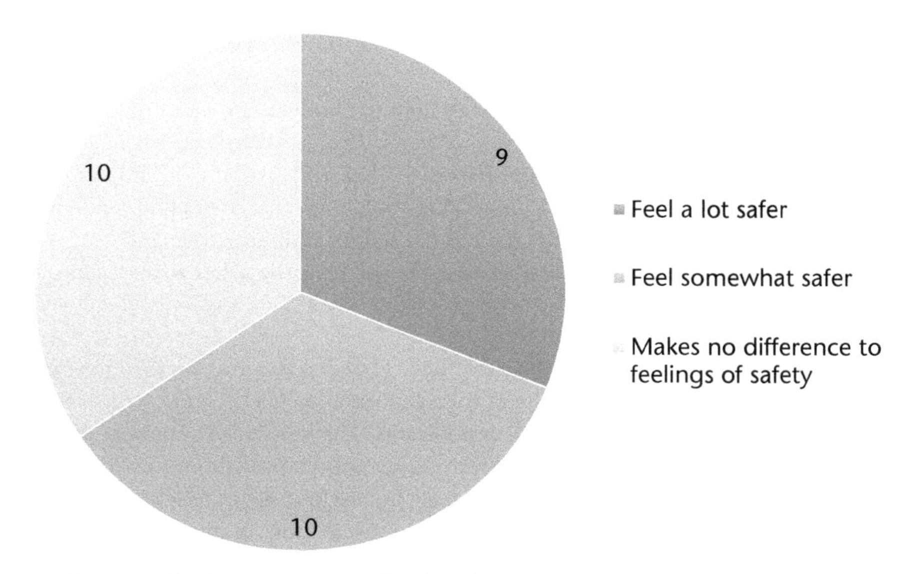

FIGURE 5.7 Impact of having an SRO in school on feelings of safety ($n = 29$)

- the presence of the SRO diminished the threat of aggression, drug dealing, and/or bullying within the school population, which increased perceptions of safety all around – both within the school ("there is a general feeling of safety because SROs are accessible") and in the community.

Those who responded that they felt somewhat safer provided a variety reasons, the most common being that the unknown threat of something bad happening was somewhat mitigated by the fact that there was an officer assigned to their school ("You never know what can happen – better to have SRO officer as an accessible resource").

Finally, the administrators who said the presence of the SRO made no difference to how safe they felt during work hours gave a variety of reasons for their opinion, with some saying that they felt safe, but would not attribute it to anything the SROs were doing, while others said their students did not make them feel unsafe, claiming "safety is a non-issue."

The following quote typifies responses to this question:

> "Yes. I don't need them here all the time, but when I do it's nice to know that they're there. And I do need them on occasion. Like even in this school, there are still occasions where large groups of people gather, and I've always joked and said when I go out that back door to the south parking lot and there's 500 kids, I'm by myself, I have a walkie talkie and I watch them scatter, I just am shocked. Why are these kids running? Like here comes (the big bad wolf) . . . with a walkie talkie and they scatter . . . And there will come a time when they won't run. And it's always nice to know that the officers are there in those situations. And they do occur. You know, at what point do you put value on that and say, okay, that only happens once a semester, maybe that's a tolerable amount. I would disagree."

Trust in SROs Assigned to the School

Finally, the value of this program and the quality of the relationship between administrators and SROs can be appreciated by noting that 100% of the administrators that we talked to indicated that they trusted the officers assigned to their school enough to talk to him or her about problems that are occurring in the school, as well as to ask him or her for personal advice.

View of the SRO Program

The final section of this chapter summarizes what the administrators at the five schools felt about the SRO program overall and whether or not they felt it should be continued.

Comparison: Schools with SROs to Schools without SROs

We began this section of the interview by asking our administrators the following: "Have you ever worked in a school that did not have an SRO assigned to the school full time? If yes, what differences have you noticed between these two schools?"

Just under half ($n = 12$) of the administrators in our sample had worked in schools that did not have an SRO assigned to the school full time. These administrators were all able to identify ways in which schools with full-time SROs differed from schools without. Key differences are summarized below.

SRO acts as a deterrent/increases sense of safety: Half of the administrators felt that the presence of the SRO in the school acts as a deterrent. They noted that having the SRO around gives both students and staff a feeling of safety. They also noted that the presence of the SRO in the school deters kids from doing "stupid" things.

Increases the trust between police and students: One in three administrators felt that there was a greater degree of trust between the police and the students in schools with an SRO than in schools without. Administrators who gave this response noted that this trust increased as the students and staff became more familiar with the officers. They also pointed out that, in their experience, this feeling of trust spread to the community and helped parents understand the severity of a particular situation.

Other benefits: Two administrators who had worked in schools with and without SROs felt that there was a better rapport between the administrators and the police in schools with SROs. Another two administrators talked about how, in their experience, schools without an SRO spent more time dealing with issues where students showed disrespect to teachers. They also felt that teachers in schools without SROs were more fearful than their counterparts who were in schools with SROs.

The following quote illustrates the answers given to this question:

> "The pot smoking that happened at the front of the school stopped when the SRO program started. The blatant drug use stopped. The cell phone theft stopped. I attribute this all to the police presence in the schools."

Administrators' Opinion of the SRO program

We then asked: "What is your opinion of the SRO program? What is good about this program? Is there anything about this program that you feel is problematic?"

Administrators had an overwhelmingly positive view of the SRO program and the officers that worked at their school. The following quote illustrates the types of comments made by administrators to this question:

> "So what is good about the program? For the kids, I think a lot of students in our area specifically are raised to be fearful of police authority, so it's nice for them to have that opportunity to build that relationship with an officer and to feel that sense of safety . . . For our community, again I think it's nice for them to see that we have a liaison in our building who's trying to develop that relationship and that rapport. For myself, there are so many benefits to it, it's just . . . it just makes it so much easier because we're dealing consistently with the same team, and instead of constantly just calling the police to investigate a matter that might come up and be more reactive, I think now we can be more proactive, and that's the difference I think it makes."

Administrators identified four things that they thought were "good" about the program. The most common response (provided by all but two of the administrators interviewed) related to the feeling on the part of those in the school that the SRO program allowed officers to become part of the school community and establish trusting relationships with students, staff, teachers, and administration. Those who gave this response appreciated the fact that the program made SROs aware of school protocols and how to deal with teenagers. They also noted that students were more forthcoming in terms of sharing information with police whom they knew compared to those officers they did not know.

One in three administrators gave one of three additional responses to this question:

- the program is good because it increases student's feelings of safety;
- the program is good because the SROs are always available and quick to respond to an emergency; and/or

- the administration at the school is connected to the community through the SRO program ("the SRO program means that the school is not on an island, but rather can be viewed as a support system for the community").

One in three administrators identified factors that they felt were problematic about the SRO program. The most common response to this question was that officer turnover was, in their opinion, too rapid (Peel Police move officers every two to three years), which meant that the relationship between administration, teaching staff, and the SROs were often severed. The following quote illustrates this challenge:

> "The problematic piece to me is we are not sustaining the existing SRO officers in a particular school – there's a rotation that occurs every two years. And there is a learning curve for officers that come into secondary schools . . . How they go about transitioning to work in a school so we can have officers that are more skilled at working with teenagers. And it's a skill, trust me, I've been doing this a long time . . . You can show up and do it, but that doesn't mean you do it effectively. So, I've always felt that it was a challenge when this rotation of officers is coming in."

The administrators who spoke about this issue wanted the officers left in the school longer.

Finally, there was also a small group of administrators ($n = 4$) that felt that the presence of the SRO in schools had the potential to unnecessarily escalate a situation that would in turn create hostility between police and the students, as well as the families of these students. It should be noted, however, that these same administrators also talked about how the program benefited the school, suggesting perhaps that their opinion on the issue was mixed.

Perceived Importance of Having SROs in School on a Full Time Basis

We asked: "In your view, how important is it for the Peel Regional Police to assign an officer to work in your school on a full-time basis? Why do you say this?"

All 29 administrators we talked to felt it was important for Peel Regional Police to assign an officer to work in the school on a full-time basis. For example:

> "Why? Because we're an educational venue, but we're doing so much more than that, and . . . a lot of things fall to the school . . . if they're not attending school . . . if there's drugs in the community . . . no matter what, the justice system sends them back here. So there is no rehab component, right, so they all just fall here. So we are where the kids [who] are dealing with all of that have to come. A breakdown of home, and social support . . . they still come here, this is their normalcy, right, so we are more than a school. You know, we work very closely with our community partners dealing [with] mental health and addictions and with social workers . . . the police facilitate this . . . so we need them, because we are all playing a very important role in these students' lives."

Respondents gave various justifications for their response, many of which are consistent with what we heard in response to earlier questions. Half stated that by assigning the SRO to the school full time, Peel Police supported the development of a relationship between the police and the school and created a sense of community that included the police. They observed that the SROs they deal with felt connected to and responsible for the school and its students, and that the relationships they developed with the students worked to change existing prejudices students and their families might have towards police.

Perceived Impact on the School of Discontinuing the SRO Program

We began by asking the administrators to imagine what it would be like at their school if the SROs were not in the school on a daily basis. Administrators identified three major things (all negative) that would change if that were to occur. First, school administrators would have to deal with the Peel Police switchboard or 911 when problems occurred. Peel Police would then send officers who had limited familiarity with the school/students to deal with this issue. This would, in the opinion of virtually all the administrators, be problematic because:

> "police involvement in schools would be a series of one-offs"
>
> "the level of concern would be different"
>
> "investigations would be drawn out and slower"

Second, school administrators would lose the personal relationship they currently enjoyed with Peel Police. Third, many felt that they would lose a key asset in their efforts to run safe schools.

We then asked our administrators to imagine what would happen if police officers were not in the school on a full-time basis. All of the responses referenced what the administrators felt would increase in the absence of an SRO, not decrease. There was a strong consensus within the group that we spoke to that: (1) unlawful activity in schools would increase without the SRO as a deterrent (e.g., inappropriate behavior, drug dealing, drug using, drug dealers entering schools, incidents involving students outside of schools at community centres); and (2) the administrator's job would become more difficult and stressful (e.g., anxiety would increase, there would be more paperwork for the administrator to do, the administrator would have to spend more time managing problematic students and dealing with attendance conditions of students with 'Do Not Associate,' administrators would have to spend significantly more time providing and explaining students' circumstances to different police officers).

Finally, one in five administrators repeated the concern that we heard earlier – that the volume of calls to Peel Police switchboard and 911 would increase as the focus in the school changed from preventing and diverting to reacting and enforcing.

Likes and Dislikes of Having an SRO Working in Their School

All of the administrators we interviewed were able to identify things that they liked about having an SRO working in their school. There was a strong consensus within this group that they liked:

- the positive relationship that existed at their school between school administration and the SRO ("we have a good rapport. . .we chat on regular basis. . .they are easy to talk to");
- that the SRO was available and very able to assist school administration by either enforcing the law when needed ("they are another voice, another perspective in creating solutions to difficult situations") or using diversion when appropriate to help "put wayward youth back on the right path"; and
- that the SRO understands how to deal with students (e.g., they offer a trained professional voice, they understand the issues youth are facing).

One in three administrators also mentioned that they appreciated how the SROs were able to create a sense of safety within the school. The following quote again speaks to what administrators like about the SRO program:

> "I think most is just having that connection with them so that if there is something going on here, it's another voice. It's a trained voice. It's a route to a solution that we might not be aware of."

One in three administrators were unable to identify anything that they did not like about having an SRO in the school. One in four disliked the fact that the SROs were not always available and wanted a greater police presence in their school ("two SROs between two schools means that we have to share with another school"). A similar number felt than having an SRO at the school could either unnecessarily escalate a situation or be misinterpreted by families/the community ("parents may think the school is bad because a cruiser is parked out front"). As one administrator observed:

> "I do think that they are a lot better at relating with students but there are times . . . and not that I expect them all to be friends because I know that they're here for a different purpose I guess. But I do think finding a bit of balance with the kids would be good. I think just recognizing that they are teenagers."

Do You Prefer to Work in a School With or Without an SRO?

All 29 administrators indicated that they would prefer to work in a school with an SRO. Why? Because the officer offered an extra level of support for the administrators, which, in turn, gave them peace of mind, a sense of safety, and more material support when things went seriously wrong in the schools. They also felt it helped to open channels of dialogue between students and police, which in turn led to healthier relationships between students and the police. For example:

> "I'm basing my answer on 15 years of administration in seven different Peel schools that have had SRO officers. It just . . . it makes life easier. It's a connection, it's a peace of mind that kids know that they're connected, and I think they make kids feel safer just knowing that they're connected to schools. I think once you explain to parents that when there's a police car out front it's not a bad thing, people feel better knowing that there are police around if you need them."

Should the SRO Program Be Continued?

Only one administrator felt that the program should be discontinued, stating that it was both a waste of money and a way to criminalize young people. There was a strong degree of consensus among the other 28 administrators, both that it should be continued, and why. The vast majority (80%) noted that the program was of real value to the school and iterated many of the reasons noted throughout this chapter to support their view (e.g., beneficial to have a point of contact in the police, the SRO is familiar with the school, the personalized approach to policing within the school). The vast majority (80%) also talked about how the program was of real value to the students, again citing reasons that were talked about earlier in this chapter (e.g., the police are perceived as caring adults, the police build relationships with students within the school, the police can help errant students get back on track, the police protect the victims, the police assist with mental health issues).

One in four administrators stated that the increased sense of safety in the school was an important reason to continue the program (i.e., safe schools provide a better learning environment, the youth in the region have a history of becoming unsafe and the SRO is an effective deterrent).

One in five felt that the program added value to the Peel Police department, and as such, should be continued (i.e., enhances the public's perception of the police, the SRO is more aware of what is going on in the community than road patrol, the program provides a good training ground for SROs to develop social skills and investigation skills).

Administrators spoke passionately about why the program should be retained, as reflected in the following three quotes:

> "Oh, yes, 100%. And that's why I literally laugh when I hear in Toronto where the schools are balking against having police involved. I think, you're crazy, because the fundamental thing we believe in Catholic schools is a safe school, is a school where kids can learn, that's the fundamental. It doesn't matter what you're teaching kids - if they're not safe, they're not going to learn jack and the SRO increases this sense of safety."

> "I am a strong advocate of this program and I would be very upset if they were to pull it out of the school because it would be doing a disservice to the youth of today. We are a society that has a positive policing presence but how do we get our youth to understand it if they are coming from immigrant backgrounds that don't have a positive view of policing. How then do we teach them that police can have a positive presence? We have to introduce it somewhere before these youths become adults."

> "Yes, I mean, again, we know that for our young people their mental health is not getting better. In fact, we're seeing more and more young people in mental health crisis so, again, being able to have someone to do wellness checks, to be able to accompany to the hospital. We're also seeing, again, cyber stuff is not getting better. I mean there is more awareness but having officers to liaise and to interrupt that where we can, is huge."

Is There Anything You Would Like to Add?

We ended our interview by asking the administrators if there was anything they wanted to add. The following comments and suggestions reflect what we heard:

> "The SRO really adds to the sense of safety so that everyone in the school can focus on education. Administration can only do so much to ensure the safety of students – what is administration going to do against a person with a gun?"

> "The proactive approach may be costly but it is totally worth it. The feeling of safety is important but it is really about making everyone in the school feel like they don't even need the SRO because there is nothing going on anymore – because they know right from wrong."

> "The programme needs to be consistent across all schools. The officers should make a point of being in the school during lunch times so that they have the opportunity to interact with students and develop those relationships."

> "Don't cancel the programme and then expect the schools to be the same in five years. Communities can expect real problems if the SRO program is discontinued."

> "The SRO is a link to all the silos that exist in a new bedroom community such as Brampton. If it weren't for the SRO, there would not be a network connecting the school to much of the information about what is going on in Brampton because it is such a new community that it lacks an established community infrastructure. Everyone is a stranger who just moved into the community – there is a lack of connection between people."

> "The Education Act requires students to be in schools, regardless of that student's individual problems. As a result, the school has become a treatment centre for all kinds of problems. A population struggling with myriad problems absolutely need the police."

Reviewing these comments, it is again clear that administrators in the schools with full-time SROs had a very positive view of the program and felt that the program delivered real value to the schools and the students.

The fact that the majority of administrators began their interviews by saying that their biggest "brag" about their schools was that they are safe and caring communities show that administrators truly value safety in their schools. The fact that virtually all administrators talked about how the SROs presence in the school increased their sense of safety makes it clear that the SRO is delivering value in the form of safety to many school administrators. Also noteworthy is the response that we got when we asked what the administrators liked least about the program – it was not extensive enough or large enough! It would appear, then, that the administrators see a strong link between the SRO program and safe schools.

Summary and Conclusions

Peel Police's SRO program seeks to create safe school environments that promote respect, responsibility, and learning. According to the administrators working in the five schools who participated in this study, the SROs are delivering on this goal.

The data analyzed in this phase of our research shows that, from the perspective of the school administrator, the value of having an SRO assigned to work full time in the school is multi-faceted and varied. A plurality of administrators stated that the SROs offer value within the school in the following ways:

They can enforce the law: Students are not being deterred by threat of school suspensions but think twice when involved in a discussion with the police; parents are more likely to appreciate the severity of an issue when the police are involved.

Having a good relationship in place between police and school increases police effectiveness: Any investigation is more effective when the SRO is involved rather than uniform patrol, as parents, students, and administrators are more likely to communicate with the SRO than an officer that they do not know.

Information sharing: Police have information or have access to information that the school administrators might not have (e.g., assaults that occur off-campus, graffiti and gang-tagging that occurs on and off school grounds).

Bring a different perspective: Police bring a different perspective to the issues going on at the school than do the school administrators, who are often too close to the situation.

Deter crime: The presence of the police in the schools acts as a deterrent to those students who are thinking of behaving inappropriately.

Enhanced perceptions of safety: The quick/easy access to the police ensured by the presence of the SRO makes students/parents feel safer.

SRO decreases administrators' workloads: Having the SRO in the school decreased administrators' workloads by reducing the number of discipline issues within the school. SROs also perform a number of other critical duties (e.g., conducting wellness checks, researching 'Do Not Attends,' and providing security within the school) that would otherwise need to be done by the administrators.

SRO increases administrators' job satisfaction: Administrators attributed this increase in job satisfaction to the fact that the SRO was a valuable resource that helped the administrators successfully resolve issues that they faced, assisted in the creation of a better learning environment within the school, gave administrators information about what their students were up to in the community, made it easier for school administrators to deal with parents of children who have committed an offense, and provided the school with a personal connection to Peel Police.

SRO increases administrators' ability to do their job: Administrators attributed this increase in effectiveness to the assistance the SRO gave them in establishing and maintaining a safe and caring learning environment within the school and responding effectively to crises and problems as they arose.

Other indicators of value can be identified by considering what our administrators envisioned would happen if the SRO program was discontinued. Administrators stated that if the SRO was not present in the school:

- victims of a crime/bullying might not come forward and report the issue;
- it would be harder to coordinate any response to a challenging incident at the school between the police and the school;
- students would not be diverted and would end up dealing with the criminal justice system;
- the amount of unlawful activity occurring in the schools would increase;
- school administrators would have to deal with the Peel Police switchboard or 911 when problems occurred;
- school administrators would not have a personal relationship within anyone within Peel Police;
- school administrators would lose a key asset in their effort to run safe schools; and
- the school administrator's job would become more difficult and stressful.

Also noteworthy are the data showing that none of the administrators anticipated any positive outcomes that would occur if the SROs were taken out of the school. This reinforces the notion that the SRO program brings value to the schools within Peel Region and underscores the importance of the SRO program in the eyes of school administrators.

Notes

1 The Program Performance Evaluation Office (PPEO): www.cdc.gov/eval/guide/step1/index.htm

2 Diversion consists of strategies that seek to avoid the formal processing (i.e., criminal prosecution) of a youth by the criminal justice system.

6

THE VALUE OF SROS

Views from Within (School Resource Officers)

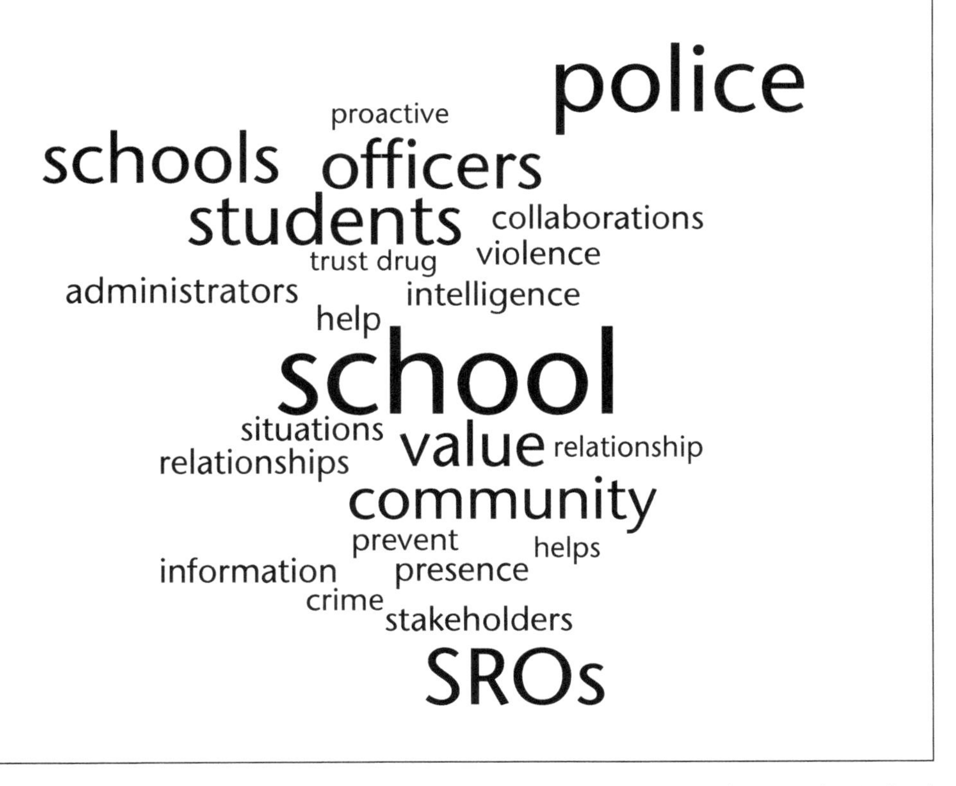

WordMap: 25 most common words in Chapter 6: "The Value of SROs: Views from Within (School Resource Officers)"

Key Learnings

This chapter summarizes key findings with respect to the value of the School Resource Officer (SRO) program as seen by one of the stakeholders most intimately involved with the initiative – the SROs themselves. The data analyzed in this chapter comes from two sets of interviews conducted with the eight SROs working in the five Peel District high schools participating in our study.

Most Important Activities Undertaken by the SROs: The SROs' Perspective

The SROs awarded more importance to activities associated with preventing crime than those associated with enforcement. In fact, all the SROs we interviewed agreed that the most important aspect of their role could be linked to:

- relationship building: activities that encourage positive relationships to be developed and maintained between the police and students, staff, and community members (i.e., engaging in conversations, asking questions, listening);
- enhancing visibility: activities that increase the visibility of the SRO in the school and the community (i.e., walking the school with the administrators, patrolling the community, being present at school events and functions).

What Value Do these Activities Deliver?

According to the SROs, relationship building activities add value by: (1) increasing the extent to which high school students and school administration trust the police and (2) enhancing perceptions of safety. Being visible in the school delivers value by: (1) deterring misbehavior and criminal activity and (2) enhancing relationship building, which helps increase trust in the police.

Value Delivered by the SRO Program: The SROs' Perspective

Analysis of the data presented in this chapter can be used to make the case that the SRO program provides value to high-school students, to high-school administrators, to the community surrounding the school, to the police service which offers the program (i.e., Peel Police), and to the SROs themselves.

Value of the SRO program – students, school administrators and community stakeholders: The data strongly supports the following conclusions with respect to the value that accrues to students, schools, communities, and society from programs such as the one implemented in Peel Region:

- The presence of the SRO in the school helps prevent or deter crime in the school and surrounding areas (gang violence, threats, fights, drugs, and robberies in particular) in the following three ways:
    - the SRO acts as a deterrent (people think before they act when they see the police);
    - the SRO intercepts and stops crimes from happening; and
    - the SRO intervenes early with troubled youth and helps guide them towards more positive behavior.

- The SRO is at the school and/or in the community and can act quickly to reduce the severity of crimes/de-escalate problematic situations.
- SROs are more able (and more likely) to recommend diversion to students when appropriate. This gives young people a chance for a meaningful future as it reduces the likelihood that a student will get a criminal record.
- The presence of the SRO in the school helps prevent or minimize property damage in the school and surrounding areas.
- The presence of the SRO in the school reduces the likelihood that a student will suffer physical or psychological harm when at school by reducing the incidence of physical violence, bullying, and cyberbullying.
- The presence of the SRO in the school increases the likelihood that students will get the help they need from the social service and health care systems.
- SROs provide school and community stakeholders with a resource that they can easily consult if they need information or advice on matters of the law.
- SROs make it easier for students and citizens to see the police as someone they can talk to if they have a problem rather than someone to fear.
- SROs increase the level of trust between key community stakeholders and the police. This increases the likelihood these individuals will seek help from the police or share information with the police as required.
- The SROs' knowledge of the community and the school enhances their ability to effectively investigate criminal activity in the area.
- The SROs provide school administrators with important information on what their students are doing outside the time they are in school as well as provide information on the law and how the police operate.
- The SROs provide invaluable support for administrations that are having difficulties enforcing school rules and managing the behavior of problematic students.

The value of the SRO to the Peel Police: The data strongly support the following conclusions with respect to the value realized by the SRO's employer – Peel Police – from the program:

- The personal relationships that the SRO has formed with members of the school community (administrators, students) facilitates the collection of intelligence and information that is valuable to other units within Peel Police.
- The SROs can use their social networks to obtain information and intelligence that would have been time consuming or impossible for other police officers to acquire. The following units seem to gain the most value from the SROs' ability to make connections and gather information: robbery, drugs, and Special Victims.
- The presence of the SROs in the schools and the SROs' information networks decrease the number of 911 calls and calls for service coming from the high schools.
- Proactive policing in the high schools decreases the total number of investigations required.
- The actions taken by the SROs increase the efficiency of police investigations as well as solvency rates (i.e., investigations experience fewer delays and take less time).

The value of the SRO program to the SROs: SROs working in the SRO program report that their job offers them a number of benefits that they personally value:

(continued)

(continued)

- They find the job personally fulfilling as they are often able to make a real difference in the lives of students that they interact with.
- They appreciate and value the personal relationships they develop in the course of their work.
- They enjoy the fact that their job helps people see police in a different, more positive light (i.e., "we can show the person behind the badge").
- They benefit from the opportunity to engage with average citizens ("we get to work with some good people, whereas on patrol we often only deal with people who have committed a crime"). This gives them a more complete perspective of who lives in their community.
- Performance of the SRO job helps them develop key skills, such as how to deal with students, communicate effectively with a variety of different audiences, work collaboratively with both the police and the community, and gain experience with investigations. Officers believe that the skills they gain from the job of SRO prepares them for other desirable positions within Peel Police (e.g., investigative units) and helps them advance within the service.

What Would Change if Police Officers Were not in High Schools on a Daily Basis?

Officers agreed that if the SROs were not in the schools, there would be an observable increase in:

- drug use (smoking weed in particular), drug trafficking and thefts, and the amount of violence, particularly in the form of fights that occurred in the schools;
- crime in the community as students skipped classes, trespassed, etc.;
- the workload of uniform patrol officers (more 911 calls); and
- police response time to the schools.

In addition, the SROs believed the following would decrease if SROs were not in the schools:

- the number of preventative interventions undertaken with high school students in the region;
- the number of diversions; and
- the amount of intelligence available for other Peel Police units.

As noted in Chapter 4, sound program evaluation requires the evaluator to "reach out" to all key program stakeholders in order to get a clear and consensual understanding of the program's activities and outcomes. This chapter provides the results from our engagement of the SROs in the evaluation process.

A Peel police officer spends, on average, two years working as an SRO. They spend these two years working with one other SRO. SRO pairs work in partnership with school administrators to promote a safe learning environment in the high schools in Peel Region. They do this by making efforts to reduce incidents of crime and by investigating criminal activities in the secondary schools that they are assigned to, along with areas in the surrounding community where students congregate. After two years, the officer rotates out of the SRO role and is replaced by a new SRO recruit. This rotation is done so that there is always one officer in the school who has experience in the SRO role and one officer that is new to the role and to the school. The more experienced SRO is supposed to coach and mentor the new recruit to ease their transition into the role.

In January and February 2016, we conducted five interviews with the eight SROs working in the five Peel District high schools participating in our study. Six of these officers worked in pairs in three of the schools involved in the study. During the interviews with these officers, we asked them to focus their answers on the three schools that they worked in that were included in our research. The other two officers worked together in the other two schools in the study. These two schools were located in very close proximity to each other. These two officers were asked to give us information on both of these high schools.

Three of the five interviews were conducted in person. The remaining two interviews were conducted over Skype. The same interview script was followed in all cases. Interviews were content coded using the methodology outlined in Cooper and Schindler (2006), and the responses examined for commonalities of views and opinions. In this chapter, we use terms such as "your school" and "their school" to refer to the school that the SRO works in that is included in this study. In all cases where the SRO was asked to think about "their school" before responding to the question, the unit of analysis is the school (i.e., $n = 5$). In cases where we ask questions that are more general in nature (e.g., what makes a good SRO), the unit of analysis is the officer ($n = 8$). In most cases, officers offered multiple responses to the questions asked, which means frequencies may add up to more than five (i.e., the number of schools represented in the study) or eight (i.e., number of officers we interviewed).

The SROs who were interviewed for this study have been in their respective schools for varying periods of time. One SRO had been at their school for nearly three years at the time of the interview. Three of the officers had been in their schools since September 2014 (i.e., were second-year SROs), while the other three officers had been in their current schools from September 2015 onwards (i.e., were first-year SROs). These time periods are consistent with how Peel Police administer the SRO program.

The remainder of the chapter is divided into eight sections. The chapter begins with a short description of how the SROs perceive the schools they work in. The second section examines data that speak to the training and skills that is/are necessary for effective performance of the SRO role. The third section focuses on what the SROs have found to be the key challenges and rewards associated with working as an SRO. In the fourth section, we look at collaborations between the SROs and school administrators/staff, as well as collaborations between the SROs and other units within the Peel Police. The fifth section continues this line of investigation by discussing key findings with respect to what the SROs in our study perceive to be the three most important activities that they perform in Peel Region high schools. In the sixth section we focus on what the SROs perceive to be the key value delivered by the SRO program to the following program stakeholders: students, school administrators, the community, Peel Regional Police, and the SRO. The penultimate section discusses data that speaks to the SROs' views of the SRO program, and the chapter ends by summarizing key findings with respect to the value offered by the SRO program as articulated by those doing the job.

SROs' Perceptions of the Schools in the Study

Strengths of the School

We began our interview by asking the SROs the following question: "If you were bragging about your school to a friend or colleague, what would you mention?" All SROs gave the same two responses to this question: great students and great staff.

Officers who bragged about the students attending the schools in our study talked about how friendly they were and how respectfully they treated the police. All of the SROs also spoke enthusiastically about the strong working relationship they had with the administrative staff at the schools in our study, describing them as collaborative and fantastic people who were fair and who made the SRO feel as if they were "part of the school family." Consider the following quotes from SROs working at two different schools:

> "At XXX, they're really big on building a team environment with us. They'll have us to the events, we'll be with the kids, we'll walk the halls, we feel like we're part of the XXX family. You're included with everything. They treat us very well, we have a great relationship."

> "I'm a big fan of the staff. We work really well together and I think they're very fair . . . It's just a really good working relationship, I find."

What Makes Your School Unique?

SROs highlighted several things that they felt made their schools different from others. Officers in three of the five schools felt that the quality of the sports programs offered at their school made them unique. Officers at two of the five schools felt that the quality of the leadership team at their school (principal and vice principals) set them apart from other schools. What made this leadership team great? According to these officers, school leaders had a low tolerance for student misbehavior, made an effort to stay on top of their students' issues and concerns, were very inclusive, and worked as a team. One officer appreciated the quality of the policies governing the school he/she worked in (the school is inclusive and requires school uniforms).

Challenges Facing Students and Staff in the Schools that Are in the Study

We then asked the SROs to tell us what they perceived to be the main challenges facing the students and staff at the school they worked in at this time. One challenge was identified as problematic by all eight of the officers: high levels of social media use and cyberbullying. Officers felt that the challenge presented by social media was exacerbated by the fact that many of the school staff did not use social media themselves, were unaware of how it was being misused, and had little idea of how to address the problem.

The relationship between the students at the school and their parents was seen to contribute to the challenging environment present in three of the five schools. Officers talked about how some of the parents of the children at the school they worked in were overly protective and did not support discipline of their children by either the administrators in the school or the SRO. The following quotes, given by officers at two different schools, illustrate this challenge:

> "They don't support any type of disciplinary action that involves their child. They have no respect for the administration at the school and make every effort to make their kid's problems go away."

> "A challenge for the staff that I see is dealing with the parents of some of these youth . . . we see when these kids are being pulled in for a negative reason and when they [school administrators] call their parents they're [the parents] extremely difficult to deal with . . ."

Three pairs of officers mentioned that challenges arose because of high levels of student entitlement within the school. Two pairs of officers identified students' lack of respect for any form of authority (i.e., authority wielded by teachers, SROs, school administration, parents) as a factor that contributed to issues within their school.

Two pairs of officers noted that high levels of recreational drug use at their schools (e.g., prescriptions, MDNA, cocaine) was of concern to them and the school administrators. Officers felt that in the schools they worked in, the large student body made things challenging ("there are lots of students in many different programs . . . Too many kids to keep track of who should be where when"). Finally, in one school, officers identified high levels of racial tension between two different groups of recent immigrants to Canada as problematic (i.e., "students from different cultures not seeing eye to eye").

In summary, the SROs identified the following list of challenges being dealt with in the schools in our study: social media use/cyberbullying, overprotective parents, high levels of student entitlement, students with no respect for authority, high levels of recreational drug use, and racial tensions between different groups of recent immigrants to Canada. The fact that most schools experience some combination of these issues suggests that they are linked in some manner.

On a reassuring note, none of the officers we talked to felt that there were any serious safety problems at their school. It may be, however, that their response can be in part attributed to the fact that "serious safety problems" has a different meaning for a police officer than a school administrator or parent, a conclusion that is supported by the follow quote from one officer:

> "Yes – like the incidents that happen . . . I don't know if I'd necessarily deem it as a safety concern for the general school, but obviously we do deal with fights and assaults and, you know, other threats and cyberbullying and stuff like that. I wouldn't necessarily say often, but I would say often enough. But I wouldn't generally say that the school is unsafe, no."

Skills and Training Required for Effective Performance of the SRO Role

Who best to find out what traits, skills, and training are required for effective performance in the SRO role than those who have experience in the job? Their thoughts on these issues are summarized in the section below. Since each SRO has experience in all of these areas, the unit of analysis for these questions is the officer themselves (i.e., $n = 8$).

Personality Traits that Are Critical for Effective Performance of the SRO Role

SROs identified seven personality traits that they feel are critical for anyone doing this type of job. In descending order of importance (measured by the number of times they were cited) these traits include:

- compassion (understanding) ($n = 7$);
- patience ($n = 7$);
- dedication to their job (hardworking, professional) ($n = 6$);
- friendly (approachable, easy to talk to) ($n = 5$);
- decisive (able to make tough decisions, self-confident, fair, able to use discretion) ($n = 5$);
- self-disciplined (hardworking, self motivated, able to manage time) ($n = 4$); and
- able to keep things in perspective (sees the big picture) ($n = 4$).

The following quotes illustrate these traits and demonstrate how challenging the job of the SRO really is:

> "You have to have discretion because they are minors; you have to understand that they're not necessarily making adult decisions."

> "Somebody who's approachable. Easy to talk to. Can communicate with the kids. I think a big thing is patience because you're going to be dealing with a lot of parents. Yes. I just think approachable and patient. Those are two great qualities to have in my opinion."

> ". . . you don't want to make mountains out of molehills because a lot of the stuff we deal with is not a big deal and shouldn't be made a big deal of . . . even though it gets presented to us that way . . . So being able to kind of figure out what can be dealt with in a conversation as opposed to opening up a big investigation."

Two other responses were given to this question, neither of which is, strictly speaking, a personality trait. Four officers felt that the SRO should be a role model that students could emulate and look up to, an idea that is related to being professional, fair, compassionate, and dedicated. Another officer felt that an SRO needed to be smart/intelligent. The fact that many of these traits are very difficult, if not impossible, to train for (e.g., compassion, patience, friendly, dedication) emphasizes the importance of the SRO selection process.

Operational Skills that Are Critical for Effective Performance of SRO Role

SROs identified five operational skills that they felt were essential for anyone doing the job of SRO. All eight spoke about the need for an SRO to be a highly skilled communicator. In this context, they talked about how the job required that they communicate clearly and effectively with both the public and other police officers (i.e., "know your audience"). They felt that an effective SRO had the ability to adjust their communication style to suit their audience (i.e., communicate one way when dealing with civilians, another way with police officers; one way with adults, another way with teens). They also noted the importance of good tactical communication skills. The following quote speaks to the importance of this skill:

> "I think interpersonal skills are huge because you deal with a wide variety of personalities . . . You are dealing with students, dealing with principals, and also relaying that information to bosses and other police officers. . . So I think interpersonal skills, communication skills are huge."

Six out of the eight officers mentioned organizational skills – the ability to manage their time well, keep track of various obligations and duties, work alone but also work with others, and be organized. Six out of the eight officers also felt that it was critical for an SRO to have a good knowledge of the relevant laws and statutes (i.e., "know what you are and are not able to do"). They noted that often they were the only ones on the scene and if they dealt with the issue inappropriately, then there were likely to be legal consequences. The other two operational skills, being a good team player and having a good knowledge of the context (i.e., know school policies and procedures), were each mentioned by two officers.

The fact that there was such a high degree of consensus within this group of officers of what they thought were essential operational skills again speaks to the importance of the SRO selection and training processes.

Training Officers to Take on the SRO Role

We began this section by asking officers what types of training they get to prepare them for the SRO role. All of the officers we talked to noted that every officer received one week of job-specific training prior to taking on the SRO role. During this week, they were given instruction on how to deal with students and how to deal with school specific situations that they were likely to face (e.g., bullying, cyberbullying, social media related crimes). They were also given material and tools associated with SPEAR (School Police Emergency Action Response), which has been described as follows:

> SPEAR is designed to provide police and other emergency services with critical and accurate school information to assist in responding to school emergencies. This innovative and comprehensive computer database was the first of its kind in Canada, and highlights the lead that Peel Regional Police has taken in proactive school security and emergency preparedness.[1]

Also included in this one week of training were sessions on proactive policing and dealing with students with mental health issues.

All officers also receive training in Immediate Rapid Deployment (IRD), which trains first responders how to actively confront a developing high-risk crisis, and one year of "on the job training" from the senior officer of their SRO team, which is more specific to the schools and communities where these officers worked. This training was described by one SRO as follows:

> "So for the training, yes, you get the week of training from our headquarters which deals with a wide variety of topics relating to school policy and issues that stem from the schools. Like you get gang stuff, prostitution. And then also you usually partner with someone who's been there before, and you kind of shadow what they do, and you learn a lot. Most of what you learn is kind of the informal process of how you deal with principals and how you handle certain situations and so the biggest part is learning from your partner."

Challenges and Rewards of Working as an SRO

The SRO is likely to face a number of challenges in the course of their work in the school and the community. Ideally, they also find aspects of the job rewarding and gratifying. To help us better understand the "peaks and valleys" of the job, we asked our group of SROs: (1) "What is the biggest challenge faced by those doing a job such as yours? How do you deal with this challenge?" (2) "What is the greatest reward?" Responses to these questions are provided below.

Biggest Challenge

The officers we talked to identified a number of challenges they faced during the course of their work. All eight officers agreed that the negative image the public and young people have of the police makes it more challenging for them to do their job. They noted that this negative image sometimes resulted in them being stigmatized by the youth with whom they were seeking to develop relationships. They also stated that they often encountered a lack of respect and outright hostility when trying to do their job, negativity that they felt was triggered by the uniform they wore. They attributed these negative attitudes to the media, which, in their opinion, was swaying many youths to hold unconstructive views of the police. The following quote typifies what we heard:

> "I think one big challenge is connecting with the kids because there's a lot of kids just through watching like music videos and watching TV . . . there is just a lot of negativity about the police on TV . . . they don't like police. So you kind of try to break that barrier, and try to build positive relationships with them and show them like we're here for them, we're here to help."

The second challenge (mentioned by all but one SRO) relates to the first – it is hard to establish relationships of trust with young people today (i.e., "it is hard to connect"). This is unfortunate, as positive relationships are critical to successful performance of the job of SRO.

The third challenge talked about by all but one of the officers in our sample relates to the difficulties SROs experienced educating students and school staff on the law. They mentioned that both of these groups had problems distinguishing between an action that was against the rules versus against the law. The following quotes speak to this challenge:

> "So I think a lot of people misunderstand, or they don't really know, right, what actually constitutes certain crimes. They want people charged for something that is not technically a criminal offense . . . and explaining that to them tactfully, right? While still sort of being sensitive to their issues. I think that's a challenge . . . So if you can articulate what you're doing, nine times out of ten you can smooth most things over with people. Or at least walk away and they know what happened to them and why, and it changes everything."
>
> ". . . when two people fight, that doesn't always constitute assault. There's not always a criminal offense there. So you need to know the difference between a fight and an assault, and you know, everybody's definition of harassment is different, but the definition of criminal harassment is specific, so . . . And the same thing with threats. Everybody can say they feel threatened by anything, which everybody always does. So you need to know the difference between that stuff . . ."

Two other challenges were each noted by officers in two different schools. In the first case, officers discussed how hard it was to manage all the different and varied demands of their job in a limited time frame ("I often need to be in two places at the same time"); a challenge that relates to the need for SROs to be good at time management. In the second case, officers mentioned how the Young Offenders Act makes enforcement of the law difficult.

How Do Officers Deal with These Challenges?

Officers mentioned that the Peel Police's SRO selection process focuses on identifying people for the positions who have the right personality and skill set to manage their own time, set priorities, and build relationships of trust. This made it easier for them to manage the various challenges inherent in the job. These officers felt it was vitally important that such practices continue. Other responses included working overtime and building relationships of trust:

> "Build a rapport . . . be consistently present at the school and its events and put the effort in as it takes time . . . every day. Just keep going in . . . just keep trying to talk to them. Like you're not going to win over every kid, but you put the effort in. You're at the school every day, you're walking the hallways, you're connecting with them . . . I think that's all you can do is just keep trying."
>
> "Yes, I think the best way to deal with it is talking to them and reaching out as much as possible and reassuring them that you're not out there to arrest them. You're not looking to arrest kids . . . you're not . . . You don't benefit from that. You're actually trying to help them out."

Greatest Reward

There was a strong consensus within the sample of SROs that we talked to that the greatest reward that an officer experienced while being an SRO was making a difference in the lives of the students. All officers we talked to mentioned this reward in one way or another. They talked about how great they felt when "kids who had hated police now say hi" when they see the officer in the yard or hall. How great it was to see "kids learn from the police and make better choices." How great it was to change people's negative perceptions of police officers. How good it felt "working with young people and stopping them from getting a criminal record." The following quotes speak to this reward:

> "Yes. There's a lot of kids that when we look at last names . . . you know, their one brother is in jail for first degree murder, their other brother is in jail for drugs and guns, and their cousin and their stepdad and . . . your this and that. I mean, they're all so closely tied to a lot of people who are in bad spots. They're either dead or doing hard time. Just I think for me, it's those tough kids . . . If you can crack that nut . . . it's connecting with them. Helping them with their problems. Being somebody that they feel they can approach you . . . I think that's the most rewarding part is helping that kid and making a difference in their life, as cheesy as that sounds."

> ". . . when we deal with this kid who could easily be charged for a criminal offence. If he was dealing with somebody, just like an officer on the street, he'd likely be charged, but we have the ability to sit down with him, take the time and work it out with him and maybe work out a plan that doesn't include a charge. And when the year ends and we haven't run into that student again in a negative way, I'd say that's pretty rewarding."

All but one officer also talked about how rewarding it was for them to feel really connected with the community that they serve. These officers talked about how they found it really satisfying to "get involved with the community" and "deal with good people." They also appreciated it when they received recognition from the community ("great to feel appreciated," "love it that they know who I am," "thumbs up and smiles when I go by"). Again, in their own words:

> "I think getting more in touch with the community; like I find that we're not perceived in such a negative way; they see us and they get to know us, they call us by first names. We get to know the schools, we get to know the students as well as their parents and extended families, and you're not seen as such a negative thing."

Finally, two officers talked about how they found it rewarding being assigned to the NPU and working with a group of people with the "same mindsets" where everyone is happy to help each other out. In other words, they are rewarded by the sense of team they experience within the NPU.

Collaboration between SROs and Key Stakeholders

The next set of questions relates to collaborations between the SRO and two sets of key stakeholders: school administrators and other Peel Police units. Key findings on collaborations with school officials are presented first, followed by our data on collaborations with other Peel Police units.

Collaborations between the SROs and School Administrators

We began this section of the interview by asking our SROs how often they collaborated with school administrators. All of the officers stated that such collaborations took place on a daily basis. We then asked the SROs to describe the nature of these collaborations. Analysis of the data showed that these collaborations were either:

- *Proactive/Preventive*: Such collaborations involved SROs and administrators working together to prevent something from happening. Examples mentioned in the interviews included developing a communication plan for a student drill, doing a patrol of the school property together with the administrator, sharing information on a student that seemed to be having problems, and just checking in with the administration in case they needed the officer for anything.
- *Reactive/Enforcement*: Such collaborations involved SROs and administrators working together to react to something that had happened. Examples mentioned in the interviews included dealing with a crime that had occurred on school property, dealing with a student who had a mental health issue, and responding to a call for service in the community.

While the officers estimated that proactive/preventive collaborations outnumbered interactions with a reactive/enforcement flavor by a ratio of two to one, they also acknowledged that the type of collaboration they had with the school administrator depended on what was "going on that week."

Working Collaboratively: The Details

To increase our understanding of the collaboration process, we then asked our respondents to: "Think back to a time that you worked collaboratively with the administrators at your school that you remember clearly. Can you please describe this situation to us? What do you think was the value to the school of having an SRO work with you on this issue? What do you think would have happened if you were not around?" The information we got using this approach was very detailed and rich. In fact, the officers gave so many examples of positive collaborations it was hard to decide on which ones to include in this report. The list we selected as illustrative is provided below.

Situation One: Summary Worked together to investigate and prevent organized fighting within the school. While the group fight did not happen, two students started fighting anyway. SRO and administrators worked together to break up the fight and then took the student to the administration office where they focused on calming the student down before he damaged any property. The officer's telling of the story is as follows:

> "So it was during the time when we had some problems with . . . organized fighting between a few schools. The staff had brought three students that were fighting within the school together and we were called in. During the course of our investigation . . . we found out that there was a fight scheduled to happen within the next hour involving the students that we were initially dealing with. The administration left us to deal with the three students and went looking for the other half of the fight. And they found it . . . it was just about to break out . . . and we were able to intercept the students during the fight. And then, when we left to patrol the school, another student that was involved in the fight had been taken down to the office and started to cause problems . . . and the vice principal was able to just call us over the PA system and we were able to get to the office really quickly in order to assist in calming the student down before he damaged any property or anything like that.
>
> Both times we were already present at the school and were able to defuse the situation before it became widespread, instead of something having to occur and then having to call 911, and wait for the officers to respond."

What would have happened if the SRO were not there? The fight would have occurred. Students would likely have been injured and property would have been damaged. If a major fight broke out (highly likely if the officer was not there) the school would have had to call 911 and Peel Police would have needed to divert officers from the road to the school. This would take time.

Situation Two: Summary Worked together to avoid having to lay criminal charges against a student after an assault had occurred on a school bus. The administrators shared information from the school's initial investigation of the situation with the SROs and discussed this student's background. While the SROs could have charged the student (he/she committed an offense) they allowed the school to determine what was to be done and identify appropriate consequences. The SROs were convinced that this approach was in the best interest of not only the youth, but also society.

What would have happened if the SRO were not there? The student would have been charged with a criminal offense with all that entails. The school would also have had to call 911 and Peel Police would have needed to divert officers from the road to the school. This would take time. In the officer's own words:

> "If that same assault had happened on a bus or in public, he would likely have been charged criminally . . . as it is he won't have any consequences other than penalties imposed by the school. So, because we know what the school's doing . . . and we know the background on the suspect . . . we decided that a criminal charge would probably not be in the best interests of him or society . . ."

Situation Three: Summary Worked together to prevent fights in the school by being a visible presence at the right time and place in the school. This allowed the school to lay suspensions for inciting the fights rather than criminal charges for fighting. In the words of the SRO:

> "Yes, I'm thinking about a big sort of fight that was happening here. They [the administration] told us it was going down, and they showed us the video of what was happening, the big standoff basically in the hallway, and it was right before Christmas break, so we kind of wanted to make sure that it didn't spill out into the community . . . So, we were there and administration was there . . . and it just never really happened. The VPs were out there with us, walking the schools, and they ended up IDing some kids and suspending them . . . for sort of the inciting of other kids."

What would have happened if the SRO were not there? The fight would have occurred. Students would likely have been injured and property would have been damaged. The school would have had to call 911 when the fight broke out and Peel Police would have needed to divert officers from the road to the school. This would take time. The students involved in the fight would have been charged with a criminal offense with all that entails.

Situation Four: Summary Worked together to resolve a drug problem in the school by jointly liaising with the community and sharing information. This situation involved collaboration between school administrators, the community, and the police. Here is the situation as told by the SRO:

> "At the beginning of my tenure . . . there was a significant drug problem that was going on in the school, and we interacted with the administrators, just basically trying to gather as much information as we could, and trying to get them to help us with how we were going to perform our investigation. And they helped us liaise with community, people in the community who were also concerned and had information to share with us. That went really well, we had a really good interaction between administrators, community, and the police, and we put some really big dents in the problem that was going on in the school and the community.

> What would have happened if the officer was not there? An increased risk that students would drop out of school, overdose, or die . . . because they've had several in the last couple of years. So, we think that we put a pretty big dent in that, we protected people, you know, hopefully we helped stop kids from getting into the drug thing . . ."

What would have happened if the SRO were not there? Students would have continued to buy and sell drugs and the risk that students would overdose would continue. Perceptions of safety within the school would decline.

Situation Five: Summary Worked together to identify resources for a girl who needed help to leave her parents' home so that she could return to school after going missing. This collaboration resulted in the girl getting safe shelter, a steady source of food, and everything else she needed to return to school. The student returned to school after this assistance was provided. Here is the story in the officer's words, with the name of the girl removed:

> "There's one kid who has mental health issues who's been emancipated from her parents and we check up on her through Instagram and by going to her house and information sharing. The first time we heard about this girl she went missing for the weekend and her parents called it in and the school administration heard through her friend that she was sleeping rough. So we worked with the school administrators to come up with a plan on how to protect her and get her to come to school, because she hadn't been attending school. So, we looked after her safety, eventually locating her and . . . we dealt with her parents while the school worked to emancipate her from her parents by getting her what she needed, bus tickets, school supplies, food, getting the right connections. But between all of us . . . the school, my partner . . . we were able to go down the checklist and check everything that we needed to do to make sure that she had shelter, food, and everything she needed for school too, and to come back."

What would have happened if the officer were not there? It is highly likely that the girl would not have returned to school and her mental health issues would not have been treated. If the school had called uniform patrol they would have opened a missing persons file and made every attempt to locate her, but they would not have made an effort to return her to school or get the mental health issues treated because they were unaware of the context.

Situation Six: Summary Worked together on a situation where two students were selling drugs and extorting money from other students. One student's mother became aware of the situation because of Facebook conversations she had seen. She brought it to the attention of the school, as she was concerned that her son was involved with someone who was doing and selling drugs. The SROs were brought into the school to try to identify some of the names on the Facebook conversations. The SROs could identify some of the students. They shared the names of the students with the school, but did not make any arrests. A day later, the SRO found out by talking to officers in another unit that these same students were extorting money at a variety of schools as part of a "drug game they were playing." The SROs alerted the school administrators, who caught these two students in one of the high school washrooms selling drugs to other students. Both had a pocket full of cash. These students were charged with extortion and possession. This illustrates collaboration on several levels. First, the SROs would not have been involved in the issue if they had not been brought in by the administration. Second, the administrators would not have been aware of the severity of the issue if they had not been alerted by the SROs. Finally, the SROs would not have had the complete picture on what was going on if they had not talked to officers working in other units within Peel Police. The following quote illustrates not only the impact of the cooperation, but hints at what would have happened if the officer were not there:

> "They took it seriously because we had come to them only a day earlier . . . saying you know that these kids may be involved in taking money and selling drugs in your school . . . so I think having us there and working with the school helped everyone deal with it faster. And those kids, essentially because of the arrests, those two kids will have to be moved to other schools. Which is good as it will get them away from each other, and get them out of that school. And you know, while one has to hope we would have caught them eventually, but I mean, how long would it have gone on for if we sort of hadn't had that collaboration? If we hadn't have come together on this issue . . . how much more money would they have taken, how many more kids would they have victimized . . . It's just so detrimental . . . to the victimized kids, right? They're coming to school Monday to Friday, like just probably paranoid, scared, don't want to be there. Which of course affects their studies and their grades and everything else and . . . A month could feel like a year to them. Right?"

Scanning the above list, one is struck by the diversity and complexity of the different situations in which collaboration is required. Some related to the SROs' ability to enforce the law, some are illustrative of proactive efforts to prevent a crime or injury. Many combine elements of both proactive community-based policing with reactive attempts to enforce the law. In all cases, however, the fact that the SRO was present in the school prevented any or all of the following from occurring:

- the student from getting a criminal record;
- students getting injured or perhaps even dying (fights, drug overdoses);
- property damage (school or community);
- calls to 911;
- a reduction in the number of uniform officers on the road (they would be at the school);
- slower response by the police; and
- students with mental health issues being unable to get needed help.

Quality of the Collaboration

Seven out of eight of the SROs we interviewed rated the quality of the collaborations between themselves and the administrators at their school as excellent. These officers attributed their positive experiences to three factors: we trust each other, we have formed a strong relationship over time, and communication between the SROs and school administrators is excellent:

> "We have a very good relationship and rapport with all of the staff that . . . we work very well together and we trust each other . . . we understand each other . . . we're on the same page."

One SRO stated that the quality of the collaboration was "okay". He/she explained that the challenges had more to do with the school they were in and the type of issues they faced (they were working in one of the urban grant high schools) than with the relationship they had with the school administrators.

Value to the School of Having an SRO Work with Them on this Issue

What value did the school realize because of the SRO program? While the answer may be apparent to anyone who reads the above set of scenarios, the list below summarizes what the SROs told us with respect to the value the SRO offers not only the school, but the community and society:

- their presence helps prevent or deter crime in the school and surrounding areas;
- they can act quickly to reduce the severity of crimes/de-escalate problematic situations;
- the problem-solving capacity of the police and the schools is enhanced as both groups are more aware of any potential problems within the schools and this awareness increases the ability of the police and the school administrators to act proactively to address issues before they occur;
- the police are more aware of students' "backstories" so they are able to respond faster and with more discretion to incidents where the law is broken;
- they can recommend that a student go through diversion, when appropriate, which reduces the likelihood that a student will get a criminal record;
- their presence helps prevent or minimize property damage in the school and surrounding areas;
- their presence minimizes the likelihood that a student will suffer physical harm; and
- the police have access to community resources and partners which the school does not, and this access increases the likelihood that students will get the help they need.

The following quotes illustrate some of the sources of the value offered by SRO officers:

> "They had one less kid dying of a drug overdose because we were there."
>
> "Well, it has the potential of stopping young students who have been arrested getting criminal records for just bad decisions that they're making as kids . . ."

Collaborations between the SROs and other Units within Peel Police

We began this section of the interview by asking the SROs how often they collaborated with other sections within Peel Police. Responses show that the frequency of SRO–Peel Police collaborations varied from school to school with some officers reporting daily collaborations, others providing an estimate of three or four times a week, and yet other officers estimating that such collaborations occur once or twice a week. One officer put it well: "there is no average –we collaborate as needed depending on the file."

Nature of the Collaboration

We then asked the SROs to describe the nature of these collaborations. Analysis of the data showed that collaborations were of two types: information sharing and investigations. All officers in all five schools mentioned both types of collaborations, often when describing the same situation. The following quotes help the reader appreciate what is involved in a collaboration involving information sharing and investigations:

> "Our breaking and entry unit . . . 100% I'm talking to them every day about kids that could be potentially doing B and E's in certain areas and stuff I've seen on Twitter . . . Helps them know who to look at."
>
> "Yes, it goes both ways. Sometimes there's circumstances where you have to pass off what we're dealing with . . . like a sex assault incident where we have units that specialize in just that and who will be able to take care of our students better than we can just as SROs. But also we're used as a resource because we know our students and in the case where the break and enters were good with solid information they would ask us because we know who the students are and who they hang around with."
>
> "Our gang unit, our street crime gang unit has thanked us because we give them information on possible new gangs coming out, what the relationship is, and we gather a lot

> of information for them that they use later on. And they use us in the same capacity, you know, can you guys check to see if this person still goes to this school? Can you guys see where this person is now? So we're able to do that a lot easier than . . . or a lot more efficiently than if they would have to do . . . If they were to come out and do that."

> "It's mostly CID that we're dealing with . . . it's at least a couple times a week and that could be as simple as, like an email, like, hey, you're going to your school, do you know if you could show this to the art teacher and see if, like, basically it's a graffiti tag, and see if she's seen this work before and stuff like that. And the art teacher at our school would say yes or no or who she thought it was or, yes, I think that's what's typically the information . . ."

Working Collaboratively: The Details

To increase our understanding of the collaboration process, we then asked our respondents to: "Think back to a time that you worked collaboratively with the officers in other units that you remember clearly. Can you please describe this situation to us? What do you think was the value to Peel Police of having an SRO work with them on this issue? What do you think would have happened if you were not around?" In the section below we provide a summary of four such collaborations that we found to be instructive in understanding how the SROs collaborate with other units to contribute value.

Situation One: Worked with the Special Victims Unit (SVU) to investigate a sex assault and get help for the victim. In the words of the officer involved:

> "Well, we just recently had a case that involved an alleged sex assault with a student . . . She was making some allegations, and it took us a few days to kind of break down exactly what she was saying, but we were able to collaborate with SVU and get her upstairs to get some help. And CAS [Children's Aid Services] was involved, and so we worked hand in hand with them as well."

What was the value to Peel Police of having the SRO involved?

> "Well, because we work with the schools . . . we've more of a wealth of information regarding this student . . . I mean, yes, they're the subject matter experts when it comes to the actual offense, but in this investigation we become the resource because they're going to want to inquire about the student . . . we care about our students, right? . . . We feel more of a connection to them and we can put a lot more time and effort into dealing with them than those guys in SVU who have a lot of other calls . . . and she talked to us but was kind of shy with them . . ."

What would have happened if the SROs were not in place?

> "I think the investigation would have been longer . . . been way more drawn out because of the sensitivity of the incident, which was a sex assault to a young person, a minor; it had to be handled very delicately . . . I guess, without us there it probably would cause a little bit more stress on a victim . . . she knew us but she did not know them."

Situation Two: Worked on a project to investigate break and enters by assigning SROs to assist in the investigation:

> "Every robbery is, you know, hours of investigation, because especially when somebody calls and says I was just robbed, that turns into maybe five, six, ten, twenty officers setting up perimeters, checking the area. You call in canine . . . it's hard on a time frame . . . So, there's a big issue in Brampton with a lot of break and enters . . . and there's no indication that these were stopping. They weren't. They were ramping up . . . they were getting more frequent. The young guys were getting more ballsy about it . . . because you do so many, you keep getting away with it, you keep getting away, and you're getting stuff . . . and so it started spiraling out of control . . . so they came to us for extra manpower . . . It's commonplace for them to come to the SROs for help . . . We're the default unit. So we're a resource for everyone all the time. So, whenever somebody needs something, uniform's always too busy answering calls and doing everything else. You've got your CIB [Criminal Investigations Bureau] guys who have task lists a mile long. We're that middle ground. You know, we're not tied to the radio, we don't have task lists that are a mile long, so basically, you know, we're the ones who are available for all things at all times. So, we helped out on this . . . spent extra hours . . . and helped until the guys were arrested."

What was the value to Peel Police of having the SROs involved? The SROs provide trained officers in times of emergency or crisis. Having these extra resources speeds up the investigation process and, in this case, resulted in an arrest.

What would have happened if the SROs were not available? Peel Police would have either had to pay hundreds of hours of overtime to make the arrests in a timely manner or accept that the robberies would continue at the current pace until the culprits were identified and arrested.

Situation Three: Worked with the CIB on a case that involved sharing of information with schools to find missing students:

> "Yes, on multiple occasions we have worked with our CIB, with regards to missing students . . . so the CIB officer would be pursuing their own leads and they would contact us to try and find information at the school level, you know, speak to people who are friends of the missing party, speak to administrators and try to come up with other avenues to pursue and try to locate them, and make sure they are healthy and safe."

What was the value to the Peel Police of having an SRO to work with on that issue?

> "Well . . . it's information that can be garnered at a level that normal officers who aren't at the school wouldn't have, because that relationship isn't there, you know, the relationship, the trust level, just the facial recognition. You know, students see that we're there all the time, so when we go speak to them, if we are concerned about a student . . . then they have a bit more faith in us because they know we are there every day, we are part of the community, we are part of that school community, so they are more than willing to help us out."

What would have happened if the SRO were not in place?

> "Well, I think it would just have caused delays in their investigation for sure . . ."

Situation Four: Worked with CIB to locate a student in the school and arrest him for mischief after Uniform Patrol [Road] was called to investigate a domestic disturbance. The SRO then transported the student to Division where Road took custody:

> "Yes, I can remember a few months ago. I was at my school and speaking with the VP in the office and I could hear a domestic happening over the radio and it was basically a young kid who smashed the house, smashed a bunch of things in the house. And this was on a Friday. It was close to the end of the day . . . I heard that call over the radio, but they didn't go into any details. Shortly after that I got a call from an officer on the Road who was at the house . . . it turned out that it was a domestic between a mother and her son – the son was a student at my school and he knew I was the officer for this school . . . and he asked me if I was at the school, which I was, and he said if I could find out if this student was inside the school because he was "arrestable" for mischief, because he had smashed things at his house. And it being the end of school day . . . I think we had probably ten minutes or less to get him . . . so I asked the VP if he was in class. They checked and he wasn't. The VP then paged him and told him to come down to the office . . . He came down and I arrested him . . . and I subsequently transported him back to Division where the Road took over and transported him."

What would have happened if the SRO were not in place?

> "I think the average officer on the Road who probably hasn't been in SRO wouldn't even know off-hand where the school was or know where to park or know where the main office is, and little things like that would not make that situation fluid. And even going to school administration and explaining look, I'm an officer from the Road, I'd like to speak to someone and find this kid . . . I think we've had issues in past where school administration is kind of put off by the officer from the Road's attitude or maybe aggressiveness because they just want to go in and grab this student from class . . . but we have this mutual respect, so as much as school administration is willing to help us out, in exchange we can kind of wait or bend our procedures to help them. So, we're not going to go to class and rip this kid out because that's not what school administration wants to do. So, we'll let them call the parents and have this kid come down, kind of thing."

What was the value to the Peel Police of having an SRO to work with on that issue?

> "And without that, I think to coordinate someone from the Road to get to the school, to go find school administration, to get the barrier over what they're looking for and go through all those steps that we've already cemented over the past couple years, would take longer than 15 minutes . . . And that kid could be gone. He had a concert, he was going to some concert that day. We wouldn't have found him until maybe the next day . . ."

Value to Peel Police of Having an SRO Work with Them on this Issue

What value do other units in Peel Police realize because of the SRO program? While the reader has likely gotten an appreciation for the answer to this question from reading the above scenarios, we also have data that speak to the SROs' impressions of the value they add. The SROs themselves identify several ways that they add value. First, the personal relationships that they have formed with members of the school community (students, administrators) facilitate the collection of important intelligence and information (i.e., students are only willing to talk to police that they know and trust). Second (and as a direct consequence of the first), their ability to tap into their personal networks and gather information that would otherwise have been time consuming or impossible for other police officers to acquire increases the efficiency of police investigations as well as solvency rates (i.e., and investigations experience fewer delays and take less time).

Quality of the Collaboration

All but one of the officers we interviewed described the quality of the collaboration between themselves and other units within Peel Police as being excellent or very good. Those who gave the collaboration positive ratings did so because they felt appreciated and valued (i.e., "So I'd go to SVU, the detectives' office, with information I had, and it's usually . . . thank you very much . . . pat on the back"), and because they felt that the officers in the other units had their backs (i.e., "if I need help or information they are there for me – just like I am there for them"). One officer felt that the quality of the relationship was okay. This officer felt that information from the other units was not adequately shared with the SRO unit.

Most Important Activities Undertaken by SROs: The SROs' Perspectives

Our work with the SROs revealed that these officers perform a multitude of different activities each week (see Chapter 3). We asked a number of questions in the interview to help us determine which of these activities the officers think are the most useful or important. More specifically, we asked: "What do you feel are the three most important activities you perform as an SRO? Why are each of these activities important? What value do they add?"

SROs at each of our five schools were in complete agreement that the most important activities performed by the SRO involved:

- *Relationship building*: Actions that encourage positive relationships to be developed and maintained between the police, students, staff, and community members (e.g., engaging in conversations, asking questions, listening).
- *Enhancing visibility*: Activities that increase the visibility of the SRO in the school and the community (e.g., walking the school with the administrators, patrolling the community, being present at school events and functions).

The following comment illustrates the SROs perspective on these two activities:

> "Presence. Just presence and socializing with the staff and students. Building relationships and trust. I don't know, it kind of ties into other things like crime prevention, right? Being present prevents crime."
>
> "One I think is walking the school with the administration. I think the value of that is you're there, you're with the kids, you're trying to break the barriers as far as showing police in a positive light. But at the same time, while you're doing that, you can gather the intel . . . you can see who hangs out with who. You can kind of see where groups hang out, the layout of the school. If there's an emergency happening, you'll be ready to go. That activity I think is very important. That way you know the kids, you know who they hang out with . . . you're breaking barriers, helping to make students see police in a positive light as well as you're out in the school, and getting to know the layout."

There was less agreement on the third activity to include in the list of top three, with the following activities all being identified by three SROs: collaborating with students, staff, and other police units to make the schools safer; educating students and staff on the role of the police and the law, and intelligence gathering to proactively deal with crime; and solving crimes (i.e., more traditional police work). It is interesting to note that the SROs awarded more importance to activities associated with preventing crime than activities typically considered part of policing (law enforcement).

Why Are these Activities Important? What Value Do They Add?

Officers gave four reasons for identifying these activities as critically important to effective enactment of the SRO role: (1) they deter crime/misbehavior, (2) they create a sense of trust between the police and the community, (3) they enhance feelings of safety in the school and in the community, and (4) they facilitate more effective police work in a number of ways, including the gathering of community intelligence that can expedite the solving of a crime and reduce police response times.

Each of the four activities adds value in a number of ways, as shown in Table 6.1 and discussed below.

The value of activities supporting relationship building: All of the officers we talked to felt that relationship building activities added value in a number of interrelated ways. More specifically, they talked about how relationship building fostered trust between the SRO, high school students, and school administration:

> "I can almost guarantee that my school hasn't called 911 in over a year, because they just call me . . . like major incidences have happened at the school, but they have so much trust and faith that I'll be there and show up and deal with it . . . they just call me directly."

They then linked the increased trust between themselves and the school to a number of indicators of enhanced police effectiveness,

> "I guess, I would hope at some level that it breaks down, like, any negative beliefs about the police, about us being, like, assholes or, like, authority junkies and stuff like that and . . . that they can approach us for things and the incidents or ten years down the road when something happens to them or they witness something that they wouldn't normally call the police, but they would because they believe just that we can be trusted . . . because they remember us."
>
> "Well, I think it's huge; I think it has a great value, because if we weren't there, there'd be numerous 911 calls, I'd say, at schools throughout the region. Having officers respond

TABLE 6.1 Activities deemed to be critically important to performance of SRO role

Value of these activities	*Activities that support:*			
	Relationship building	*Visibility*	*Collaboration*	*Education*
Deters misbehaviour				
Enhances police effectiveness: • Faster response • Enhanced intelligence gathering				
Fosters feelings of safety				
Creates trust				

> and liaise with the staff or speak with the students when there's no relationship between them ... with us having that relationship, that rapport, with the students and the staff, makes our investigation a whole lot easier . . . They talk to us, give us the heads up."
>
> "It's kind of that time saver too that kind of allows them to get what they need from the police without having to get on the phone or call an emergency or non-emergency, and then wait for an hour, two hours, for an officer."

and enhanced perceptions of safety:

> "It makes the school feel safer. It makes the staff feel safe knowing that they can come to us day or night . . . they've been able to contact us even on our days off . . . they trust us to deal with the incident, right? Like they always feel that they can contact us at any time and they're going to get the answer that they need . . . they feel safer because of the connection with us."

The value of being visible: The SROs felt that being visible in the school added value in a number of ways. They talked, for example, about how their being visible in the schools and the community deters misbehavior and criminal activity while at the same time enhancing perceptions of trust in the police:

> "Just our mere presence in the school . . . just that alone. I mean, who knows how much we deter just from that? How much bullying or criminal offences and misbehaviors do not happen because of us just being there."
>
> "I think foot patrol with school admin is extremely beneficial. Like, getting to know, like, kids' faces and it seems like you become more approachable the more you do it because you don't seem like an officer who's there to enforce something or to investigate something. Because sometimes they do ask oh, why are you here, because they think that you're there for an issue, but the more often they see you in the cafeteria and just hanging out and answering questions, the more approachable I believe that you appear . . . the more you appear just like a regular person, that you're not just like this authority figure."

The value of collaborations: The SROs felt that collaborations between the SRO, the school, and other units in Peel Police increased police effectiveness:

> "Information sharing for sure, and both ways. It seems like school admin is a plug for CIB and vice versa, the other way. When we hear that a student was arrested we let the school administration know and they can monitor him. For example, there's a kid . . . and CIB heard that this kid's involved in drug dealing, so they let the SRO know, who let the school admin know . . . there's no way CIB would just call the school . . . that would be non-existent. But having this two-way information sharing and the relationship . . . I think it helps out CIB and school administration equally."
>
> "They may have problems with social media or bullying, right? With us being there, we can help facilitate Crime Stopper presentations, anti-bullying presentations, have people from different bureaus like Youth Education come in and give those presentations, right? Sit down and mastermind like a plan of attack, a game plan of how we can fix whatever problems they have."

The value of education: The SROs felt that by spending time educating students, staff, and community members they reduced the amount of crime/misbehavior within the schools and the community while also enhancing police effectiveness and increasing feelings of safety within the school and the community:

> "I'd say educating the students on, you know, the role of police and things that they may not necessarily consider to be a criminal offence . . . and being able to educate them so they can make intelligent decisions."

> "Hopefully it's a deterrent, where they're going to think before they act because there is always a potential for criminal charges to be laid in a lot of circumstances."

> "I think the value is just awareness; like having those resources available to the schools to educate the kids, it just builds awareness."

Value Delivered by the SRO Program

This section summarizes key findings with respect to the value of this program as seen by the officers most intimately involved with the program at this time – the SROs themselves. The data covered in this section augments other discussions of value offered earlier in this chapter and elsewhere. The section is divided into two sections. In the first section, the discussion of value is situation specific. In the second section, we look more broadly at the value of the program to each of the key stakeholders described above.

Illustration of the Value of the SRO

We asked our SROs to describe a specific situation that they felt provided a good illustration of the value that comes from Peel Police's SRO program. Analysis of the situations identified by each pair of officers provided us with a wealth of rich data to help us better appreciate the many ways that this program makes a difference. In the section below, we first summarize one narrative for each of the high schools in the study. We then identify the various sources of value illustrated by these descriptions.

Situation One: The situation involved a gang problem that had previously led to regular fights between three schools. SROs were able to prevent the fights from taking place through a visible presence after school and in the community ("we would flood the areas"; "stick around our schools"):

> "So, at the beginning of the school year we had somewhat of a gang problem involving three different schools . . . and within a few weeks there'd be almost daily fights between the three schools. If it wasn't for the SROs being present and patrolling the area of those three schools, things might have gotten a lot worse. If we weren't there, there would have to be uniformed guys responding to calls . . . a reactive response instead of being proactive. With us there a lot of fights were avoided. We knew when these things were going to happen, and we were able to show up before the fights started and intercept. If we weren't there for those things . . . I mean, again, the only way police would be involved would be 911 calls from citizens observing kids fighting."

The SRO then spoke about how this situation illustrates the value of the program to stakeholders:

> "We were able to intercede and stop potential fights . . . these young students did not get arrested and gain criminal records for making bad decisions . . . you know we're catching kids with metal bars and knives and baseball bats . . . right? I mean, carloads of kids with

weapons in their trunks on the way to these fights, and we're able to stop them because we have the time to investigate the issue . . . to dedicate to the schools . . . Students potentially could have been killed. At the very least it seems like if they've got knives and bars and bats . . . then that's an Emergency Room visit for sure . . . And I think we definitely turned it around if not made it stop, because since then we haven't had any organized kind of gang street fighting with those schools involved."

Situation Two: This situation involved two SROs on patrol in the neighborhood around the school recovering a loaded firearm from a student who was in the back of a taxi in the area:

> "So we were on our way to the school and patrolling as we went. We saw this younger looking guy who wasn't wearing his seat belt, back of a taxi cab. So we pulled him over and he was just about to light a joint . . . and when we looked in the back seat we saw a loaded firearm in his backpack . . . Just someone at traffic, stopped, a loaded firearm."

According to the SROs this situation illustrates the following ways in which the program provides value to stakeholders:

> "So our presence at the school allowed us to be proactive and led to a firearm being seized. And we're not the only ones who've done that . . . there have been other SROs . . . from our division alone there's been about three or four firearms that were seized just last year."

Situation Three: Situation three involved a series of robberies that were happening in a nearby green space. SROs recognized the suspect descriptions from witness reports matched the descriptions of students who became known to the SROs after they were called in to investigate a fight that had occurred at the school. Investigation of this fight resulted in the SROs identifying the group of friends who were committing the robberies and arresting them. This stopped the robberies:

> "There was a group of 'our students' . . . there were four of them . . . and every day they would rob somebody in the green space around the school. They would pick a target and they would rob them . . . Basically we had 11–12 robberies over a span of two weeks. And then we [the SRO and his/her partner] got involved . . . we knew the robberies were happening . . . but we had nothing to go on in terms of who these guys were, how to track them down. At the same time, there was a student at the school we were dealing with and he was involved in a fight . . . nothing major, but the principal asked us to try and locate him as he had left the school before the administrators could talk to him . . . so we went looking for him. All we wanted to do was talk to him . . . and so we went to XXX [green space near the school] because we know that's a hang out spot, and we ended up finding the kid . . . he was with these three other guys . . . a group of four . . . and we were able to look at them and put it all together. We knew them as individuals through the school but we'd never made the connection to them as a group of friends . . . seeing them all together hanging out at a place which actually backs onto the green space where all these robberies were happening . . . that was kind of the click . . . they're all hanging out right where these robberies are happening. We started looking at and reading over these reports of all these robberies and realized, wait, they're describing one guy who's really, really tall and skinny, well that's that guy. Then describing another guy who's a little bit shorter, well that's that

> guy. And . . . that's that guy. So then knowing who they all were from seeing them at the school . . . it just it came together real quick . . . and we arrested them for 12 counts of robbery. And that's that . . . And there hasn't been a robbery since, they were all arrested. So they stopped completely. Went from 12 robberies to none."

This situation illustrates the following ways in which the SRO provides value to stakeholders:

> "So the value is that we were able to read the reports of crimes in the community and make that bridge . . . That connection . . . general knowledge of the school . . . we were able to put it together pretty quick . . . If this program wasn't here, you would have had probably different officers on different days dealing with the different incidents . . . it would be hard to make this connection, even for a really good investigator, it'd be a big leap . . . But it's easy when we're there every day, and we already know who they are. You know, it took us about a day."

Situation Four: This situation involved a known drug trafficking problem in the school. The SROs were able to resolve the problem and remove the traffickers from the school through investigation and prosecution:

> "Sure, when we first started at school X two years ago, they had a significant drug problem – marijuana and cocaine – and this was something that was identified to us by not only school administrators, but also by outside informants as well. So we identified that as a problem and conducted an investigation. We ended up making arrests of the people who were trafficking, and those people were prosecuted. They also were removed from the school. Since that time, we have not had any more issues of that degree, other than the one-offs here and there, but we have not had a significant organized drug problem in the school as far as we know."

According to the SROs, this situation illustrates the following source of value to stakeholders:

> "Our presence there shows that there is enforcement of the law when it comes to drug dealing. . . and I think it makes people wary of doing those kinds of things when they know the police are going to be walking around the school and you know, walking into bathrooms and walking into change rooms . . . the places they deal."

Situation Five: This situation involved resolving a threat of violence made against the school. SROs were able to resolve the concern by using information they had about the personal relationships of the students to identify the source of the threat and stop him:

> "We're basically on an 'on-call' basis with our school admin. Any time there's an issue they can call us. They don't call the Road, they don't call the office, they call us and we come in and deal with it. And I was just about on my way to work, actually, and I got a call from XXX [vice principal at this school] and he said that he had heard about a threat against the school where someone's going to basically come and shoot up the school with a shotgun. The rumor was very vague, but he heard it through a student. And he was coming in early to see what was going on. So, knowing that this was going on, I just put my uniform on and headed down there. He had already called 911 at this point and even though I hadn't started work yet, I acted as kind of a liaison between him and the rest of the guys on the Road and we ended up going and picking up this guy after finding out who it was . . . in the end, he was arrested for that threat against the school."

This situation illustrates the following ways in which the SRO provides value to stakeholders:

> "We started with a rumor, someone walked into the office, and worked backwards all the way to the person who was the source of the threat and the only reason we could do that was we had the knowledge of who knows who and who hangs out with who and where do they live . . . we could do this but uniform couldn't . . . because we're familiar with that school."

To summarize, the above stories illustrate a number of ways in which the SRO program provides value, the most common of which (mentioned by the officers in four out of five schools) include:

- the visibility of the SRO in the school acts as a deterrent to crime in the school (gang violence, threats, drug trafficking, gun seizure);
- the relationships that the SRO has developed in the schools (knows students, trusted by the administrators) means that these officers are able to gather intelligence (knowledge, information) that makes it possible for the police to either prevent crimes from occurring and/or enforce the law in a timely fashion;
- the SRO's ability and willingness to divert students rather than charge them reduces the number of young people in the community with criminal records and helps keep kids in school; and
- the SRO reduces the number of young people experiencing physical harm by preventing violence and controlling the number of firearms in the community.

Value the SRO Program Offers to Different Stakeholders

We concluded this section of the interview by asking SRO officers: "What value does the SRO program provide to: students, school administrators, the community, Peel Police, and you personally"?

The Value of the SRO to the Community and School Stakeholders

Data on the value the SRO program is perceived to provide to the students and school administrators in Peel Region, along with the communities surrounding these schools, are summarized in Table 6.2. For school and community stakeholders, much of the value of the SRO program

TABLE 6.2 Value of SRO to students, administrators, and the community

Value of these activities	*Value to following stakeholders*		
	Students	*Administrators*	*Community*
Positive relationships with police			
Crime prevention			
Feeling of safety at school and in the community			
Police are able to do their job more efficiently			
Avoidance of criminal record			
Important source of intelligence and information			
Support in managing problematic students			

arises from the personal relationships they develop with the SROs who work in their school/community. These personal relationships deliver value in a number of ways:

- they provide stakeholders with a resource that they can easily consult if they need information or advise on matters of the law;
- they make it easier for students and citizens to see the police as someone they can talk to if they have a problem rather than someone to fear; and
- they increase the level of trust between these key community stakeholders and the police, which has value in that it increases the likelihood these individuals will seek help from the police or share information with the police as required.

As one SRO put it:

> "The students find out that they can approach me, trust me, and they realize that we [the police] aren't bad people, right? We can hopefully start getting rid of the stigma of how officers are looked at these days."

Community and school stakeholders also agree that the SRO provides value by preventing crime within the school/community (fights, drugs, and robberies in particular). They noted several mechanisms by which the presence of the SRO in their communities reduces crime, including factors we have highlighted before (e.g., the SRO is a deterrent, the SRO can intercept and stop a crime from happening) and others that have been flagged less frequently (e.g., the SRO is able to intervene early with troubled youth and guide them towards more positive behavior). No matter how it happens, all agree that having the SRO in their community makes it a safer place. This results in another outcome that all stakeholders value – an increased sense of safety and security (i.e., peace of mind). This source of value is hard to quantify, but easier to appreciate by reading the following set of quotes from officers:

> "I think it's just a matter of peace of mind for them as well. You know . . . knowing that your kid is happy to come to school and feel safe."
>
> "I think it provides parents with some sense of safety knowing that their kids that they send to school every day have police officers that are allocated to their schools, and that can deal with things right away instead of being you know, five, ten minutes away . . . They are there to deal with something like a stabbing or a possible shooter in the school."
>
> "I think it should help with the community being a lot safer as well as we know the area. Also we'll be in the streets around the area, and just quick response time, knowledge of the kids and who's doing the criminal activity, I think that's what the community kind of values from the program."

Finally, school and community stakeholders receive value from the fact that the consistent presence of the SRO at the school, and in the environment around the school, facilitates more effective police work because of any or all of the following factors: faster response time ("we are right there") and an increased ability to effectively investigate crimes that can be attributed to intelligence gathered through consistent contact with community members and knowledge of the community.

We also identified one way that the SRO uniquely provides value to high school students in the region: diversion. SROs agreed that their ability to put a student into a diversion program provides real value to "the good kids in the school who get carried away and do something stupid" in that their rash actions do not result in a criminal record that would follow them for the rest of their lives. The following quote illustrates the value students realize by having a police officer "know their backstory" and make decisions accordingly:

> "And we have an investment in these kids, too. Like XXX . . . He's a good kid, and he'll . . . I mean, if he can figure it out he'll probably be pretty successful in life. Like he's a smart kid, he's charismatic. He's got a lot of things going for him, but if he didn't have somebody who was invested in him, who wanted to see him succeed from a police point of view, I mean, he'd probably already have a handful of criminal charges. You know, he'd be fighting an uphill battle already. Where at this point he's made it this far with, you know, a clean record, and we are working to make sure he gets out of high school without [spoiling that], so . . . It depends on him. But he's a lot better off that he's got officers in school who know him and can work with him . . ."

Finally, the SROs identified two ways that they add value for the school's administrators: (1) they are an important source of information and intelligence on the law, how police operate, and what their students are doing outside of the time they are in school, and (2) they provide invaluable support for administrators who are having difficulties enforcing school rules and managing the behavior of problematic students. Greater details on these two sources of value can be found in the chapter on school administrators (see Chapter 5) as they, too, mentioned these activities as being of great value to them.

The Value of the SRO to the Peel Police

According to the officers we spoke to, the SRO provides value to the Peel Police in the following three ways. First, the program reduces the demands placed on uniform patrol officers by reducing call volume and the number of 911 calls:

> "You're not having to hire a whole bunch of extra officers to be able to deal with the call volume, because the call volume on a road officer would increase drastically if there was not a specific officer assigned to each school. So they're saving money in that way, I think."

Second, it improves Peel Police's investigation process by helping investigative officers in the robbery, drugs, and special victim units make connections and gather information in a timely fashion. Much of the intelligence provided by the SRO depends on the relationships they have built up over time and would be difficult or impossible to gather in any other way ("being around, you pick up little pieces of information that later fit together"):

> "I think it gives the service better opportunity to investigate an incident properly."

Finally, the program helps develop a positive image of Peel Police within their communities:

> "It helps the public relations. It gets us out there. It allows people to speak to you . . . it humanizes us . . . and I really think that it helps build better relationships between the community and the police service."

The Value to the SRO

Officers working in the SRO program report that they benefit personally from the role they play in many ways. First, they all mentioned that they find it personally very fulfilling when they are able to make a real difference in the lives of the students that they interact with:

> "And I think that there's occasions where we do make a real difference . . . most of the time that's in relation to like one specific student, right? I mean, you may have a student that may be hanging out with a group of say, thugs, and he might have some drugs on him or weapons; we pull him to the side. We have a good talking to him, and he realizes that, you know, like what am I doing? Why am I hanging out with these guys? I'm going to land myself in trouble. And then he, you know, disassociates from these people."

Second, they appreciate and value the personal relationships they develop in the course of their work and their ability to help people see police in a different, more positive light ("we can show the person behind the badge") as well as engage with people who help them appreciate why they took the job in the first place ("we get to work with some good people, whereas on patrol we often only deal with people who have committed a crime").

Finally, the SRO benefits by holding a job that develops key skills, such as how to deal with students, communicate with a variety of different audiences, work collaboratively with both the police and the community, and gain experience with investigations. Officers believe that the skills they gain from the job of SRO prepare them for other desirable positions within Peel Police (e.g., investigative units) and help them advance within the service.

Evaluation of the SRO: The View from Within

We included one final set of questions to augment the others noted above and obtain a more comprehensive sense of the value of having a police officer assigned on a full-time basis to each of the high schools located in Peel Region: "What if police officers were not in high schools on a daily basis?"

What if Police Officers Were not in High Schools on a Daily Basis?

All of the officers we talked to identified three things that they thought would increase and three that they thought would decrease if SROs were not in high schools on a daily basis.

What would increase? The SROs said that drug use (smoking weed in particular), drug trafficking, and thefts would increase, as would the amount of violence, particularly in the form of fights, on school property.

> "I think just our mere presence in the schools deters a lot of crime from happening. I think, without us there, problem students would probably feel they need to act out more . . . we could potentially stop something from happening before it starts, rather than just responding to a call that's happening."

Not only would the amount of crime in the schools increase, according to the SROs, so would the amount of crime in the community, as students skipped classes, trespassed, and engaged in other forms of criminal behavior.

Finally, the SROs were unanimous that, if they were removed from the high schools, the workload of uniform patrol officers would increase, as would time spent on calls for service to the schools.

> "I think it would increase the workload on the road, on the patrol officers, because the issues at the schools take a lot of time; they take a lot of investigation, and to be using patrol officers off the road, there's only so many, and also they're also dealing with all the regular call volume as well as calls from the school and they would likely not be able to get to the schools right away."

What would decrease? Interviewees agreed that, without SROs in the schools, there would be a decrease in the number of preventative interventions undertaken with high school students in the region (i.e., "no one there to prevent the escalation of misbehavior"). They also said that the number of diversions would also decline, as uniform patrol would have less knowledge of the context in which the misconduct occurred and be more likely to charge the culprit with a criminal offense. Almost all the officers also felt that taking the SROs out of the school would mean less intelligence available for other police bureaus. Finally, one pair of officers felt that removal of officers from the high schools would mean there was "one less resource in the high schools to deal with special concerns like mental health."

Should the SRO Program Continue in its Current Form?

One hundred percent of the SROs we interviewed responded that they thought the SRO program should continue in its current format:

> "I think yes, absolutely, I think they should keep it, and I think it speaks for itself."

The reasons for this opinion were varied. Most commonly, SROs justified their response by pointing to the program's track record of success. They noted that the SRO program is well run and that the SROs "make a difference" and "problems get fixed." They talked about how the community appreciates them, how they are able to build valuable positive relationships between schools, the community, and police, and how their presence in the school increases the sense of safety among students, administrators, and parents:

> "I believe that we have made a difference . . . whether it's to, you know, change the behavior of one student in the school or to help students feel that the school is a safe place . . . This is because there's a police officer who spends most of their time in the school – right? The staff love us there; I think . . . even for the parents it's just like knowing that the police are in the school gives them a sense of security. With everything that's been in the news . . . like, mass killings, school shootings, terrorism . . . I think it's a plus."

Half the officers also felt that the SRO program ensures that Peel Police officers are aware of what is going on in the school and the surrounding community. This awareness has two possible benefits. First, this knowledge improves the police's ability to deal quickly and effectively with any emergency in the school. Second, this knowledge serves as an important source of intelligence for other Peel Police units as they seek to investigate criminal occurrences in the school and the community.

Possible Changes to the Program

Not surprisingly, given the positive view of the SRO program expressed by these officers, there was little that they felt was problematic about the program:

> "I really don't think I would change anything; I'm pretty happy with the way the programs run."

Only two issues were mentioned. The first (noted by officers at one school) related to these officers' sense of obligation to respond to any request of them made by the school, however minor. These officers felt that sometimes the schools use the police to circumvent "their own bureaucratic processes." The second problematic issue (noted by officers at two schools) related to the lack of officer coverage of the school in the evenings and on weekends (coverage is limited to school hours). One challenging offshoot of this schedule was that there was no SRO available to respond to problems with students that happen overnight or on the weekends. These issues tended to be dealt with by uniform patrol. The SROs worried that these officers would not deal with the situation in the same way that they did because of their lack of familiarity with the students. The officers that raised this issue stated that they would change the way that the schedules were designed so that there were more SRO officers on duty during evening and weekend time periods:

> "I think probably just getting more flexibility in the schedule. I like the difference between days and afternoons, 7 to 3 and 12 to 8, to have that coverage between 7 a.m. and 8 p.m., but the inability to switch to a weekend to look after kind of those things, like when we have, like, a drug dealer at one of our schools that we're supposed to tackle . . . it's a problem that we're restricted to Monday to Friday, 7 a.m. to 8 p.m. So, any night time drug dealing, any weekend drug dealing is untouched . . . so I think the schedule is the number one thing for me."

Summary and Conclusions

This research initiative had one main objective in mind: to identify, and where possible quantify, the value that Peel Police's SRO Program offers to key stakeholders, including students and administrators working in the region's high schools, communities surrounding these schools, Peel Police, and the SROs themselves. This section summarizes key findings with respect to the value of this program as seen by the officers most intimately involved with the program – the SROs.

Activities that Deliver Value

The SROs identified four ways in which they perceive that they add value:

- They engage in relationship building activities, which add value by: (1) increasing the extent to which high school students and school administration trust the police, and (2) enhancing perceptions of safety.
- The fact that they are visible within the school delivers value by: (1) deterring misbehavior and criminal activity, and (2) enhancing relationship building and helping increase trust in the police.
- Collaborations between the SRO, the school, and other units in Peel Police bring value by increasing police effectiveness.
- By spending time educating students, staff, and community members, SROs provide value by: (1) reducing the amount of crime/misbehavior within the schools and the community, (2) enhancing police effectiveness, and (3) increasing feelings of safety within the school and the community.

Collaboration between SROs and School Administrators Add Value

All of the SROs we talked to collaborated with the administrators at their school on a daily basis. Analysis of the data showed that these collaborations were either proactive and preventive in nature, or reactive interactions that involved enforcement. Proactive collaborations outnumbered interactions with a reactive/enforcement flavor by a ratio of two to one.

Analysis of the interview data supports the following conclusions about the nature of the collaborations that occur between SROs and school administrators, as well as the impact these collaborations have on key school and community stakeholders.

Collaboration is required in a variety of different situations, many of which are quite complex. While some relate to an SRO's ability to enforce the law, others are illustrative of proactive efforts to prevent a crime or injury, or combine elements of the two. In all cases, however, the fact that the SRO was present in the school helped prevent any or all of the following from occurring:

- the student from getting a criminal record;
- students getting injured or perhaps even dying (fights, drug overdoses);
- property damage (to the school or in the community);
- the school from having to call 911 and wait for the police to arrive at the school;
- Peel Police having to take officers from the road and send them to the school in response to a call for service; and
- students with mental heath issues being unable to get help.

In other words, the value of having an SRO assigned on a full-time basis to high schools in Peel District is realized in a number of different ways by a number of different stakeholders.

Value of the SRO Program to the School and Community Stakeholders

The data strongly support the following conclusions with respect to the value that accrues to schools, communities, and society from SRO programs such as the one implemented in Peel Region:

- The presence of the SRO in the school helps prevent or deter crime in the school and surrounding areas (fights, drugs, and robberies in particular) in the following three ways:
    - the SRO acts as a deterrent (people think before they act when they see the police);
    - the SRO intercepts and stops crimes from happening; and
    - the SRO intervenes early with troubled youth and helps guide them towards more positive behavior.
- The SRO is present in the school and/or in the community and can act quickly to reduce the severity of crimes/de-escalate problematic situations.
- SROs are more able (and more likely) to recommend diversion to students when appropriate. This gives young people a chance for a meaningful future as it reduces the likelihood that a student will get a criminal record.
- The presence of the SRO in the school helps prevent or minimize property damage in the school and surrounding areas.
- The presence of the SRO in the school reduces the likelihood that a student will suffer physical or psychological harm when at school by reducing the incidence of physical violence, bullying, and cyberbullying.
- The presence of the SRO in the school increases the likelihood that students will get the help they need from the social service and health care systems.
- SROs provide school and community stakeholders with a resource that they can easily consult if they need information or advice on matters of the law.

- SROs make it easier for students and citizens to see the police as someone they can talk to if they have a problem rather than someone to fear.
- SROs increase the level of trust between key community stakeholders and the police, which increases the likelihood these individuals will seek help from the police or share information with the police as required.
- The SRO's knowledge of the community and the school enhances their ability to effectively investigate criminal activity in the area.
- The SROs provide school administrators with important information on what their students are doing outside of the time they are in school, as well as provide information about the law and how the police operate.
- The SROs provide invaluable support for administrators who are having difficulties enforcing school rules and managing the behavior of problematic students.

The Value of the SRO to the Peel Police

The data strongly support the following conclusions with respect to the value realized by Peel Police from the SRO program:

- The personal relationships that the SRO has formed with members of the school community (administrators, students) facilitates the collection of intelligence and information that is valuable to other units within Peel Police.
- The SROs can use their social networks to obtain information and intelligence that would have been time consuming or impossible for other police officers to acquire. The following units seem to gain the most value from the SROs' ability to make connections and gather information: robbery, drugs, and special victims.
- The presence of the SROs in the schools and the SROs' information networks decrease the number of 911 calls and calls for service coming from the high schools.
- Proactive policing in the high schools decreases the total number of investigations required.
- The actions taken by the SRO increases the efficiency of police investigations as well as solvency rates (i.e., investigations experience fewer delays and take less time).

The Value of the SRO to the SRO

SROs working in the SRO report that their job offers them a number of benefits that they personally value:

- they find the job personally very fulfilling;
- they enjoy the fact that their job and how they behave helps people see police in a different, more positive light;
- they benefit from the opportunity to engage with average citizens. This gives them a more complete perspective of who lives in their community;
- performance of the SRO job helps them develops key skills, such as how to deal with students, communicate effectively with a variety of different audiences, work collaboratively with both the police and the community, and gain experience with investigations. Officers believe that the skills they gain from the job of an SRO prepare them for other desirable positions within Peel Police (e.g., investigative units) and help them advance within the service.

What Would Change if Police Officers Were not in High Schools on a Daily Basis?

Finally, a list of what would and would not happen if the SRO was not in the schools on a daily basis provides us with yet another set of indicators of the value of this program. Officers agreed that if they were not in the schools, the following negative outcomes would increase:

- drug use (smoking weed in particular), drug trafficking and thefts, and the amount of violence, particularly in the form of fights that occurred in the schools;
- crime in the community as students skip classes, trespass, and engage in other forms of criminal behavior;
- the workload of uniform patrol officers (more 911 calls); and
- police response time to the schools.

while the following positive outcomes would decline:

- the number of preventative interventions undertaken with high school students in the region;
- the number of diversions; and
- the amount of intelligence available for other Peel Police units.

Note

1 www.thebramptonnews.com/articles/1836/1/Peel-Regional-Police-SPEAR-Program/Page1.html

7

THE VALUE OF SROS

Views from Above (Staff Sergeants)

police patrol
officers collaborations collaboration calls skills
program students reduces trust
role investigation ability encouraging
Value Drugs service support
officer strong SRO work
relationships benefits Robbery
Victims
good young schools law
activities community
crime positive social
information
school
sergeants

WordMap: 35 most common words in Chapter 7: "The Value of SROs: Views from Above (Staff Sergeants)"

Key Learnings

Police staff sergeants take on the role of front-line supervisors in police services. As such, their views of the value offered by the School Resource Officer (SRO) program is critical to our evaluation. This chapter presents key findings from our interviews with 11 Peel Police staff sergeants who had high familiarity with the SRO program.

Most Important Activities Undertaken by the SRO: The Staff Sergeant's Perspective

Virtually all of the staff sergeants interviewed agreed that three sets of activities were critical to the role of SRO:

- activities directed to building strong positive relationships between the police, students, and school staff, such as spending time interacting with students and liaising with staff;
- activities that actively involve the SRO in the community, such as going to events, being seen around the neighborhood, and participating in outreach activities; and
- education, such as delivering presentations in the school and community on how the law views issues of importance or relevance (e.g., bullying, cyberbullying, drugs).

Value Delivered by the SRO Program: The Staff Sergeant's Perspective

Staff sergeants identified the following ways that the NPU and the SROs offer value:

- *Gives police access to information that they cannot get any other way*: The trust the SRO has built up within the school creates cooperation between the school and the police and encourages students and school staff to share what they have heard/know.
- *Increases the efficiency of police investigations*: The relationship the SRO has with the school reduces the amount of time that the police need to spend in information gathering, which contributes to a reduction in the total amount of time required to investigate an infraction.
- *Increases awareness of criminal activity in Peel region*: The SROs' information network ensures that these officers hear about criminal activities that would otherwise remain unreported. The SROs report these crimes to the appropriate unit for investigation, which reduces the amount of unsolved crime in the region.
- *Prevention of crime*: The information gathered by the SROs helps the police intervene and prevent a crime from occurring (e.g., robbery, drug trafficking).
- *Mitigation of harm*: SROs offer education and counselling, which helps to mitigate the harm resulting from negative activities, such as bullying, cyberbullying, fighting, and drugs. These interventions also increase perceptions of safety in the student population.
- *Extra resources*: SROs offer a source of skilled back-up when needed (often during a crisis).
- *Diversion*: When a youth commits a crime, SROs can use their discretion to intercede without laying charges. Diversion offers value in two ways. First, it prevents or stops criminal activity within the school and community. Second, it reduces the number of young people with criminal records.
- *Career development*: Collaboration with the community, other police units, and community associations develops the skill base of the SRO and helps them learn the role of investigator more quickly and efficiently.

- *Increases the efficiency of the service overall*: SROs are more able to prioritize a call from the school correctly. This results in a reduction of calls for service associated with false emergency situations that need to be attended by uniform patrol. The program also reduces the total number of calls for service to patrol, as the school staff call the SRO directly when they require police services rather than 911.
- *Enhances the reputation of the service*: The positive interactions that SROs have with schools, teachers, and school boards demonstrate that Peel Police cares about the community.

Police sergeants and staff sergeants take on the role of first-line or front-line supervisors in police services, and are generally recognized to hold one of the most important roles in any police department. To be successful, staff sergeants must act on behalf of the police department and its leaders, train and develop the officers under their command, coordinate the efforts of the officers in their section, coordinate the efforts of the officers in their units with the work of officers in other units, place employees in positions appropriate to their capabilities and interests, resolve any internal conflicts, be they personal or job-oriented, and provide leadership to the officers in their unit by taking on the management functions of planning, organizing, directing, and controlling. They must also evaluate the effort of those who work under their command and correct any deficiencies. The roles and responsibilities of those working as staff sergeants uniquely positions these officers to comprehensively pass judgment on the value of those officers working within the Neighborhood Police Unit (NPU) – SROs.

Accordingly, in January and February 2016, we conducted interviews with 11 Peel Police staff sergeants who had high familiarity with the SRO program. More specifically, we interviewed the four staff sergeants who directly supervised the efforts of the SROs who worked in the five schools that were participating in this study (i.e., staff sergeant – NPU). These four officers work in three different Divisions (11, 21, 22) within Peel Police. We also interviewed a staff sergeant in charge of administration (i.e., administrative staff sergeant) who interfaced with the SROs in our study, as well as the other staff sergeants in terms of scheduling. Finally, we interviewed six staff sergeants who represent units (or bureaus) within Peel Police whose work is likely to be impacted by the work of the SRO (i.e., Robbery, Drugs, Special Victims, Street Crime, and Uniform Patrol).

The 30- to 60-minute interviews were conducted in person at one of Peel Police's buildings, recorded, and transcribed. The same interview script was followed in all cases. Interviews were content coded using the methodology outlined in Cooper and Schindler (2006), and the responses examined for commonalities of views and opinions. Many of the staff sergeants provided multiple answers to a number of interview questions, which explains why response frequencies often exceed 11. Please note that, to maintain confidentiality, we do not attribute the quotes to any one type of officer.

To help us interpret the data, we started the interview by asking the 11 staff sergeants in our sample for information about themselves and their background. The sample was well distributed with respect to the number of years these officers had spent in their current role: four had been in their position for approximately six months, five had spent 12–18 months in their current job, and two had almost two years' experience in the role.

We then asked the 11 staff sergeants in our sample to describe their job and tell us what their job entailed. These officers stated that they engaged in the seven different activities highlighted in Table 7.1. The activities undertaken by the four officers who manage the work of the SROs working in the schools in our study are shaded in this table.

TABLE 7.1 What does your job as staff sergeant entail?*

What does your job as a staff sergeant entail?	*n*	*% of sample*
Supervise and manage officers in my unit	11	100%
Supervision of officers responding to calls for service by allocating resources appropriately	4	36%
Supervision of officers conducting investigations by providing access to information and other units in the police service	4	36%
Provide personal and professional support to staff	4	36%
Provide oversight and quality control of operations	4	36%
Provide the administrative functions of management to ensure accepted procedures are followed	3	28%
Engage with community	3	28%

* Shaded rows represent activities that were undertaken by all NPU staff sergeants

All of the staff sergeants in our sample supervised and managed the work of the officers in their unit (i.e., manage a team of officers, manage a special unit, run parade). Just over one in three perform one or all of the following four job functions: supervise calls to service (i.e., law enforcement, traffic, drugs), supervise investigations (i.e., robbery, drugs, gangs, special victims), provide personal and professional support to the staff under their command (i.e., offer advice, be a sounding board, facilitate the exchange of information), and provide oversight for operations undertaken within their unit (i.e., hold officers accountable, do performance evaluations, give feedback about performance, set goals). Three officers provide administrative oversight (i.e., review reports, process evidence, staff the unit) and also undertake activities to encourage community engagement (i.e., attend community events, be involved in community activities, build relationships with key community partners).

The staff sergeants of the SROs in our sample engage in all but two of the activities we identified. They are also the only staff sergeants to indicate that they participate in activities that directly involve the community.

Familiarity with SRO Program: The officers in our sample all had a high level of familiarity with Peel Police's SRO program. This familiarity is not surprising given the fact that virtually everyone in the sample was either: (1) supervising SROs at the time the interview was being conducted, (2) had previously supervised within the NPU, and/or (3) had direct experience coordinating work between their unit and SROs. The fact that the SRO position is often a pathway to promotion is consistent with the fact that all but three of the staff sergeants we interviewed had worked as an SRO prior to their promotion. It is also interesting to note that four of the staff sergeants we talked to were one of the original SROs in the region (i.e., worked in the job 20 years ago). The rest had worked in the position more than a decade ago.

Changes in SRO program over time: The SRO program has been in place in the Peel Region for more than two decades. Given these officers long years of experience with the program, and with the Peel Police, we felt it appropriate to ask them if they had noticed any changes in the program over time. Six officers agreed that such changes had occurred and talked about how the SRO program had altered its focus over time so that the emphasis was now more on the officer's relationship and work with the schools and less on the neighborhood (i.e., "moved from stopping into schools once a week to stopping in daily"). Four other officers (those who had worked as an SRO more recently) felt that, although the focus of the program was essentially the same as when it started (i.e., "the core components have not changed"), subtle changes in operations had been implemented over time. Finally, one officer talked at length about the history of the SRO program:

> "I think we were known as a School Liaison Unit and the Chief at that time was Lunney and, I guess, just for budgetary reasons, he took the officers out of the schools and put them back in front line policing. And, I mean, the school board, they were not happy. They were even willing to pick up the cost of the salaries of the officers to keep them in the schools . . . And that protest lasted maybe a year or two and we started the programme back up and they were back in the schools."

This chapter includes eight sections. We begin by examining data that speak to what duties the staff sergeants we talked to perceive should be performed as part of the SRO role. In the second section we discuss the attributes and skills that the staff sergeants have found typify a "great SRO officer." The third section discusses the staff sergeants' views of the most important activities undertaken by the SRO, while the fourth and fifth sections examine data that speak to how officers in the NPU interact and collaborate with officers in other Peel Police units. The sixth section summarizes our key findings with respect to staff sergeants' assessments of the impact the SRO program has on the following stakeholders: the SROs themselves, Peel Police, and the schools/community. The interview included a number of questions designed to give us a fairly comprehensive understanding of how staff sergeants see the SRO program. These data are reviewed in the penultimate section. The chapter ends by summarizing key findings with respect to the value offered by the SRO program as articulated by the staff sergeants within Peel Police with high familiarity with the SRO role.

Duties of the SRO

We asked our 11 staff sergeants to describe what they understood to be the duties required of an SRO. Analysis of their responses produced a list that included the 12 activities shown in Table 7.2.

There was a high degree of consensus within our sample of staff sergeants with respect to half of the activities on this list. All staff sergeants agreed that the job of an SRO was to provide police services (i.e., law enforcement, patrolling, education) to secondary schools and the schools' catchment areas:

> "The idea is to form a strong bond between the officers assigned to the school and the students and staff there so that the officers can be aware of any issues playing out at the school that may impact the safety and tranquility of the school. They are also tasked to view the school as a component of the larger community and try to address any problems that might exist from a system standpoint if you will – how the school fits into the community."

The vast majority also agreed that the SRO should:

- act as a liaison between Peel Police and the administrative staff at the school: "They're responsible for most of the communication between the organisation [Peel Police] and the schools [administrators], and the community";
- investigate any issues occurring either at the school and/or in the community surrounding the school that students or staff bring to their attention;
- organize and/or attend activities within the school or in the community that bring the police and community together ("They're also involved in charitable events, like Cram-a-Cruiser, which is a food drive that we run every Christmas");
- educate those in the school and the surrounding community with respect to the law; and
- act as a resource for students (i.e., provide guidance on how to deal with situations).

TABLE 7.2 What are the duties of an SRO?

What are the duties of an SRO?	*n*	*% of sample*
To service secondary schools and the neighboring area around the school	11	100%
To liaise between the police and the administrative staff of the school	9	82%
To investigate issues brought to their attention by students and staff	8	73%
To organize and/or attend activities within the school or in the community	8	73%
To educate those within the school and/or in the community on issues of concern (e.g., prepare presentations on bullying, theft, the Criminal Code)	8	73%
To liaise between Peel Regional Police and the students	7	64%
To create a safe school environment through non-enforcement contact with staff and students	5	45%
To make proactive efforts to address problems in the school and in the community	5	45%
To attend to the specific needs of the community surrounding the school they are assigned to	3	27%
To operate as a uniform function	3	27%
To provide support and intelligence to other bureaus	3	27%
To project a positive image of the police service in schools	3	27%

This last activity was described by a staff sergeant as follows:

> "If you can identify a kid that's struggling or having some issues and you can hopefully find out what they are, and you can get them back on the right track or keep them from falling off the rails, so to speak, and getting involved in crime, then that's the primary mandate."

Half of the respondents felt that a key part of the SRO job was to create a safe school environment. Half felt that that the role of the SRO was to act proactively to address problems within the school. In both of these cases, the staff sergeants felt that the SRO's role was one that focused on prevention rather than enforcement, a sentiment that is illustrated by the following quote:

> "In most families both parents work full-time, and, in some cases, there is not much parental supervision, so getting the officers involved in the school, it's more of a proactive effort to have the officers involved in the schools to prevent things from happening rather than dealing with problems after the fact."

The final four aspects of the role of the SRO were identified by a minority (one in four) of our staff sergeants, none of whom, it should be noted, is currently supervising SROs. These officers felt that the SRO should modify what they do to reflect the social, economic, and cultural needs of the community surrounding the school they are assigned to, operate as a uniform function, provide support and intelligence to other bureaus (i.e., Homicide, Break and Enter, Drugs), and project a positive image of Peel Police in the schools and the community.

The following quote provides a vivid illustration of the myriad activities and responsibilities that the staff sergeants believe are part of the SRO role:

> "It's their responsibility to oversee their high schools, assist with general events, give school lectures and deal with any criminal activity that takes place in or around the school and neighboring area. They also identify at risk youth and attempt to work with the school to prevent them from entering the criminal justice system. They also look after issues that arise in classes and parks surrounding the school that may be affected by students travelling to and from the school."

Attributes of a Great SRO Officer

The SRO program is only as good as the officers who work within the unit. This poses the question: "What are the skills and attributes of a successful SRO?" We asked our staff sergeants to help us better understand this issue by asking them to identify for us what traits, skills, and qualities were key to success in the SRO role. Responses to this question are summarized in Table 7.3 and discussed below.

The vast majority of the staff sergeants that we talked to felt that all successful SROs had good interpersonal skills. They were friendly, approachable, personable, compassionate, and good listeners. All officers who gave this response talked about how such skills were critical to the officers' ability to establish trust with the students, parents, and school personnel that they had to deal with in the course of their duties. These characteristics also helped these officers engage with the students as necessary:

> "Communication is critical and the ability to problem solve collaboratively with the schools and the school system."

Half of the staff sergeants also felt that a good SRO officer was able to act independently. Along these lines, they described an officer who was disciplined, self-motivated, able to act responsibly without constant supervision, willing to take initiative, able to conduct his/her own investigations, and manage his/her time well. Such descriptors are consistent with the fact that SROs are "on their own" in the schools and must be self-sufficient and manage their time and tasks independently:

> "The ideal officer to have for this unit has a good work ethic . . . they're in to work on time. They look professional. They conduct themselves professionally, but they also have their heart attached to their brain."

Just under half of the staff sergeants felt that a successful SRO had good presentation skills. More specifically, they were articulate communicators who were good presenters and were able to think on their feet. This skill is seen as critically important, given the expectation that the SRO will deliver lectures and programs within the school they work in as well as the surrounding community:

> "The fact that they're liaising every day with the school staff and the students, they're going to need to have, for sure, great communication skills . . . an ability to conduct presentations, a high comfort level speaking, you know, in front of other people."

TABLE 7.3 Skills and attributes of a successful SRO*

Skills and attributes of a successful SRO	*n*	*% of sample*
Good interpersonal skills	8	73%
Able to work independently	6	54%
Good presentation skills	5	45%
Strong policing skills	5	45%
Good judgment	4	36%
Strong knowledge of legislation	4	36%
Professional	4	36%
Community conscious (have a vested interest in their school)	2	18%

* Shaded responses were mentioned by all NPU staff sergeants who are currently supervising an SRO

Most of the staff sergeants who were attached to units outside the NPU felt that SROs needed to be good police officers. They wanted an SRO who had enthusiasm for the investigation role, experience testifying in court, who had dealt and interacted with bureaus outside of Peel Police, who had worked as a uniform patrol officer, and had great performance indicators prior to getting the job of SRO. According to these officers, good team working skills would also be an asset in this job. This set of responses reflects what other units want from these officers – the ability to help them do their own jobs effectively and reliably.

All of the staff sergeants working within the NPU wanted an officer who was able to demonstrate good judgment. By this they meant an officer who was good at decision making, used common sense when making decisions, was able to do the tough parts of the job and the unpopular things when necessary, but also able to be flexible and use discretion as the situation warranted it:

> "You know they have to have enough common sense to realise that not everything has to be dealt with by a hammer, that you can if you get in there early enough, you can head off a lot of these issues before they escalate."

The last three attributes and skills were noted by a minority of the officers, all of whom worked outside the NPU. In these cases, officers felt it was important for an SRO to have a strong knowledge of legislation ("they have to know the law"), have a professional demeanor ("they are ambassadors for Peel Police"), and be willing to be involved with, and invest their time in, the community. The following comment again speaks to these attributes and skills:

> "You know, they can be dealing with thefts, assaults, minor robberies so they have to be current on the legislation and knowledge base."

Most Important Activities Undertaken by the SRO

As noted in Chapter 3, SROs perform myriad activities during the course of a week. We asked two questions in the interview with staff sergeants to help us determine which these activities are perceived to be most useful from the point of view of the staff sergeants. We asked: "In your opinion, what are the three most important activities undertaken by the SRO? Why are these activities important?" Answers to these questions are listed in Table 7.4 and discussed below.

Relationship Building

All of the staff sergeants we spoke to agreed that the most important activities of the SRO related to building strong positive relationships between the Peel Police and the high school

TABLE 7.4 Most important activities of the SRO*

Most important activities of the SRO	*n*	*% of sample*
Building relationships in schools	11	100%
Community involvement	8	73%
Education	6	54%
Intelligence gathering	3	27%
Visibility	3	27%
Law enforcement	2	18%

* Shaded responses were mentioned by all NPU staff sergeants who are currently supervising an SRO

communities operating within Peel Region. All agreed that it was critically important that the SRO spend time interacting with students, liaising with staff, and acting as a mentor and a resource to students and staff in the school to which they were assigned. Why do staff sergeants feel that relationship building is so important? According to the officers, such activities builds trust between the students and the police ("if we can remove the stigma attached to talking to the police, the kids will come to us with a problem") and between the police and parents who may be new immigrants and come from cultures where trust in the police is rare. Relationship building was also felt to help the police identify potential victims and work with them to reduce the likelihood that they would be harmed and increase their sense of safety. The following three quotes speak to the importance of such activities:

> "The most important thing they do is attending the schools and interacting with the students."

> ". . . with the multicultural component comes . . . new immigrants to the country who, you know, a lot of the immigrants come from countries where policing is not respected, it's not professional, and it can be very corrupt, absolutely, and very oppressive to society. So, it's important that the officers develop relationships, get their trust . . . you know, they've never experienced anything different, they just see police through their experiences before they came here."

> ". . . viewing of the school as a component of the community at large is tremendously important and again it all kind of relies on number one being successful in building those relationships."

Get Involved with the Community

Three-quarters of staff sergeants we interviewed felt that activities that visibly involved the SRO with the community (i.e., going to events, being seen around the neighborhood, participating in outreach activities) were critically important. They justified this pick by describing how such activities go a long way to improve the public image of the police in the community (i.e., "it's not just about putting handcuffs on people") as well as encouraging community members to cooperate with police investigations.

Education

Half the staff sergeants identified one last activity as belonging in the top three: education. They felt that it is critically important that the SRO deliver presentations and classes on how the law views issues of importance or relevance to students in the school. Examples of presentations seen as vital by this group of officers include: cyberbullying, anti-bullying, the internet and social media, drug dealing, and theft. They gave a number of reasons for selecting education as a critically important activity. First, they believe in the idea of "forewarned is forearmed" and argued that students who were educated in the law were more likely to be "kept out of the system" and less likely to commit crime. Second, they felt that education would increase students' ability to cope effectively with the problems that they faced in school and in the community.

There was no consensus with respect to other "important" activities. One in four felt that intelligence gathering in the community was an important activity, arguing that such information allowed the police to be more proactive and take actions to minimize the occurrence of crime. One in four staff sergeants noted that, above all else, the SRO had to be a visible presence within the school, not only because this would deter crime, but also because it would promote relationship building:

> "Information flows from the communication between officers, staff, and students – and that comes from being there to establish strong relationships within the school."

Finally, two staff sergeants felt that it was critical that the SROs enforce the law (i.e., timely response to calls for safety) even if that meant that they were diverted from the school to an area where the staff sergeants in patrol felt their presence was needed.

Interactions between SROs and Officers in Other Units

We asked several questions to help us understand how SROs fit into, and support, the work of other units within Peel Police. The focus here was on how often the SROs interacted with their counterparts in other units.

Frequency of Interactions between Staff Sergeants and SROs

We began by asking our officers to estimate how often they interacted with the SROs. Responses to this question are shown in Figure 7.1.

Examination of these data show that the number of interactions between the staff sergeants in our sample (and, hence, other units within the Peel Police) and the SROs varies from daily to monthly, depending on the role of the staff sergeant. Those who supervise the work of the SRO, the administrative staff sergeant, and one of the staff sergeants in Uniform Patrol stated that they talked with SROs on a daily basis. One individual (the staff sergeant working in the Street Crime unit) interacted with the SROs a couple of times a week. Officers in charge of Robbery and Special Victims units, along with the other staff sergeant in Uniform Patrol, interacted with the SROs less frequently (a couple of times a month). Finally, the staff sergeant in the Drugs unit stated that he did not interact directly with the SROs, but instead went through the chain of command if they wanted information from a particular SRO. The following quote illustrates this last response:

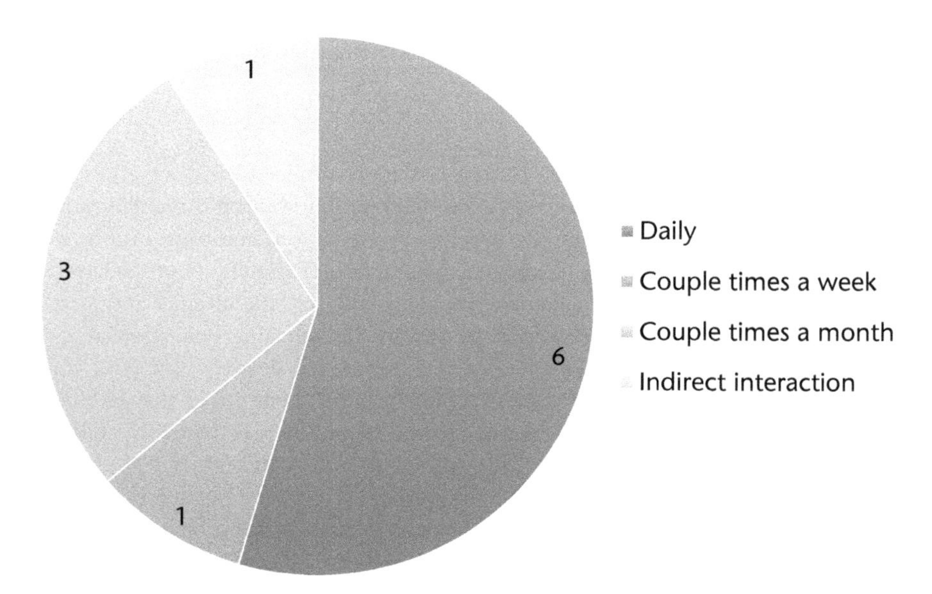

FIGURE 7.1 How often, on average, would you interact with the SROs? (n = 11)

> "I, myself, as a Staff Sergeant, would interact more with their supervisors. If I require them because there's a major call around a school or if it's a scene around the school such as a suicide at a lake, I can pull those officers and use them as security around that area instead of tying up my cars for hours while dive teams go in and search the lake."

These data support the following conclusion: SROs interact with many other bureaus in the police service on a regular basis.

The Nature of Interactions between SROs and Officers in Other Units

We then asked the staff sergeants to describe the nature of these interactions and coded the descriptions, as shown in Figure 7.2. Nine staff sergeants talked about how officers in their unit shared information with the SROs. Eight staff sergeants talked about how their officers (i.e., officers in Special Victims, Drug, and Street Crime units) liaised with the SROs during an investigation. The four NPU staff sergeants mentioned that the SROs often collaborated with other bureaus, most frequently officers in the Drug and Special Victims units. Finally, the officers working in Uniform Patrol and the administrative staff sergeant described situations where SROs were asked to provide backup/assist road officers in their enforcement activities. This was more likely to occur at the end of the school day when calls for service on the road are higher. The following quotes illustrate the complexity of many of these interactions:

> "It could be ranging from a missing person, to a school threat, to some sort of enforcement activity, to drug activity to, you know, lawless public behavior, to a robbery, the whole scope of events that can happen . . . can happen in a school setting or in and around the area. The SRO can have to work with other bureaus on any of these things."

> "Crime Stopper tips are managed through my office and when they involve students of the school or activities happening at that school, those are then forwarded to the respective NPU office where it's happening and then the SRO at the appropriate school. So, anything that's happening in the schools, drug-wise, we'll coordinate and deal with NPU in regards to that."

> "Actually, the SROs are a tremendous asset to our unit. We meet with them biweekly; we have a biweekly meeting with SROs for the purposes of sharing information. And I would say that, on average, we probably receive two or three phone calls a week from SROs that are passing information on just for further investigation. One of the areas that they're a real asset to us is . . . they monitor potential gang activity in the schools at youth level and make us aware of any potential trends that they may see or potential gang members . . . youth that are falling off the track."

The four staff sergeants who managed the SROs in 11th, 21st and 22nd Divisions also talked about interactions that were either: (1) more administrative in nature (e.g., reporting, giving instructions, parade, supervising timesheets, managing evidence and seizures, receiving prisoners and releasing them from custody) and/or (2) positive recognition of one of the officers under their command's performance and/or investigating complaints that came to their attention.

Finally, six staff sergeants (supervisors of the SROs and the staff sergeants of the Special Victims and Street Crime units) discussed more informal interactions where they talked to the SRO, either face-to-face or by phone/radio. These officers noted that they were either asking the SRO for their advice on something that they were dealing with or were offering the SRO a different perspective on an issue that the SRO was facing. These conversations were often described as occurring "on the fly."

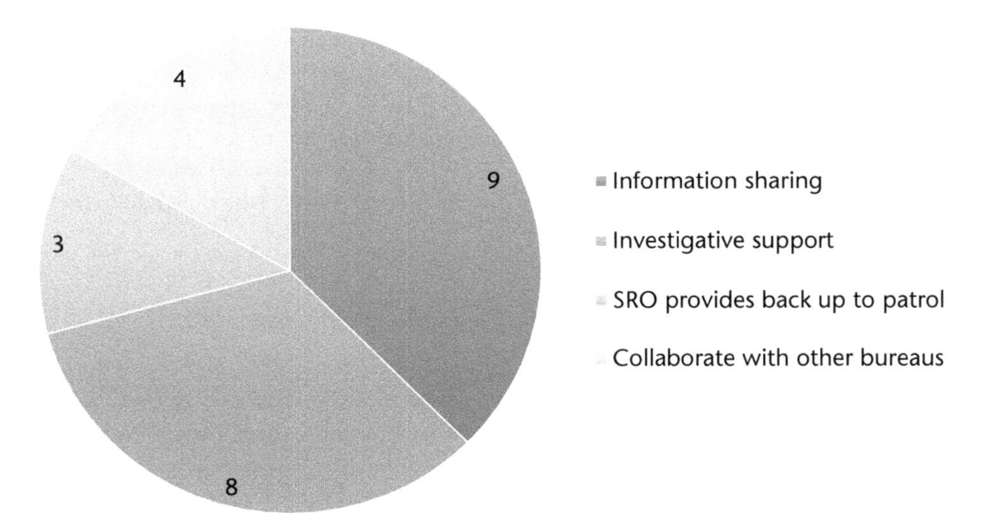

FIGURE 7.2 Nature of the interactions: SROs and officers in other Peel Bureaus (n = 11)*

* There were multiple responses from some participants.

Collaboration between SROs and Officers in Other Units

We also asked a number of questions to help us understand how SROs collaborate with officers in other units within Peel Police.

Describe a Situation

We began this line of questioning by asking the staff sergeants to: "Think back to a time that one of the officers who report to you worked collaboratively with the SROs that you remember clearly. Please describe this situation. What was the value to you of having the SRO as a resource on this occasion?" This provided very rich data that illustrate quite clearly the essential role the SROs relationship with the school plays in the how Peel Police perform their work. Details are provided below.

Situation One – Staff Sergeant NPU: This situation involved students being robbed as they were leaving the school property. The SRO had acquired some photographs of the incidents and other information that they shared with investigators. As a result, the thief was identified and arrested.

Situation Two – Staff Sergeant NPU: This situation involved human trafficking of underaged girls. The situation was discovered by an SRO who brought in the Vice unit to help with the investigation. The girl was "rescued" from the control of the pimp and criminal charges were laid.

Situation Three – Staff Sergeant NPU: This situation involved a street gang that was recruiting high school students into prostitution. These students were then tasked to recruit other students into the prostitution ring. In this case, the SROs became aware of the situation and asked their staff sergeant for advice on how to put a stop to this situation. Under the staff sergeant's direction, the SROs collaborated with officers from the Vice unit to identify at-risk girls within the school and to provide education and advice to them on how to deal with the situation. Then officers from the Vice and Street Gang units collaborated with the SROs to set up surveillance on the pimps. The story can be summarized as follows:

"... a couple of girls are working on the side as prostitutes, they're trying to entice other students into the trade as well. So, the officers approached me with this. Obviously, it's beyond the scope of anything they've dealt with. I put them in touch with the officers that I know in the Vice unit. We've set up a program where the Vice unit is coming around to speak to the girls we've identified as at risk of being brought into this trade."

Situation Four – Staff Sergeant NPU: This sergeant did not describe a specific situation, noting instead that they occurred daily.

Situation Five – Administrative Staff Sergeant: This staff sergeant described a Problem Oriented Policing (POP) project involving drug trafficking, where descriptions of suspects were shared between the SRO and investigators working within the Drug unit. This sharing of information increased the efficiency of the investigation and resulted in a number of convictions.

Situation Six – Detective in Robbery: The staff sergeant described a situation where the officers in the Robbery unit shared a video that showed an individual trafficking in stolen property (mostly electronics) to the SROs in hopes that they could identify the individual. Regular contact with the students meant that one of the SROs was able to identify this individual because of the clothing they wore, their facial features, and their gait. This resulted in the arrest of the offender.

Situation Seven – Staff Sergeant in Drugs: In this case, the situation involved a tip from Crime Stoppers about drug trafficking in a high school. Information was passed to the SRO, who did not have enough evidence to lay charges, but did share information on what was happening with the school's administration. The administrators were then able to intercede to provide counsel to the students, which led to the activity stopping and the placement of the student who was selling the drugs into a diversion program:

"Now, in that case, they weren't able to lay a charge because they didn't have enough evidence, but they were able to bring that information forward to school staff. And you know in Ontario, school staff have the power to intercede especially if they believe that any type of drug offenses are occurring or affecting their students. In this case they brought the students in, spoke to the students involved, counseled them ... The SRO officer spoke to the student as well [put him in a diversion program] ... and the trafficking ceased at that school without anyone being arrested."

Situation Eight – Staff Sergeant in Special Victims: This incident involved a Special Victims unit investigation that sought help from an SRO to identify a student who had sexually assaulted a young female. This female did not know the name of her assailant but knew the name of the school that he attended. They also knew the individual's nicknames, what he looked like, and who he hung around with. The involvement of the SRO helped the officers within the Special Victims unit identify and arrest the offender:

"I'm thinking of a particular case where a victim of a sex crime did not know the name of the student who sexually assaulted her, however was aware that the student attended a certain school and therefore, the SRO, at that point, becomes a valuable resource to us in that we can use nicknames, descriptions and, you know, possible associates and leave them with that information and they can often piece together who that suspect is. And in this case, I believe they were able to do that for us, so they assisted us in our investigation."

Situation Nine – Staff Sergeant in Street Crime: In this case, the SRO became aware of an individual dealing drugs near the school property. The SRO provided information to the Street

Crime unit. This information resulted in surveillance, a search warrant, and, ultimately, an arrest. The SRO continued the collaboration during the surveillance and through the arrest. The staff sergeant noted that this type of situation occurs regularly and observed that, in many cases, Peel Police would not know about crimes involving young people if SROs did not bring them to the service's attention. They also noted that the willingness of the SRO to collaborate throughout the investigation helped develop the skills of the SRO and prepared him/her for a future role in an investigative unit.

Situation Ten – Staff Sergeant in Uniform Patrol: In this case, the SRO took part in an incident that involved a missing person's body found in a lake. The SRO was available to provide skilled back-up by assisting with scene control for four hours.

Situation Eleven – Staff Sergeant in Uniform Patrol: This situation involved a young lady who was reported missing from one of the high schools. The SRO knew the missing student and took the lead on the investigation (i.e., talked to her friends, her teachers, and her parents) collaborating with uniformed patrol along the way. The girl was ultimately found, unharmed.

The Value Offered by the SRO in this Collaboration

While some ($n = 4$) of the sources of value identified by the staff sergeants were idiosyncratic and seemed to be situation dependent, other examples of the value of collaborations between SROs and officers in other police units came up several times and, as such, deserve attention.

The relationship the SRO has with the school and with the students: The most commonly mentioned source of value ($n = 6$) offered by the SRO to other units within Peel Police relates to the relationship these officers have with students and staff at the schools to which they are assigned. According to the staff sergeants we spoke to, these relationships help the SRO gain intelligence that was critical to resolving the issue under discussion. The staff sergeants talked more specifically about how the trust the SRO has built up within the school creates cooperation between the school and the police and encourages students and school staff to share what they have heard/know. They also observed that the SROs' network within the school has proven "time and again" to be an invaluable (and unique) source of information that the police can use to address criminal activity in and around the school. Finally, the staff sergeants noted that SROs have learnt how to communicate with youth. This skill is, they feel, vital in any investigation that involves young people and helps the police gather information that they would not be able to get any other way.

Increases the efficiency of the investigation: The next most commonly mentioned source of value ($n = 4$) of collaborations between SROs and other units within Peel Police relates to the efficiency with which the incident/crime can be solved. In all cases where this was mentioned, the staff sergeants linked the presence of the SRO to an increase in cooperation between the school, the students, and Peel Police, and a concomitant decline in the amount of time required to investigate a crime.

Prevention, mitigation, and extra resources: Two other types of value were mentioned by several staff sergeants. The first related again to the relationship that SROs had with the students and staff in their schools. In this case, officers talked about how the SROs used their relationships to prevent an activity (i.e., robbery, drug trafficking) from occurring or mitigated the harm resulting from such an activity once it had occurred (i.e., education, coping resources, counselling). The second (offered by both staff sergeants in Uniform Patrol) related to the idea that the SRO offered a source of skilled back-up when needed.

Diversion, awareness of criminal activity, and career development: Other sources of value described by the staff sergeants included the ability the SRO had to divert students when appropriate:

"SROs can work with school staff to intercede in activities without laying charges to prevent or stop criminal activities. Activities stop and kids stay out of the corrections system."

the fact that they bring awareness of crimes to the appropriate unit:

"Wouldn't know about crimes without them."

and the value that having them work collaboratively on an investigation offers in terms of career development:

"Collaboration develops the skills base of the SRO, which prepares them for their next roles in investigative units like the Street Gangs unit. They are able to assume these roles more quickly and efficiently saving time and improving performance of the unit."

The Quality of the Collaboration

All officers rated the quality of the collaboration between their unit and the SROs as "excellent" ($n = 9$) or "very, very good" ($n = 2$). They used a number of arguments to justify these ratings. The most common reason for evaluating the collaboration as excellent revolved around the attributes of the SROs themselves. Two-thirds of the staff sergeants praised the SROs for their willingness to assist other units (i.e., they are quick to assist, willing to help, motivated to cooperate), especially if such assistance produced results for their school or the community surrounding their school. Half stated that the results of the collaboration spoke directly to this issue (i.e., "we see the results").

One in three staff sergeants attributed their excellent collaboration rating to the fact that many officers in their current unit used to be SROs themselves. This offers several advantages when it comes to their ability to work together, not the least of which seems to be the high level of trust officers in other units have for those working in the NPU (i.e., "there is an established relationship which facilitates a productive work relationship"):

"Because most of my officers that are in here now used to be SROs, so they know what they have to do out there. These SROs are motivated officers."

While two of the staff sergeants in the NPU praised the collaboration, they did feel that there "were some hiccups" that they attributed to the fact that officers in the other units did not recognize the special requirements on SROs in their dealings with the community ("the relationship that has been created needs to be respected").

Finally, it is interesting to note that four staff sergeants took some credit for the success of the collaboration:

"You know what, I think the collaboration is more me putting them in touch with the resources that we have within regional policing, kind of getting that to work. I would say that it's excellent, we work very well as a department together, so I can make a phone call to whatever bureau I need, and you know, within a matter of half an hour, have resources available to these guys."

"I am very insistent that these guys take ownership of their schools, and they take ownership of their investigations, make it clear to them that I am well aware of what their abilities and non-abilities are. And then if there's something that's ever . . . that they feel is beyond their scope of being able to deal with, there's no embarrassment to be found in asking for help. In fact, it is to be encouraged."

Impact of the SRO Program

We included several questions in our interview to help us appreciate the staff sergeant's perceptions with respect to the impact the SRO program had on three key stakeholders: the officers working in the NPU (i.e., SROs), the Peel Police, and the communities in which they work (i.e., high school, catchment area). Key conclusions supported from this stage of the analysis follow.

Impact on the SRO

We began by asking our staff sergeants: "What skills does an officer acquire through their time and work as an SRO?" Responses to this question are presented in Table 7.5 and discussed below.

A substantial number of the staff sergeants we interviewed agreed that the job of SRO helped develop the following skills and awareness in the officers who hold this role:

- community policing skills – the job teaches them how to build relationships with members of the outside community, how to maintain, develop, and build good community relations, and how to network with the community;
- a comprehensive knowledge of the different dimensions of police work – the job gives them the opportunity to gain experience by working on teams with police officers in a wide variety of units and service areas and augments their networking skills;
- good investigative skills – the job allows them to gain the experience they need to conduct investigations, including writing warrants and reports;
- intelligence gathering skills – the job gives them the opportunity to learn how to conduct interviews and engage in meaningful intelligence gathering activities;
- problem solving skills – the job requires them to learn how to analyze information and come up with conclusions and recognize early warning signs of problems;
- communication skills – the job helps them develop public speaking skills, presentation skills, report writing skills;
- time management skills – a good SRO has to learn how to manage unpredictable workloads; and
- social media skills – students make extensive use of social media as do the SROs who work in the schools.

We then asked the staff sergeants if they could suggest other ways in which young police officers could acquire the above list of skills if they were not SROs. All but four officers felt that there

TABLE 7.5 Skills developed by working as an SRO*

Skills developed by working as an SRO	*n*	*% of sample*
Community policing skills	8	73%
A comprehensive knowledge of the different dimensions of police work	6	54%
Investigative skills	6	54%
Intelligence gathering skills	5	45%
Problem solving skills	5	45%
Communication skills (public speaking skills, presentations, report writing)	4	36%
Time management skills (managing workload)	4	36%
Social media skills (Snapchat, Instagram)	2	18%

*Shaded responses were mentioned by all NPU staff sergeants who are currently supervising an SRO

was nowhere else that young police officers could acquire this set of skills. The following quotes illustrate why the staff sergeants felt this way:

> "They can't, not to the same level that they pick them up as an SRO because nowhere else would they get the opportunity to work so closely with the individual members of the community and other areas within the service on such an array of issues."
>
> "Obviously you're going to build on your communication skills when you're doing front-line work, but not at the level that the SROs are exposed to here."
>
> "There is less opportunity to develop these skills in Uniform Patrol because we are governed by the calls for service and we rarely get to devote the time that would be needed to acquire these skills."

Four staff sergeants felt that these same skills could be obtained if one worked in a smaller town or on a project devoted to community engagement. These findings support the following conclusion: the job of SRO provides Peel Police officers with valuable job-related skills that they would not be able to obtain elsewhere.

Finally, we asked the staff sergeants to give us their view of the importance of the skills noted above to the ability of these officers to get ahead within Peel Police. Six staff sergeants felt that the acquisition of these skills was very important to the ability of these officers' (or any officer's for that matter) career progression within the police. Eight staff sergeants felt that assignment to the NPU is a key stepping-stone to advancement within Peel Police. These officers talked about how experience as an SRO was a "launch pad into the Criminal Investigation Bureau" and stated that, at this time, 80% of investigative officers within Peel Police were once SROs.

Staff sergeants identified five reasons (shown in Table 7.6) to explain why they felt that the SRO program was a stepping-stone to advancement within the police. Key reasons include the fact that the job of the SRO allows an officer to:

- gain experience with all stages of the investigative process (i.e., get to run the investigation from start to trial; handle all the administrative elements, such as search warrants);
- gain experience managing a variety of challenging situations (i.e., get the opportunity to engage in problem-oriented policing [POP] projects; they are responsible for their entire community, not just calls that come in on the radio; they get exposed to a wide variety of issues);
- develop critical communication and relationship building skills (i.e., skills that are needed on the front line, organizational skills, interviewing skills, project management skills);
- gain exposure within the service (i.e., it is a career stepping-stone to an investigative bureau); and
- demonstrate the skills they have developed in a public forum (i.e., show that they have the ability to build community relationships, take initiative, manage their time).

TABLE 7.6 Reasons why SRO role is seen as a stepping-stone to advancement

Reasons why SRO role is seen as a stepping-stone to advancement	*n*	*% of sample*
Gain experience with all stages of the investigative process	7	64%
Gain experience managing a variety of challenging situations	5	45%
Development of critical communication and relationship building skills	5	45%
Gain exposure within the service	4	36%
Gives them the opportunity to demonstrate their skills	4	36%

Again, a quote can be used to illustrate these points:

> "I think that, just the empathy level that these officers develop for, you know, our victims, and the community. I think it's easier to become a little disconnected from the community when you're just running around from call to call. And I think the fact that these guys have to engage with the community, it provides them with a better insight into how to deal with the concerns of the public, and . . . I would say they probably generate a lot less complaints, because they don't become crusty habituated cynics . . . like oh no, not another accident, kind of thing. And it's like . . . there's a greater sympathy level because they've had that community involvement, and they feel that connection."

Impact of the NPU (and the SRO) on Peel Police

So, the development of these skills is critical to the career advancement of the SRO, but are they important to Peel Police overall? While it makes intuitive sense that Peel Police will benefit when officers within their command gain the skills and abilities outlined in the previous section, we checked our perception by asking the staff sergeants two questions: "How important is the development of these skills to the Peel Police overall, and why do you say this? How does the SRO program benefit other Peel Police officers?" Responses to these questions are summarized below.

Importance of the development of these skills to the Peel Police: All 11 of the staff sergeants in our sample unequivocally stated that the development of the skills listed in Table 7.5 are very important to the Peel Police Service; in fact, some stated that such skills were fundamental to the ability of the Service to do their job effectively. They gave a wide variety of reasons for this view (see Table 7.7).

Two answers were given by two-thirds of the staff sergeants in the sample. In the first case, all of the staff sergeants in the NPU, along with the staff sergeants in the Special Victim and Street Crime units, felt that the skills developed by SROs working within the NPU encouraged long-lasting positive relationships with the community. More specifically, they felt that the skills SROs acquired through their work in the schools helped them better understand how to: (1) interact with the public, (2) build trust between the police and the community, and (3) reduce the barriers that often exist between the community and the police. Staff sergeants also talked about how the job of the SRO often resulted in the development of a sense of empathy for victims and the community within this group of officers; a skill that is notoriously hard to train for using conventional methods. They went on to note that officers who behaved empathetically towards victims and offenders generated fewer complaints from the community.

TABLE 7.7 Reasons why development of these skills are important to Peel Police*

Reasons why development of these skills are important to Peel Police	*n*	*% of sample*
Such skills promote long-lasting positive community relationships	7	64%
Builds the skills for the future service	7	64%
Promotes organizational learning	5	45%
Relieves pressure on front-line officers	4	36%
Solve problems sooner	3	27%
Benefits future investigations	3	27%

* Shaded responses were mentioned by all NPU staff sergeants who are currently supervising an SRO

A similar number of staff sergeants feel that the skills that an officer learns when working as an SRO are critical to the demands that any police service is likely to face in the future. These officers noted that communities are changing (e.g., they are more socio-economically and demographically diverse; citizens are more dependent on, and conversant with, technology; officers are exposed to a higher number of mental health issues within the community) and felt that police services have to make changes inside the organization to accommodate these shifts that are happening outside. This group of staff sergeants argued that changes at the level of the community require a new type of "well-rounded" police officer who appreciates the importance of relationship building. They went on to note that, in their experience, the job of SRO instilled such skills in younger police officers.

Half of the staff sergeants felt that the way that the program was designed promoted organizational learning. To explain, Peel Police SROs work in pairs (two officers job-share two schools). Each Fall, the more senior SRO of the pair (i.e., the one who has spent two years working as an SRO) is rotated out of the NPU and is replaced by a new officer. While this new officer has received formal training on the duties of an SRO, the senior officer in the pair (i.e., the officer who is in their second year as an SRO) is expected to share their skills with their new partner and coach and mentor them during the one-year overlap on the assignment. Half of the staff sergeants we talked to spoke about how this arrangement encouraged the development of a culture of learning with the population of officers who had been and/or are SROs.

Three other ways that the program benefits Peel Police were identified by the staff sergeants we talked to: (1) the program relieves pressure on front-line officers by giving them additional informational or physical resources when needed, (2) the program facilities fast solutions of problems (i.e., direct communication with school staff alerts the officers to issues that can be solved more readily in their infancy than when "full blown"), and (3) the SRO provides information that benefits investigations by those working in Special Victims, Drug, and Robbery units.

Benefits of the SRO program – other Peel Police officers: Staff sergeants identified five ways in which other Peel Police officers benefited from the NPU program. Four of these benefits were identified by approximately half of the officers we talked to:

- the SRO reinforces a positive image of the police which makes "all of our jobs easier";
- the SRO provides us with knowledge and intelligence that helps our investigations;
- the SRO establishes good relationships with one of our key community partners, the schools, which makes investigations involving students and youth much easier; and
- the SRO program reduces the number of 911 calls, which frees up front-line police officers for other duties.

The following quote speaks to this last point:

> "First and foremost, it frees up the front-line response officers from having to attend schools. There's a number of calls for service at senior schools and high schools, for fights, for mischiefs, for swarmings, etc., around the school. The SRO looks after most of these issues . . . so that helps to free up my front line to deal with other issues within the community."

Two officers also felt that the program increased the skills within the police force in a more efficient way than other types of training.

The above data provide further support for the idea that the SRO provides a tremendous amount of value to Peel Police, and, by extrapolation, any other service that adopts this proactive/preventative approach to policing.

Impact of the SRO: The Community and the School

We asked the following two additional questions to help us gain a more complete view of the benefit that the SRO has on other key stakeholders: "What benefits does the SRO offer to the community? What benefits does the SRO offer to the schools in which the officers are placed?"

Benefits to the community: Half of the staff sergeants felt that the NPU benefited the community by:

- helping build positive relationships between the police and the community;
- increasing the amount of trust the community has in its police service which, in turn, makes it more likely that community members will go to the police if they need assistance; and
- increasing the likelihood that students will be placed in a diversion program rather than charged with a crime, which benefits not only the students, who are kept out of the system, but also reduces crime in the community and the costs to society associated with incarceration.

Other benefits to the community mentioned by these officers included:

- the SRO helps create a safer community;
- the SRO provides a dedicated resource to an important part of the community, the schools;
- the SRO educates members of the community in important aspects of the law (i.e., cyberbullying, internet safety); and
- the SRO enables police to solve crimes more quickly and efficiently by facilitating information gathering.

The following quote speaks to the value the SRO offers to the community:

> "These officers, they develop strong community partnerships. They've got a good understanding of the local neighborhoods that they're responsible for. They engage with the community, you know, promoting a flow of information between the community and the police. And they can either take that information and act on it themselves or they can provide that information to other units such as mine. And we act on it. To me having SROs is a win–win."

Benefits to the schools: What benefits does the SRO offer to the schools in which the officers are placed? As shown in Table 7.8, the staff sergeants identified eight ways that they felt high schools benefited from the NPU and SROs.

The benefit identified by the greatest number of staff sergeants ($n = 8$) was one that has come up before in other contexts: the SRO program helps build positive relationships between the police, school staff, and students. It builds trust, encourages open communication channels, and provides students with the ability to interact with police officers who can be seen as positive role models.

Three-quarters of the staff sergeants also identified a benefit to the program that was very specific to the fact that it operates within high schools: the program creates a feeling of safety within Peel Regional high schools. Officers who identified this benefit noted that the SRO acts as a deterrent to criminal activity within the schools and enforces the law, such that students benefit from a safer environment and feel more secure. The following quote talks about this issue:

> "Well, I think it provides the schools with a resource there for them to use in the event that they have, sort of, any kind of criminal activity, for community outreach and for mentoring young people as positive role models."

TABLE 7.8 Benefits of the NPU: the schools*

Benefits the schools realize from the NPU (the SRO)	*n*	*% of sample*
Builds positive relationships between police, school staff, and students	8	73%
Creates a feeling of safety within the schools (i.e., officer acts as a deterrent to criminal activity within the schools, officer enforces the law, students benefit from a safer environment, students feel more secure)	8	73%
Removes police stigma	3	27%
Reduces need to make calls to police as NPU knows when to follow-up proactively on situations	3	27%
Provides information sharing	3	27%
Provides education	2	18%

*Shaded responses were mentioned by all NPU staff sergeants who are currently supervising an SRO

The other four benefits were identified much less frequently: the SRO reduces the stigma young people often attach to the police (i.e., students have more positive perceptions of the police and are more able to interact with them comfortably), the SRO reduces the need for the school to call the police (911) when something goes wrong (i.e., school benefits from faster response times as the officer is already in the school), the SRO is able to share information on students in the school with school administration, and the SRO provides education to students on issues of importance to this age group (e.g., cyberbullying, drugs).

Evaluation of the SRO Program

We concluded the interview with a number of questions designed to give us information on how the staff sergeants who either supervised or worked with SROs viewed the SRO program. We began this section of the interview by asking: "All things considered, what is your opinion of the SRO program? Why do you say this?" Answers here ranged from very general favourable opinions ("there are a lot of benefits," "it is invaluable") to more specific answers, including:

- the program is invaluable when it comes to early intervention and prevention;
- it is great – it "humanizes the police department" and "alleviates misconceptions many young people have toward the police";
- really positive as it "engages the community with the police"; and
- it is really valuable – "the relationships developed between school administrators and students and the SRO bring in information about issues that would not be available otherwise."

This last view was held by staff sergeants working in three units: Street Crime, Robbery, and Drugs. The following quotes are reflective of the responses we received to this question:

> "The problem with law enforcement in general, is the measurement of what you prevent. Crime prevention has always been one of the biggest things that law enforcement struggles with, right? This program delivers on the prevention piece."
>
> "They represent Peel Police to the youth and if we can break down any type of barriers or stereotypes, the earlier that we can do it, the better."

Also important are the data showing that, while all of the staff sergeants we interviewed felt that the SRO program should be continued, many appreciated the challenges of showing the value of the program to others. While all of these officers were confident that the program was effective, they also felt that the ways in which the program positively impacted the police and the community were difficult to measure (i.e., "how do you measure the absence of something?"). These officers all talked about how they had personally seen the positive results the program was having and felt strongly that having the SROs in the school reduced crime within the community. Comments such as, "the SRO is a terrific use of police resources" and "there would be a lot of negative impacts if we removed it" reflect this view.

Four officers (those in Robbery, Special Victims, Drugs, and one NPU staff sergeant) lauded the SROs ability to provide intelligence when investigations involve young people. This increased the efficiency of their units and also increased the likelihood of a successful resolution of the issue:

> "We're not allowed to use – and we do not use – confidential informants that are under the age of 18. It's just not done. So, that intelligence information has to come from our SROs who are in the schools."

The staff sergeants in the NPU also felt that the SRO program creates value by enhancing officer development, building relationships with schools and the community, and by having the officers participate in proactive Problem Oriented Policing (POP) projects.

Problems with the SRO Program

We then asked: "Is there anything about the SRO program that you feel is problematic? Why do you say this? Can you think of any way that this problem could be addressed?" Two-thirds of the staff sergeants responded that they could not think of anything about the SRO program that was problematic. The five staff sergeants who are currently supervising SROs were, however, all able to think of challenges with the program – probably because they were involved in the program on a daily basis. Challenges that were identified by NPU staff sergeants, along with the reasons that these officers provided as to why they saw this issue as problematic, are discussed below. Also included in this section are solutions these officers provided on ways to address the issue.

A lack of understanding of why the SROs are in the schools: One officer felt that the fact that parents, as well as some school staff, really don't have enough information about why SROs are in the schools was problematic. In their experience, this lack of understanding meant that some schools were negatively stigmatized within the neighborhood. The most common example given by these officers involved parents' negative reactions to having police cruisers parked outside a school. The staff sergeants think this issue can be minimized by providing information explaining the program and the benefits it offers to the school and the students to parents and school staff at the beginning of the year and at school events.

Keeping SROs time in the schools protected: One staff sergeant talked at length about how difficult he finds it to maintain the scope of the program:

> "It's maintaining the scope of what we do. We tend to get farmed out on many things that don't fall under our mandate . . ."

He noted that in a police environment where there are not enough police resources, SROs are often called upon to assist Uniform Patrol, which makes it hard for those in his position to "keep to the mandate." Time away to work on other police tasks is, in his opinion, problematic as it takes the SRO away from the school, which often means these officers no longer have the time to "do what they are there to do." He says that more effort needs to be made to avoid having SROs being seen as a resource that anyone can call when they have a problem.

SRO tenure within the schools: As noted in the interviews with school administrators, the schools really do not like to see SROs rotating out of their school every two years. Rather, school personnel want to "keep the ones they have" under the assumption that it is more challenging and time consuming to rebuild relationships and trust every year with a new officer. Peel Police, on the other hand, want to stick with the current two-year assignment as an SRO (one new officer rotates in each year and one is placed elsewhere). Peel Police based their rotation schedule on the desire to have other bureaus and units within the service benefit from the skills developed and experience gained from working in the NPU. The NPU staff sergeant who gave this response, while appreciating the challenges inherent in the current structure, felt that the cost of keeping the officers in place for more than two years is too high and that many SROs themselves often want to move on after two years. He advocated for greater discussions with the school explaining the value of the program as it was currently administered.

Balancing relationship building with need to enforce the law: In this case, two NPU staff sergeants talked about how challenging it is for the SRO to balance the maintenance of positive relationships with their duty to the law (i.e., "it is often very hard for the officers when they have to be tough – when unpopular arrests have to be made"). They felt that enforcement activities, while part of the job, could contribute to a loss of trust between the SRO and the students. It was suggested that this should be addressed by having an SRO from another school do the actual arrest so as to "preserve the positive relationships developed within the school." The following quote illustrates this suggestion:

> "So sometimes it's almost better, when it comes to arrests and that kind of thing, where you take a step back and somebody else, maybe another SRO that's not at that school, does the actual arrest and leaves the guy that's associated with that school out of it."

Importance of Having an Officer Working in the High Schools on a Full-Time Basis

Staff sergeants were asked to tell us how important they think it is for the Peel Regional Police to continue to assign an officer to work full-time in and around the high schools in the region. With the exception of one staff sergeant in Uniform Patrol, all the staff sergeants in our sample felt that it was very important for Peel Police to assign an officer to work full-time in and around all of the high schools in Peel Region. They gave a number of reasons for feeling this way. More than half of the staff sergeants talked about how their experience both as an SRO and an officer supervising SROs had convinced them of the value of the program. For example:

> "I've seen the difference the program makes . . . I have been on the job long enough to remember what it was like before the NPU was introduced . . . it has a proven track record as far as I am concerned."
>
> "Having the same officer at the school and building that rapport gets things done, it gets people comfortable and not afraid to share with you . . . that trust level is huge."

Half the staff sergeants stated that the program was critically important as the consistent presence of the same officers in the school strengthens relationships and collaboration between the school, the police, and the students. These officers perceived that if this consistency was not there, such relationships would not form and the value of the program would be lost (i.e. "we wouldn't know the backstories . . . the context;" "we would not be told anything . . . trust is key"). They also worried that if officers were not assigned to schools on a full-time basis, they would not take ownership of their school assignment and Peel Police would lose the in-depth understanding of the high schools in the region and the communities that surround them that currently exists:

> "I think it is important that there's one school and one or two officers assigned to it. They need to take ownership . . . ."

Just under half of the staff sergeants linked the consistent presence of SROs to the school's ability to provide a good education to students who want to learn ("education would not be as possible if the officer was not there") and to perceptions of safety. Along these lines, these staff sergeants also talked about how the SRO could work to "steer youth in the right direction early" so they did not make a "silly" mistake that followed them for the rest of their life.

Finally, one officer felt that, without the SRO, all policing within the school would be reactionary in nature and more youth would be charged. The officer who did not feel that the program was critically important felt that these officers were needed in Patrol.

Suggested Changes to the SRO Program

We ended the interview by asking the staff sergeants: "If you could make one change to the SRO program, what would it be?" Five staff sergeants stated that they would not change anything about the program, a finding that again emphasizes the value offered by this program in the minds of those working in other units within Peel Police.

The staff sergeants within the NPU suggested a number of changes that are consistent to ones we heard when we talked to the school administrators:

- Peel Police should assign officers to middle schools (i.e., "they should dedicate an officer per each middle school instead of treating them as a group of feeder schools handled by the bike unit in off-bike season"); and
- Peel Police should create an option that would make it possible to keep officers in schools longer than their two-year assignment ("the schools would really like this").

The rest of the suggestions were very idiosyncratic and related to the function of the units that made the suggestion.

We end our discussion of the interview findings with the following comment made by a staff sergeant in the NPU which, we think, articulates the value of this program, not only now, but moving forward:

> "There is so much need in communities right now. Early intervention and social interaction with young offenders give the program the most value . . . you know . . . when I'm interacting with an 18-year- and 20-year-old that's been involved in some pretty serious crime and stuff like that, or you know, he's got himself in a bad place or hanging with a bad crowd, it's pretty difficult to get those guys back on track, right? I really do believe that if you're going to change society . . . the earlier the intervention component of it the better. These early interactions give it (the SRO program) the most value. It's not perfect but we have a much better chance of saving somebody early on than we do much later, right? It's a much bigger uphill battle. Once they've already played in the mud puddle and they've got some dirt on them, it's tough to wash it off."

Summary and Conclusions

This section summarizes key findings with respect to the value of this program as seen by staff sergeants who have personal knowledge of the program (i.e., they supervise SROs or they work in units that frequently collaborate with SROs).

Activities that Deliver Value

Virtually all of the staff sergeants interviewed agreed that three sets of activities performed by the SRO were critical to their ability to deliver value:

- activities directed to building strong positive relationships between the police, students, and school staff: spending time interacting with students and liaising with staff;
- activities that actively involve the SRO in the community: going to events, being seen around the neighborhood, and participating in outreach activities;
- education: delivering presentations in the school and community on how the law views issues of importance or relevance such as bullying, cyberbullying, and drugs.

Value: Collaboration between SROs and Officers in Other Units

SROs interact and collaborate with many other bureaus in the police service on a regular basis. They share information, liaise with other units during an investigation, and provide back-up/assist patrol officers in their enforcement activities.

The perceived value of these collaborations is multi-faceted, varied, and often somewhat idiosyncratic (i.e., unit specific). Staff sergeants identified the following ways that the NPU and the SROs offered value to their unit/Peel Police:

- *Gives police access to information that they cannot get any other way*: The trust the SRO has built up within the school creates cooperation between the school and the police and encourages students and school staff to share what they have heard/know.
- *Increases the efficiency of the investigation*: The relationship the SRO has with the school reduces the amount of time that the police need to spend on information gathering, which contributes to a reduction in the total amount of time required to investigate an infraction.
- *Increases awareness of criminal activity in Peel region*: The SROs' information network ensures that these officers hear about criminal activities that would otherwise remain unreported. The SROs report these crimes to the appropriate unit for investigation, which reduces the amount of unsolved crime in the region.
- *Prevention of crime*: The information gathered by the SROs helps the police intervene and prevent a crime from occurring (i.e., robbery, drug trafficking).
- *Mitigation of harm*: SROs offer education and counselling, which helps to mitigate the harm resulting from negative activities such as bullying, cyberbullying, fighting, and drugs. These interventions also increase perceptions of safety in the student population.
- *Extra resources*: SROs offer a source of skilled back-up when needed (often during a crisis).
- *Diversion*: When a youth commits a crime, SROs can use their discretion to intercede without laying charges. Diversion offers value in two ways. First, it prevents or stops criminal activity within the school and community. Second, it reduces the number of young people with criminal records.

- *Career development*: Collaboration with the community, other police units, and community associations develops the skill base of the SROs and helps them learn the role of investigator more quickly and efficiently.
- *Increases the efficiency of the service overall*: SROs are more able to prioritize a call from the school correctly. This results in a reduction of calls for service associated with false emergency situations that need to be attended by uniform patrol. The program also reduces the total number of calls for service to patrol, as the school staff call the SRO directly when they require police service rather than 911.
- *Enhances the reputation of the service*: The positive interactions that SROs have with schools, teachers, and school boards demonstrate that Peel Police cares about the community.

Value of the SRO Program on Key Stakeholders

The SRO: The job of the SRO provides a unique opportunity to learn a wide range of skills that are critical to effective police work and critical to career advancement. Key skills they acquire on the job include an understanding of community policing, how to conduct an investigation, how to gather intelligence, problem solving, communication, time management, and social media. They also gain a very comprehensive knowledge of the different dimensions of police work during their two years in the role.

Peel Police: Almost all of the staff sergeants felt strongly that the skills developed by SROs encouraged the development of long-lasting positive relationships with the community, which gave these officers the ability to: (1) interact effectively with the public, (2) build trust between the police and the community, and (3) reduce the barriers that often exist between the community and the police. The majority also saw a link between the skills developed within the NPU and the demand they were seeing from the community for a new type of police officer who appreciated the importance of relationship building.

The program also benefits Peel Police by encouraging the development of a culture of learning with the population of officers who had been and/or are SROs, reducing the pressure on the front line by reducing the number of 911 calls, and facilitating investigations by developing sound information sharing mechanisms between the NPU, Special Victims, Street Crime, Drugs, and Robbery units. Finally, many staff sergeants spoke about how the SRO program reinforces a positive police image, which makes "all of our jobs easier."

The community: Staff sergeants indicated that SROs provided three sources of value to the community. First, this program humanizes the police and increases the amount of trust the community has in its police service. This benefits the community as it increases the likelihood that community members will go to the police if they need assistance. Second, the diversion program offers value not only to the students who are kept out of the system, but also reduces crime in the community and the costs to society associated with incarceration. When these two things are considered together, the third source of value becomes clear: the NPU program helps the police create a safer community.

The schools: Staff sergeants agreed that the SRO provides value to the high schools they police in a number of ways, most of which result from the fact that this program promotes positive relationships between the police, school staff, and students. It builds trust, encourages open communication channels, and provides students with the ability to interact with police officers in situations that are non-confrontational. The fact that the SRO acts as a deterrent to criminal activity within the schools and enforces the law means that both students and staff experience a safer environment and feel more secure. Many officers also felt that the NPU program reduces the stigma young people often attach to the police and reduces the need for the school to call 911 when something goes wrong. Having an officer on site also means that the school benefits from faster police response times and an ability to de-escalate problems quickly. Finally, officers noted the benefits of having an SRO in the school who is able to share information on their student population and what is happening in the catchment area with school administration, as well as educate students on issues of importance to this age group (e.g., cyberbullying, drugs).

8

THE VALUE OF SROS

Insider Views from Officer Ride-Alongs

WordMap: 35 most common words in Chapter 8: "The Value of SROs: Insider Views from Officer Ride-Alongs"

Key Learnings

This chapter presents key findings from an ethnographic study of the School Resource Officer role. The goal of this phase of the research was twofold. First, we wanted to identify and describe any activities undertaken by the SRO that might create social value (i.e., stopping a fight at a school). Second, we wanted to help the reader understand the job of the SRO by "telling their story."

Value Delivered by the SRO program: The Ethnographer's Perspective

A myriad of ways in which SROs create value were observed or discussed during the ride-alongs. Details on each are provided below.

Source of intelligence: This phase of the research uncovered multiple instances where the SROs were an invaluable source of intelligence because of the relationships they had built within their school and the community. This intelligence was used to benefit the school and the community.

Stopping or following up on an assault of any kind: There was a mix of real-time observations and second-hand accounts of the SROs dealing with multiple incidents of assault.

Stopping a suicide attempt: During one of the ride-alongs, the ethnographer witnessed the SROs stopping a suicide attempt.

Dealing with bullying: During one of the ride-alongs, the ethnographer witnessed the SROs dealing with a bullying situation at the school.

Managing a rape threat: During one of the ride-alongs, the ethnographer witnessed an SRO assist a colleague who was dealing with a rape threat.

Youth diversion: The ethnographer observed the SROs placing a juvenile who distributes drugs into a diversion program, thereby offering the student the opportunity to pursue a healthier life track without a criminal record.

Crimes solved more efficiently: There is value in the fact that the SRO has a fine-grained knowledge of the community. During the ride-alongs, the ethnographer observed how the SROs' in-depth knowledge of youth gang members operating within the school's catchment area is a real asset when solving crimes. Their knowledge allowed for a rapid response to a crime that might have otherwise taken up officer resources for days/weeks in both the uniform patrol and robbery bureaus of the Peel Regional Police.

Providing extra authority to school administrators: In an effort to make safer schools, the SROs were often asked to attend meetings with students and parents. These officers were able to make the students aware of the consequences of their behavior in a more direct way than either the school administrators or the parents could administer.

De-escalation: The ethnographer observed the SROs help school administrators de-escalate heated situations.

Encourage young people, particularly visible minorities, to consider joining the police: The SRO program creates the opportunity for youth to meet police officers in a non-threatening way. Some of these youth, who may otherwise not have thought about careers in law enforcement, may now consider the profession. Subsequently, the Peel Regional Police may have gained an opportunity to increase its ability to be representative of the population in Peel.

(continued)

(continued)

Providing peace of mind to the school administrators/teachers: The fact that school administrators have the ability to call their SROs when a serious problem occurs in the school or the community around the school provides these individuals with an increased sense of security and peace of mind.

Establishing a positive view of police in the minds of young people: By interacting with young people in non-threatening circumstances, the SROs are creating positive impressions of police that contrast with the many negative examples of policing that are communicated through the media and the anecdotal experiences of dissatisfied community members.

This chapter is based on field notes taken by Gregory Dole, a PhD student in the Sprott School of Business at Carleton University at the time this book was written. These notes represent his interpretation of observations made during the course of ten full-day "ride-alongs," an arrangement whereby a civilian spends a shift in the passenger seat of an emergency vehicle, observing the workday of a police officer. These ride-alongs were undertaken with four Neighborhood Police Units (NPUs) from October 9, 2015 to March 21, 2016. During these ride-alongs, Greg observed the SROs working in all five schools that were participating in this study. Three of the schools were visited twice and two schools were visited three times.

The goal of this phase of the research was twofold. First, we wanted to identify and describe any activities undertaken by the NPU that might create social value (e.g., stopping a fight at a school). Second, we wanted to help the reader understand the job of the SRO by "telling their story."

The chapter is divided into four main sections. We begin by describing the ethnographic approach used in this stage of the study. The material in this section of the chapter is taken from two main sources: (1) the web center for Social Science Research[1] and (2) Brian Hoey's (2014) introduction to the practice of ethnography. In the second section, we highlight the ways in which the SRO was observed to provide social value. Ethnographic writing tends to take on the form of stories, which "intertwine" the lives of the ethnographer with his or her subjects (Hoey, 2014); in the third section, Greg tells 11 stories of value creation by SROs that were produced using his field notes. The final section of the chapter provides a summary of the key findings with respect to the value of the NPU program in Peel, as revealed using ethnographic methods.

Ethnographic Research

Ethnography, simply stated, is the study of people in their own environment. While the ethnographic approach to qualitative research was originally used only by anthropologists, it has recently been broadened to support the study of virtually any group or organization. In this case, we use the technique to describe interactions between the SROs and various groups of individuals: the high school students who go to the schools in our study, school staff working at the five high schools in our study, and community members. All interactions were witnessed in the course of ten ride-alongs, as described above.

Ethnographers typically spend a considerable amount of time in the places where they conduct their research and ethnographic research requires a lot of time and energy from the researchers who are carrying out the study. Ethnographers generate understanding by taking what researchers call an emic perspective (i.e., an "insider's point of view"). They do this by engaging in a research methodology called participant observation. This form of research requires the researcher to take on two roles: (1) a participant in the setting, and (2) an observer who can describe the experience with a measure of objectivity. Participant observation requires the researcher to take copious field notes: summaries created when the investigator is "in the field" to record (and, hence, remember) the behaviors, activities, events, and other features of an observation. Many consider ethnography to be an interpretative science, as ethnographic accounts are both descriptive (details are crucial) and interpretative (the ethnographer must determine the significance of what he or she observes without gathering broad, statistical information).

In this case study, the ethnographer, PhD student Greg Dole, collected field data in two ways: (1) he audio-recorded impressions during the event, and (2) he took field notes where he jotted down what was going on. Field notes allow the researcher "to turn the events of the moment into an account that can be consulted again (and again) later" (Hoey, 2014, p. 5). In his time in the field, Greg took detailed notes describing: (1) *who* (key actors in a given context), (2) *what* (what happened in a given place and time?; what was going on?; what was being said/body language?), (3) *where* (where did things take place?), (4) *when* (when did things happen?; what did people do to prompt observed actions?), (5) *how* (how do things work?; how do different groups of people behave?), and (6) *why* (why did things unfold the way they did?). These notes were analyzed, patterns were identified in what was going on, and conclusions were drawn. These notes and recordings were used to create the stories included in the third part of this chapter. These stories allow you, the reader, to experience – through the ethnographer's account – what he witnessed and encountered.

Examples of How SROs Add Value

This section of the report was created using Greg Dole's field notes. In this section, we identify SRO activities that add value, particularly those that were not described in other data collection efforts. What is not discussed in this section of the report is the time spent on certain activities, such as parade (scheduled before the SRO heads out on the road in the morning; officers are briefed before they go to their schools) and report writing (typically done at the police station to which the SRO is assigned at the end of the day; this activity is triggered by other activities taking place throughout the day).

Areas of value creation observed or discussed during the ride-alongs, in descending order by frequency, include:

- dealing with criminal activity occurring either in the school or the surrounding neighborhoods (i.e., theft, robbery, break and enter) ($n = 16$);
- responding to calls for service (includes providing back-up, working in operations, responding to radio calls) ($n = 14$);
- actions that contributed to students feeling safer ($n = 13$);
- relationship building (i.e., participation in school events, education) ($n = 12$);
- gathering intelligence and providing it to other Peel police bureaus ($n = 8$);
- stopping or following up on an assault of any kind ($n = 6$);
- stopping a suicide attempt ($n = 1$);
- dealing with bullying ($n = 1$); and
- investigating threats of rape ($n = 1$).

Details of each are provided in the sections below. It should be noted that in this section we clearly distinguish between activities that were observed in *real time* during the ride-along (RT) as compared to *second-hand* accounts of value added activities that were mentioned during discussions between the SROs and the researcher during the ride-along (SH). It should also be noted that

Greg observed the SROs responding to calls from radio dispatch (i.e., instigated by Peel Police) and on their phones (i.e., instigated by the vice principals (VPs)s in their school) throughout the day. These types of activities are also identified in the discussion below.

Dealing with Criminal Activity in the School and/or in Catchment Area

The SRO adds value by dealing with criminal activity occurring in either the school or in the neighborhoods surrounding the school. The data in Table 8.1 illustrate the types of criminal activity that the SRO commonly encounters: drugs, theft, and break-and-enters. More specifically, eight of the observations/stories related to drug dealing on school property, four pertained to theft (cell phones, a car), and two were associated with robberies and break-and-enters. These crimes took place in the schools and in the surrounding neighborhoods.

The ethnographic study revealed the myriad ways that the officers address drug dealing on school property: they follow up on information provided to them by the school administrators, they invested their own time working on POP projects relating to drug crimes in their catchment area, and they used social media to identify and charge drug dealers operating in the schools. Their efforts to reduce crime in their area was described by one SRO as follows:

> "We hit the known areas where kids will hang out and do drugs (e.g., parks and plazas). Then we have POP projects that are planned in advance. These projects include targeting issues that affect the schools such as: (a) drug dealers that sell to students, (b) cell phone thefts that target students, and (c) anything that affects the schools and student body."

Another SRO reported that there had been no drug overdoses in his school in the past year, a fact he attributed to the work of himself and his colleague. Yet another SRO talked about the value of using social media to set up drug busts: "we have now had three busts of dealers in the parking lots at [this school]."

Finally, the value of the SRO program was summarized by one SRO who observed that investigations into one crime, in combination with the SROs knowledge of interviewing techniques, familiarity with high school students, and their knowledge of the social networks in the schools, often led to arrests in other areas. One officer gave an example that involved drugs, robberies, and break-and-enters (B and E's):

TABLE 8.1 Dealing with criminal activity

Dealing with Criminal Activity in the School and/or in Catchment Area	*RT*	*SH*
Investigated drug dealing on school property	$n = 3$	
Investigated drug crimes (as part of problem-oriented policing [POP] project)*		$n = 3$
Investigated theft of cell phones	$n = 1$	$n = 1$
Dealt with situation where students were stealing from English as a second language (ESL) students	$n = 1$	$n = 1$
Arrested youths in possession of drugs and stolen goods		$n = 2$
Investigated drug dealing networks using social media		$n = 2$
Investigated possible stolen car		$n = 1$
Responded to robberies and break-and-enters in the neighborhood		$n = 1$

* A POP, or problem oriented policing project, is a tactical investigative project designed to identify the contributing factors, underlying conditions, and causes for a particular problem – in this case, drugs in the schools.

> "Knowing people in the neighborhood, who lived and hung out there led to us solving a couple of B and E's (Break and Enters) in seven minutes."

One officer talked about how this ability to deal with criminal code offenses means that SROs can offer value to the school that is not available from private security guards:

> "We are trained to investigate criminal matters. A security guard has nothing in their mandate on how to investigate criminal matters so the only thing they could enforce is trespassing – the Trespass to Property Act."

Responding to Calls for Service

Greg noted that, when the SROs do not have planned activities at their schools, they may work in support of other Peel Police Bureaus responding to calls for service that come through by radio dispatch. This could happen on a quiet day at the schools, but also occurred when the school was closed during school holidays and before and after school hours. The types of calls for service that Greg observed or heard about during the ride-alongs are listed in Table 8.2.

One type of value observed for the first time through the ride-along process related to the fact that many of the school administrators at the high school where the officer worked (as well in elementary schools in their catchment area) were in possession of the SROs' phone numbers. Greg notes that, in five cases, the SROs talked with him about responding to calls for assistance from either elementary school administrators (n = 3) or the Principal/VP at the high school they were assigned to (n = 2). The SROs stated that the schools called the SROs directly to avoid having to call 911 and to ensure that the officer who responded to the call had knowledge of the schools and experience of dealing with younger people. The response was also faster when the SRO was approached directly than it was when the call was a 911. This strategy is, in some ways, unfortunate, as calls to cell phones, and calls where the officer has to deal with issues at elementary schools, do not generate statistics for either Peel Police or the NPU (i.e., they can be considered *invisible* work).

Other responses to calls for service noted in this phase of the study (see Table 8.2) included serving warrants, working on proactive police work associated with POP projects, responding to calls for back-up over the police radio, responding to Amber alerts, and spending time in court. Some of these specific activities (i.e., Amber alerts, serving warrants) had not been noticed previously and give us a better understanding of the wide range of tasks that fall under the purview of the SRO. The following comments illustrate how SROs prioritize these various activities:

TABLE 8.2 Responding to calls for service

Responding to calls for service	*RT*	*SH*
Respond to personal calls from elementary school administrators		n = 3
Serving warrants	n = 1	n = 2
Proactive police work (patrol, personal projects, POP projects)	n = 1	n = 2
Responding to request for back-up over the radio	n = 2	
School administrator calls officer directly on their cell phone		n = 2
Spending a day in criminal court for cases that might have been worked on before the officer became an SRO or involved a trial of a student		n = 2
Responding specifically to missing child calls (Amber alerts)		n = 1

"Patrolling the neighborhoods as well as checking in at the schools are the most important activities. When we finish that we go do whatever is of most value to the community."

Activities that Result in Students Feeling Safer

As summarized in Table 8.3, the link between the presence of the SRO in the school and students' feelings of safety was observed on multiple occasions during the actual ride-alongs (n = 9) and in the second-hand accounts discussed in the car (n = 4).

The most common way (n = 4) in which the police make students feel safer seems to be "by just showing up." Greg personally observed three instances where this relationship was apparent: police attended the school's basketball game, were visible after school hours on school property, and/or in the community surrounding the school. It was noted that having the police at the game promoted safety by reducing public drinking and/or the selling and consuming of drugs. The visible presence of the police on school property and in the community, on the other hand, acted as a deterrent to assaults, bullying, and drug trafficking.

Also common were feelings of safety associated with the police's ability to visibly investigate threats of gun violence (n = 4). During the ride-alongs, Greg witnessed the police dealing with an episode where a gun was seen by other students on school property and an episode where there were reports of gunshots fired in the neighborhood. Police officers also talked about two other episodes involving threats of guns in the school or in the catchment area during the ride-alongs.

Greg also observed three other actions that were associated with students' feelings of safety: (1) the SROs confronted strangers and trespassers who were on the school grounds, (2) the SROs ticketed vehicles that were parked in the school's parking lot that did not belong to someone associated with the school, and (3) the SROs responded to a mental health call at the school where the student had become violent and threatening to other students.

Relationship-building Activities

The SROs engaged in a number of activities with the goal of building relationships with key stakeholders in the community (see Table 8.4). Greg witnessed or heard about diverse efforts on the part of the SROs to develop rapport. Greg and the SROs attended a community event and played sports with the students. The SROs told Greg about the different seminars and training they offered at the school and described how they help the school organize charity events as well as attend school dances. The SROs also act as a liaison between the school and other police bureaus and they help school administrators communicate with students' parents on matters of the law.

Greg concluded that not only were the relationship-building activities carried out by the SRO diverse and wide ranging, many of them are not captured in management metrics collected by

TABLE 8.3 Activities to make students feel safer

Activities that Result in Students Feeling Safer	*RT*	*SH*
Provide police presence as a deterrent	$n = 3$	$n = 1$
Investigate threats of gun violence	$n = 2$	$n = 2$
Policing school grounds	$n = 2$	$n = 1$
Responding to a call from a school about violent outbursts from a student with mental health issues	$n = 1$	

TABLE 8.4 Activities related to relationship building

Activities related to relationship building	*RT*	*SH*
Attending events/playing sports at the (secondary/ elementary) school and in the community	$n = 2$	
Education and training in the schools (emergency preparedness training in the schools, lockdown training)		$n = 3$
Help school organize charity and community events (mapping a walk)	$n = 1$	$n = 2$
Paid duties like monitoring school dances allow networking with teachers		$n = 1$
Acting as a liaison between other police bureaus and schools		$n = 2$
Police asked by administrators to communicate with parents on matters of the law		$n = 2$

Peel Police, as the SROs appear to engage in them opportunistically. Greg also noted that the SROs appear to genuinely take interest in the schools and communities that they serve and often do not include personal relationship-building activities in their activity logs as they do not view such activities as work!

Gathering Intelligence

SROs are uniquely able, because of the relationships they have built within their school and the community, to engage in intelligence-gathering activities that benefit the community and the students. As shown in Table 8.5, the types of activities included within this group are, again, quite diverse, but depend on the high levels of trust the SRO has nurtured within the school. It would be difficult (if not impossible) for Peel Police to get the intelligence provided by the SRO any other way.

The following quotes help justify this claim:

> "Knowing who is friends with who and who hangs out with who else is really very useful."

> "Another big one is the work we do with social media monitoring because we can connect students with their online profiles and if these students are committing serious crimes, bullying others, or just even showing, for example, lots of money, then we can usually identify those students and work on the situation . . . it's amazing how the drug dealers find each other. They can show up at a new school and they will find each other through social media and make friends."

TABLE 8.5 Intelligence-gathering activities

Gathering intelligence	*RT*	*SH*
Monitoring social media	$n = 3$	
Track information on people who trespass onto school property and hang around the school after school hours	$n = 1$	
Track instances of crimes being committed by students in their school (female students acting as prostitutes, males committing thefts)		$n = 2$
Providing information on criminal activity to other Peel Police bureaus		$n = 1$

Stopping or Following Up on an Assault of any Kind

As shown in Table 8.6, there was a real mix of real-time observations ($n = 3$) and second-hand accounts ($n = 5$) of SROs dealing with incidents of assaults. One officer related this story that Greg captured:

> "One of the incidents that we dealt with at a school was a student alleging rape. She went to the extreme because she wanted to go home. We knew the administration at the school, and they had let us know that she was a student with learning disabilities that was more happy at home than in school. Imagine if that had been an officer who did not have a history of the student. They would have reacted to the rape charge on the basis of that information alone. Instead, knowing background, we could deal with the situation in a more informed way. We showed up to the school knowing all the staff. We knew the student's history. We were able to get to the bottom of the story relatively quickly."

SRO Stopped Suicide Attempt

During one of the ride-alongs, Greg witnessed the SROs stopping a suicide attempt. For confidentiality reasons, we have elected not to describe this situation here.

Bullying

During one of the ride-alongs, Greg witnessed the SROs dealing with a bullying situation. He describes the situation as follows:

> "The SROs visited a student at her home at the request of the school's administration. This girl's mother had taken her out of school because she had been bullied by five other students. The officers spoke to the girl about the causes of bullying and gave her advice on what to do if this happened again."

During the ride-along, the officers told Greg that the SRO is more likely to be called in to deal with more serious cases of bullying. They noted that this is done as a deterrent and a way for school administrators and parents to escalate the severity of the situation (i.e., charges are possible when the police are brought in).

Dealing with a Rape Threat

During one of the ride-alongs, Greg witnessed an SRO assist a colleague who was dealing with a rape threat. He describes the situation as follows:

TABLE 8.6 Stopping or following up on an assault of any kind

Stopping or following up on an assault of any kind	*RT*	*SH*
Interviews of students who were involved in an assault situation (witness, assault victim, rape threat, alleged child abuse)	$n = 2$	$n = 2$
Investigated an assault that had occurred in the community (community center, grocery store, mall)		$n = 3$
Arrested a student who was charged with assault	$n = 1$	

"A father had phoned the school the previous afternoon to investigate a rape threat that his daughter received while riding the bus home from school. Apparently, one of the Grade Nine students said, "I am going to rape you and make you my sex slave." The father was outraged as well as scared for his daughter. The officer talked to the father and daughter and then spoke to the boy who made the threat along with the boy's mother. While the boy claimed he was just joking, the officers made the boy aware that such a statement is not funny and could have negative consequences for him if it happened again."

Stories of Value Creation by SROs[2]

Capturing human interaction is a fundamental part of understanding the value being created by the Peel Regional Police. Over the course of several months, Greg Dole intermittently spent time in job shadowing and tracking the work lives of a group of SROs from the Peel Regional Police. What follows are 11 stories from the road that Greg wrote which demonstrate ways in which the SROs create value for the schools, the police, and the community at large. In each case, the story is told and then the types of values created highlighted.

Story One: "The Wall"

At XXX Secondary School there was an incident where the SRO was able to solve a theft in the surrounding community that led to addressing a school safety issue and a larger illegal drug distribution problem in the school.

What had happened is that a resident in the community around XXX Secondary School had contacted the police regarding a theft of his patio furniture. The SRO was advised of this complaint and looked into the matter. The resident had noted that, on occasion, students were emerging from the wooded ravine at the bottom of his street and speculated that the presence of those students was connected to the theft. After a search of the wooded area, the SRO came upon a secluded area behind a building that backed onto the wooded area. Walking into this secluded area he came upon several students, lounging on the stolen patio furniture, smoking marijuana and socializing. The SRO subsequently arrested two of these students because they had prior drug conditions that had been placed on them. A subsequent search revealed that one of the youths had $335 in small bills as well as a small scale and dime bags (to package the drugs in 1 gram packets). It eventually came out that this youth was a drug dealer who had set up a conveniently located "drug den" for his clients from XXX Secondary School to engage in drug use during and/or after school hours. He had stolen patio furniture to make a comfortable place for his clients to lounge around as they purchased and partook in drugs.

This youth was known to the SRO because the officer had been following the youth on Instagram. The youth was also known to the school administration as a suspected drug dealer at XXX Secondary School. Owing to a familiarity with the youth through conversations with the school administration, as well as having been aware of the youth's social media presence, the SRO was able to both solve a petty crime and unearth a larger problem of drug distribution in the high school.

A knock-on effect of the creation of this "drug den" was that the students were found to be leaving school during school hours to go to the den. To get to the "drug den" quickly, they would cut across a set of busy train tracks. This was an especially dangerous crossing because of the high frequency of GO commuter trains that travelled this route.

Value creation #1 – making connections between unknown yet connected incidents: The value of the presence of the SRO was that he was able to connect a petty theft crime in the community with a larger issue affecting the health and safety of the students in the local high school. Specifically, by identifying and apprehending a school drug dealer, the SRO was able to both limit (however temporarily) the flow of drugs into a school with a long history of drug problems (drug overdoses have been a consistent problem at this high school). By seeing the drug bust in context, it turned from being a problem involving 4–7 youths at the scene of the crime to something connected to a community of over 1000 youths at XXX Secondary School. If a uniform patrol officer had happened upon the "drug den," the arrests could have foreseeably been made in isolation and never connected back to larger issues at XXX Secondary School. Knowledge of the context of the crime allowed the SRO to disambiguate a larger issue.

Value creation #2 – youth diversion: In this case, there was the possibility of some form of diversion for one of the juveniles who was dealing drugs.

Value creation #3 – preventing dangerous circumstances: The potential for loss of life by having "stoned" students crossing this set of train tracks during school hours represented a serious threat to the lives of XXX students. By eliminating this threat, the SROs actions may have prevented loss of life.

Story Two: "Solving a Crime in Seven Minutes or Less"

The SRO was in a community near BBB High School. The officer knew of the gangs in and around the school. One day, a call came over the radio regarding a break-and-enter and the theft of jewelry. Uniform patrol was dispatched to the scene of the crime. The SRO heard the call and decided not to attend the scene. Instead, given the SRO's knowledge of the youth gangs operating in the area, the officer headed over to a known address of one of the suspected members of the youth gang. Approaching the address, the officer asked an older man standing on a corner if he had seen anything strange within the last few minutes. The older man responded that he had seen some youths running across a yard and into a garage across the street. The SRO proceeded to that location. He opened up the garage to find the stolen jewelry and the gang of thieves inside. The officer solved the crime in seven minutes from the time the call came over the radio dispatch.

Value creation #1 – tacit knowledge: There is value in the fact that the SRO has a fine-grained knowledge of the community. Having an in-depth knowledge of youth gang members is an asset when solving crimes. In this particular case, the SRO had awareness of all of the gangs operating in and around a local high school. This knowledge base allowed for a rapid response to a crime that might have otherwise consumed officer resources in both the uniform patrol and robbery bureaus of the Peel Regional Police for days/weeks on end.

Value creation #2 – deterrence: Given the speed that the crime was solved, one might optimistically hope that gang members might be deterred from committing other crimes in the community because of the fear of being caught.

Story Three: "Meeting with Troublesome Students"

The Vice Principals communicate frequently with the SROs. Sometimes it happens that the VPs ask the SROs to assist them by participating in joint talks with troublesome students. In this particular instance, the school administration was dealing with a student that they suspected of drug dealing but could not catch or find a way to discipline. The VP decided to call in the SROs to educate the student about the law and the consequences of dealing drugs. The SROs were unable to convince the student to stop selling drugs, a conclusion that was determined when school administrators found that this student had drugs in his/her possession. This then led to a drawn-out afternoon with the parents of the student, who themselves admitted they could not communicate with their child and convince him/her to stop selling and using drugs. In this case, both the parents and the school turned to the SROs when nothing else seemed to work.

Value creation #1 – providing extra authority to school administrators: In an effort to make safer schools, the SROs are brought in to deliver a level of discipline and consequence that, in this case, neither the school administrators nor the parents could administer. In some cases, the recognition of there being legal consequences for your actions is valuable. Establishing an authority that can mete out consequences for antisocial behavior can be seen as a deterrent for future actions on the part of the offending students.

In this particular example, it is clear that school administrators benefit from this access to that extra level of authority when it is required. From the school administrators' perspective, the SROs are an effective tool in their toolkit that they can use in their efforts to create safer school environments.

Story Four: "De-escalation"

A serious incident had taken place in the school's lunchroom. A student had assaulted another student and the injury to the victim was quite severe. As a result of the injuries, the SROs were forced to arrest the student who had started the fight. The mitigating factor in what would seem to be a straightforward case of assault was that the perpetrating student had been previously bullied by a group of students – a group which included the victim. The initial bullying situation had not been brought forward by the student and no one identified the potential for an escalation of this situation. Following the arrest, the SROs returned to the school to give an update and discuss the incident with school administration. The administration expressed appreciation that it was an SRO who was familiar with the school and the students who was available to deal with the fall-out from the assault. In fact, the school administrators noted that they felt that the outcome for the perpetrator would not have been the same if the arresting officers had come from uniform patrol and were unaware of the background of this situation. They felt that, in this case, the officers would likely treat the perpetrator as someone who had assaulted another student.

Given a full understanding of the context, the arresting SROs dealt with the perpetrator in a more nuanced manner. They realized that the perpetrator had been the victim of bullying by several classmates and that his response was that of an adolescent boy who had grown frustrated with being victimized. This contextual information influenced how they dealt with the perpetrator (diversion). Instead of further victimizing the perpetrator, the SROs were much more understanding, demonstrating both empathy and compassion.

Value creation #1 – solving serious problems in the schools: This case is one of many examples of how SROs help school administrators solve serious problems that happen in the schools. In fact, the SROs who participated in this study indicated that they were often responsible for dealing with the aftermath of bullying within the schools. Armed with the history of the situation, as well as the background of the school administration, the SROs were able to deftly navigate what was/is a complicated situation. The SROs demonstrated great interpersonal skills and refrained from being confrontational with the perpetrator, the victim, the parents, or the administrators. In fact, by taking an empathetic approach, the SROs neutralized the frustrations of all participants and de-escalated a heated situation.

Story Five: "Officer Recruiting at AAA High School"

The SROs at AAA High School seem to make a point of stopping and chatting in the school's meeting area. AAA is a neighborhood school that draws specifically from the surrounding community, as opposed to bringing in students for specialized programs from across the Peel Region. Demographically, many students are members of either the Southeast Asian community or the Caribbean–Canadian community. Based on feedback from the officers, as well as documented interactions, a consistent topic of conversation between police and students at AAA High School is that of careers in the area of law enforcement. In this example, two students of Southeast Asian background, as well as four female students of Afro/Caribbean–Canadian background, were very keen to start careers in law enforcement. All students seemed grateful to have the opportunity to talk to the SROs and get advice on how they could get into law enforcement. The officers were very happy to give advice on this issue and had discussions with the students on how they could position themselves with their post-secondary education plans to better their chances of being successful applicants to the Peel Regional Police.

Value creation #1 – direct marketing of job opportunities for visible minorities in Peel Regional Police: Students who are interested in a career in law enforcement may not have access to information on how to proceed into that type of career. They may also be discouraged from learning about how to get into law enforcement because of a variety of myriad cultural and/or personal reasons. At the same time, there are calls from the community for greater representation of different diversity groups in Peel Regional Police. By creating the opportunity for youth to meet police officers in a non-threatening way, youth who may otherwise not have thought about careers in law enforcement may now consider the profession. Subsequently, the Peel Regional Police may have gained an opportunity to increase its ability to be representative of the population in Peel.

Story Six: "Lockdown at an Elementary School"

In the early afternoon, the SROs received an unexpected text from a school superintendent on their cell phone. This administrator asked the SROs to show up at their school to resolve a serious situation. No other information was given. The officers then proceeded to the school. Upon arrival, they were greeted at the doors by the superintendent, who proceeded to give a lengthy explanation of what had transpired in the school that afternoon. Just inside the entrance, it was clear that something bad had happened. The floors were littered with papers and broken potted plants. Venturing further down the hallway, a teacher was peering around a corner, observing what turned out to be a young student that had acted out and created the mess in the hallways. The superintendent went on to explain that the student in question had earlier in the day tried to harm herself by running out into oncoming traffic on a busy street. When stopped by teachers, this student then lashed out against her fellow students, ripping posters off walls, and throwing potted plants to the ground. The student would not stop her aggressive behavior. Nor would the mother of the student agree to come to the school. This escalation sent the elementary school into lockdown.

The SROs dealt with the situation with great expertise. They first engaged the troubled student and then brought the student into the main office, where the student subsequently relaxed enough that the police could then focus on getting the mother down to the school. While the mother eventually showed up, she was not prepared to help the school handle the situation and left without her daughter. The SROs then coordinated with the school administrators to get the student's home address so that the officers could bring the student home themselves. The girl was subsequently driven home. The SROs and the school administration then coordinated to advise the relevant authorities, such as the Children's Aid Society, to investigate further into this matter.

Value creation #1 – resolving serious problems within the school: The administrators and the superintendent turned to the SROs because they could not resolve the problem themselves. Without the assistance of the SROs, the administration would have had to call 911 or the Peel Police switchboard.

Value creation #2 – providing support for the young person: This young person was categorized as being suicidal. The young person's mother did not seem to be able to help her daughter and the school administration could not proceed on their own. The SROs were then inserted into this sensitive situation to try to comfort and care for the troubled/scared young person. Now involved in the matter, the SROs advised the Children's Aid Society in the hope that it could bring about a workable solution so that this young person would be given the attention that she needs to move forward in a more positive way.

Value creation #3 – providing peace of mind to the school administrators/teachers: Witnessing the activities of that afternoon, it was clear that neither the teachers nor the administrators could solve this situation by themselves. The ability to call on SROs when such problems arise (the SROs had given their cell number to the school principal) likely provided these individuals with an increased sense of security and peace of mind.

Story Seven: "SROs Attend the 'Big' Game"

During the morning parade at XX Division, the staff sergeant asks that the SRO be present at the basketball game taking place that day at MMM Secondary School. The staff sergeant mentions that 400 tickets have been sold to the game and that there will need to be a security presence. There has been a history of conflict between the home school and their opponent and Peel Police fear an escalation of this conflict at the game or after the game.

We then head to the school around noon. The parking lot is packed and it is hard to find a place to park. We enter the gym and it, too, is packed. The other SROs are all standing along the wall in one corner of the gym. Their presence is clearly noted by the students in the vicinity. The crowd is animated, but under control. The SRO responsible for AAA High School is clearly cheering on his school as they take on MMM Secondary School. The VP from AAA High School recognizes his SRO's enthusiasm and beams with happiness.

After the game, the officers mill around before heading out to their cars. The game has ended without incident and the students and families disperse. Afterwards, in conversation with the SROs, they relate that the presence of the different officers in the gym was important and a great way of showing the community that the police care about the school. They concluded that it is important for young people to interact or be around police in non-threatening circumstances.

Value creation #1 – establishing a positive view of police in the minds of young people: By interacting with young people in non-threatening circumstances, the SROs are creating positive impressions of police that contrast with the many negative examples of policing that are communicated through the media and the anecdotal experiences of dissatisfied community members. To counter these perceptions, it is important for the police to seek out ways to create positive interactions with the communities they serve. In this particular instance, the sight of an SRO enthusiastically cheering along "his" school is a positive experience for students.

Story Eight: "Diverting Problematic Youth"

A disturbing incident occurs at a school that is assigned to a colleague of the SRO I am riding with. Early that morning, we head over to the school to find out that a Grade Nine male student had been threatening one of his female classmates. The parents of the female student called the school administration to demand that the student be investigated. The SROs spent the morning investigating the incident. They were able to determine that the male student was living with his mother and siblings. The father was out of the country studying and the male student effectively ran the house and did not respect his mother's authority. The mother told the police that she could not control her son.

The police recognized that this was a situation that needed attention and met with the male student in his family home. After much discussion, during which time the male student continually misrepresented the truth, the SROs were able to get the male student to agree to submit to a youth diversion program to address his problematic behavior. Afterwards, the SROs were hopeful that they were able to head off further bad behavior from the male student, whose own mother had expressed real concern that he was becoming uncontrollable. Given that the boy was only a Grade Nine student, the SROs hoped that they had reached him in time to divert him from a path that would lead him to more destructive behavior.

Value creation #1 – youth diversion from unlawful activities and onto a better path: Prior to the SROs intervention, this young male student appeared to be on the wrong path. As the home visit indicated, the situation is complex. The father is not present and the youth does not respect the mother's authority. By treating the offending young person with compassion and understanding, the hope is that this youth can be diverted from the path he is on and directed towards more positive activities and outcomes. By reaching this young person at a tender age (Grade Nines are typically 13–14), there is the potential for this young person to get his life together and pursue an education that will lead to a more positive outcome. This student would have been charged with a criminal offense if diversion was not available.

Story Nine: "Student with the 'Bad Haircut'"

The SRO received a call from a Vice Principal regarding a potential case of child abuse. A student had shown up at school with a patch of hair missing from the side of his head. When the boy explained to the VP that his father had pulled out his hair in response to the bad grades that the boy had earned in school, the VP contacted the SRO. The VP also contacted by phone the student's mother, who claimed that the missing patch of hair was the result of a mishap she had while cutting her son's hair.

The SRO arrived at the school to meet with the student and the mother. The VP gave the background on the student – he had committed academic dishonesty on several occasions and had been caught telling lies on numerous occasions. In one instance, the boy had set off a fire alarm to cancel a meeting regarding his falsification of his report card. The VP also mentions to the SRO that the student is under a great deal of pressure from his parents to succeed in school.

The mother and her son come into the office. Immediately, the mother explains that this is all a big misunderstanding. The son meekly corroborates his mother's story that the missing clump of hair is from a bad haircut. He then says that he made the story up. Bewildered by what has transpired, the VP and SRO end the meeting.

Value creation #1 – providing additional authority to the school administration: The VP was frustrated by the dishonesty of this youth, but was ethically and legally bound to investigate the allegation of child abuse made by the youth against his father, alleging that this was due to the youth's bad marks in school. To the outside observer, the family supported this behavior. The mother expressed no disappointment with her son's continuous dishonesty and explained away the cheating. The blatant disregard of the school's rules exhibited by this student forced the VP to turn to the SRO as they considered the actions of the son to be threatening to the order in the school (e.g., setting off fire alarms to interrupt school proceedings). By calling in the SROs, the VP forced the mother and son to deal with the police. It would appear that this was the intent of the VP, who indicated he had run out of options to address the student's behavior. The VP did not have the authority to stop the student's continual disregard for the school's rules. The expectation was that, by involving the police, the family in question would take more seriously the actions of their son.

Story Ten: "The Problems with Private Security Guards in Schools"

During a regular trip to one of the SRO's schools, we sit down with one of the VPs while waiting for the SRO's usual VP contact to get out of a meeting. This other VP relates her enthusiasm for the presence of the SROs in schools. She brings up an example of how it used to be at another school that she worked at where the school had hired private security guards because they did not have access to an NPU program. In her role as VP, she was faced with dealing with many problems created by the private security guards. She noted that these guards were routinely found smoking marijuana with students and socializing with/hitting on female students. As the VP commented, "we needed to manage them to get them to do a job."

Value creation #1 – SROs independently foster a safe environment: As the example illustrates, private security guards need to be managed by the school administration. Hiring private security guards assigns more work to the school administrators. It should also be noted that their limited power in the eyes of the law also restricts what these guards are able to do. The SROs are police officers, first and foremost. They are working on community safety all day long – they do not need to be prompted or managed by the school administration to work on ensuring community safety.

Story Eleven: "Young Man Hanging Out in School Parking Lot"

Upon exiting the school, the SRO comes across an illegally parked car painted in electric blue. The SRO knows the driver and approaches him. With great skill, the SRO engages the young man in friendly banter, persistently asking the young man what he is up to and what he is doing. The SRO later explains that the young man is known to police because of a record of drug charges as well as break-and-enters. The young man is also associated with a gang that is contributing to problems in the community. The SRO goes on to say that the purpose of the interaction that day was to associate the young man with the car he was driving. If, in future, that car was cited near a break and enter, then it could be tied to that young person. The entire interaction was an information-gathering session to associate a known criminal with a car.

Value creation #1 – information gathering for the future: The SRO's ability to tie in a known criminal with a particular car might someday be of use to other Peel Regional Police bureaus. This small event might save the police service a great deal of time and money by being able to quickly solve a crime such as a future break and enter.

Value creation #2 – interaction with criminals sends message: The fact that the SRO interacted with the known criminal sends a message to this individual that he is being watched. Second, given this student's background, the fact that the SRO engaged with him on school grounds is useful as it may dissuade the youth from showing up on school grounds in future (i.e., his track record would suggest his presence on school grounds could only be considered a negative to the safety of that school's students). By confronting this individual, the SRO might deter the person from returning to the school property in the future.

Summary and Conclusions

Activities Performed by SROs that Add Value

SROs engage in a variety of activities that add value within the schools and communities they serve. Details on each are provided below.

Dealing with criminal activity occurring either in the school or the surrounding neighborhoods: The most common criminal activities that the SRO encounters include (in order of frequency) drugs, thefts, and break-and-enters (B and E's). The ethnographic study revealed the myriad ways that the officers address drug dealing on school property: they follow up on information provided to them by the school administrators, they invest their own time working on POP projects relating to drug crimes in their catchment area, and they use social media to identify and charge drug dealers operating in the schools.

Responding to calls for service: Many of the SROs' calls for service were made directly to the officer's personal cell phone by school administrators in high schools and elementary schools in the catchment area. The schools used this strategy to avoid having to call 911, thereby ensuring a fast response from an officer who had knowledge of the schools and experience of dealing with younger people. Other activities grouped under this heading include serving warrants, working on proactive police work associated with POP projects, responding to calls for back-up over the police radio, responding to Amber alerts, and spending time in court.

Activities that result in students feeling safer: The most common way in which the police make students feel safer is by "just showing up." It was noted that the visible presence of the police at the school and in the catchment area acted as a deterrent to the commission of assaults, bullying, and drug trafficking by young offenders. Other activities that the ethnographer saw the SRO perform that enhanced student safety included investigating threats of gun violence in the school and in the community, monitoring the school grounds, confronting trespassers, and responding to mental health calls at the school.

Relationship building: The SROs engage in a number of activities with the goal of building relationships with key stakeholders in the community. Relationship-building activities noted by the ethnographer included the SROs' attendance at community events, participation in sports with the students, offering seminars and training to students and community members, helping organize community charity events, attending school dances, acting as a liaison between the school and other police bureaus, and helping school administrators communicate with parents on matters of the law.

Ways in which SROs Add Value

The myriad ways in which SROs create value were observed or discussed during the ride-alongs. Details on each are provided below.

Source of intelligence: This study uncovered multiple instances where the SROs provided key intelligence that was then used to benefit the school or the community.

Stopping or following up on assaults: SROs dealt with a number of situations involving assaults.

Stopped a suicide attempt: The ethnographer witnessed the SROs stopping a suicide attempt.

Dealt with bullying: SROs were called in by the school administrators to deal with more serious cases of bullying. The SROs serve as a deterrent in this situation and are a way for school administrators and parents to make the bully aware of the severity of the situation (i.e., charges are possible when the police are brought in).

Managed a rape threat: The ethnographer witnessed an SRO assist a colleague who was dealing with a rape threat.

Youth diversion: The ethnographer observed the SROs placing a juvenile who distributes drugs into a diversion program, thereby offering the student the opportunity to pursue a healthier life track without a criminal record.

Crimes solved more efficiently: There is value in the fact that the SRO has a fine-grained knowledge of the community. The ethnographer observed how the SROs in-depth knowledge of youth gang members operating within the school's catchment area is a real asset when solving crimes. Their knowledge allowed for a rapid response to a crime that might have otherwise taken up officer resources in both the uniform patrol and robbery bureaus of the Peel Regional Police for days/weeks on end.

Providing extra authority to school administrators: In an effort to make safer schools, the SROs were often asked by the administrators to attend meetings with students and parents. This strategy was used when the school administrators wanted to increase the student's awareness of the consequences of their behavior in a more direct way than either they or the parents could administer. We note the value to the school administrators of having access to this extra level of authority when they require it. The opportunity to use the SROs in these types of situations is valuable, as it enhances the school administrator's abilities to make the schools safer.

De-escalation: On several occasions, we observed SROs help school administrators solve serious problems that arose in their schools. Armed with the history of the situation, as well as the background of the school administration, the SROs were able to deftly navigate complicated situations. By remaining calm, refraining from confrontational behavior, and taking an empathetic approach, the SROs were observed to de-escalate heated situations.

Encourage young people, particularly visible minorities, to consider joining the police: Students that are interested in a career in law enforcement may not have access to information on how to proceed into that type of career. They may also be discouraged from learning about how to get into law enforcement by a myriad cultural and/or personal reasons. At the same time, there are calls from the community for greater diversity within the Peel Regional Police. By creating the opportunity for youth to meet police officers in a non-threatening way, the youth who may otherwise not have thought about careers in law enforcement may now consider the profession.

Providing peace of mind to the school administrators/teachers: The fact that school administrators have the ability to call their SROs when a serious problem occurs in the school or the community around the school provides these individuals with an increased sense of security and peace of mind.

Establishing a positive view of police in the minds of young people: By interacting with young people in non-threatening circumstances, the SROs are creating positive impressions of police that contrast with the many negative examples of policing that are communicated through the media and the anecdotal experiences of dissatisfied community members. To counter these perceptions, it is important for the police to seek out ways to create positive interactions with the communities they serve.

Notes

1 www.socialresearchmethods.net/kb/qualapp.php
2 It should be noted that in this section we have changed certain details of the stories to protect the anonymity of the school, the officers, and the students.

9

THE VALUE OF SROS

Social Return on Investment (SROI)

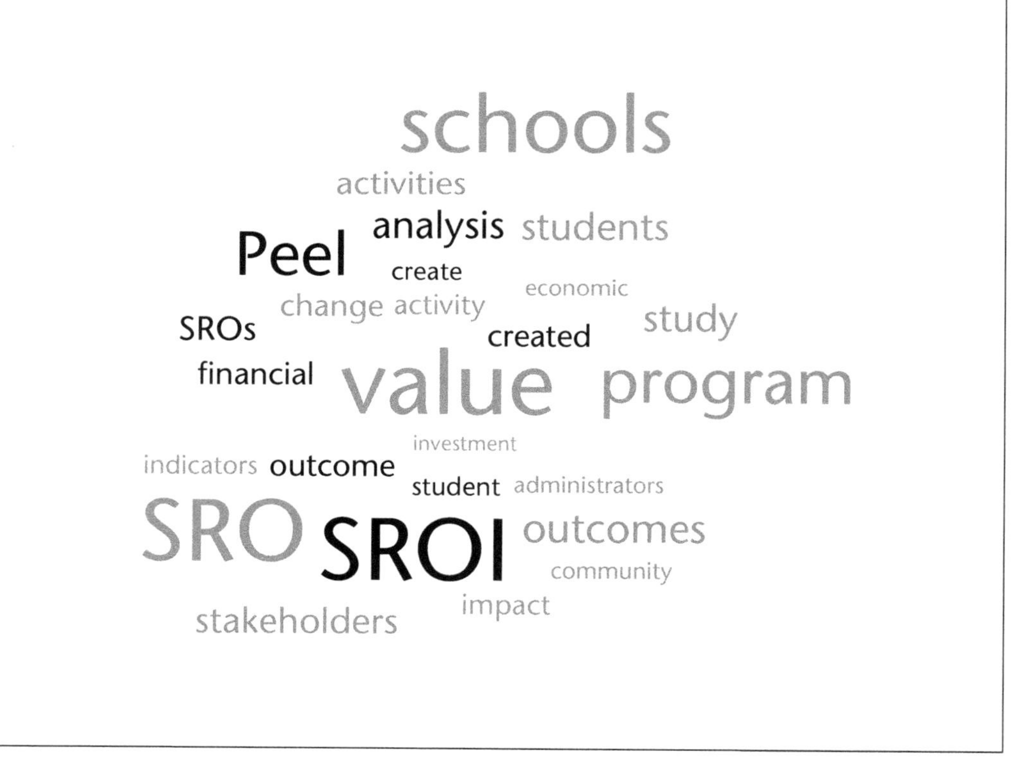

WordMap: 25 most common words in Chapter 9: "The Value of SROs: Social Return on Investment (SROI)"

Key Learnings

Social Return on Investment (SROI) is an outcomes-based measurement tool that helps organizations understand and quantify the social, environmental, and economic value they are creating. In this chapter we use SROI to assess the value that Peel Regional Police create by having a police officer (an SRO) assigned to work on a full-time basis in every high school in Peel Region.

A SROI analysis consists of six main steps: (1) establishing scope and identifying stakeholders to establish the parameters of the study, (2) identifying inputs, clarifying outputs, and describing outcomes, (3) evidencing outcomes and giving them value, (4) establishing impact (Impact = Outcomes – (Attribution, Deadweight, Displacement), (5) calculating SROI, and (6) reporting.

Scope: The value the SROs provide to the following key stakeholders: students, school administrators (principals, vice principals), Peel Police, and the SRO.

Inputs: Inputs are resources used to run the activities – money, people, facilities, and equipment. This is the investment against which the value of the impact is compared. In this case, we are looking at the amount Peel Police invests to deliver the SRO program in the five schools in our study (i.e., $660,289).

Activities: Activities are the intervention or program that is provided. In this case, the SROs engage in a variety of proactive and reactive activities ($n = 20$) to deliver on the desired outcome – "to create a safe learning environment for Peel Region Secondary School Students."

Outputs: Outputs are the direct and tangible products from the activity.

Outcomes: Outcomes are changes that occur for stakeholders as a result of the activity. Outcome indicators are measurable signs, signals, or pieces of information that allow the researchers to determine whether a specific change has taken place. In this study, we identified both qualitative (interviews) and quantitative (survey) indicators and relied on both subjective (self-reported) and objective (activity) data.

Evidencing value: In all cases, value created is calculated by linking the outcomes experienced by stakeholders to proxies that represent the value of change that they (the stakeholders) have experienced. The rule of thumb with SROI is: do not overclaim, a rule that was followed religiously in this analysis.

Value of the SRO Program: SROI Analysis

SROI calculations (done by SiMPACT Strategy Group[1]) determined that the social and economic return on the total investment of $660,289 (the cost of running the SRO program in the five schools in the study) yielded a total present value of $7,349,301.

In other words, we estimate that for every dollar invested in the Peel SRO program, a minimum of $11.13 of social and economic value is created.

> SROI measures change in ways that are relevant to the people or organizations that experience or contribute to it. It tells the story of how change is being created by measuring social, environmental and economic outcomes and uses monetary values to represent them.
>
> *(Nef, 2012, p. 1)*

SROI is about value rather than money (Nef, 2012). SROI is the method of analyzing and putting a monetary value on the worth of a program or an intervention (Arvidson, Battye, & Salisbury, 2014). According to Emerson, Wachowicz, and Chun (2000), SROI is based on the premise that money invested in public value creation will generate a return that exceeds the initial monetary investment. This return in value creation, therefore, needs to be captured during any program evaluation. According to the developers of this technique, the actual value created by public investments in programs such as the one offered by the Peel Regional Police is either under-valued or never documented (Emerson, Wachowicz, & Chun, 2000). They attribute this problem to the fact that it is difficult to assign a market value to a public good using traditional metrics (Arvidson et al., 2014) and recommended that SROI methodologies be used as a way to identify and capture forms of value that have previously gone unmeasured (King, 2014; Ryan & Lyne, 2008). As noted by MBA Associates (2015): "SROI analyses show value for money in terms that go beyond the financial. They assess a 'triple-bottom-line' of financial, social and environmental returns and compare them with cash and other investments to create a ratio" (p. 5).

REDF (formerly known as the Roberts Enterprise Development Fund) was created to provide assistance to nonprofit organizations on the measurement of value. REDF aimed to create something more complex, realistic, and nuanced than was possible with a simple "bean-counting" technique – a new metric that would provide credible data for both practitioners and investors. This metric became SROI, "a complex construct that essentially measures cost-savings and changes in either a society or individuals' lives as a result of social purpose enterprise employment" (Twersky, 2002, p. 14). SROI has grown in scope to become a measurement tool that is used in both the public and private sectors (Nef, 2012).

An SROI analysis consists of six main steps: (1) establishing scope and identifying stakeholders to establish the parameters of the study, (2) identifying inputs, clarifying outputs, and describing outcomes, (3) evidencing outcomes and giving them value, (4) establishing impact (Impact = Outcomes – (Attribution, Deadweight, Displacement)), (5) calculating SROI, and (6) reporting. The interested reader is referred to Nef (2012) for an excellent review of the different steps required to complete an SROI analysis. The actual SROI calculations for this project were done by SiMPACT Strategy Group,[2] which specializes in measuring and valuing social impact. SROI was calculated using the data presented in previous chapters in this book.

This chapter provides details on how SROI techniques were used by the authors to measure the value that results from Peel Police's SRO program. The chapter is divided into seven sections, each of which describes a different step in the SRO evaluation process. We strongly recommend that any public organization that wishes to assign value to a program that they offer follow these steps. The first thing we did when undertaking this project was to establish an advisory board to guide the research. How this was done is described in Chapter 1 and in the first section of this chapter. The second section presents important details on how we went about establishing the scope of this evaluation (i.e., deciding what is "in-scope" and what is "out of scope," and why). The third and fourth sections describe how we arrived at consensus with respect to inputs into the SROI process (i.e., activities performed by the SRO) as well as the desired outcomes and outputs. The fifth section briefly outlines the process used to determine how best to establish what SROI methodologists call "the change story" (i.e., what data to collect and from whom). The heart of this chapter is the material presented in the final two sections. Information on how the SROI analysis was undertaken by SiMPACT and how value was calculated are provided in the sixth section. The results of this analysis are provided in the last section with the articulation of the value of the SRO program realized by key stakeholders, including high school students in Peel Region, the SRO, school administrators, the community, and Peel Police.

Establishment of an Advisory Board to Guide the Research

Our research team of academics are not experts in either operational policing or in secondary school environments. As such, we needed the cooperation and help of those that were experienced in these environments to complete the SROI analysis. Accordingly, before beginning the investigation, we created an advisory board to guide the research as well as inform our interpretation of key findings.

The composition of this group was key. There was a need for senior leadership representing the police and the school boards, as well as guidance from SROs and experienced school administrators. With this in mind, the researchers recruited a Research Advisory Board to guide the SROI research (SROI RAB). The SROI RAB included representatives from Peel Regional Police (deputy chief, inspector, NPU staff sergeant, the SROs working in the five schools participating in this study) as well as ten of the region's school administrators (principals, vice principals, superintendents, school board researchers). Initial conversations with the members of the SROI RAB determined that none of them was familiar with the SROI research methodology and wanted to learn more. This issue was addressed by having the research team give a presentation on the SROI methodology before discussing how to proceed with the project.

Following the presentation on the SROI methodology to the SROI RAB, we discussed, as a group, how they wanted to proceed. Many pointed out that it would be very difficult to get the senior people in the room to attend multiple meetings, given their busy schedules. The group decided that this could be addressed by the creation of a subcommittee of the SROI RAB that would be tasked with steering the project along during the initial months. All members of this subcommittee committed to meeting with the research team at least once a month and to give feedback on any findings that were sent out by email between these meetings. This group, which is referred to throughout the rest of the report as the SROI Steering Committee, included two SROs, an inspector who was involved with the NPU program, a sergeant in charge of coordination, one high school vice principal, two school board superintendents, and one school board researcher ($n = 8$). We chaired all SROI Steering Committee meetings. At the beginning stages of the research, the SROI Steering Committee focused on stakeholder identification. As the project evolved, the SROI steering committee worked with the researchers to create a set of key indicators that would be applied to all five schools.

Step One: Establishing Scope

"The scope of an SROI analysis is an explicit statement about the boundary of what is being considered. It is often the result of negotiations about what is feasible to measure and what you would like to be able to improve or communicate" (Nicholls, 2009, p. 18). A list of the steps we followed to determine the scope of our SROI analysis is provided below.

Create a List of all Stakeholders

The research team first took the SROI RAB through an exercise to identify all of the stakeholders who needed to be considered in the SROI process. This step was accomplished by engaging in a brainstorming exercise with the entire group, with the goal of generating a list of all potential stakeholders.

The initial list of possible stakeholders identified through this brainstorming exercise included a very diverse group, including: students, parents and families, police, educators, school administrators, school staff, student support workers (e.g., social workers, child youth workers, psychologists), the surrounding community, community services, athletic coaches, and students not yet in secondary school (i.e., Grade 8 students).

This initial list of stakeholders was somewhat unwieldy, and, as such, it was decided that it needed to be reduced for the purposes of this evaluation. Consequently, we went back to the SROI RAB with the goal of reducing our initial list to a more manageable number. This was accomplished by giving each of them a copy of the full list of possible stakeholders and asking them to help us identify from among this list who we: (1) absolutely needed to include in the study, (2) who would be nice to include in the study, and (3) individuals or groups who were only peripherally of interest to our SROI analysis.

We began this exercise by splitting the SROI RAB into four smaller groups. Each subgroup included representatives from both the police and the school boards. These four groups were then asked to discuss the list of the potential stakeholders and classify them into the three groups noted above. They were also asked to justify why they felt a given stakeholder was important/ less important to the study. There was little agreement within the room and in the four hours allocated for this exercise the group only reached consensus in one area, with everyone agreeing that high-school students were the primary stakeholders of the SRO program. The SROI RAB decided to refer the matter back to the SROI Steering Committee for further discussion.

Decide which Stakeholders Should Be Included in the SROI Exercise

To ensure that the scope of the study was neither too narrow, nor too broad, a follow-up meeting was scheduled for the Steering Committee that was tasked by the advisory board with responsibility for determining the key stakeholders. To accomplish this goal, the research team led the Steering Committee through a mapping exercise using a "Level of Importance Matrix"[3] to guide the discussion. The one axis of this matrix considers the level of power or influence each stakeholder has over the NPU program. The other axis considers the importance of the stakeholder to the NPU program (see Figure 9.1).

Level of Importance	Level of Influence: Low	Level of Influence: High
High	**Primary Beneficiaries** The school The surrounding community Parents of students Students Students: Victims	**Ones who can make a difference** SRO VP in charge of discipline School administrators Youth Support Workers (social worker, child youth worker (CYW), psychological support) Peel Police
Low	**Bystanders**	**At risk group** Students: Mental health issues Students: Behavioral issues Students: "Record of problematic behavior in the past" (i.e., in public school) Students: Bystanders

FIGURE 9.1 Level of importance matrix

The SROI Steering Committee was asked to map the stakeholders onto the two-by-two matrix using the following definitions to guide their decision making:

- *Primary beneficiaries*: These are the main stakeholders whose interests need to be protected.
- *Ones that make a difference*: Stakeholders that are key to the success of the SRO program. These are stakeholders that the SRO needs to build good working relationships with to ensure effective delivery of, and support for, the program.
- *The at-risk group*: Stakeholders who may be at risk and require careful attention (either monitoring or assistance from the SRO officer).
- *Bystanders*: Those that are unlikely to be a focus of the NPU program, but may have some indirect influence over its success.

Discussion within the group determined that the student stakeholder group likely included a number of important subgroups that had to be identified and classified in terms of importance and influence. After much discussion, the Steering Committee arrived at the schematic shown in Figure 9.2 below, which they felt represented the various groups of students in the school that are likely to be impacted by SROs in quite different ways.

By placing the various stakeholders into the labeled quadrants, it became clear which groups could be considered 'critical stakeholders' who needed to be consulted during the evaluation process versus groups who had less familiarity with the workings of the SRO program. Based on the perceived importance and influence that each of the potential stakeholders have on the SRO program/the SRO has on them, this mapping exercise led the Steering Committee to land upon a consensus that consultation with representatives from each of the following stakeholder groups was key to any SROI analysis:

- students (see Chapter 4);
- school administrators (principals, vice principals) and student support workers (see Chapter 5);
- SROs (see Chapter 6); and
- staff sergeants (see Chapter 7).

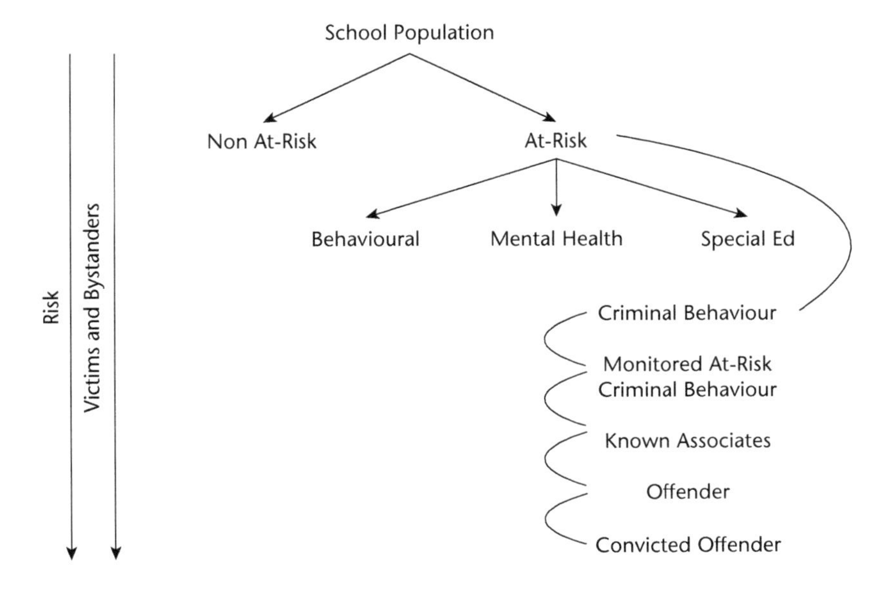

FIGURE 9.2 Subgroups of students

The four quadrants of the matrix are as shown in Figure 9.1, along with the final classification of the various stakeholders that was agreed upon at the end of the consultation.

Some stakeholders, such as the surrounding community and the parents of students attending the school, were not included as stakeholders in the SROI analysis because: (1) it would be hard (if not impossible) to gather information from a representative sample of parents, and (2) these stakeholders have limited, if any, familiarity with the SRO program. The Steering Committee also felt that the teachers had limited familiarity with the SRO program and were considered to have relatively little influence on how the SRO program is administered and run. That being said, it was noted that this evaluation might lead to greater understanding of the SRO program and subsequently greater interaction between teachers and SROs.

Get Buy-In from Key Stakeholders (i.e., the School Boards)

To collect the data needed for the SROI analysis it was necessary to get the participation of both of Peel Region's school boards in the research project. The fact that we were able to obtain excellent buy-in from these groups was, in retrospect, a central element to the success of the research.

The first step the research team took to obtain the necessary levels of participation was to ask the Peel Regional Police to raise the topic with the school boards on behalf of the research team. The senior leadership of Peel Police approached director-level representatives from the Peel District School Board (PDSB) and the Dufferin–Peel Catholic District School Board (DPCDSB) to begin the conversation of creating a research partnership. The Deputy Chief from Peel Police, as well as a participating police inspector, met with the school board directors to begin the dialogue. This meeting was followed up by a formal invitation to both school boards from the director of the research team, Professor Linda Duxbury. The invitation emphasized the topical nature of the research and the opportunity to participate in cutting edge applied research. The point was also made that policing investments across Canada are increasingly under scrutiny, and that it would be helpful if those who perhaps benefit from specific policing programs participated in endeavors that increased the understanding of the program's impact.

Select the Schools that Will Be Involved in the SROI Analysis

Resource constraints on all sides meant that we had to select from the 62 high schools in the region a subset of schools to participate in the SROI research initiative. These schools had to agree to participate in all data collection exercises that were required by the SROI methodology. Selection of the schools was done as follows. We began by asking for volunteers. The fact that a number of high schools wanted to participate in this exercise can be considered a reflection of the reputation of the SRO program in the Peel Region high schools. To narrow this list down, we asked both the Peel Regional Police and the directors of research at both school boards to nominate secondary schools that would help us best understand the phenomena being studied. We then, with the help of the school boards and Peel Regional Police, selected schools that reflected the region's diversity. The senior administrators at each of these schools were then contacted by the researchers, the project explained, and the demands on their time outlined. We ended the call by asking for their support. Ultimately, five schools agreed to participate in the study. It should be noted that none of the schools we asked to participate turned us down. We again feel that this reflects the high level of value those working within the schools accord to the SRO program.

Get a Good Understanding of the Context Within which the SROI Analysis Is Being Undertaken

Contextualizing the data collection process is an important step. In this particular case, the researchers needed to develop an understanding of the five schools that were selected to participate in the study. The issues in the school that the SROs were reacting to, or proactively trying to counteract, could be the result of any number of factors, including, but not limited to, location, community characteristics, and demographics. It could also be the result of the physical, social, or academic environment of the school. To this end, our team researched each school and their surrounding areas to create a document on the backgrounds of each school. Data were pulled from a variety of publicly available reports (e.g., the Fraser Institute's school rankings), reports from the participating school boards, and interviews with participating SROs, vice principals, and principals. These profiles provided the context to interpret any data collected as part of the SROI evaluation process.

As noted above, five Peel Region high schools participated in the SRO evaluation. Three secondary schools were part of the public school board (PDSB) and two secondary schools belonged to the Catholic school board (DPCDSB). The demographic mix of the selected secondary schools varied greatly as well. Among Canadian school districts, the Peel Boards have among the most ethnically and culturally diverse student population in Canada. According to the available statistics, the schools that participated in this study were no different. Two schools featured a significant majority of students from Southeast Asia who did not speak English at home. One school featured a significant majority of students from Caribbean and African families. One school featured a significant majority of students from families of European heritage. The final school had an extremely diverse student population and included students of African, European, East Asian, and Caribbean heritage.

Two of the selected secondary schools are classified as "Urban and Priority High Schools." This term means that these schools receive additional funding because they have been recognized by the province of Ontario to be located in areas that experience complications from poverty, criminal and gang activity, and a lack of community resources. The additional funding allows these schools to offer programs in a number of vital areas, such as: (1) breakfast and lunch programs, (2) student leadership and engagement programming (e.g., Grade 9 orientation camps, leadership training), (3) lunch-time and after-school programming (e.g., intramural sports, music ensembles, special interest clubs, summer camps), (4) staffing (e.g., student success teachers, social workers, child and youth workers), and (5) improving student achievement (e.g., helping all students afford the basics of school life, including class trips and transportation).

Effectively, then, the sample of secondary schools participating in the study ran the gamut of the region's cultural, religious, and socioeconomic spectrum. This was considered important, given the diversity within Peel Region. By ensuring that the schools that participated in this research varied on a wide range of contextual variables of possible relevance to the value provided by the SROs, we hope that the study's SROI story will reflect the realities of Peel Region, as well as increase the generalizability of the findings.

Identify the Time Frame for the SROI Evaluation

School administrators from the five schools were brought together to decide for how long the research initiative should run in their schools. After much discussion, the group of administrators decided that the study should run over the course of the first semester of the 2015–2016 high school year (i.e., the beginning of September 2015 to the end of January 2016).

Establishing the Goal of the Program Being Evaluated

SROI is considered a stakeholder-informed methodology. One of the foundations of SROI analysis is to identify what social value means to the stakeholders (i.e., what they see as the value of the SRO program). Such information is critical to the identification of the types of data that need to be collected to evaluate the program and from whom this data needs to be collected. Both the SROI RAB and the SROI Steering Committee were involved in this step of the research.

We started by acknowledging that the SRO program was put in place to benefit the students (the primary stakeholder group). To emphasize this lens, the research team began this stage of the study by asking the SROI RAB to tell us, in their opinion, what they thought were the goals of the SRO program.

The response from the committee was that the SRO program was designed to meet the following goals and objectives: (1) create a caring and inclusive learning environment within the high schools in Peel Region, (2) establish a connection between the Peel Regional Police and the high schools in Peel Region, (3) create, in all stakeholders, a feeling of ownership and pride in their school and in the surrounding community, and (4) create a safe learning environment in all the high schools in Peel Region. After much discussion, it was agreed that, above all else, the goal of the SRO program is: "To create a safe learning environment for Peel Region Secondary School students."

Step Two: Identifying Inputs – Activities Performed by the SRO

A central element of the SROI methodology is the creation of an impact map (see Figure 9.3), which is defined as: "A table that captures how an activity makes a difference: that is, how it uses its resources to provide activities that then lead to particular outcomes for different stakeholders" (Nef, 2012). More specifically, an impact map is a table that captures how an activity makes a difference (i.e., how different activities lead to particular outcomes for different stakeholders).

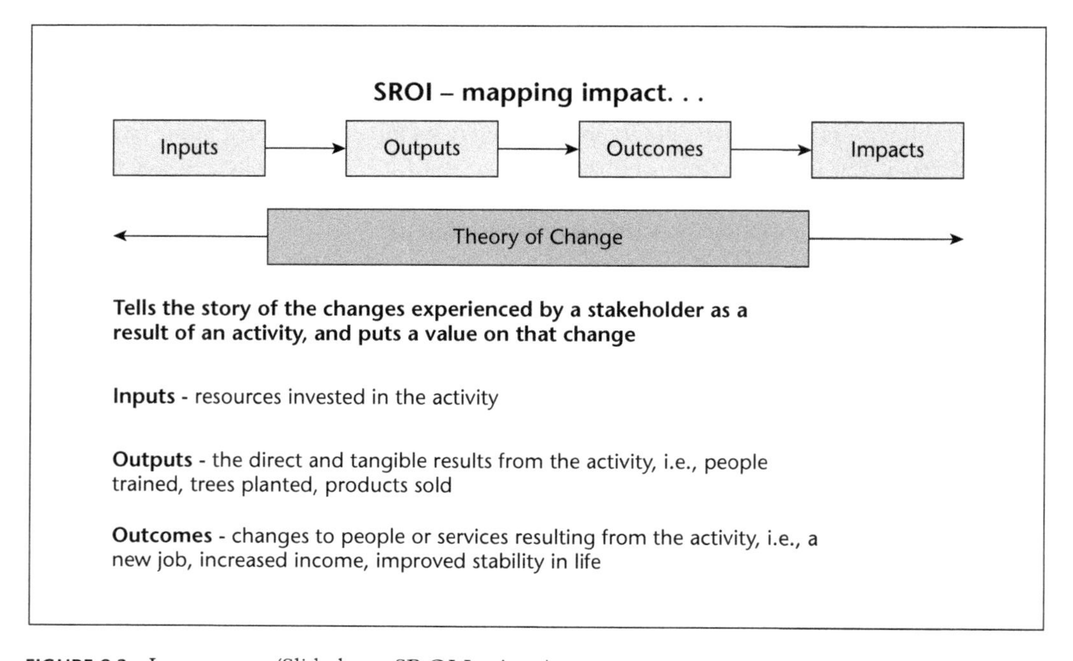

FIGURE 9.3 Impact map (Slideshare, SROI Institute)

TABLE 9.1 Mapping key terms to SROI analysis of the SRO program (Source: Peel Regional Police)

Goal	To create a safe learning environment at Peel Secondary Schools
Inputs	Assigned NPU Officer to each secondary school in Peel
Activities	1. Enforcement of federal, provincial, and municipal statutes
	2. Investigation of all incidents and related follow-ups by NPO at assigned secondary school
	3. Create and implement POP (Problem Oriented Policing) projects targeting behavior that interferes with the safe learning environment of the school.
	4. Monitor youth gang activity
	5. Lectures
	6. Liaison between school and police
Outputs	Tickets/charges by NPOs.
	Master occurrences for each secondary school, cross-referencing all occurrences at the school
	Investigation of all school occurrences by assigned NPO
	POP projects
	Youth gang reports
	Lectures at schools
	School/Principal awareness and satisfaction with officer involvement
Outcomes	Safer environment at secondary schools
	Fewer occurrences at secondary schools
	Improved relationship and communication between students–officers
	Safer community
	Improved police presence/visibility in secondary schools

The following pieces of information are included on an impact map:

- *Inputs*: Inputs are resources used to run the activities – money, people, facilities, and equipment. This is the investment against which the value of the impact is compared.
- *Activities*: This is the intervention or program that is provided (i.e., what SROs do to fulfil their mandate).
- *Outputs*: These are the direct and tangible products from the activity.
- *Outcomes*: Outcomes are changes that occur for stakeholders as a result of the activity.

In Table 9.1, we provide an example of how each of the elements of a SROI impact map can be conceptualized in our study. The process used to determine the various activities performed by the SROs during the course of their work was discussed in Chapter 3. The 20 activities identified from that process were used as the inputs to the SROI process.

Step Three: Identifying Desired Outcomes and Outputs

The SROI methodology also requires the identification and the measurement of outcomes, which are defined as the likely or achieved short-term (first level) and longer-term (second level) effects of the total intervention/activity. In this stage of the SROI analysis, the researcher seeks to determine if the activities included in the SROI analysis have the desired effect. The principle at work here is "understand what changes." Indicators are "ways of knowing that the change has happened" (Nicholls, 2009, p. 38). SROI requires that indicators of outcomes are found for all changes that are significant to stakeholders.

It should be noted that, in terms of a process, the SROI methodology recommends that the desired outcomes be identified *before* one seeks to identify the outputs. This is done because experience has shown it is logically easier to establish desired outcomes than it is to identify outputs.

Outputs are, by definition, the direct and tangible results that result from engaging in the activities included in the SROI. In other words, the outputs are the evidence that a given activity (typically measured in terms of numbers of hours) has occurred.

When constructing an impact map (see Figure 9.3), the practitioner is looking for the changes in outcomes (i.e., behaviors, attitudes, awareness) that occur for stakeholders as a result of the activities (Nef, 2012). To put the above information into the context of this exercise, according to the SROI RAB, the goal of the Peel Regional Police's NPU program is to ensure safe schools. The SROs engage in a variety of proactive and reactive activities (see Chapter 3) to deliver on this desired outcome. This outcome can either be realized directly or indirectly through a number of intermediate outcomes.

The 2012 guide to SROI uses the example of the Wheels-to-Meals program that required participants to come to a community center to get their meals rather than have the meals delivered to the individual's home to illustrate first-level and second-level outcomes of an intervention/activity (Nef, 2012). Three outcomes were identified as shown in Figure 9.4. The researchers first noted that those involved in this program benefited from better physical fitness (outcome 1). Several months later they noted that as a result of their improved levels of fitness, these individuals fell less often (outcome 2) and were, as a result, hospitalized less often (outcome 3).

The research team worked with the SROs, school administrators, and the SROI Steering Committee to generate a complete list of the desired outcomes of the SRO program. We interviewed the SROs and asked them to tell us a story that typified an interaction with a student or students in the school they were working at (see Chapter 6). During this story-telling experience, we probed to determine the outcomes of all such interactions. Similarly, we asked the school administrators to tell us a story about the SROs at their school (see Chapter 5). Again, we probed to determine the outcomes of the interaction observed by the administrators.

With the SROI Steering Committee, we took another approach. More specifically, we went through each of the activities discussed in Chapter 3 of this report and asked variants of the following question: "What changes (outcome) for each stakeholder in the school because the SRO engages in X activity (input)?"

For example, when we asked what changes for the student (the stakeholder) because the Neighborhood Policing Unit (NPU) walks around school with school administrators (proactive activity), we were told the students feel safer (outcome). The outcome chain was as follows. The first-level outcomes of this activity were that the students–parents–teachers became more aware of the police's presence in the school and the SROs developed greater situational awareness (e.g., more knowledge of the school's layout, such as where the exits were, where things [including people] could be hidden, etc.). We also identified the following possible second-level outcomes: (1) several stakeholder groups within the school community now feel safer (e.g., students who are victims, teachers, administrators), (2) some stakeholder groups within the school community are now less likely to be disruptive or engage in criminal activity (e.g., the at-risk student), and

Activity	Example of Output	Outcome 1	Outcome 2	Outcome 3
Luncheon Club (Wheels on Meals)	Group activities, including exercise sessions	As a result residents were fitter	As a result they fell less often	As a result they were in hospital less often

FIGURE 9.4 Outputs of Wheels-to-Meals program*

* *Source*: Nef (2012).

(3) several stakeholder groups within the school community have developed a positive relationship with the police (e.g., students, administrators, teachers that deal with the SRO, some parents).

Step Four: Establishing Impact through Data Collection

This stage of the SROI methodology involves evidencing the outcomes and giving them a value (i.e., identifying outcome indicators that can provide evidence that the outcome is or is not occurring). Outcome indicators are measurable signs, signals, or pieces of information that allow the researchers to determine whether a specific change has taken place. In this study, we followed the advice of SROI experts (Nef, 2012) who recommend that practitioners seeking to measure more complicated outcomes should use multiple, complementary indicators. Accordingly, in this study, we identified both qualitative (interviews) and quantitative (survey) indicators and relied on both subjective (self-reported) and objective (activity) data. A complete discussion of the data collection process used in this evaluation is provided in the Introduction (Chapter 1). Details on how the indicators used in this study were identified are reviewed below.

We began this step by again meeting with the SROI Steering Committee to discuss and agree on the relevant outcome indicators. We provided the group with an overview of various data collection techniques and measures used by other SROI practitioners to quantify some of the constructs we were including in our analysis. This process took many hours and much discussion, and the actual detail of how this was done is beyond the scope of this book. These discussions did eventually result in a consensus on how to collect the SRO activity data (see Chapter 3), as well as desired outcome and indicator data to be collected from students, administrators, SROs, and Peel Police staff sergeants (the data that are reported in Chapters 4 through 8). For illustrative purposes, we provide in Table 9.2 the end results of the discussions we had with the group with respect

TABLE 9.2 Expected outcomes/indicators of "SRO walks around the school with administrators"

Outcomes: What changed as a result of this activity?		*Indicators*
1st Level	*2nd Level*	
Students, parents, and teachers more aware of the police's presence in the school SROs have greater situational awareness (i.e., knowledge of the school's layout – doors, exits, places to hide)	Following groups feel safer at school: student, student who is a victim, teachers, administrators Following groups are less likely to engage in disruptive or criminal activity (police as deterrent): at-risk students Following groups are more likely to develop a positive relationship with the police: students (all types), administrators, some teachers (i.e., the ones that the SRO deals with), some parents Administrators have greater situational awareness Ultimate outcomes: students feel safer at school, school environment more likely to promote learning Teachers have more control over their classroom	Students, teachers (to a slightly lesser extent), and parents are more aware of police presence in the school (survey – Have you seen a police officer in your school?) Student and teachers report more positive feelings towards the police (survey) Students and teachers spend time talking to, and joking with, police officer (interviews) Students and teachers are able to identify (by name) the police officers who work in their school (survey) Administrators spending less time on issues related to student discipline (interviews) Reduction of criminal and non-criminal incidents on school property (quantitative data) Learning and student wellness outcomes (survey)

to the outcomes and indicators associated with one proactive SRO activity: SRO walks around the school with the administration. Examination of this table demonstrates the kind of thinking required in this stage of the SROI exercise.

Finally, it should be noted that in the SROI analysis completed in this study, we used the Time 1 and Time 2 Grade 9 student survey data (see Chapter 4) to identify changes in student's attitudes and behaviors over time that we can attribute to the presence of the SRO in the high school.

Step Five: Evidencing the Outcomes and Giving Them Value

SROI requires that indicators of outcomes are found for all changes that are significant to stakeholders, and then, once evidence of change is collected, the researcher develops financial proxies or approximations of value. As noted by Nicholls (2009), what one needs to do here is value the things that matter – use financial proxies to allow the value of the outcomes to be recognized.

An example from our SROI analysis (see Table 9.3) may prove illustrative. The interviews with the SROs, the school administrators, and the students indicated that the SROs can elect not to charge a student with a criminal offense, but can instead recommend the student attend a diversion program that is designed to remedy the behavior leading to the arrest. Diversion allows the student to avoid a criminal record. Peel Regional Police indicated that there had been 49 diversions in the five schools participating in our study from September 2015 to February 2016.

The students who are diverted are the stakeholders in this example. The outcomes associated with this diversion include the following: the student can continue their education/not drop out of school and will have the opportunity to avoid a criminal record. Two financial proxies are, therefore, used by SiMPACT in the SROI calculations: the personal costs of dropping out of school and the value of never having been arrested.

In all cases, value created is calculated by linking the outcomes experienced by stakeholders to proxies that represent the value of change that they (the stakeholders) have experienced. Other examples of the valuation outcomes process used in our analysis are shown in Table 9.4.

The final steps in the SROI evaluation process involve establishing impact and calculating SROI. Establishing impact involves assessing whether the outcomes being analyzed result from the activities. With respect to this evaluation, this involved making sure that the changes in the outcomes can be attributed to the SRO program. To do this, the analyst has to take into account the following (Nicholls, 2009):

- *Deadweight*: Consideration of what would have happened anyway.
- *Displacement*: The extent to which the outcome has been shifted from elsewhere.
- *Attribution*: The extent to which the change can be credited to others.
- *Drop-off*: The extent to which outcomes that last beyond the intervention reduce in effect over time.

TABLE 9.3 Evidencing the outcomes and giving them value: an example

Stakeholder	*Outcome*	*Indicator*	*Financial Proxies*	*Proxy Value*	*Proxy Source*
Students who are diverted (rather than charged)	Pursue their education Do not drop out of school Avoidance of a criminal life trajectory	Number of students in the five schools who are diverted Sept. 2015–Feb. 2016	Personal costs of dropping out of school Value of never being arrested	\$13,370 \$9,772	HACT Table ENV 1403 HACT Table YOU 1605

TABLE 9.4 Examples of valuing outcomes

Stakeholder	*Outcome*	*# reaching the outcome*	*Financial proxy*	*Proxy value per person per year*
Students at risk of being victimized	Reduced anxiety as a result of not being worried about becoming a victim of crime	185	Value of not being worried about being victimized	$13,338
School administrators	Increased job satisfaction	12	Cost of career counselling sessions that enable increased job satisfaction	$1,622
SROs	Increased employability as a result of utilizing skills gained while in SRO position	8	Value of the skills obtained and value of a promotion/ advancement within the NPU	$39,330
Peel Police	Reduction in the amount of time spent responding to incidents and/or offenses/ calls for service	935	Cost of a police call out	$310
Criminal justice system	Resources reallocated for youth probation officer	49	Youth probation officer wages	$1,017

The SROI is then calculated after deadweight, displacement, attribution, and drop-off (which may reduce the value claimed) are taken into account. The rule of thumb with SROI is *do not over-claim*; a rule that SiMPACT followed religiously in this analysis.

Value created for each outcome is calculated by first multiplying the quantity reaching the outcome under consideration by the financial proxy, and then subtracting the drop-off, attribution, and deadweight values. This step is repeated for all years where value has been projected. All the values for each outcome for all years are then added. This value is the total present value. The spreadsheets describing the SROI analysis undertaken in this study are available from the authors upon request.

Step Six: Reporting on the Value of SROs – Social Return on Investment (SROI)

The theory of change that guided our SROI analysis is summarized as follows:

Theory of Change *Create a one-sentence statement that describes your theory of change*
IF secondary schools that have safety concerns due to issues such as drug dealing, bullying/cyberbullying, assault, and theft are offered the services of a skilled full-time police officer who engages in prevention and enforcement related activities in and around the school, THEN students will feel safe, be engaged, have a positive educational/academic/school experience, will be deterred from crime, and will not be victimized. They will embark on their young adulthood successfully, while the community surrounding the school will feel safer and the police and criminal justice system will be able to reallocate resources for other priorities.

SROI calculations (see Figure 9.5) determined that the social and economic return on the total investment of $660,289, (the cost of running the SRO program in the five schools in the study) yielded a total present value of $7,349,301.

This means that, for every dollar invested in the Peel SRO program, a minimum of $11.13 of social and economic value is created.

As SiMPACT selected conservative estimates for all financial proxies, this ratio represents the minimum amount of value created by the SRO program. While the SROI ratio demonstrates a real value created, there are various outcomes that cannot be represented in financial terms (e.g., workloads of the social workers and psychologist in the school might increase as result of SROs assisting students who have mental health problems, the Peel Regional District School Board may benefit from an improvement in the quality of the schools' environment and safety, the value of reduced victimization, increased trust, and a more positive view of the police among people living in the catchment areas of the five schools). Finally, this ratio is relatively high and many SROI evaluations that use the same approach as followed in this analysis (i.e., ensure no exaggeration, double-counting, or overstatement) are calculated to yield $3 to $5 dollars of social and economic value for every dollar spent.[4]

Finally, it should be noted that, while this ratio was calculated using the data from the five schools that participated in the study, we feel confident that it can be generalized to schools across Peel Region (at a minimum). We base this assumption on the fact that we took great care to select schools that varied with respect to key socio-economic indicators that are likely to impact the value of this program. The diversity of the schools in our sample also suggest that a SRO program like the one administered by the Peel Regional Police will also add value in other communities. This ratio can, however, be expected to differ if the context is very different from the schools in our study (i.e., there were some factors that made the schools different, the communities where students live different) or the job of the SRO is different (i.e., officers are assigned to work in multiple schools).

Students Gain the Most Value from the SRO Program

Who receives the greatest value from the SRO program? The answer to this question is unequivocal: the student. As shown in Figure 9.6, just over 80% of the value of the SRO program is to the students, particularly those who have been victimized (i.e., bullied, cyberbullied, physically assaulted).

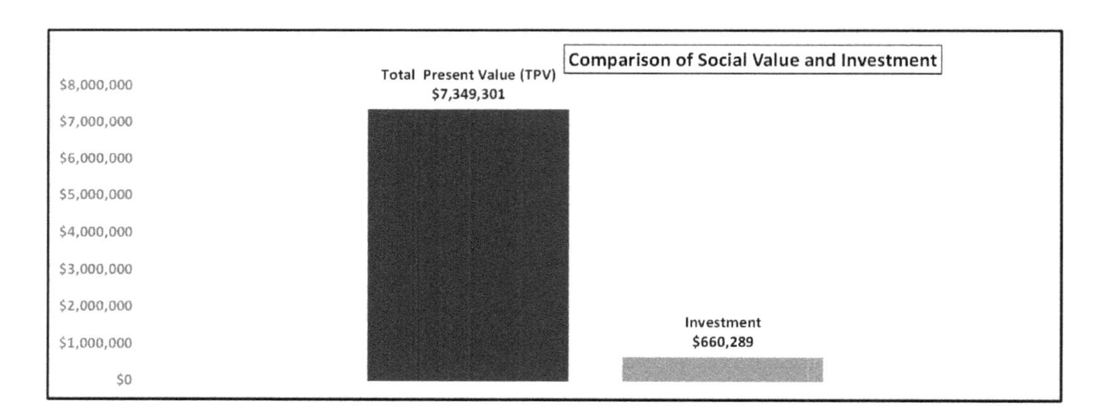

FIGURE 9.5 Comparison of social value and investment

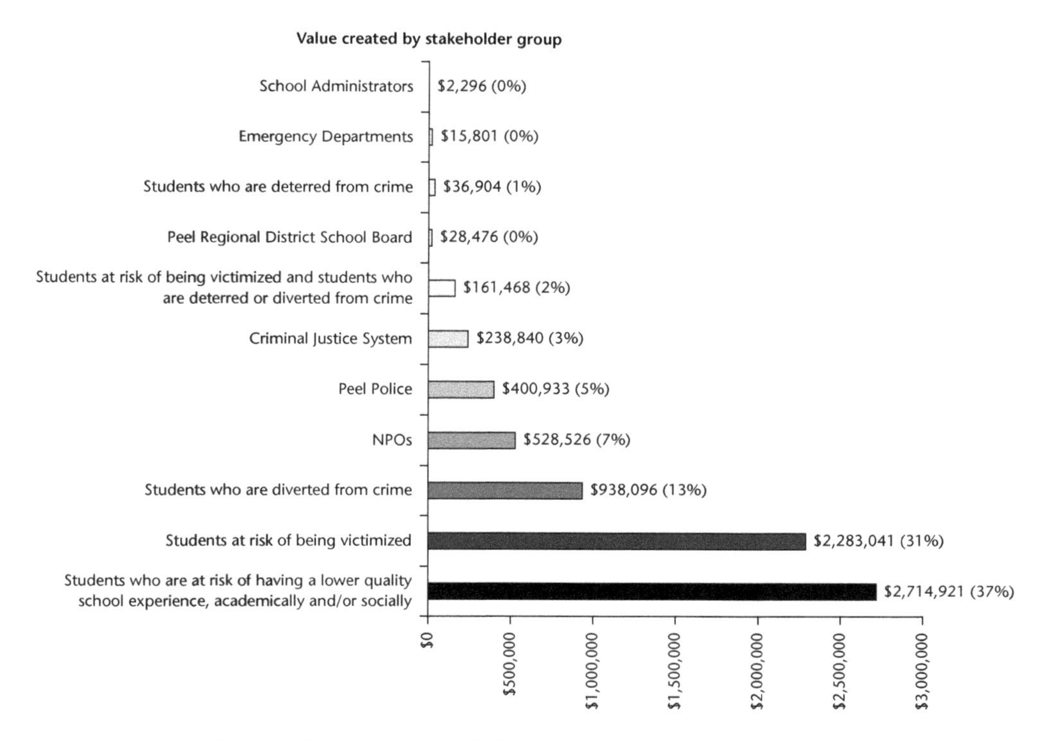

FIGURE 9.6 Value of the SRO program by stakeholder group

Also noteworthy are the data showing that students who are diverted also achieve substantive value from the SRO program.

The data in Figures 9.7 and 9.8 illustrate the value of having police officers engaging in pro-active and preventative policing activities as compared to enforcement. Our calculations show that activities directed towards prevention offer approximately twice as much value to students as those targeted at enforcement. These findings support the need for such a program in high schools where youth can benefit from exposure to officers with a community policing mandate.

Finally, included in the Appendix at the end of this book is a summary of the SROI analysis process followed by SiMPACT and ourselves in this report. This Appendix summarizes the various decisions we made during the course of this analysis. It is hoped that this information will help those who wish to use this methodology to demonstrate the value of other social programs.

Summary and Conclusions

This chapter presented an SROI analysis of Peel Regional Police's SRO program. The SROI analysis consists of six main steps: (1) establishing scope and identifying stakeholders to establish the parameters of the study, (2) identifying inputs, clarifying outputs, and describing outcomes, (3) evidencing outcomes and giving them value, (4) establishing impact (Impact = Outcomes – (Attribution, Deadweight, Displacement), (5) calculating SROI, and (6) reporting.

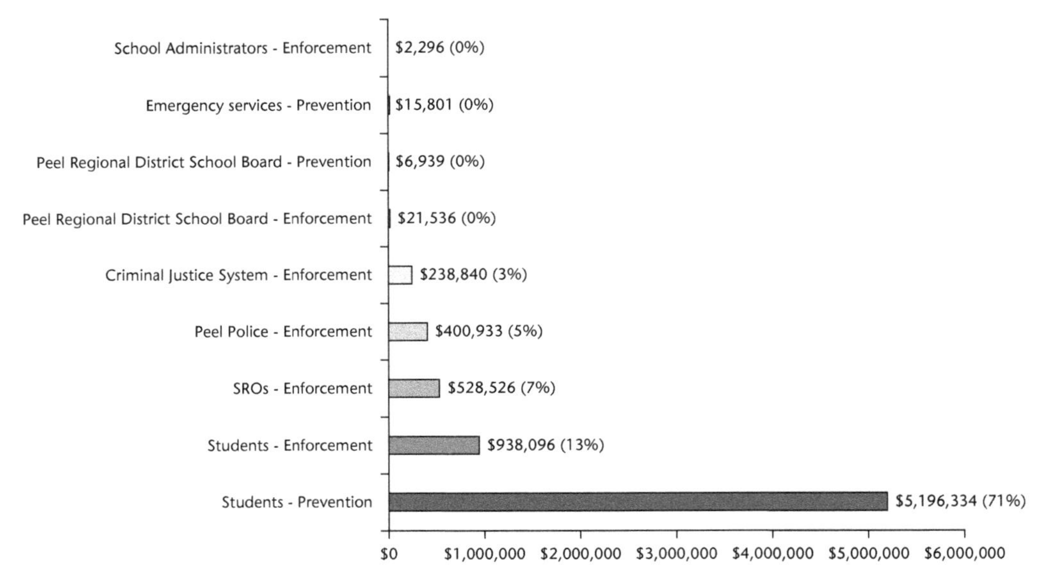

FIGURE 9.7 Value creation by type of SRO activity and stakeholder group*

* The value created through "enforcement" or "prevention" outcomes for each stakeholder group was added up, resulting in a total value created for each stakeholder group by type of outcome ("enforcement" or "prevention"). After much debate, we elected to consider "diversion" to be a preventative activity (as it reduced the likelihood that the student would commit future crimes, which would result in costs to the criminal justice system) rather than one reflecting enforcement. This decision also reflects the fact that SROs only used diversion when they knew the student and felt that the program would benefit them (i.e., prevention).

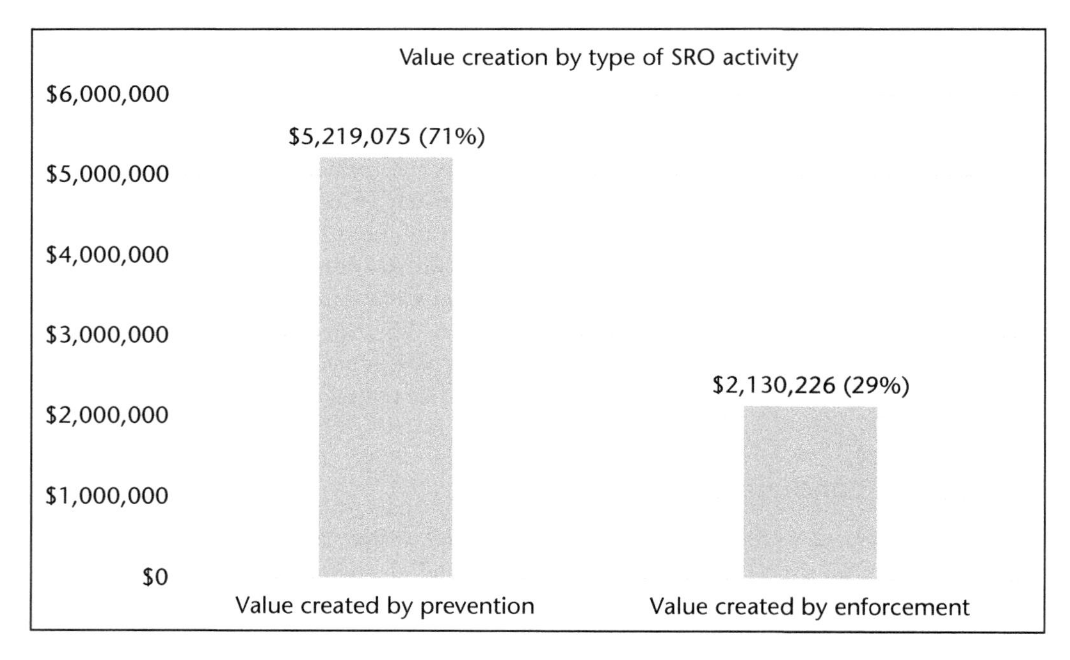

FIGURE 9.8 Value creation by type of SRO activity (for the five schools in the study)

In collaboration with an SROI Research Advisory Board (SROI RAB) and an SROI Steering Committee, both made up of of representatives from Peel Regional Police and Peel's school boards, the above six steps were undertaken. It was decided that the following stakeholder groups would be focused on in the SROI analysis: students, school administrators, SROs, and staff sergeants that had some type of involvement with the SRO program. It was also decided that the SROI analysis would focus on five high schools in Peel region during the first semester of the 2015–2016 high school year to determine if the SRO program is creating a safe learning environment within these schools. Together with the SROI RAB and Steering Committee, we identified relevant inputs, outputs, and outcomes associated with the SRO program and, as described in the previous chapters, we collected both qualitative and quantitative data related to the outcomes in order to assign value to them and carry out the SROI calculations.

SROI calculations (done by SiMPACT Strategy Group) determined that the social and economic return on the total investment of $660,289 (the cost of running the SRO program in the five schools in the study) yielded a total present value of $7,349,301. In other words, we estimate that for every dollar invested in the Peel SRO program, a minimum of $11.13 of social and economic value is created. In addition, the SROI analysis indicated that, out of all stakeholders, students gain the most value from the SRO program. Furthermore, the SROI analysis indicates that SRO activities directed towards prevention offer more value to students than those activities that target enforcement.

Notes

1 https://simpactsg.com
2 https://simpactsg.com
3 www.managingforimpact.org/tool/influence-and-importance-matrix
4 Personal communication, SiMPACT.

10

THE VALUE OF SROS

Summary of Key Findings and Conclusions

SRO
Police
administrators information
community activity
time
students analysis
officers
officer
proactive school value
crime criminal SROI
activities program
positive safety catchment
Peel ethnographic
stakeholders

WordMap: 25 most common words in Chapter 10: "The Value of SROs: Summary of Key Findings and Conclusions"

In an era where the costs of policing are constantly under scrutiny from governing municipalities, the time has come for police agencies to re-evaluate the services they provide. To do this, they need to answer questions relating to the value the different activities they perform create in the communities they serve. In other words, they need to change the focus of the conversation from "what does this service cost" to "what value does this service provide."

This book summarizes key findings from a longitudinal (2014–2017), multi-method (quantitative, qualitative, ethnographic, and Social Return on Investment [SROI] analyses) case study undertaken to identify the value of School Resource Officers (SROs) that are employed by Peel Regional Police and work in the service's Neighborhood Police Unit (NPU). Of particular note is the application of SROI techniques in this evaluation process. SROI, a methodology that emerged from the not-for-profit sector, helps researchers identify sources of value outside of those considered through traditional valuation techniques, such as cost–benefit analysis.

Evaluation of Peel Police's SRO program was motivated by a number of factors. First, the cost of this program is both easy to identify and significant (just over $9 million per year). Second, it is very challenging to identify the value that this program provides to students and the community (i.e., how do you assign value to something not happening, such as crimes being prevented?). The challenges of quantifying the value offered by assigning full-time SROs to high schools is evidenced by the fact that such programs are rare, as police services around the world have responded to pressures to economize by removing officers from schools through either eliminating the role of the SRO or having one officer attend to many schools.

Research Objectives: There appears to be a real need for research examining the value offered by SRO programs. The communities which have "protected" the SRO role spend considerable resources on such services and need to be able to communicate to their key stakeholders: (1) whether these investments are meeting their stated goals, and (2) the value such programs create and for whom. This book had two main objectives. First, it seeks to provide answers to communities, politicians, and school boards who question the value of SRO programs. Second, it adds to the existing body of work on the subject of public value measurement in general and SROI techniques in particular. This study fills a critical gap in our understanding of the value of assigning police officers to work in high schools (i.e., the SRO role) and should assist other police services and communities in making informed decisions on how to spend their resources.

Peel Regional Police's SRO Program: Peel Regional Police assign a full-time police officer to all secondary schools operating in the area policed by their service through their NPU. The officers who are assigned to area high schools are known as SROs.

On their web site, Peel Regional Police describe the program as follows:

> The primary responsibility of the School Resource Officer (S.R.O.) is to strive to create a safe learning environment at our Secondary Schools. This is achieved by forming positive partnerships with students and school administration. It is encouraged that officers use a proactive style of policing and interact with youth in a non-enforcement manner on a regular basis.

While the program has gone through a few iterations of its mandate over time, the core objectives are to assign sworn police officers to work in the region's high schools with the goal of facilitating the development of positive relationships with the youth living in the region and to enhance perceptions of safety and security in high schools and the community. In that capacity, the SROs work directly with school administrators, teachers, parents, and the community to ensure that the youth are either on the right path to a positive future or that they can get back to the right path.

There are 60 SROs working in the schools and school catchment areas in Peel Region. They are supervised by eight sergeants and four staff sergeants. There are also nine civilians involved with the NPU program. The total cost of the program is $9,004,880[1] per year (excluding costs for uniforms, law enforcement supplies, etc.). The staff sergeants have other NPU responsibilities as well.

Peel Police officers spend, on average, two years working as an SRO. SROs in Peel Region work in pairs. Each SRO pair are assigned to two high schools and work in partnership with the administrators in these schools to promote a safe learning environment. After two years, one officer rotates out of the SRO role and is replaced by a new SRO recruit. This rotation is done so that there is always one officer in the school who has experience in the SRO role and with the school and the community, and one officer that is new to the role and to the school. Finally, the more experienced SRO is tasked with coaching and mentoring the first-year SRO to ease their transition into the role.

Data that inform our conclusions: SROI analysis requires the collection of a variety of indicators of value (i.e., desired outcomes of the SRO program). Value was determined in this study in a number of ways using a variety of different sources of data (see Table 10.1).

Indicator data were collected over several years and in several formats, and required tremendous cooperation and commitment from the various stakeholders. The challenges we faced when designing our study were exacerbated by the fact that the SRO program in Peel Region has been in place for more than two decades. This makes it impossible for us to calculate value using pre–post comparisons. The fact that Peel Police's NPU program does not, however, operate in middle or elementary schools gave us another option on how to evaluate the program as it implies that students would not regularly interact with a school police officer until they began Grade 9. Accordingly, in this study, we collected survey data that enabled us to compare relevant student attitudes and outcomes at two points in time: (1) when the student started in Grade 9 (i.e., September 2015) and (2) at the end of the first semester of Grade 9 (i.e., March 2016).

TABLE 10.1 Summary of data

	2014	*2015*	*2016*
Qualitative data (interview data)	10 SROs	5 SROs and 5 school administrators (August); 10 school administrators (December)	29 school administrators (January–March); 8 SROs (January–March); 11 Peel police stakeholders (sergeants and staff sergeants) (March–April); 8 student interviews (April)
SRO activity data		Daily records kept by SROs working in the 5 participating high schools (September–December)	Daily records kept by SROs working in the 5 participating high schools (January–February)
Quantitative data (student surveys)		Surveyed students in Grade 9 in the 5 participating high schools in September (beginning of term) (n = 610)	Surveyed students in Grade 9 in the 5 participating high schools in March (end of term) (n = 655)
Ethnographic data		5 out of 10	5 out of 10

The final chapter of the book is divided into two main sections. We begin by summarizing the key findings from this study with respect to what SROs do in the course of a day. We present our typology for classifying the different activities undertaken by the SROs and summarize the findings on how the SROs in our study spend their time. We then identify those activities that the analysis determined provided the most value to the various stakeholders considered in this analysis. The second part of this chapter summarizes what the data tells us about the value the SRO program offers students, school administrators, the community, Peel Regional Police, and the SROs themselves. We begin by summarizing our findings with respect to the SRO's ability to create a safe school environment. We then discuss the other forms of value offered by the SRO program, identified in the analysis of our data, including: the establishment of positive relationships with the police, diversion, enhanced police effectiveness, and impacts on the performance of the school administrators. The chapter concludes with a summary of the value of the SRO program as determined using SROI methodology.

Activity Data: What Do SROs Do During the Day?

The role of the SRO involves participation in 20 different activities (see Figure 10.1), which can be classified along two different continua.

Reactive (n = 9) versus proactive (n = 11) activities: Officers engage in reactive activities as a response to something that has already happened at the school or the school's catchment area. In all reactive situations, SROs undertake a variety of actions to resolve the matter effectively and re-establish a safe school learning environment. All the activities in the proactive grouping, on the other hand, are taken by the SROs to prevent a crime, avert the victimization of other students, or forestall anti-social activity.

Intelligence gathering activities (n = 9) versus activities that use information skills and training (n = 11): Information and intelligence gathering activities contribute to the development of positive relationships with key stakeholders, while the activities that involve the use of information, skills, and training enhance the credibility of these officers within a variety of stakeholder groups.

Where Do the SROs Spend Most of Their Time?

Analysis of the activity data resulted in the following important conclusions. First, SROs spend their time in myriad different activities. Second, SROs spend almost a quarter of their time on administrative work (i.e., report writing, filling out property tags, lodging property, informing supervisors of cases, writing notes, court package preparation, disclosure requests from Crown/Defense, email correspondence with co-workers/Crowns/other police services, reading alerts that have been distributed). Third, Peel Regional Police SROs spend more of their time on activities associated with proactive policing/crime prevention (44% of their time) than they do on reactive activities involving enforcement of the law and/or calls for service (34% of their time). Fourth, a substantial amount of the SROs' time (30%) is spent on information gathering activities to help prevent crime. These activities also serve to enhance relationships with key stakeholders. Finally, analysis of the activity data showed that Peel Regional Police SROs spend approximately 5 to 10% of their time at work engaged in the following seven activities:

- criminal calls for service at or around the school (reactive);
- general patrol in the neighborhood around the school (proactive);
- acting as a liaison between school administrators and Peel Regional Police (proactive);
- engaged in patrol work in the community (proactive);

- engaged in foot patrol with school administrators in the school (proactive);
- working on Problem Oriented Policing (POP) projects (proactive); and
- appearing in court (reactive).

The other activities that are part of the SRO role appear to be performed on an "as needs" basis and consume relatively small amounts of the officer's time over the course of a semester.

	Gather Information → Relationship Building	**Use Information and Expertise → Credibility Building**
Proactive (prevention)	• SROs walk around the school with school administrators • SROs walk around other targeted areas where students congregate • Police monitor social media • SROs patrol the neighborhood around the school • SROs conduct patrol work not related to NPU • SROs engage in extra-curricular activities with students (e.g., sports, charity events) and in the community	• SROs respond to requests from members of the school's broader community • SROs play an educational role in their school • SROs act as a liaison between Peel Police and administrators in the school • SROs use information they have gathered to prevent criminal activity from occurring (in the school and in the school's catchment area) • SROs engage in emergency preparedness exercises within the school
Reactive (enforcement)	• SROs participate in Problem Oriented Policing (POP) projects within their community • SROs pass on relevant information to other members of Peel Police, as appropriate • SROs assist other bureaus with NPU-related investigations	• SROs respond to criminal (e.g., drugs, robberies) and non-criminal (e.g., trespassing, liquor, fighting, suicide attempts) calls for service at the school and in the school's catchment area; in other words, they use their training and information they have gathered to enforce the law • SROs deal with non-criminal critical incidents in the school (e.g., trespass, suicide attempts, criminal activity) • SROs spend time dealing with critical incidents at the school and in the school's catchment area (behavioural and mental health issues) • SROs enforce federal/provincial/municipal laws in the school and in the school's catchment area • SROs attend court • SROs write reports and complete administrative duties

FIGURE 10.1 Typology classifying the different activities undertaken by SROs

Which of These Activities Deliver Value?

During the interviews we asked the SROs, the school administrators, Peel Police staff sergeants, and students to identify the SRO activities that they perceived produced value. Ethnographic data were also collected to inform this issue. There was a strong degree of consensus between these various groups in terms of the key value-adding activities undertaken by the SRO.

Relationship-building activities: All stakeholders spoke to the importance of SRO engagement in activities directed towards building strong positive relationships between the SRO and the students and school staff (i.e., getting involved in student activities, counseling the students individually or in groups, running workshops, and having pleasant conversations with the students, staff, and parents). Such activities were felt to add value by: (1) increasing the level of trust between the SRO (and by extrapolation the police) and high school students, school administrators, and members of the school community, and (2) enhancing perceptions of safety in and around the school.

Activities that increase the visibility of the SRO within the school and community: All stakeholders spoke to the importance of activities that increased the visibility of the SRO within the school and in the adjoining community (i.e., walking around the school with the administrator, attending school events, being seen around the neighborhood, participating in outreach activities). These types of activities were seen to deliver value by: (1) deterring misbehavior and criminal activity, (2) increasing students' and school staffs' sense of safety, and (3) enhancing relationship building between the SRO (and by extrapolation the police) and high school students, school administrators, and members of the school community. The visible presence of the police at the school and in the catchment area was also seen to be a valuable deterrent to the commission of assaults, bullying, and drug trafficking within the school and the surrounding community. During the ethnographic phase of the study, the researchers saw the SRO perform a number of activities that enhanced student safety, including investigating threats of gun violence in the school and in the community, monitoring the school grounds, confronting trespassers, and responding to mental health calls at the school.

Educating students, community members, and school staff: All stakeholders spoke to the value of having the SRO spend time delivering presentations in the school and community. All identified seminars designed to educate students, staff, parents, and community members on how the law views issues of importance or relevance to them, such as bullying, cyberbullying, drugs, and the role of police in Canadian society as being appreciated. These activities were seen as providing value by: (1) reducing the amount of crime/misbehavior within the high schools and the community, (2) enhancing perceptions of police effectiveness, and (3) increasing feelings of safety within the school and the community.

Collaborating with Peel Police: Two stakeholder groups (Peel Police staff sergeants and SROs) saw value in collaborative activities between the SRO, the school, and other units in Peel Police. Peel Regional Police use the SRO to serve warrants, work on proactive police work associated with POP projects (typically drugs), respond to calls for back-up over the police radio, and respond to Amber alerts and other emergencies. These activities provide value to both Peel Police and citizens in the region by increasing the effectiveness of the service overall.

Enforcing the law: School administrators were the only stakeholder group to highlight the value of having SROs, who were familiar with the youth attending the school and knew how to interact with young adults, engaging in enforcement activities to deal with criminal activity occurring either in the school or the surrounding neighborhoods. Enforcement activities mentioned explicitly by this group of stakeholders included charging and arresting students who were committing crimes such as drug dealing, thefts, and break-and-enters, and diverting students from the justice system when appropriate. These activities provide value by: (1) enhancing perceptions of safety in the school and in the school's catchment area, (2) improving the relationship between Peel Police and students who are diverted from crime, as well as school administrators, and (3) increasing the effectiveness of Peel Police.

Activities which Deliver Value: SROI Analysis

SROI analysis shows that high school students realize just over 80% of the value of the SRO program (Figure 10.2). Students who have been victimized in the past (i.e., bullied, cyberbullied, physically assaulted), in particular, benefit from the program. Also of note are data from the SROI analysis showing that proactive SRO activities directed towards prevention offer just over twice as much value to key stakeholders (i.e., students, administrators, the community) as reactive activities linked to enforcement.

The Value of the SRO Program

This research initiative had one main objective in mind: to identify, and, where possible, quantify, the value that Peel Police's NPU offers to key stakeholders, including students and administrators working in the region's high schools, communities surrounding these schools, Peel Regional Police, and the SRO officers themselves. This section summarizes key findings with respect to the value of this program. We start by identifying sources of value identified by all stakeholder groups (i.e., areas of consensus). This is followed by the identification of sources of value unique to various stakeholder groups. This section concludes by articulating the value of this program as calculated using SROI analysis.

Value of the SRO Program: Increased Sense of Safety

As noted earlier, the primary responsibility of the SRO is to create a safe learning environment in Peel Region Secondary Schools. The data presented in this book provide strong support for the idea that the SRO program administered by Peel Police meets its goals of increasing perceptions of safety both within the school and in the school's catchment area. The fact that each of the stakeholders included in this study spoke at length during the interviews about how the SRO added value by making students and school staff feel safer reinforces our confidence in this conclusion. The fact that the student survey data as well as the ethnographic data mirror these findings provides additional support for this conclusion.

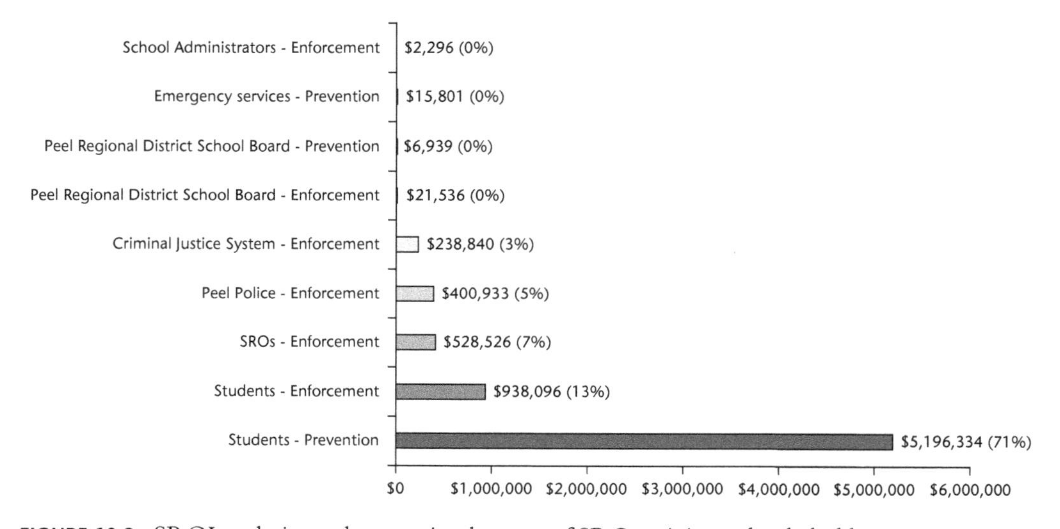

FIGURE 10.2 SROI analysis – value creation by type of SRO activity and stakeholder group

Is safety a problem in Peel Region secondary schools? According to the SROs and the school administrators we interviewed, the answer to this question is a definite yes. Seventy percent of the administrators flagged school safety as either a serious (10%) or moderately serious (60%) issue in their school at the time the study was being conducted. Administrators identified several underlying issues that contributed to these safety concerns, including the socio-economic environment in their high school's catchment area, the fact that some parents do not support attempts on the part of the school to discipline their children, and mental health issues within the student body. The view of these administrators was that the presence of the SRO in the school diminishes the severity of the safety issue within their school (from serious to moderately serious) and that "Without the SRO, we would be calling 911 frequently."

Why Does Having an SRO in the School Make Students–School Administrators Feel Safer?

During the interviews, a majority of students and school administrators stated that having an SRO assigned to their school makes administrators, teachers, and students feel safer when they are at school – "just by being there." The data identified a number of mechanisms that help us understand why the presence of an SRO within the school increases perceptions of safety.

Deterrence: Every stakeholder group felt that the SROs acted as a deterrent to the manifestation of criminal and inappropriate behavior simply by being visibly present at the school and in the community. Moreover, they all agreed that it was the SROs' ability to deter inappropriate behavior that resulted in increased perceptions of safety. Students talked about how the presence of the SROs at the school and in the community acted as a constraint to students who bully or physically harm other students. They also felt that the presence of the SROs reduced the likelihood that students (including themselves) would behave inappropriately on school property, and engage in bullying or fighting ("the SROs stop students from making bad choices, doing stupid things, and getting into trouble"). Students stated unequivocally that if the officers were not in the school on a daily basis there would be more fights, thefts, and drugs in the school and more school rules would be broken.

Of note are data showing that both the administrators and the students that we talked to felt that the SROs were more effective than school administrators at deterring bullying, assaults, and other criminal behavior, stating that: "SROs can enforce the law – while teachers, vice principals, and the principal can only enforce school rules." Administrators concurred. They noted that, in their experience, students who were not deterred by threat of school suspensions thought twice about their behavior when involved in a discussion with the police. They also noted that parents were more likely to appreciate the severity of an issue when the police were involved than they were when the discussion was just with the administrators.

Data from the student survey strongly supports the idea that the SRO program is effective at reducing the amount of bullying taking place on school property and in the surrounding area (see Figures 10.3, 10.4, and 10.5). Six months after moving from a school without an SRO to a school with a full-time SRO, the number of students reporting that they were afraid of being bullied or physically harmed by other students or by gang members either at school or during the commute to and from school decreased significantly, as did the number of students reporting that they either avoided going to school and/or skipped classes because they had been bullied or feared being bullied.

Other stakeholders spoke about the ability of the SRO to deter crime and inappropriate behavior at the school. School administrators attributed their feelings of safety at work to their belief that the presence of the SRO within the school acted as a deterrent to those students who were thinking of behaving inappropriately. This, in turn, diminished the threat of aggression, drug dealing, and bullying within the school population – all of which increased perceptions of safety all around. This view was particularly strong in the 50% of school administrators who had worked in schools that did not have a full-time SRO prior to their transfer to a high school within Peel Region.

Similarly, the SROs themselves felt that their presence at the school and in the community helped prevent or deter crime (i.e., bullying, fights, drugs, and robberies) by increasing the likelihood that people would think before they act. They felt that their presence in the school reduced

FIGURE 10.3 The likelihood that students will miss school because of bullying decreases over time

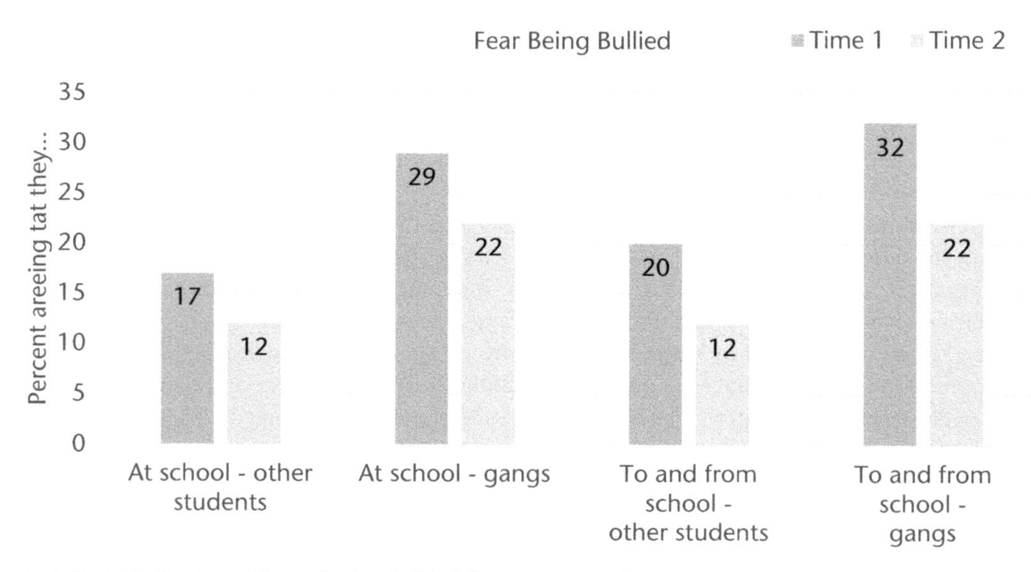

FIGURE 10.4 Students' fear of being bullied decreases over time

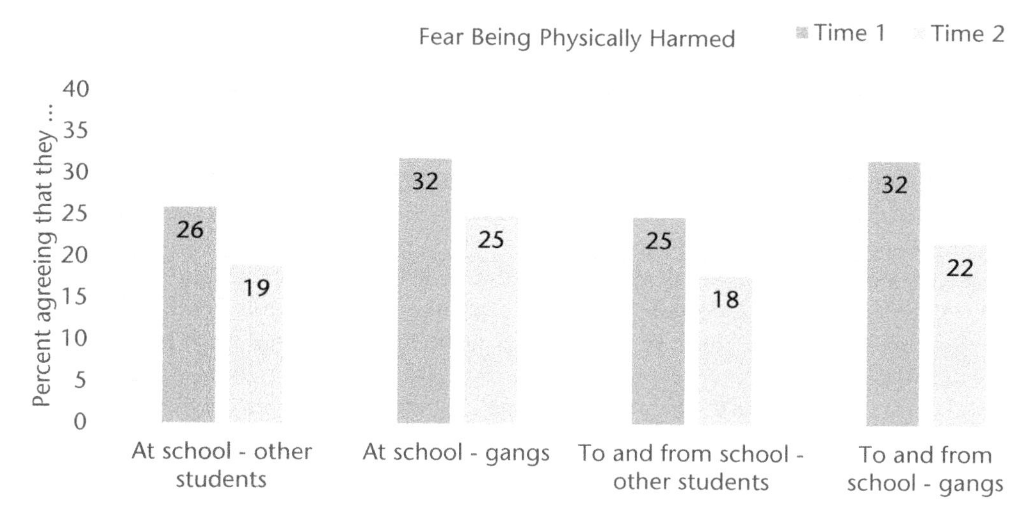

FIGURE 10.5 Students' fear of being physically harmed decreases over time

the likelihood that a student would suffer physical or psychological harm when at school by reducing the incidence of physical violence, bullying, and cyberbullying. Officers agreed that if they were not in the schools, drug use (e.g., smoking weed), drug trafficking, thefts, and the amount of violence, particularly in the form of fights that occurred in the schools, would increase. They also felt that crime in the community would also increase as students skipped classes, trespassed, and engaged in other forms of criminal behavior.

These findings were mirrored in the ethnographic study, where it was noted that SROs are often asked by school administrators to help them deal with more serious cases of bullying. Administrators felt that by involving the SRO in the discussions, they were more able to make the bully and their parents aware of the severity of the situation (i.e., charges are possible when the police are brought in).

Faster response time: Students and administrators who responded that they felt a lot safer at school because of the SROs linked this to their belief that they could count on these officers to be available if they were needed and act quickly to stop or reduce the severity of the situation. Students felt safer knowing that the officer was "there when the students needed them" and could respond immediately when issues arose and something unsafe happened in the school. The officers themselves also felt that their presence in the school and/or in the community enabled them to act quickly to reduce the severity of crimes/de-escalate problematic situations and stated that if they were not in the schools, response time to a 911 call from the school would be longer. The ethnographic data provides further support for this source of value as we witnessed an SRO assist a colleague who was dealing with a rape threat and an SRO stopping a suicide attempt.

De-escalation: Students, school administrators, and SROs all attributed their feelings of safety to their belief that the SRO understood the school and the students within the school and could defuse problematic situations or stop them before they escalated. SROs felt that they could prevent crime in the school and surrounding areas by using intelligence or information that they had gathered to intercept and stop crimes from happening. They also felt that they could intervene early with youth and help guide them towards more positive behavior. They felt that if SROs were not in the schools on a full-time basis, the number of preventative interventions undertaken with high school students in the region would decrease, as there would be fewer resources within the school to prevent the escalation of misbehavior. The ethnographic data reinforces these impressions, as the researchers observed a number of occasions where the SROs dealt with assaults.

Three other mechanisms, whereby the presence of the SRO contributed to perceptions of safety, were identified by one or two stakeholders only. School administrators felt that, if the SRO was not around, the victim of a crime/bullying might not come forward and report the issue. They also felt that, if the SRO program stopped, they would lose a key asset in their efforts to run safe schools.

The SROs and the staff sergeants felt that the SROs' ability to prevent crime and mitigate harm was a key predictor of perceptions of safety, a perception that might drive the large amount of time these officers spend in proactive policing activities in the school. These staff sergeants also felt that the SROs were uniquely able to offer education and counseling to help to mitigate the harm resulting from negative activities such as bullying, cyberbullying, fighting, and drugs that the students had experienced.

The ethnographic study also provided us with the opportunity to observe firsthand situations where the SROs helped school administrators de-escalate potentially problematic situations. In all of these cases, the SROs' understanding of the situation and their ability to remain calm, refrain from confrontational behavior, and their empathetic approach facilitated the de-escalation of heated situations.

Consequences of Feeling Unsafe

The above data draw a strong and compelling link between the SRO program and enhanced perceptions of safety for students and administrators. But, what value does feeling safer in a high school with a full-time police officer provide to these two important stakeholders (and, by extrapolation, the community and Canadian society)? The data from this study (see Figure 10.6) is

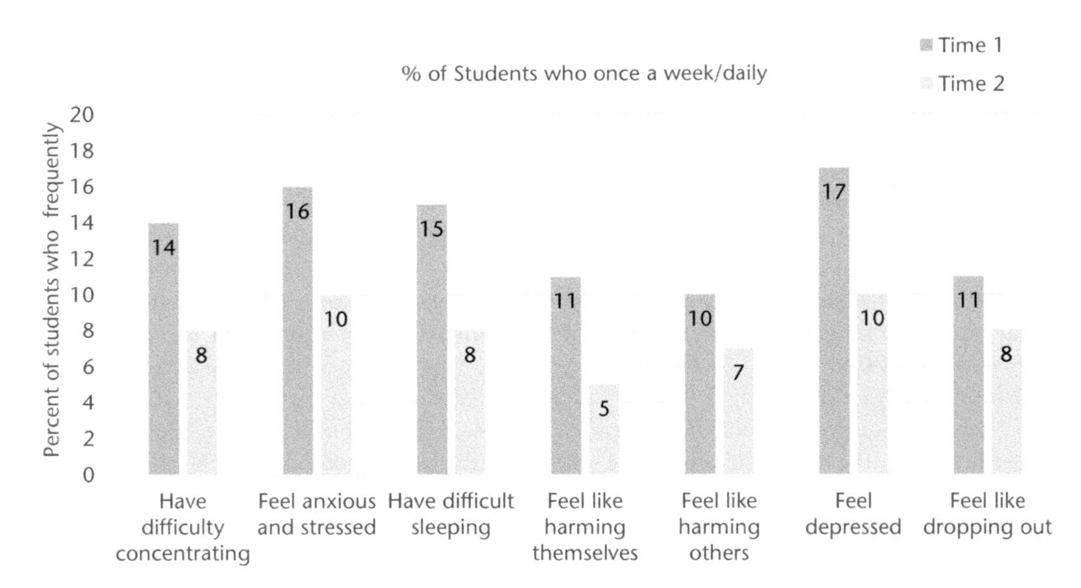

FIGURE 10.6 Students' mental health improves over time

unequivocal in this regard. Five months after becoming a student at a high school with a full-time SRO, the students who responded to our survey were significantly more able to concentrate, in better mental health (i.e., reported less anxiety, stress, and feeling depressed), less likely to report difficulties sleeping, and less likely to think about harming themselves or others. Given the data showing that these students who feel safer are also less likely to skip class, miss school, and be thinking of dropping out, we also expect that students who feel safer are also more able to take advantage of the learning opportunities offered in the school.

While follow-up analysis determined that some groups realized more value from the SRO program than others, it is important to note that our comparison of the Time 1 and Time 2 data determined that all students, regardless of their gender, regardless of whether or not they have made contact with their SRO, regardless of whether or not they have been arrested/stopped by the police, and regardless of whether or not they have been victimized, indicated that they felt significantly safer at school and less stress and anxiety five+ months after exposure to the SRO program than at the beginning of the semester (i.e., when they had no exposure to the NPU program). These findings support the following conclusion: all surveyed students realize measureable benefits from the presence of SROs in their school. That being said, the data also indicate that students who have been victimized (i.e., bullied, physically harassed) can expect to gain the most benefits from the presence of police in the high schools.

The students we interviewed offered another benefit of feeling safer: better academic achievement. They reported that they would prefer to go to a high school that had a full-time SRO because the presence of the officer gave them an increased ability to focus on their school work without distraction from feelings of insecurity.

Also noteworthy are the data showing that half of the administrators we talked to stated that they personally felt stressed or anxious at work because they felt their safety or security was compromised and one in five mentioned that concerns about their safety and security at work sometimes made it difficult for them to get a good night's sleep. These individuals also noted that having the SRO in the school helped alleviate their stress.

Value of the SRO Program: Positive Relationships with the Police

All the stakeholders we consulted agreed that the relationships the SROs develop with the community add tremendous value. From the students' point of view, the relationship they form with their SROs increases their faith in, and trust of, the police and provides a resource that students can tap into when they need advice, help, or information. In fact, the survey data showed that a substantial number of students (one in ten of the Grade 9 students in both our Time 1 and Time 2 samples) indicated that they had turned to their SROs for help when they had a problem. Also noteworthy are the survey data showing that the students in our sample relate to the SROs at their school in a different (and more positive) fashion than they do to the police in general and that their views of the NPU program became significantly more favorable over time. This supports the idea that students who have more exposure to the police in a non-confrontational environment (i.e., SROs working in a high school) are more likely to form positive relationships with the police and see beyond the stereotypes of police that are common in our society.

The views of the school administrators are very like those offered by the students. Of note are data showing that 100% of the administrators that we talked to indicated that they trusted the officers assigned to their school enough to talk to him or her about problems that are occurring in the school as well as to ask him or her for personal advice. The school administrators working in the five schools in the study noted that the SRO program allows school police officers to become part of the school community and establish trusting relationships with students, staff, teachers, and administration.

The ethnographic study provided additional data that reinforces the idea that, by interacting with young people in non-threatening circumstances, the SROs are creating positive impressions of police that contrast with the many negative examples of policing that are communicated through the media and the anecdotal experiences of dissatisfied community members.

Value of the SRO Program: Diversion

When a youth commits a crime, SROs can use their discretion to intercede without laying charges through a process called diversion. A diversion program in the criminal justice system has two goals: (1) to find a solution for the behavior leading to the original arrest and (2) to reduce the number of young people who are convicted of a crime and have a criminal record. It is in the SROs' power to divert high school students who have committed a crime away from the criminal justice system. All but one of the stakeholders (the students) talked about the value this ability provides to the students. Diversion offers value in at least two ways. First, it prevents or stops criminal activity within the school and community. Second, it gives young people a chance for a meaningful future, as it reduces the likelihood that a student will get a criminal record.

Value of the SRO Program: Enhanced Police Effectiveness

School administrators and Peel Police staff sergeants agreed that the SRO program increased the effectiveness of Peel Regional Police. They felt that the in-depth tacit knowledge that the SRO has developed in the community helps the Peel Police solve crimes and respond to emergencies more efficiently. One in five of the school administrators indicated that they never had to contact Peel Police, as their SRO was able to handle all of their policing needs. Administrators also stated that if the SRO was not around, the volume of 911 calls and calls to the Peel Police would increase dramatically. They also appreciated that the relationship that they had developed with their SRO facilitated a fast response to any emergency occurring at the school or in the surrounding community. Staff sergeants noted that any police investigation that involved high school students in the region was more effective when the SRO was involved (rather than uniform patrol) as the parents and students and administrators are more likely to communicate with the SRO than an officer whom they do not know.

Finally, the ethnographic study showed how the SROs' in-depth knowledge of youth gang members operating within the school's catchment area was a real asset for Peel Police with respect to the service's ability to solve crimes. The SROs' knowledge allowed for a rapid response to a crime that might have otherwise taken up officer resources for days/weeks on end in both the uniform patrol and Robbery bureaus of the Peel Regional Police.

Value of the SRO Program: Increased Effectiveness of the School Administrators

During the interviews, the school administrators identified a number of ways in which they uniquely benefited from the SRO program. One in four administrators stated that having the SROs in their school decreased their workload by reducing the number of discipline issues within the school and by performing several critical duties (e.g., conducting wellness checks, researching 'Do Not Attends') that would otherwise need to be done by the administrators. Two-thirds of the administrators we talked to felt that the SROs had positively impacted their ability to do their job effectively and increased their job satisfaction. These increases were attributed to the assistance the SROs gave them in establishing and maintaining a safe and caring learning environment within the school and responding effectively to crises and problems as they arose.

Value of the SRO Program: Encourages Young People to Consider Joining the Police

Students who are interested in a career in law enforcement may not have access to information on how to proceed into that type of career. They may also be discouraged from learning about how to get into law enforcement for a myriad cultural and/or personal reasons. At the same time, there are calls from the community for greater diversity within the Peel Regional Police. The ethnographic study showed that the SRO program addressed this issue by creating the opportunity for youth to meet police officers in a non-threatening way. This creates value, as youth who might otherwise not have thought about careers in law enforcement could now, with the encouragement of their SROs, consider the profession.

Value of the SRO Program: SROI Analysis

SROI calculations determined that the social and economic return on the total investment of $660,289, (the cost of running the SRO program in the five schools in the study) yielded a total present value of $7,349,301. *This means that for every dollar invested in the Peel SRO program, a minimum of $11.13 of social and economic value was created.*

This ratio represents a minimum value created, as conservative estimates were selected for all financial proxies. It also compares favorably to the value created by other social programs, which typically yield $3 to $5 dollars of social and economic value for every dollar spent. The SROI ratio demonstrates a real value created; however, there are various outcomes that cannot be represented in financial terms, such as the fact that the workloads of the social worker and psychologist in the school might increase as result of SROs assisting students who have mental health problems, the Peel Regional District School Board benefiting from an improvement in the quality of the schools' environment and safety, and the reduced victimization and the increased trust and positive view of the police among people living in the catchment areas of the five schools.

Finally, it should be noted that, while this ratio was calculated using the data from the five schools that participated in the study, we feel confident that it can be generalized to schools across Peel Region (at a minimum). We base this assumption on the fact that we took great care to select schools that varied with respect to key socio-economic indicators that are likely to impact the value of this program. The diversity of the schools in our sample also suggest that an SRO program like the one administered by the Peel Regional Police will also add value in other communities.

The ratio can be expected to differ from what we calculated if the context is very different from that considered in our study (i.e., the schools differ from the ones we studied, the communities where students live are different from those considered in this study, the SRO works part-time or covers many schools).

Finally, while the above data are compelling in their own right, we believe that the following quote illustrates in quite a poignant manner why Peel Regional Police believe in the program and support its continuation:

> "There is so much need in communities right now. Early intervention and social interaction with young offenders give the program the most value . . . you know . . . when I'm interacting with an 18- and 20-year-old that's been involved in some pretty serious crime and stuff like that, or you know, he's got himself in a bad place or hanging with a bad crowd, it's pretty difficult to get those guys back on track, right? I really do believe that if you're going to change society . . . the earlier the intervention component of it the better. These early interactions, give it [the SRO program] the most value. It's not perfect but we have a much better chance of saving somebody early on than we do much later, right? It's a much bigger uphill battle. Once they've already played in the mud puddle and they've got some dirt on them, it's tough to wash it off."

Note

1 Deputy Chief McCord, Peel Regional Police, September, 2017.

APPENDIX A

Summary of the SROI Analysis

Please provide a short description of your organization
The Neighborhood Police Unit is a unit of Peel Police. Its responsibility is to strive to create a safe and positive environment in which to live, work, visit, and learn at secondary schools. The Peel District School Board (PDSB) and the Dufferin–Peel Catholic District School Board (DPCDSB) emphasize the importance of student safety. Five high schools from these two school boards operating in the region are participating in this study. These five schools are located in a variety of neighborhoods. Two are designated "urban-grant" schools and are located in socio-economically challenged areas in Peel Region, one school is in an affluent community, and two schools are situated in "middle class" communities. All five schools have student populations that are ethnically diverse. These schools have strengths, such as their extra-curricular activities and the variety of programming, as well as their dedicated teachers and support staff.
Please provide a short description of the project that is the subject of your SROI
The Peel Police's Neighborhood Policing Unit (NPU) program was set up to "ensure that, through cooperative programs between the schools, community, and the police, the SRO shall strive to create a safe and positive environment in which to live, work, visit, and learn." The NPU includes School Resource Officers (SROs) who are assigned to work on a full-time basis in the school. The SROs work with the school and Peel Regional Police to create a safe and secure learning environment, and to enhance safety and security within the community surrounding the school. They do this by: (1) forming positive partnerships with students and high school administrators, (2) using a proactive style of policing whenever possible, and (3) interacting with youth in a non-enforcement manner on a regular basis. The NPU program has been operating in Peel for over two decades. In the midst of concerns about the cost of policing in general and the high cost of the NPU program specifically, Carleton University embarked on a large research project to examine the value of the work of the SROs in 2015. This research includes: a literature review on school violence; perception of violence and their effects on academic achievement; student surveys; ride-alongs with the SROs; and interviews with SROs, school administrators, high school students, and Peel Police staff sergeants who have high familiarity with the SRO program. The SROI, which demonstrates the value of the SRO program, is part of this research.

(continued)

(continued)

What is the purpose of this SROI?

The purpose of the SROI is to assess the value that Peel Regional Police creates by having a full-time SRO assigned to work on a full-time basis in every high school in Peel Region.

Who is your target audience?

- Peel Police.
- Peel Regional Government.
- Peel District School Board, Dufferin–Peel Catholic School Board.
- Stakeholders in five "partner" schools.
- Other school boards, other police services.
- Community (particularly in catchment area).

Create a general profile of the person/people who are the focus point of the program you are evaluating. This is your "target stakeholder"

The most serious issues facing the schools, according to school administrators and SROs, are: the selling and using of drugs, bullying/cyberbullying, and theft. These issues create safety concerns for the schools. There are also secondary issues such as trespassing, assaults, and gang fights. The stakeholder groups that are the focal point of the SRO program are a direct reflection of the issues facing the school community: (1) the groups that are not at risk, (2) the groups that are at risk of creating problems/crime in the school, and (3) the groups that are at risk of being victims of these issues.

(1) Stakeholder groups that are not at risk:

- Students who may experience a lower quality educational experience academically and/or socially may benefit from the work of the SROs in the school.
- School administrators are responsible for the safety of the school and they benefit from the support of the SROs in their duties.
- SROs are responsible for the prevention and enforcement of crime occurrences facing the school and they benefit from the skills they gain and use in their work.

(2) Stakeholder groups that are at risk of creating problems/issues in the school:

- These students are deterred or diverted from crime. They may have behavioral issues or a history of criminal behavior.

(3) Stakeholder groups that are at risk of being victims of these issues:

- Students who are at risk of being victimized: they are at risk of being bullied, assaulted, or having their property stolen. They may also experience mental health issues that make them vulnerable and easy targets/victims.

What activities are you offering the stakeholders of your program?

SROs' activities can be categorized as prevention related and enforcement related activities:

(1) Prevention related activities:

- Walk around the school and around other areas where students congregate, patrol outside the school, and engage in extra-curricular activities with students, within the school.
- Spend time counseling parents, students, school administrators and others on issues related to the school.
- Run workshops on bullying and other issues.
- Divert from criminal justice system when appropriate.

These activities deter the occurrence of crime (theft, gang activity, drug dealing, etc.) within the school and increase the sense of safety for those at the school.

(2) Enforcement related activities:

- Enforce the law: charge and arrest students who are committing crimes such as drug dealing.
- Pass on relevant information to other members of the Peel Police as appropriate; engage with other police units to follow-up on critical incidents.

34% of officers' time is spent in enforcement related activities, while 44% of the time spent is in prevention related activities, and 23% is spent on paperwork and training.

What changes do you expect your target stakeholder to experience as a result of these activities and their exposure to the SRO Program?

Stakeholder Group 1: Students who are at risk of having a lower quality school experience, academically and/or socially:

- Enjoyment of school and school-related activities.
- Increased socialization with peers.
- Experience of well-being as a student.
- Increased ability to focus on schoolwork/learn well.
- Are prepared for further education.

Stakeholder Group 2: Students who are deterred or diverted from crime:

- Avoidance of a criminal life trajectory.
- More prepared for life after high school.

Stakeholder Group 3: Students at risk of being victimized:

- Continued avoidance of being victimized or no longer at risk of being victimized.
- Improved overall quality of life (no longer anxious and worried as a result of being or becoming a victim of crime).

Stakeholder Group 4: School administrators:

- Increased ability to do their job effectively.
- Increased job satisfaction.

Stakeholder Group 5: SROs:

- Increased employability as a result of utilizing skills gained while in SRO position.

Describe the future circumstances of your target stakeholder if they are not *able to participate in your program. How would their circumstances be different than they are today?*

Stakeholder Group 1 : Students who are at risk of having a lower quality school experience, academically and/or socially:

- Would be less likely to have an increased well-being as students.
- Would be less likely to be engaged in school.
- Would be more fearful.
- Would be less able to focus on their studies (with the results that their marks go down).
- Would be less likely to achieve their educational/career goals.

Stakeholder Group 2: Students who are deterred or diverted from crime:

- Would commit illegal activities and have a criminal record.
- Would be engaged in the criminal justice system.

(continued)

(continued)

Stakeholder Group 3: Students at risk of being victimized:

- Would be at risk of being picked on or victimized.
- Would engage in self-harm behaviors/would more likely commit suicide.

Stakeholder Group 4: School administrators:

- Would not be as engaged in the school.

Stakeholder Group 5: SROs:

- Would not have such an opportunity to increase skills and to become more employable.

List other stakeholders who will be impacted either directly or indirectly by the changes experienced by your target stakeholder

- Peel Regional District School Boards.
- Peel Police.
- Teachers.
- Parents.
- People living in the catchment areas for the five schools (vicinity of the schools).

Do target stakeholders currently use services provided by any level of government?

Emergency health care services.

Does the result of your activity change or reduce use of any of the services described above now in the future? Is so, how?

- Emergency health care services: reduced use.
- Criminal justice system: reduced use.

Theory of Change
Create a one-sentence statement that describes your theory of change

IF secondary schools that have safety concerns due to issues such as drug dealing, bullying/cyberbullying, assault and theft are offered the services of a skilled full-time police officer who engages in prevention and enforcement related activities in and around the school, THEN students will feel safe, be engaged, have a positive educational/academic/school experience, will be deterred from crime, and will not be victimized. They will embark on their young adulthood successfully, while the community surrounding the school will feel safer and the police and criminal justice system will be able to re-allocate resources for other priorities.

REFERENCES

Arvidson, M., Battye, F., & Salisbury, D. (2014). The social return on investment and community befriending. *International Journal of Public Sector Management, 27*(3), 225–240.

Berger, R. R. (2002). Expansion of police power in public schools and the vanishing rights of students. *Social Justice, 29*(1), 119–130.

Botelho, G., & Ellis, R. (2015). Police in schools: Why are they there? *CNN*. Retrieved from: www.cnn.com/2015/10/27/us/south-carolina-school-resource-officers/index.html

Bough, A. G. (1998). Searches and seizures in schools: Should reasonable suspicion or probable cause apply to school resource/liaison officers? *UMKC Law Review, 67*, 543.

Bowen, N. K., & Bowen, G. L. (1999). Effects of crime and violence in neighbourhoods and schools on the school behavior and performance of adolescents. *Journal of Adolescent Research, 14*(3), 319–342.

Bracy, N. L. (2011). Student perceptions of high-security school environments. *Youth & Society, 43*(1), 365–395.

Broll, R. (2016). Collaborative responses to cyberbullying: Preventing and responding to cyberbullying through nodes and clusters. *Policing and Society, 26*(7), 735–752.

Broll, R., & Huey, L. (2015). "Just being mean to somebody isn't a police matter": Police perspectives on policing cyberbullying. *Journal of School Violence, 14*(2), 155–176.

Brown, B. (2006). Understanding and assessing school police officers: A conceptual and methodological comment. *Journal of Criminal Justice, 34*, 591–604.

Burdick-Will, J. (2016). Neighbourhood violent crime and academic growth in Chicago: Lasting effects of early exposure. *Social Forces, 95*(1), 133–158.

Carroll, J., Ben-Zadok, E., & McCue, C. (2010). Evaluation of efficiency in crime control and crime prevention programs. *American Journal of Criminal Justice, 35*(4), 219–235.

Choi, K. S., Cronin, S., & Correia, H. (2016). The assessment of capable guardianship measures against bullying victimization in the school environment. *Police Practice and Research, 17*(2), 149–159.

Chrusciel, M., Wolfe, S., Hansen, J. A., Rojek, J., & Kaminski, R. (2015). Law enforcement executive and principal perspectives on school safety measures: School resource officers and armed school employees, *Policing: An International Journal, 38*(1), 24–39.

Coon, J. K., & Travis III, L. F. (2012). The role of police in public schools: A comparison of principal and police reports of activities in schools. *Police Practice and Research, 13*(1), 15–30.

Cooper, D., & Schindler, P. (2006). *Business Research Methods* (11th edition). New York: McGraw Hill.

Cornell, D. G., & Mayer, M. J. (2010). Why do school order and safety matter? *Educational Researcher, 39*(1), 7–15.

Crawford, C., & Burns, R. (2016). Reducing school violence: Considering school characteristics and the impacts of law enforcement, school security, and environmental factors. *Policing: An International Journal, 39*(3), 455–477.

Cray, M., & Weiler, S. C. (2011). Policy to practice: A look at national and state implementation of school resource officer programs. *The Clearing House: A Journal of Educational Strategies, Issues and Ideas, 84*(4), 164–170.

Daniels, J. A., Bilksy, K. D., Chamberlain, S., & Haist, J. (2011). School barricaded captive-takings: An exploratory investigation of school resource officer responses. *Psychological Services, 8*(3), 178–188.

Dogutas, C. (2008). Reactive vs. proactive strategies: The effectiveness of school resource officers to prevent violence in schools. Unpublished doctoral dissertation, Kent State University.

Dohrn, B. (2001). "Look out kid/It's something you did": Zero tolerance for children. In W. Ayers, B. Dohrn, & R. Ayers (Eds.), *Zero tolerance: Resisting the drive for punishment in our schools* (pp. 89–113). New York: New Press.

Eklund, K., Meyer, L., & Bosworth, K. (2018). Examining the role of school resource officers on school safety and crisis response teams. *Journal of School Violence, 17*(2), 139–151.

Emerson, J., Wachowicz, J., & Chun, S. (2000). Social return on investment: Exploring aspects of value creation in the nonprofit sector. *The Box Set: Social Purpose Enterprises and Venture Philanthropy in the New Millennium, 2*, 130–173.

Finn, P., McDevitt, J., Lassiter, W., Shively, M., & Rich, T. (2004). *Case studies of 19 school resource officer (SRO) programs*. Washington, DC: US Department of Justice.

Flannery, D. J., Wester, K. L., & Singer, M. I. (2004). Impact of exposure to violence in school on child and adolescent mental health and behavior. *Journal of Community Psychology, 32*(5), 559–573.

Gill, C., Gottfredson, D., & Hutzell, K. (2016). Can school policing be trauma-informed? Lessons from Seattle. *Policing: An International Journal of Police Strategies & Management, 39*(3), 551–565.

Graham, H. R., Minhas, R. S., & Paxton, G. (2016). Learning problems in children of refugee background: A systematic review. *Pediatrics, 137*(6), e20153994. Retrieved from: http://pediatrics.aappublications.org/content/137/6/e20153994

Gronna, S. S., & Chin-Chance, S. A. (1999). Effects of school safety and school characteristics on grade 8 achievement: A multilevel analysis. Retrieved from: https://eric.ed.gov/?id=ED430292

Hoey, B. (2014). A simple introduction to the practice of ethnography and guide to ethnographic field notes. *Marshall University Digital Scholar*. Retrieved from: http://works.bepress.com/brian_hoey/12/

Hopkins, N., Hewstone, M., & Hantzi, A. (1992). Police–school liaison and young people's image of the police: An intervention evaluation. *British Journal of Psychology, 83*(2), 203–220.

Hopson, L. M., Schiller, K. S., & Lawson, H. A. (2014). Exploring linkages between school climate, behavioral norms, social supports, and academic success. *Social Work Research, 38*(4), 197–209.

Jackson, A. (2002). Police–school resource officers' and students' perception of the police and offending. *Policing: An International Journal of Police Strategies & Management, 25*(3), 631–650.

James, N., & McCallion, G. (2013). School resource officers: Law enforcement officers in schools. *Congressional Research Service, 26*(201), 3.

James, R. K., Logan, J., & Davis, S. A. (2011). Including school resource officers in school-based crisis intervention: Strengthening student support. *School Psychology International, 32*(2), 210–224.

Jennings, W. G., Khey, D. N., Maskaly, J., & Donner, C. M. (2011). Evaluating the relationship between law enforcement and school security measures and violent crime in schools. *Journal of Police Crisis Negotiations, 11*(2), 109–124.

Johnson, I. M. (1999). School violence: The effectiveness of a school resource officer program in a southern city. *Journal of Criminal Justice, 27*(2), 173–192.

Kaplan Research Associates (2014). *Formative evaluation of the SRO program in the Winnipeg school division*. Retrieved from: www.winnipegsd.ca/Governance/BoardReports/Documents/WSD%20SRO%20FULL%20EVALUATION%20REPORT.pdf

King, N. (2014). Making the case for sport and recreation services: The utility of social return on investment (SROI) analysis. *International Journal of Public Sector Management, 27*(2), 152–164.

Kupchik, A., & Monahan, T. (2006). The new American school: Preparation for post-industrial discipline. *British Journal of Sociology of Education*, 27(5), 617–631.

Lambert, R. D., & McGinty, D. (2002). Law enforcement officers in schools: Setting priorities. *Journal of Educational Administration, 40*(3), 257–273.

Lynch, C. G., Gainey, R. R., & Chappell, A. T. (2016). The effects of social and educational disadvantage on the roles and functions of school resource officers. *Policing: An International Journal of Police Strategies & Management, 39*(3), 521–535.

Margolin, G., & Gordis, E. B. (2000). The effects of family and community violence on children. *Annual Review of Psychology, 51*(1), 445–479.

Maskaly, J., Donner, C. M., Lanterman, J., & Jennings, W. G. (2011). On the association between SROs, private security guards, use-of-force capabilities, and violent crime in schools. *Journal of Police Crisis Negotiations, 11*(2), 159–176.

May, D., & Higgins, G. (2011). The characteristics and activities of school resource officers: Are newbies different than veterans? *Journal of Police Crisis Negotiations, 11*(2), 96–108.

May, D. C., Fessel, S. D., & Means, S. (2004). Predictors of principals' perceptions of school resource officer effectiveness in Kentucky. *American Journal of Criminal Justice, 29*(1), 75–93.

May, D. C., Hart, T. A., & Ruddell, R. (2011). School resource officers in financial crisis: Which programs get cut and why. *Journal of Police Crisis Negotiations, 11*(2), 125–140.

May, D., Ruddell, R., Barranco, R., & Robertson, A. (2016). Do rural school resource officers contribute to net-widening? Evidence from a southern state. *Journal of Rural Social Sciences, 31*(2), 62–85.

MBA Associates (2015). *An introduction to social return on investment.* Retrieved from: http://mbassociates.org/wp-content/uploads/2015/10/An-introduction-to-SROI_MBAssocs_2012.pdf

McDevitt, J., & Panniello, J. (2005). *National assessment of school resource officer programs: Survey of students in three large new SRO programs.* Document number 209270. Washington, DC: US Department of Justice.

Merkwae, A. (2015). Schooling the police: Race, disability, and the conduct of school resource officers. *Michigan Journal of Race & Law, 21*, 147–181.

Na, C., & Gottfredson, D. C. (2013). Police officers in schools: Effects on school crime and the processing of offending behaviors. *Justice Quarterly, 30*(4), 619–650.

Nance, J. P. (2016). Rethinking law enforcement officers in schools. *The George Washington Law Review Arguendo, 84*, 151–159.

Nef (New Economic Foundation) (2012). *A guide to social return on investment.* Office of the Third Sector, Government of Scotland. Retrieved from: http://b.3cdn.net/nefoundation/aff3779953c5b88d53_cpm6v3v71.pdf

Nicholls, J. (2009). *A guide to social return on investment.* Retrieved from: www.thesroinetwork.org

Noaks, J., & Noaks, L. (2000). Violence in school: Risk, safety and fear of crime. *Educational Psychology in Practice, 16*(1), 69–73.

Osofsky, J. D. (1995). The effect of exposure to violence on young children. *American Psychologist, 50*(9), 782–788.

Owens, E. G. (2017). Testing the school-to-prison pipeline. *Journal of Policy Analysis and Management, 36*(1), 11–37.

Peel Regional Police (2003, April). PRP Regional N.P.U. mandate. Unpublished internal document.

Peel Regional Police (2011, August). Peel Regional Police directive issue No. I-B-416 (F). Unpublished internal document.

Perry, B. D. (2009). Examining child maltreatment through a neurodevelopmental lens: Clinical applications of the neurosequential model of therapeutics. *Journal of Loss and Trauma, 14*(4), 240–255.

Perumean-Chaney, S. E., & Sutton, L. M. (2013). Students and perceived school safety: The impact of school security measures. *American Journal of Criminal Justice, 38*(4), 570–588.

Petrosino, A., Guckenburg, S., & Fronius, T. (2012). 'Policing schools' strategies: A review of the evaluation evidence. *Journal of MultiDisciplinary Evaluation, 8*(17), 80–101.

Ratner, H. H., Chiodo, L., Covington, C., Sokol, R. J., Ager, J., & Delaney-Black, V. (2006). Violence exposure, IQ, academic performance, and children's perception of safety: Evidence of protective effects. *Merrill-Palmer Quarterly, 52*(2), 264–287.

Ripski, M. B., & Gregory, A. (2009). Unfair, unsafe, and unwelcome: Do high school students' perceptions of unfairness, hostility, and victimization in school predict engagement and achievement? *Journal of School Violence, 8*(4), 355–375.

Rhodes, T. N. (2015). Officers and school settings: Examining the influence of the school environment on officer roles and job satisfaction. *Police Quarterly, 18*(2),134–162.

Robles-Piña, R. A., & Denham, M. A. (2012). School resource officers for bullying interventions: A mixed-methods analysis. *Journal of School Violence, 11*(1), 38–55.

Rogers III, R. F. (2004). A study to determine if the implementation of the school resource officer (SRO) in a county school system has been effective in providing overall positive changes in school environments that have resulted in improved scholarship and decreased adverse behaviors by students. Unpublished doctoral dissertation, University of Tennessee.

Ryan, P., & Lyne, I. (2008). Social enterprise and the measurement of social value: Methodological issues with the calculation and application of the social return on investment. *Education, Knowledge & Economy, 2*(3), 223–237.

Sharkey, P. (2010). The acute effect of local homicides on children's cognitive performance. *Proceedings of the National Academy of Sciences, 107*(26), 11733–11738.

Sharkey, P. T., Tirado-Strayer, N., Papachristos, A. V., & Raver, C. C. (2012). The effect of local violence on children's attention and impulse control. *American Journal of Public Health, 102*(12), 2287–2293.

Skiba, R., Simmons, A. B., Peterson, R., McKelvey, J., Forde, S., & Gallini, S. (2004). Beyond guns, drugs and gangs: The structure of student perceptions of school safety. *Journal of School Violence, 3*(2–3), 149–171.

Solberg, V. S. H., Carlstrom, A. H., Howard, K. A., & Jones, J. E. (2007). Classifying at-risk high school youth: The influence of exposure to community violence and protective factors on academic and health outcomes. *Career Development Quarterly, 55*(4), 313–327.

Stevenson, Q. W. (2011). School resource officers and school incidents: A quantitative study. Unpublished doctoral dissertation, University of Alabama.

Theriot, M. T. (2009). School resource officers and the criminalization of student behavior. *Journal of Criminal Justice, 37*(3), 280–287.

Theriot, M. T. (2016). The impact of school resource officer interaction on students' feelings about school and school police. *Crime & Delinquency, 62*(4), 446–469.

Theriot, M. T., & Orme, J .G. (2016). School resource officers and students' feelings of safety at school. *Youth Violence and Juvenile Justice, 14*(2), 130–146.

Tillyer, M. S., Fisher, B. S., & Wilcox, P. (2011). The effects of school crime prevention on students' violent victimization, risk perception, and fear of crime: A multilevel opportunity perspective. *Justice Quarterly, 28*(2), 249–277.

Twersky, F. (2002). *An information oasis*. San Francisco, CA: Roberts Enterprise Development Fund.

Ullah, M., Ahmadullah, I., & Shahzad, S. (2016). Impact of stress on student's mental, physical health and academic achievement at secondary level due to US drone strikes in north Waziristan Agency, *Isra Medical Journal, 8*(2), 110–115.

Walkley, M., & Cox, T. L. (2013). Building trauma-informed schools and communities. *Children & Schools, 35*(2), 123–126.

Weiler, S. C., & Cray, M. (2011). Police at school: A brief history and current status of School Resource Officers. *The Clearing House: A Journal of Educational Strategies, Issues and Ideas, 84*(4), 160–163.

Wolf, K. C. (2014). Arrest decision making by school resource officers. *Youth Violence and Juvenile Justice, 12*(2), 137–151.

Wolfe, S. E., Chrusciel, M. M., Rojek, J., Hansen, J. A., & Kaminski, R. J. (2015). Procedural justice, legitimacy, and school principals' evaluations of school resource officers: Support, perceived effectiveness, trust, and satisfaction. *Criminal Justice Policy Review, 28*(2), 107–138.

Wright, M. F. (2016). Cyber victimization and psychological adjustment difficulties among adolescents: The role of technology mediation and social support from school resource officers. *Policing: An International Journal of Police Strategies & Management, 39*(3), 536–550.

INDEX

Milton Keynes UK
Ingram Content Group UK Ltd.
UKHW020641210624
444299UK00004B/12